SONIA

SONIA
A Biography

Rasheed Kidwai

PENGUIN
VIKING

VIKING

Penguin Books India (P) Ltd., 11 Community Centre, Panchsheel Park, New Delhi 110 017, India
Penguin Books Ltd., 80 Strand, London WC2R 0RL, UK
Penguin Group Inc., 375 Hudson Street, New York, NY 10014, USA
Penguin Books Australia Ltd., 250 Camberwell Road, Camberwell, Victoria 3124, Australia
Penguin Books Canada Ltd., 10 Alcorn Avenue, Suite 300, Toronto, Ontario M4V 3B2, Canada
Penguin Books (NZ) Ltd., Cnr Rosedale and Airborne Roads, Albany, Auckland, New Zealand
Penguin Books (South Africa) (Pty) Ltd., 24 Sturdee Avenue, Rosebank 2196, South Africa

First published in Viking by Penguin Books India 2003

Typeset in Aldine by Mantra Virtual Services, New Delhi
Printed at Chaman Offset Printers, New Delhi

For
Farah
who inspired me to write this book

CONTENTS

PREFACE

Sonia Gandhi is a major national political figure, the leader of a party, the Congress, which, in April 2003, was in government in fifteen states. Paradoxically, for one so prominent in public life, she remains a very private person, one about whom, in a sense, very little is known. As a leader, she has her admirers as well as detractors but seldom has there been an objective evaluation of her life.

Both these factors were obvious reasons for me to undertake writing this biography. Additionally, over the past decade, I have been covering the Congress for different newspapers, and the knowledge I have gained of its workings provided a starting point for my endeavour.

This is not an authorized biography and it posed, I must admit, its own difficulties. As a journalist, one is trained to work under adverse circumstances, but the difficulties I faced in the writing of this book far surpassed any I faced in my journalistic career. One difficulty, of course, was that Sonia was not very forthcoming, for her own reasons. Sifting the information also required care and I had to be careful what I was told was not biased or motivated. And then there were the pressures from various quarters. Dismaying and discouraging as these were, I decided to persist, given that there has been no serious, critical evaluation of a person who exercises so much influence on the destiny of a nation.

I wish to place on record my deep gratitude to hundreds of Congress party members who provided insight into the finer aspects of Sonia's

personality, her style of functioning and Congress party politics. I am
also grateful to other political leaders, including some of her worst
critics, who surprisingly often showered lavish praise on her. Since
most of them did not wish to be quoted or acknowledged, I am
constrained to withhold their identity. A special word of thanks to the
many academicians, intellectuals, opinion makers and bureaucrats
who went out of the way to help me.

I am extremely grateful to Aveek Sarkar, my editor and guide, who
generously kept telling me that I was the right person to do the book.
Bharat Bhushan, Deepayan Chatterjee, Sankarshan Thakur, Pramit
Pal Chaudhuri, S. Rajagopalan, Diptosh Majumdar and Radhika
Ramaseshan extended valuable help and patronage, which gave me
the time and confidence to do the book along with my routine
journalistic assignments. I cannot help but recall the contribution of
M.L Kotru, M.J. Akbar, Shekhar Bhatia, Vir Sanghvi, Shubbhabrata
Bhattacharya, Sumeer Lal, Pradyut Lal, Sheela Reddy, Rakesh Joshi,
Prakash Patra, Subhash Chopra, Prem and Sanjeev Prakash and
Surinder Kapoor in shaping me as a journalist.

Among friends and colleagues I wish to thank Nirmal Pathak,
Swaraj Thapa, Bhavdeep Kang, Priya Sahgal, Shikha Parihar, Diya
Kar Hazra, Askari Zaidi, Laxmi Iyer, Monobina Gupta, Kay Benedict
and Farhan Ansari who offered me useful tips. A special word of thanks
to Vaiju Naravane.

Finally, no word of thanks is enough to express my gratitude to
Krishan Chopra and Heidi Vierow at Penguin Books for their work
on this book.

New Delhi   Rasheed Kidwai
October 2003

ONE

A TRAGEDY IN SRIPERUMBUDUR

Rajiv and Sonia Gandhi arrived early at Nirman Bhawan to cast their vote on 20 May 1991. It was 7.30 in the morning, and pleasant still before the heat of the day. Behind them the line was growing. Just behind them stood Rajesh Khanna, once a Bollywood megastar and now the Congress nominee for the prestigious New Delhi constituency. They were the first to vote and the polling booth was bustling with enthusiastic Youth Congress and Sewa Dal—the party's training wing—volunteers.

Rajiv was in white cotton kurta pyjama with a tricolour angavastram draped loosely around the neck and Sonia in a flashy red salwar kameez. To the delight of the cameramen present, Priyanka too had come to vote. The Rajiv Gandhi government which was in power in 1984-89 had lowered the voting age from twenty-one to eighteen years, and Priyanka had just celebrated her nineteenth birthday.

A party worker brought a carefully prepared puja tray to start the proceedings on an auspicious note. In his nervousness, he dropped the tray as he approached Rajiv. Sonia, standing behind Rajiv, froze. It was a breezy morning, but she suddenly began perspiring. She told Priyanka to arrange for a glass of water for her, but Priyanka, in the excitement of casting her first vote, forgot.

Rajiv was quick to observe Sonia's discomfort. He gently pressed her hands, trying to reassure her, but she remained tense. Moments later, when she entered the polling booth, she could hardly find the Congress hand among the plethora of symbols in the outsized ballot paper. Confounded by the long list of candidates, she would say later, 'I thought for a moment I would have to walk away without casting my vote for him.'[1]

The snap polls in 1991 had been announced after the dramatic ouster of the Chandra Shekhar government, a weak and shaky coalition that had been surviving on Congress support for the few months that it was in power. Rajiv dumped Chandra Shekhar—a former Congressman and a bitter critic of the 'dynasty' who ironically was propped up by the Congress party's 197 MPs in Parliament to fulfil his ambition of becoming PM— on the flimsy ground that his government was spying on him. The real reason was Rajiv's political assessment that he was poised to return as India's next Prime Minister.

Soon after they returned from voting, Rajiv left to resume the back-breaking election campaign that had seen him travel several thousand miles in the past few weeks. He was putting all he had into the campaign to try and make up for the defeat in 1989.

The campaigning had left him dead tired and sleepless. His hands had swollen so much that he could not wear his wedding band. The previous week, Rajiv had returned from the Rohelkhand region of Uttar Pradesh where Muslim voters had showered him with affection, one expression of their love being to firmly grip his hands in their own, leaving them badly bruised. The present tour would take him to Orissa, Andhra Pradesh and finally to the temple town of Sriperumbudur in Tamil Nadu.

Sonia kept pleading with him to take a break, but he was unrelenting. 'A little more push and we will emerge as winners,' he told her with his disarming smile. Earlier that year, they had been to Teheran, one of the capitals Rajiv visited on his peace initiative during the Gulf War. He gently reminded her of the good time they had had there. The reference was to a quiet dinner on their wedding anniversary—their twenty-third—on 25 February 1991. They were also looking forward to Rahul's return on 23 May from the United

States, where he was doing a course in bank securities in Boston. 'We will go out and have a meal together once the elections are over,' he told her.

Twenty months in the Opposition benches had made Rajiv much wiser. He deeply regretted the way he had frittered away the massive mandate of 1984. The Congress strength in Parliament plummeted from 404 in 1984 to 197 Lok Sabha seats in 1989. However, by 1991 the Congress chances were bright as the public mood was turning against shaky coalitions and their power games.

In his zeal to win at all costs, Rajiv was defying an intelligence bureau advisory not to hold public meetings in Tamil Nadu after sunset where Sri Lankan Tamil separatists had huge pockets of support. Rajiv was on top of the extremist Liberation Tigers of Tamil Eelam (LTTE) hit list. For Rajiv, such advisories came in the way of interacting with the crowds at his rallies and were largely ignored.

Rajiv was so confident of returning as the Prime Minister that he gave extensive interviews about the qualities of a good Prime Minister. 'The Prime Minister should have vision, a national vision,' he said to *India Today*, adding that he would be able to push through a progressive, reformist agenda despite odds. Rajiv told Neena Gopal of *Gulf News* that the biggest challenge before him was to curb the divisiveness that had crept in under the stewardship of V.P. Singh, Chandra Shekhar's predecessor, whose measures to help the backward had instead deepened caste differences and led to his fall.

The next day, on 21 May, Rajiv boarded a helicopter for a whirlwind tour of the coastal areas of Bhadrak, Angul, Gunupur and Paralakhemundi in Orissa before crossing over to Vishakhapatnam in Andhra Pradesh. Uma Gajapati Raju was the Congress nominee there. Rajiv was a great votary of getting young professionals into politics, and he had made a special effort to get her a ticket.

That evening, keen to catch up on his sleep, Rajiv toyed with the idea of not going to Sriperumbudur. He was extremely hungry, and Raju invited him to her house for dinner, but he resisted the offer. His party expected an extra bit from him. Sharing his thoughts with a party functionary, he said, 'I will catch up on my sleep at leisure with

Rahul, Priyanka, Sonia around. Margetham Chandrashekhar [the Congress candidate from Sriperumbudur] is an old friend of mama [Indira Gandhi],' thereby overruling the suggestion that the former Prime Minister should not visit the constituency at night. The LTTE was known to have significant support in the area. As Prime Minister, Rajiv had drawn the LTTE's wrath when he sent in Indian troops to help the Sri Lankan government combat the group in 1987.

As Rajiv left for the airport, Raju sent Rajiv pizza, idlies and some sambhar-rasam. Rajiv boarded the plane, but there was a change of plan after a technical snag was discovered. It was decided to have a night halt at Vishakhapatnam after all. While he was driving down to the circuit house, a constable came hurrying after to inform him that the plane was now ready to take off. When the flight took off, a hungry Rajiv discovered that the food had been left in the car.

According to Suman Dubey, Rajiv's press adviser, who accompanied him on the campaign, the former Prime Minister woke up at 7.30 a.m. on 21 May. 'He was unusually late that day. But once he was up and about he took off, addressing a series of meetings in Orissa, Andhra Pradesh before moving out to Tamil Nadu.'[2]

Rajiv reached Madras at 8.30 p.m., met the press for ten minutes, had a soft drink and then hurriedly left by road for Porur to address a public meeting. At 9.30 p.m. he held another meeting before heading for Poonamallee. In between these engagements, Rajiv was giving interviews to Neena Gopal of *Gulf News* and Barbara Crossette of the *New York Times*.

When the *thalaivar* (leader) reached Sriperumbudur, there was little that could be described as security arrangements. Constables from the Tamil Nadu police watched curiously as Rajiv mingled freely with the crowd. Rajiv's personal security attendant, Pradeep Gupta, made a feeble bid to keep the mob from touching him. The senior state Congress leaders, ranging from G.K. Moopanar to Margetham Chandrashekhar, were sitting on the dais about 100 yards away. Rajiv began briskly walking on the red carpet accepting garlands from one and all.

Death stopped him when he heard a poem being recited by a young girl, Kokila, who was part of the suicide squad. His assassin, Dhanu, moved closer to him carrying a garland made of sandalwood. An edgy Rajiv sensed something unusual, signalling to Constable Anusuya to regulate the crowd. But by then Dhanu had bent, pretending to touch Rajiv's feet and triggering off the RDX strapped all around her.

Ironically, at the time of the blast, a chorus at the public meeting was still singing, 'Rajiv Gandhi's life is our life, if not for Indira Gandhi's son, there is no life for anyone.'

Number 10 Janpath was deserted at 10.25 p.m. as Rajiv and most of the party stalwarts were away from New Delhi. Rajiv's private secretary, Vincent George, had left for his Chanakyapuri residence after a long and hectic day. Since the morning, he had been on the phone taking calls from all over the country. Mostly these were election-related, partymen seeking assistance: 'Send us posters, give us a few jeeps, I am running out of money,' they would tell the ever-smiling and responsive Mr George. Some would address him as George sahib, as he was perceived to be the eyes and ears of the high command—a reputation he had earned over nine years of working with Rajiv.

George was at his residence when he got a call from a friend. 'Something terrible' had happened in Chennai involving Rajiv Gandhi, he was told. Immediately, he rushed back to 10 Janpath and called Nalini Chidambaram, wife of P. Chidambaram, who was the architect of the government's economic reform strategies as Rajiv Gandhi's right-hand man.

Sonia and Priyanka were in bed when they received a telephone call from a friend inquiring if everything was fine. Sonia picked up the intercom and asked for George, who was on the line with Nalini Chidambaram. Sonia said she would hold on till he finished his call. Nalini confirmed the news of a blast targeting Rajiv, but George couldn't bring himself to convey that to Sonia, still holding the line. As the clock touched 10.50, the telephone rang again. It was from Chennai and the caller was desperate to talk to George or 'Madam'. 'Sir, there has been a bomb attack,' the caller said identifying himself as being from the intelligence department. 'How is Rajivji?' an anxious

George inquired. There was silence for approximately five seconds, but to George the pause seemed endless. His heart sank, and in a choked voice he shouted, 'Why don't you tell me how is he?' 'Sir, he is no more' the caller said, and the line went dead. Then it rang again and again with callers from the Tamil Nadu party unit confirming the news.

The private secretary ran inside shouting 'Madam, Madam.' Sonia came out in her nightgown sensing something terrible had happened. After all, the low-key and sober George had never behaved like that. 'Madam, there has been a bomb attack,' he said. Giving him a hard stare, Sonia asked point-blank, 'Is he alive?' George's silence spoke loud and clear. She was not even listening to him after that. For the first time 10 Janpath heard her crying. The wails were so loud that they could be heard in the ante-house where party leaders had begun gathering. Former Rajya Sabha member M. Afzal was among the first to reach the house. 'Wails of Mrs Gandhi could be heard in adjoining rooms,' he said.[3]

Sonia suffered a terrible asthma attack, almost losing consciousness. Priyanka looked for her medicines, unsuccessfully trying to console her. Priyanka too was in a state of shock. Right until Rajiv's cremation there was a part of her that refused to accept that her father was dead.

The shock would continue over the next few days as Rahul arrived, accompanied by Amitabh Bachchan, a close family friend and one of the first to have received Sonia in New Delhi a few days before she married Rajiv. Although Rajiv was not occupying any official position at the time of his death, more than forty dignitaries from around the world attended his funeral and offered their condolences. Among them were royalty and heads of state. The funeral itself took place near Shakti Sthal, Indira's samadhi, and was attended by a vast crowd. The Chief Election Commissioner, T.N. Seshan recognizing the impact of the assassination on the ongoing polls, deferred the next round of voting from May to July 1991.

Sonia remembered the big fight they had in October 1984 hours after Indira was assassinated. Rajiv had just returned from Calcutta and party leaders told him to step into Indira's shoes. 'I begged him not to let them do this. I pleaded with him, with others around him too. He would be killed as well. He held my hands, hugged me, tried to soothe my desperation. He had no choice, he said, he would be killed anyway.'[4] Seven years later, Rajiv's words had come true.

TWO

THE SEARCH FOR A SUCCESSOR

At the Janpath-Akbar Road roundabout some labourers were trying hard to sleep braving the heat and the mosquitoes when the news about Rajiv's assassination became public. Soon people began to gather outside 10 Janpath, forcing the labourers to shift elsewhere. The crowd was raising slogans against former Prime Minister V.P. Singh, first associate and then Rajiv's rival, who had withdrawn Rajiv's security, Chandra Shekhar who was the current PM, Bharatiya Janata Party (BJP) leader Lal Krishna Advani and the American Central Intelligence Agency (CIA). The Gandhis' neighbour, Ram Vilas Paswan, a prominent dalit leader, had to flee when the mob attacked his 12 Janpath residence and burnt furniture hours after the assassination.

Sonia recalled the riots that had taken place after Indira's assassination and called in long-time aide R.K. Dhawan, who had risen from being an assistant to Indira Gandhi to a Union minister, and Captain Satish Sharma, one of Rajiv's flying club buddies who was close to the family. They were told to ensure that nothing untoward happened. 'Rajiv would not have liked————,' Sonia said before bursting into tears.[1]

In the power centres of Delhi, however, Congress leaders were already at work, considering the shape of things to come. Top party leaders began asking themselves: Who next? After all, general elections were on, and someone had to lead the Congress.

There was no clear mechanism for succession in the Congress. The family hold of Indira and Rajiv Gandhi had dismantled the post of number two in the party. Indira, forever suspicious, had taught Rajiv an important lesson—to keep regional satraps at bay and not to promote anyone who was not part of the Nehru–Gandhi clan.

As Prime Minister, leader of the Opposition and leader of the Congress, Rajiv may have cut regional satraps to size, but many still nursed the ambition of becoming Prime Minister. Rajiv's sudden death brought their ambitions into play. Among them was Sharad Pawar from Maharashtra, who had a knack of striking deals with his foes. Then there was Narain Dutt Tiwari, a seasoned Brahmin leader from Uttar Pradesh who was considered a politician among politicians. The Madhya Pradesh leader Arjun Singh was known for his political skills and gave Rajiv a hard time by constantly disobeying him as chief minister. When Rajiv asked him to step down following his indictment in a court case, Singh rebelled and forced Rajiv to strike a deal with him. There were also the Karnataka chief minister Veerendra Patil, and his Andhra counterpart, M. Chenna Reddy, and others who were kept at arm's length. To counter these leaders, Rajiv had promoted a set of courtiers to powerful positions who lacked a mass base of their own. They included Sardar Buta Singh, Ghulam Nabi Azad and Jitendra Prasada.

Rajiv's death altered everything. Sonia, Priyanka and a handful of party leaders may have been mourning a personal loss, but for the regional satraps, courtiers and majority of Congress MPs, the succession issue was most important. Those in the fray were hell-bent on winning the key position. While the kingmakers and courtiers were honing their skills to place their favourite in the top job, the moneybags too were openly promising party leaders and MPs that they would be suitably rewarded if their favourite won the race.

At well past midnight, Arjun Singh was outside 10 Janpath looking on as a small group of party workers, reportedly loyal to him, chanted, 'Sonia lao, desh bachao.' In grief, the political instincts of Congress leaders were as sharp as ever. Those toying with the idea of collective leadership in the post-Rajiv Congress quickly spotted Arjun's agenda.

'Oh dear, it is going to be the family again,' whispered a former Union minister from Maharashtra.[2]

It was not the first time that the Congress was faced with a leadership issue. In 1984, when Indira Gandhi was assassinated, Congressmen saw young Rajiv as the heir-apparent. Rajiv's selection was, however, not too smooth. Pranab Mukherjee, who had served as Indira's unofficial number two, projected himself as a likely successor. His miscalculation cost him dearly, forcing him to leave the party and float his own outfit. Many years later, when asked what it was called, Pranab admitted that he had even forgotten the name of his party!

Eighteen hours after Rajiv's assassination, the Congress Working Committee (CWC), the apex decision-making body of the party, consisting of twelve members, and two permanent and four special invitees, met at 24 Akbar Road, the Congress party's headquarters. Sitting cross-legged on white sheets and reclining on masnads, the party leaders left the place meant for the leader vacant as a mark of respect for Rajiv. The meeting lasted more than 100 minutes, but no tea or coffee was served.

Hours before the meeting, the regional satraps, courtiers and senior leaders held several rounds to clinch the crucial issue of who should chair the CWC meeting in the absence of the Congress president. According to the Congress constitution, the party's seniormost general secretary should head such meetings, but there was little or no agreement on the seniority of the general secretaries. Finally former Union minister Pranab Mukherjee, who was not in the succession race, proposed P.V. Narasimha Rao's name. Narasimha Rao had sought retirement from active politics on the eve of the 1991 general elections and declined to contest the polls. He was non-controversial and readily accepted by all groups and factions to chair the meet. Although Narasimha Rao was not even a CWC member, he was chosen because of his seniority, long association with Indira and Rajiv and lack of status as a contender.

Others present at the meeting were K. Karunakaran, Arjun Singh, Ghulam Nabi Azad, Balram Jakhar, Meira Kumar, Jagannath Pahadia, Rajendra Kumari Bajpai, H.K.L. Bhagat, Buta Singh, Ram Chandra

Vikal and Sitaram Kesri, permanent invitees Sharad Pawar and
Janardhan Reddy and special invitees Pranab Mukherjee, Jitendra
Prasada, M.L. Fotedar and P. Shiv Shankar.[3]

At the end of the gathering, the group unanimously requested
Rajiv's widow to take over as the All India Congress Committee
(AICC) chief. Singh proposed Sonia's name and the others endorsed
it. Many years later, Pawar claimed he had raised a mild objection—a
contention challenged by almost all those present. When asked to
spell out his objection, Pawar said he wanted to know if she had been
consulted! He was, however, partially correct in saying that Sonia's
selection as the AICC chief was not unanimous. Significantly, many
in the CWC, particularly those who knew her, were convinced that
she would not accept the job.[4]

The party also collectively ignored the basic fact that Sonia was
not even a 'char anna' member of the Congress party. Char—or four—
anna membership (the rupee was divided into annas before conversion
to the metric system) was a prerequisite for anyone joining the party.
Mahatma Gandhi, who is credited with giving the Congress a mass
base during India's freedom struggle, envisaged the concept of char
anna membership. No thought was given to Sonia's leadership
qualities or her unfamiliarity with the complexities of the political
system.

One account claimed that as Singh contemplated proposing
Sonia's name, Pawar restlessly glanced at him. At that juncture,
someone scribbled on a tiny notepad, 'She will not' and passed the
note to Pawar, much to his relief.[5]

Another account had it that Singh's camp got wind of Pawar's
move to force a vote in the CWC on who should be the leader. Unsure
of his support base among CWC members, Singh sided with some
CWC members to propose Sonia's name to check Pawar.

Arjun Singh's camp has yet another story that says that Singh had
approached Narasimha Rao to propose Sonia's name, but the latter
refused on the ground that he was presiding over the emergency CWC
meet. The insinuation was that Narasimha Rao was working on a
different agenda while projecting himself as a non-partisan person.

Years later, when Arjun Singh's group gained an upper hand under the Sonia-led Congress and Narasimha Rao was unceremoniously shown the door, Singh's supporters added Narasimha Rao's 'defiant act in 1991' in their political charge sheet against the former Prime Minister to convince Sonia to keep him out of all party fora.[6]

The deliberations took place while Rajiv's body was still lying in state. The CWC's decision was communicated to Sonia by a group of party leaders consisting of Ghulam Nabi Azad, Pranab Mukherjee and others. The meeting lasted about ten minutes. Sonia did not say anything, but she must have been taken aback by the timing of the request.

A day later she issued a small statement refusing to accept the post. It said, 'The tragedy that has befallen me and my children does not make it possible for me to accept the presidentship of the Congress.'[7] Family friends said that Sonia and her children did not even consider the offer. 'In fact, it was considered as extremely insensitive on the part of the CWC to have made such a gesture when Rajiv's funeral had not taken place,' one of them said, confirming that there was no discussion even among close friends about the CWC's offer. 'We were all too shocked and grieved to discuss politics,' said a friend of Rajiv who later opposed Sonia's entry in politics.

Amitabh Bachchan also opposed Sonia entering politics. Bachchan's opinion was greatly valued when he equated senior Congress leaders with 'mercenaries'—trying to encash tragic deaths for political ends. Bachchan, who had an unhappy brush with politics as Congress member of Parliament from 1985 to 1987, recalled how Rajiv was similarly forced to lead the party after Indira's assassination and wondered how long members of the family would continue to make such sacrifices. He made these remarks days after Rajiv's assassination in the presence of Priyanka.

Pranab Mukherjee broke the news of Sonia's selection to the media and faced a hostile press. 'She is the only person who will be able to provide leadership at this crucial juncture and under her leadership the future of the Congress is bright,' Pranab said summing up the CWC deliberations.[8]

The former finance minister had an answer for everything. 'How has the Congress accepted a leader who until 1983 was not even an Indian citizen?' he was asked. 'She is an Indian housewife and has been exercising franchise in the New Delhi constituency also,' he said.[9] When he was asked if she would be projected as the Prime Minister, Pranab said, 'We will cross the bridge when we reach it.' Had she been consulted? Would she accept the job? 'She will accept,' Mukherjee said claiming that informally she was consulted—a fact disputed by Sonia. Mukherjee later said he was misinformed!

The family faithful would not accept Sonia's refusal. The outgoing Congress Parliamentary Party (CPP) quickly endorsed the CWC's decision. In other words, if Sonia had accepted the CWC offer, she would have been the party's candidate for Prime Minister after the elections.

Each day, groups of partymen led by senior leaders called on Sonia while Sewa Dal workers raised slogans like 'Rajiv Gandhi amar rahe, Soniaji lao, desh bachao.' A disgusted Sonia summoned George and asked him to send the partymen away.

Senior leader Vasant Sathe raised the issue of acting or interim president of the Congress. According to him, the infighting and lobbying for the AICC chief's was proving to be costly for the party during elections. Sathe suggested that the AICC convene a session soon after the general elections to choose the new leader.[10] The party's chief ministers too began mounting pressure on the CWC to settle the leadership issue. They sought a leader with a good image and a national presence.

There were seven serious aspirants to succeed Rajiv as the Congress chief. Each had his own agenda, but none was willing to repeat Pranab Mukherjee's folly. For many years to come, these leaders played a pivotal role in the Congress. Some were sidelined and died as disillusioned men. The stories of these aspirants are fascinating accounts of power play and intrigue.

The senior party leaders waged a no-holds barred war against one another and finally accepted a completely inexperienced and reluctant Sonia in 1998 in order to forestall the prospects of one of them taking over. The motto was simple: If it can't be me, it cannot be you either.

P.V. Narasimha Rao was one Congress president who sought to run the party without involving the family. He failed to win assembly polls in major states like Andhra Pradesh, Karnataka, Kerala, Rajasthan, Uttar Pradesh, Bihar and Assam. According to Rao, the organizational set-up of the Congress placed the entire onus on the leadership. Rao learnt this the hard way when he faced a sustained battle of supremacy from the day he took over as Rajiv's successor.

The process of Rao's selection itself was a convoluted one. When the jockeying for Rajiv's successor began, Pawar and his camp followers were quick to take the lead. They were convinced that the time to control the Delhi durbar had come. Pawar's point man in Delhi was Suresh Kalmadi, a man who wore several hats—sports organizer, event manager, party animal, media baron and politician. A lavish dinner was organized at a five-star hotel where forty-eight Congressmen were offered the best of wine and food. The idea, of course, was to elicit support for Pawar as leader of the Congress. The poor attendance, however, further marred Pawar's prospects and many of the MPs, hailing mainly from Maharashtra, Orissa, Punjab and Tamil Nadu, became suspect in the eyes of the leadership.

The prospects of Pawar becoming Congress chief and subsequently Prime Minister got his supporters so keyed up that one of his lieutenants declared that what Pawar's mentor Y.B. Chavan, who was a towering leader in Indira's time, could not achieve, the man from Baramati would. Pawar had played a big role in the transformation of Baramati into a high-yield agriculture zone. Members of the Bombay Club—an informal group of powerful industrialists who were wary of the growing clout of multinationals—were also excited and sent word that Pawar need not bother about resources to influence the Congress party MPs.

Pawar was not as comfortable in the durbar culture of the Congress. He had deserted the Congress twice and did not get along with Rajiv on account of mutual suspicion. With Sonia he had no rapport. When he tried to break the ice with Sonia by narrating how he was the first to have discovered the 'Italian connection' when he signed a memorandum of understanding with an Italian wine company way back in the 1960s, Sonia was not impressed.[11]

Ironically, it was Arjun Singh, then AICC vice president, who brought back Pawar to the Congress during the Rajiv era. In the post-Rajiv era, however, Pawar and Singh came face to face in a no-holds barred battle for supremacy.

Singh rose from a small principality in the backward Rewa region of Madhya Pradesh. He cut his political teeth as an understudy of D.P. Mishra, who had earned the dubious distinction of being a Chanakya of MP politics by giving Indira a tough time. The Madhya Pradesh chief minister—father of the current Principal Secretary and National Security Adviser, Brajesh Mishra—outwitted Indira at a time when the Congress chief ministers used to be at the Central leadership's mercy. But Mishra succeeded in defying Indira and consolidating support among party MLAs, saving his position. Soon Singh outshone his mentor, so much so that tales of his manoeuvring replaced similar legends involving Mishra. A man of few words, he had a loyal band of partymen spread across the country. He was known to shower favours on his confidants and expect unflinching loyalty in return. He was a strong votary of power politics and credited with a view that power alone could overcome many handicaps.

Singh and his cronies thought that their moment of glory had come. They said the days of Uttar Pradesh's hegemony (the state has produced seven prime ministers) were over. Singh had all the ingredients to lead the party from the front. His supporters and even some of his critics acknowledged that he had the vision to lead the nation. His administrative skills had become part of the folklore among Madhya Pradesh bureaucrats. In his eventful political career, Singh achieved what many in the Congress could never even dream about. In 1985 Rajiv made him the governor of Punjab, an assignment brought about by his helping reach an accord with a section of Punjab separatists. Singh then became vice president of the Congress, till that point an honour that had not been accorded to anyone else. Here Singh displayed his organizational skills. Yet the coterie around Rajiv sensed trouble and began a campaign that brought about Singh's abrupt exit from party headquarters.

A great believer in astrology, Singh began to see wisdom in what many astrologers, babas and soothsayers had been telling him for long—he had 'rajyog' in his 'kundli'. 'Leave it to us and we will place all stars in your favour,' a prominent baba from Madhya Pradesh told him.[12]

However, in comparison to archrival Pawar, Singh lacked the support of even forty-odd party MPs and the kind of resources that the Maratha strongman could boast of. Pawar was counting on the support of almost all party MPs from Maharashtra, while Singh had no such luxury.

Singh decided to reach the pinnacle of Congress politics via 10 Janpath. He became a diehard Sonia loyalist in the hope that one day 'Madam' would recognize his devotion, loyalty and worth. As a reward, she would play a role in making him the most powerful man in the country—perhaps the Prime Minister.

Subsequent events showed that Singh sacrificed his promising political career, spurned rapprochement offers from Narasimha Rao, left the Congress, formed his own outfit, returned to the parent organization and plotted successfully the downfall of two coalitions headed by I.K. Gujral and Atal Behari Vajpayee respectively in 1997 and 1999.

Gujral had to go when Singh ensured that the Congress withdrew support to the mix of socialists, communists and regional parties over the Jain Commission's probe into the conspiracy angle of the Rajiv assassination. Singh insisted on the exit of two ministers belonging to the Dravida Munnetra Kazhagam (DMK), a party which was seen as sympathetic to the LTTE cause. Gujral refused, forcing the Congress to pull down the government. The Vajpayee government was brought down in an even more remarkable fashion, losing the motion of confidence by just one vote—a defeat brought about by an overnight change of stance by the Bahujan Samaj Party (BSP), which voted against the government. The Congress, however, denied having struck any deal with the BSP.

Singh continued to be a great believer in astrology. His associates said he took the theory of 'rajyog' too seriously. He used to tell his associates that he had been a chief minister, a governor, vice president of the Congress and a Central minister, so the one thing that remained was becoming Prime Minister. He firmly believed that there was a 'divine design' behind his survival when he had suffered a massive heart attack in 1989.

The doctors at Hamidia Hospital in Bhopal had almost given up on him when a call from Rajiv ensured a timely airlift to Delhi's Escorts Heart Institute. His spiritual guru, Mauni Baba of Ujjain, took credit for the miracle. The baba, who had taken a vow not to speak, reached Delhi and shut himself off to conduct various 'yagnas'. As Union communications minister, Singh gave two telephone connections to Baba. The act prompted a Hindi daily to run a headline, 'Jab Baba bolte nahin to do telephone kyon' (Why give two telephones to Baba when he does not speak)!

If Pawar was thinking of fulfilling Maratha leader Shivaji's dream of reaching the seat of power and Singh was counting on divine design, the young and dashing maharaja of Gwalior, Madhavrao Scindia, also joined the race, projecting himself as the true successor to Rajiv. The Scindias are the richest royals in the country. Scindia also had the backing of seven or eight MPs from Madhya Pradesh who were opposed to Arjun Singh. In addition, he was counting on support from a powerful newspaper and other influential lobbies.

As the Union railway minister, Scindia had become a hero of sorts for the growing middle class by introducing fast and comfortable trains like the Shatabdi between Dehi and many state capitals and installing a computerized reservation system that reduced the serpentine queues at ticket counters.

In May 1991, the news of Scindia's candidature led to a chain reaction. Rajesh Pilot, a former squadron leader from the Indian Air Force, joined the fray projecting himself as a young leader suited to step into Rajiv's shoes. Unlike Scindia, Singh and Pawar, Pilot had no locus standi in terms of experience either in the organization or in the government. Pilot was, in fact, yet to become a Cabinet minister. He was merely a minister of state in the Rajiv government. His candidature was therefore more in the nature of positioning for the future.

Many Congress leaders believed that the days of rajas and maharajas ended when India became a democratic republic. Thus Pilot tried to project himself as a man of the masses. Pilot harped on the theme of being a commoner—he was a Gujjar from western Uttar Pradesh—who made it to the power centres of Raisina Hill. Pilot, whose name was originally Rajeshwar Prasad, picked issues and campaigns that were aimed at weeding out corruption from high places. In the process, he earned the favour of the middle class, who liked his emphasis on probity in public life. Leaders of the old guard, such as Sitaram Kesri, weren't so impressed and loved to describe Pilot as 'autopilot', pointing at his inexperience in the organization.[13]

Among the contenders was also Narain Dutt Tiwari, whom many considered a politician among politicians. Panditji—he was a Brahmin, hence so addressed—was the least controversial. Most significantly, he was from UP, the heartland of Indian politics, which used to send eighty-five parliamentarians to the 545-member Parliament. He had vast experience as a four-time chief minister of the state and had held industry, finance and external affairs portfolios in the Union Cabinet.

Working against Tiwari was the difference that had cropped up with Rajiv in the course of the elections. Rajiv had asked him not to contest the Lok Sabha seat from Naini Tal as Tiwari was also a candidate for the assembly polls, but Panditji wanted to contest both as the prospects of forming a government in Uttar Pradesh, where the Congress fortunes had been on the decline, were rather bleak. Obviously, Tiwari did not want to cool his heels in Lucknow's Vidhan Sabha as the leader of the Opposition while his rivals went on to become Central ministers.

The coterie around Rajiv, however, gave a different story. They said Tiwari was hoping to edge him out as the leader of the party in case the Congress failed to get the majority. They thought he was becoming too big for his boots, and Rajiv bought the line of argument. He was not convinced by Tiwari's explanation that he could not reach the district collector in time to withdraw his nomination papers. The Tiwari camp kept its hopes alive till the results declared that a former newspaper vendor, Balraj Passi, of the BJP, had become a giant killer. It was Passi's moment of glory and the end of Tiwari's prime ministerial dreams.

Sonia finally absolved Tiwari in 2002 when, as party chief, she appointed him chief minister of the newly created state of Uttaranchal. But Tiwari was not her first choice. She wanted the party's Members of the Legislative Assembly (MLAs) to accept local leader Harish Rawat, but a rebellion from Satpalji Maharaj, a spiritual leader-cum-politician, forced her hand. Tiwari came and bowed before her. She smiled and said, 'Uttaranchal ja kar vikas kariye' (Go to Uttaranchal and help develop the state).[14]

A section of the Congressmen wanted the Vice President, Dr Shankar Dayal Sharma, to step down and take charge of the party. Sharma, a scholar of repute, freedom fighter and Nehru–Gandhi loyalist who had also been a Congress president, wanted to become Prime Minister too. The moment Sonia turned down the CWC's plea to succeed Rajiv, his followers swing into action. His son Ashutosh and wife Vimla took charge of neutralizing archrival Arjun Singh. The Singh–Sharma rivalry had its origins in their home state Madhya Pradesh, where Brahmins and thakurs were constantly locked in a battle for supremacy in the political arena. Sharma almost made it despite Arjun's opposition—he lost the battle at the last moment when another elderly Brahmin edged him out.

When Sharma realized he was nowhere in the leadership race, he made an announcement denying that he was in the running for AICC chief. He said that 'constitutional functionaries' should remain non-partisan particularly when elections were under way.[15]

The seventh contender and the unlikeliest one was P.V. Narasimha Rao. He was so low-key that the others never really considered him to be in the fray at all. But it was on him that the mantle fell. Arjun saw in him a stopgap arrangement to check Pawar. In his scheme of things,

Rao's appointment was a temporary measure to enable him to regroup his supporters before the final assault in the CPP—the Congress Parliamentary Party.

There was talk of a deal between Singh and Rao. As part of the quid pro quo, the latter was expected to appoint Singh as AICC chief. Indira's trusted lieutenant, Makhan Lal Fotedar, a former J&K bureaucrat who was known for his back-room skills and politicking, worked out the pact. Ajit Jogi, who later rose to become Chhattisgarh chief minister, claimed to be a witness when Fotedar mooted the idea of Singh as the party chief in exchange for support to Narasimha Rao as Prime Minister and Rao's endorsement of the move. According to Jogi, Rao simply went back on his word. The Rao camp denied there was any deal, saying that it may have been merely one among the many suggestions given to him.[16]

When the leadership tussle peaked four days after Rajiv's assassination, Singh wrote a letter to Rao—who was not, incidentally, holding any official post in the party—clarifying that he was not in the fray. Among other things, Singh said the 'thought of becoming Congress president never occurred' to him.[17] However, many leaders close to him openly talked about Arjun being made president of the AICC.

Unfortunately for Singh, his detractor Pawar was also working on an identical game plan, viewing Narasimha Rao as a temporary arrangement. As Maharashtra chief minister, Pawar issued a series of statements. While ruling himself out of the race for presidentship, he repeatedly insisted that the post of Congress Parliamentary Party chief should be kept open. He favoured the 'one-man, one-post' norm and said the era of towering personalities was over; the Congress should be run by collective leadership.

Narasimha Rao proved all of them wrong. He himself never believed that he would get a chance to lead the Congress and the nation at the fag end of his political career. He had been disappointed that Rajiv had allowed his opportunist friends to destroy the credibility of his government between 1984 and 1989. However, unlike V.P. Singh, Rao made no attempt to confront him, and when the party began searching for candidates for the 1991 general elections, he quietly told Rajiv that he wanted to retire from politics and go back to Andhra Pradesh to write his memoirs. Rajiv was surprised but did not insist that he stay on. He, however, sought an assurance that Rao would finalize the party manifesto.

Yet Rajiv's assassination altered everything. The kingmakers like M.L. Fotedar and Sitaram Kesri began looking for Narasimha Rao when Arjun Singh and Sharad Pawar triggered a no-holds barred competition to win over party MPs. Fotedar thought the acrimony would destroy party unity. The prospects of Shankar Dayal Sharma taking over as AICC chief rattled Arjun so much that he made a retreat favouring Rao. Pawar, who had remained adamant for a contest, also fell in line when Rao said to him philosophically, 'I will not be able to take the burden too long.'[18]

At this point, a large number of partymen sought Sonia's intervention even though she was in mourning. In the guise of offering condolences, leaders and MPs began calling on her in groups. Vincent George had assumed charge as Sonia's private secretary by this time and encouraged party functionaries to call on her. Each day some delegation would meet Sonia, besides the numerous others who went purely to offer condolences.

On her part, although Sonia may have intensely disliked politics, she continued to meet the party members who called on her. She seldom discussed politics but listened in rapt attention, reading their faces, gauging their mood, searching, looking for something.

Though Sonia did not give any clear indication of her preference for Rajiv's successor, Congressmen never tired of telling her their choices. A majority of them opposed Pawar. She was told that his promotion to AICC chief would reflect poorly for the party, which had always stood for the downtrodden and the minorities and backwards, as Pawar was seen as representing the interests of rich farmers and industrialists. Moreover, the Maratha leader was not a traditional Congressman. 'Look at the way he ditched Vasantdada Patil,' a Maharashtra leader told Sonia. In his assessment, Narasimha Rao could be trusted. He said that Rajiv had asked Rao and Mohsina

Kidwai, a former Union minister and close associate of Indira, to lead Indira's funeral procession as the two were extremely close to her. Rao 'will never let you down', the Maharashtra MP told Sonia.[19]

Sonia made it clear that she was reluctant to take responsibility and asked some senior leaders why they could not decide amongst themselves who should be the leader. The leaders smilingly admitted the party's 'inherent weaknesses' to undertake such a task—with towering personalities like Nehru, Indira and Rajiv to lead them there had been no need to develop a mechanism for succession and they wanted someone to guide them. Sonia was perplexed why they were so confident she would join politics. 'Haven't I told them I am not interested?' she asked herself.

At another level, Sonia sent enough signals to indicate that in a choice between Pawar and Narasimha Rao, her preference would be Rao. Rao's formal election as leader of the Congress was not very dramatic as the six other contenders had virtually given up. Once the Congress MPs were convinced that 'Madam' wanted Narasimha Rao, a mock election was arranged. The venue was 24 Akbar Road. Several rooms were converted into polling stations where MPs were asked to cast their vote under the watchful eyes of senior leaders like A.K. Antony, Sharad Pawar and P. Shiv Shankar. Rao polled more than 95 per cent of votes. Barring a handful of diehard Pawar supporters, everyone voted for him.

As the months passed, speculation over Sonia's role refused to die down. Congressmen did not give up hope. In an interview in July 1991, R.K. Dhawan said that she should enter politics to keep the family name alive. Dhawan, however, clarified that Sonia had no attachment to politics, adding, 'I have never in my tenure with Rajivji seen her interfering in matters of party or the government.'[20]

In August 1991 the newsmagazine *India Today* ran a special story on the enigma surrounding Sonia.[21] It praised Rajiv's widow for refusing to join politics. She would be thrown in among the hangers-on who had undermined her husband's career, it said. The article also praised her for seeing through the manipulative plans of those who were trying to persuade her.

Seven years later, these khadi clad, pan-chewing hangers-on were proved right. Sonia all along believed that she was moving in that direction as part of her historic duty and in the larger interests of the party. She was constantly told that by shunning politics, she was in fact failing a family that had made sacrifices for the Congress from the days of Nehru to Rajiv and had strengthened communal forces represented by the right-wing BJP. That she had to lead the Congress was presented as an overwhelming necessity. For the more cynical, her decision to join politics showed that the temptation of proving herself in the political arena turned out to be just too hard to resist.

THREE

A LONG JOURNEY FROM ORBASSANO

S onia was born on 9 December 1946 in Orbassano, in
northern Italy. For the family, Sonia, the second daughter, was a
little princess, their Cenerentola, or Cinderella. The nickname was
not entirely fortuitious. Unlike her sisters, Nadia and Anushka, Sonia
always wanted to be different. She was ambitious, though she confided
little about her ambitions. As a young girl she was never comfortable
in the dusty industrial town on the outskirts of Turin where she grew
up. When Sonia lived in Orbassano, the town was a muddle of
apartment blocks and houses that had come up in the early 1950s as a
result of the post-war boom in northern Italy. It was too undemanding
and lower middle class for a Cenerentola.

She was a good student but not an exceptional one, except in her
gift for languages. She could converse easily in Spanish and Russian.
She would also develop fluency in French. Nowadays she is at ease in
Hindi too and reads her speeches from texts in the Devanagri script.

The credit for teaching her Russian goes to her father, who had
fought in Russia with the Germans. He was deeply influenced by the
Russian language, culture and food and loved the country. Little wonder
then that he gave Russian names to his three daughters.

Stephano was hard working and disciplined, a quality that he
passed on to his family, especially Sonia. As a self-made man who had

been through some very tough times, he took pride in providing for his family. He had come to Orbassano from Asiago in the Veneto region as a poor mason and made good in a small construction business through his dedication and fair dealing.

Stephano brought up his daughters in the traditional Catholic way and was wary of foreigners. He was not charmed when Sonia informed him about tying the knot with the Indian Prime Minister's son. His inflexibility on this count estranged him from Sonia, so much so that he did not attend Sonia's marriage and predicted that it would end shortly. Sonia's maternal uncle, Mario Predebon, gave away the girl in the civil marriage that took place on 25 February 1968.

However, Sonia's defiance did not result in a complete breakdown in father-daughter relations. Stephano became extremely fond of Rajiv when he visited Orbassano, but Rajiv's entry in politics in 1981-82 again made the old man worried. Stephano never visited India, but he was well-versed with the political situation there and worried about religious intolerance. His friends in Orbassano claimed that Stephano, who often shared his fear of fanatics harming his daughter, would never have approved of Sonia's entry into politics.

His forceful and rather strict side often placed him at odds with his family resulting in frequent quarrels between husband and wife. The quarrels drew Sonia closer to her mother, Paola.

By Sonia's own admission, she was a naughty and 'very active' girl in her early life. She would play hopscotch for hours or join the neighbourhood boys in a game of football. She wanted to be a teacher, but Paola wanted her to pick a more paying profession.

Josto Maffeo, a friend from her youth, recalls her as one with a fiery temper. He can remember occasions when she hit him with her thick Italian-Russian-German dictionary.[1] Maffeo, a journalist with a Spanish daily, was unwilling to say anything further about Sonia. The reluctance to comment is in common with others in Orbassano who know the family.

When a group of Indian journalists visited the town in 1998, one neighbour, who claimed to have studied with Sonia, described her as a 'nice person' but one who was aware of her 'social superiority'.

According to her, after finishing school, Sonia went to a more fashionable college, the Convent of Maria Ausiliatrice in Giaveno, fifteen kilometres away.

Sister Domenica, who was an assistant when Sonia studied at the convent, remembers her well. According to her, Sonia was lively though not overexuberant, and she studied just enough to get by. Her colleague, Sister Anna Maria, recalled Sonia's visit during a school reunion. Dinner was being served when she suddenly announced she had to leave. She said that she had a special guest coming to dinner— the son of Indira Gandhi. 'She was always a little manipulative. She should do well in politics,' said Sister Anna Maria, while speaking to *Frontline* correspondent Vaiju Naravane in 1998.[2]

Family friends said that by early 1965 Stefano had made enough money that he could fund his daughter's education in Cambridge. Locals recall that the real change in the living standard of the Maino family came in the 1980s, a period which also marked the emergence of Rajiv Gandhi on the Indian political scene. Some Italian businessmen attributed Maino's success to the 1980s boom in the construction industry, but in India exaggerated reports about the Maino family's fortunes were viewed with suspicion.

Nehru–Gandhi family friend Mohammad Yunus, a journalist and administrator, was among a handful of persons from Rajiv Gandhi's side who visited the Maino house, a neat double-storey at Number 14 Via Bellini, in a neighbourhood inhabited mainly by people in the construction trade. He said, 'I can say without fear of contradiction that they are a decent middle-class family. The stories about their fabulous home and millions gained through their India link can be termed as sheer nonsense.'[3]

Sonia's sister Anushka and niece Aruna run an antique shop called Etnica two kilometres away from Orbassano at a commercial complex in Gerbola di Rivolta. The shop contains artefacts from India such as Pichwais, Tanjore paintings, silver pieces from Bikaner and expensive shawls.

Etnica served as the basis of the campaign against Sonia by her detractor Dr Subramanian Swamy, who accused her of smuggling

Indian artefacts. He followed up his charges with a slew of letters to the Prime Minister, the home minister, the Enforcement Directorate, the Central Bureau of Investigation and other investigative agencies, besides filing several petitions in the Delhi High Court. The court issued notices to the Central government and concerned agencies, and proceedings continue. The Congress is dismissive of the charges, saying they are not worth the paper they are written on. 'You know what Swamy is . . .' commented a party spokesman,[4] referring to Swamy's reputation as a maverick politician who in his career has traversed almost the entire political spectrum, as also his fierce friendships and relentless enmities.

Congress leaders said that Swamy failed to understand two things. First, during the time of Indira Gandhi, Sonia was a member of the Prime Minister's gift committee and was asked to select gift items to be given to visiting foreign dignitaries. Secondly, Sonia is herself a connoisseur of art having done an art appreciation and restoration course. She is a collector of miniature Tanjore paintings and artefacts from different states. Her friend and interior designer Sunita Kohli said, 'She has taste as also extensive knowledge of Indian arts, crafts and textiles. She is easily able to identify the designs of most Indian weaves.'

Vaiju Naravane admitted that the presence of the shop on the outskirts of Orbassano continued to nibble at her consciousness like a buzzing bee refusing to go away. She found its location incongruous. A shop like this would do well in Rome or Milan. But Orbassano? 'It's like setting up an expensive store selling Swedish furniture on the outskirts of Faizabad!' she said, drawing a comparison with a small, dusty town east of Delhi.[5]

Other aspects of Sonia's past have been questioned too. Her detractors led by Swamy alleged that the Lennox Cook School, where Sonia studied English in 1965, was a KGB outfit, which closed shop soon after she left Cambridge. The authorities at Cambridge strongly refute the charge.[6] By official accounts, the school was founded in 1961 by John Lennox Cook, a former senior tutor at the Bell School, Cambridge. Cook retired in 1985 after turning the institute into a great success, and it was then taken over by Anglo World Education Ltd., which runs a chain of such schools worldwide.

In Cambridge, Sonia stayed as a paying guest with an English family. She was homesick, and her unfamiliarity with the language didn't help. It was a difficult time for her. As she recounts in *Rajiv*, she used to feel miserable and homesick.

Her search for Italian food led her to Varsity, a Greek restaurant, the next-best option as she failed to find an Italian one, and to her introduction to Rajiv Gandhi. Each evening, noisy groups of students from Cambridge University would gather there over a pint. For Sonia, one of the boys in that large group always stood out. As she described him, 'One with big, black eyes and wonderfully innocent and disarming smile.'[7]

Rajiv made the first move using a common friend, Christian, who played the go-between. He was a German who was also doing the language course and, luckily, fluent in Italian. One day at lunchtime, he introduced Rajiv to Sonia, who recalls, 'Our eyes met for the first time directly at a close distance. I could hear my heart pounding. As far as I was concerned, it was love at first sight. He later told me that it was for him too.'[8]

Rajiv asked her out and within days, they became close. They began going out for picnics on the riverside and to jazz performances.

A year later, Rajiv visited the Maino house in Orbassano. The Prime Minister's son spent the day visiting the Orbassano city centre. Late in the evening when he met Stephano, he came straight to the point by asking for Sonia's hand. Stephano was stunned. He was suspicious of foreigners, but Stephano had no doubts about Rajiv's determination to marry his daughter. He made no concessions wondering how his daughter would possibly get used to life in India. He then told Rajiv and Sonia not to meet for a year and then see if they still wanted to spend the rest of their life together.

The one-year forced separation was the most difficult period for both Rajiv and Sonia, but a year later, they were even more deeply in love. A man of his word, Stephano had no choice but to accept the inevitable. The old man's pride, however, came in the way of his attending the marriage.

Indira Gandhi's approach was different. Rajiv wrote regularly to her and told her about Sonia. She agreed to meet her in London where she was going to inaugurate an exhibition on Jawaharlal Nehru. Sonia was extremely nervous. The meeting at India House failed to take place as on the way there Sonia completely lost her confidence. Rajiv and Indira were understanding. The meeting was re-scheduled at the residence of the Indian high commissioner. Sensing that Sonia was uncomfortable, Indira spoke to her in French, in which Sonia was much more at ease. Recalling the meeting, Sonia wrote, 'She spoke to me in French, knowing I was more fluent in it than English. She wanted to know about myself, my studies. She told me that I need not be frightened because she herself had been young, extremely shy, and in love, and she understood perfectly.'[9] Small gestures such as this from Indira gave Sonia the confidence that she could be a daughter-in-law in the distinguished family.

Sonia arrived in Delhi on 13 January 1968. She and Rajiv got engaged in a simple ceremony twelve days later. As the prospective bahu of the Nehru–Gandhi family, Indira Gandhi did not want her to stay with them and staying at a hotel was out of the question. Her aide and confidant T.N. Kaul and family friend Mohammad Yunus suggested that Teji Bachchan play host to the bride, and the matter was resolved. The proposal found immediate approval from Rajiv, Sanjay, Amitabh and Ajitabh Bachchan. Amitabh, yet to become a superstar, was Sonia's first friend in India.

The marriage took place on 25 February 1968 on the back lawns of 1 Safdarjung Road after a brief mehendi ceremony at the Bachchans'. The civil marriage was a simple affair. Rajiv wore a cream silk Patiala achkan and choodidars with a pink Bharatpuri turban while Sonia wore a pale pink khadi sari without much jewellery. In keeping with Kashmiri traditions, Sonia wore floral jewellery—jasmine garlands tied on her ankles, wrists and neck. Sanjay, like Rajiv's cousins, wore a pink turban and cream-coloured achkan. There was only light refreshment at the wedding. In the evening, however, there was a lavish dinner at Hyderabad House, off India Gate, where official banquets are held, to which about 250 guests were invited. The guests were seated on the floor and served a sumptuous Kashmiri banquet. A day later, Indira hosted a reception at the Ashok Hotel at which choice Parsi, Kashmiri and Italian cuisines were served to the one thousand invitees.

Sonia became pregnant in 1969 but suffered a miscarriage. She held Indira responsible for it, blaming her obsession with fitness and yoga. Sonia, as family sources said, had no problems with learning yoga from Swami Dhirendra Brahmachari and others, but she was not too comfortable with it during her first pregnancy.

The acrimony ended when Rahul was born in June 1970. According to Sonia, during that period Indira become her 'real mother' taking 'exemplary care' of her.[10] Sonia seldom had problems with Indira, despite her imposing personality. As she told Eric Silver of the Guardian News Service in 1986, 'My upbringing is such that I feel my husband is superior and his mother even more superior.'[11] Sonia also told a visiting Italian magazine correspondent that Indira Gandhi was as affectionate as a real mother. 'Living with her was a wonderful experience,' Sonia said, adding that she could never forget Indira's small note to her soon after her marriage when her mother left for Italy. 'I was feeling lonely and depressed. As soon as I returned from the airport, I got her note. It said: "Just to say hello and to tell you that we all love you."'[12]

Sonia admitted that she had problems in adjusting to Indian conditions. Initially, she did not like Indian food or Indian clothes, but Indira and Rajiv did not force anything on her except for one thing— speaking in Hindi at the dinner table, a custom everyone had to follow. Slowly, Sonia began liking Indian food. Nowadays, pasta, lasagna and spaghetti are rarely cooked at 10 Janpath.

Indira too did not have any problems getting along with Sonia. She repeatedly told close associates like Pupul Jayakar, Mohammad Yunus, Mohsina Kidwai and others how comfortable she was with Sonia. She used to say, 'It is amazing to know how easygoing Sonia is.

Somehow she gets to know what I want. The beauty of it is that I do not have to tell her about these things.'[13] She may have been referring to the change in Sonia's style of dress after Rajiv entered politics. She discarded jeans and skirts in 1981, opting for sarees and salwar kameez, a gesture that Indira Gandhi appreciated.

Sonia and Sanjay also used to get along very well. Rajiv, Amitabh, Ajitabh, Sonia and Sanjay would go out for drives, movies or have ice-cream on the India Gate lawns. When Sonia was pregnant with Rahul and Rajiv was away on flights, Sanjay was extremely caring, sitting with her at mealtimes and keeping her entertained with his talk.

On 20 June 1975 Sonia Gandhi had a first brush with politics, coming face to face with a crowd of about 100,000 at Delhi's Boat Club. It was eight days after the famous Allahabad High Court verdict setting aside Indira's election from Rae Bareli. Sanjay, who was chief organizer of the solidarity rally, broached the subject of the entire family attending it. 'We must all be seen together,' he argued. Both Sonia and Rajiv felt awkward but agreed to go along. Sonia wore a khadi saree and stood next to Rajiv, Maneka and Sanjay on the stage, behind Indira. While Maneka was thrilled, enjoying every bit, Sonia could not muster the courage even to wave at the crowd. She was amazed at how Indira could mesmerize a crowd as she recalled the services of the Nehru–Gandhi family and vowed to continue to serve the people till her last breath.

Later, after the lifting of the Emergency and the election defeat in 1977, Rajiv and Sanjay began having bitter fights. Somehow Rajiv was convinced that Sanjay was responsible for the downfall of 'Mummy'. Rajiv had all along disliked Sanjay's extra-constitutional authority. During the Emergency, one day as he was returning from Bombay, he was stopped and diverted because of a VIP movement. The VIP turned out to be his younger brother. Rajiv's companions asked, 'Younger brother is going; elder brother is diverted to a lane. How do you like it?' Rajiv was quick to reply, 'That's politics.'[14]

In a sense, however, the process of political orientation for Rajiv and Sonia had already begun once they moved to Indira's house. Much as they disliked the world of politics, they were already being sucked into it.

FOUR

A TALE OF TWO BAHUS

At first Sanjay's marriage with Maneka in March 1974 did not bring about much change in Indira's household. There were occasional tantrums, but both Indira and Sonia were sympathetic towards Maneka, young as she was. As in a typical Indian family, as the elder 'bahu' (daughter-in-law), Sonia had a special place. She was responsible for running the kitchen and deciding the menu. Maneka had little interest in the kitchen, so there were no clashes on that count, but she enjoyed helping Indira getting quotations for her speeches. After the Emergency, in 1977, when Indira was out of power and under attack from the Janata government, she managed *Surya* magazine and used it as a tool to run down Indira's opponents. Maneka proved a staunch defender of the family's interests and gave back as good as Indira received through the magazine, running a series of exposés that did immense damage to those who were arrayed against Indira.

Occasionally there were big fights inside Indira's house. On one occasion, Maneka got so angry with Sanjay that she removed her wedding ring and threw it at him. Indira lost her temper too, as the ring had belonged to her mother, Kamla Nehru. Sonia picked up the ring and said she would keep it for Priyanka.[1] These days, Priyanka wears it.

The ring, inset with diamonds and other precious stones, twenty-one exquisite saris, two sets of gold jewellery and a khadi saree made of yarn spun by Jawaharlal Nehru in jail were Indira's gifts to Maneka when she married Sanjay.

Another big fight was witnessed by B.K. Nehru when Sanjay threw a fit at Sonia because an egg was not properly fried. According to Nehru, Indira did not reprimand Sanjay, but she appeared acutely embarrassed by Sanjay's conduct. In his memoir *Nice Guys Finish Second*, Nehru described the scene at Indira's 12 Willingdon Crescent house: 'More often than not, there was servant trouble. Sonia was the cook, Maneka merely ate. Indira's two sons and their wives were certainly not on the best terms with each other.'[2]

Journalist and author Khushwant Singh too recalls that Rajiv and Sanjay had their differences. 'Once I happened to be there when Rajiv and Sonia were celebrating one of their children's birthdays. I noticed that the two brothers and their wives occupied different ends of the house and had very little to do with each other.'[3]

Both Rajiv and Sonia had not liked the imposition of the Emergency, but they chose to remain silent. At one party during this time, Sonia met Naveen Patnaik, son of Biju Patnaik, the towering Orissa politician and head of the regional Utkal Congress (currently known as Biju Janata Dal and headed by Naveen) who was jailed in the round-up of Opposition leaders. Sonia had no hesitation in sympathizing with Biju's son. 'It must be terrible for you that your father is in jail. I am sorry about it.'[4]

Friends of Indira said her two bahus were completely different since they came from diverse backgrounds. Sonia had been taught not to raise her voice or show dissent; Maneka was more outspoken. Maneka hardly measured her words before speaking. The Gandhi–Anand households were never at ease except during the Emergency when Maneka's mother, Amteshwar Anand, became a close companion of Indira.

Maneka and Sanjay used to have the usual family arguments over minor things like food, but many times they were witnessed by the entire family. Exaggerated accounts were later given to show Maneka as irresponsible, but sources close to Sonia maintained that at least in the first few years, the family had adjusted and they had a good time.

Maneka had a keen interest in politics, a fact that she never tried to hide. Yet over the years, Indira started trusting Sonia more, seeking her advice on everything from the choice of menu to her selection of sarees. She also valued Sonia's aloofness towards politics and matters of statecraft.

Sonia got along well with Sanjay except when he appointed her as a director in Maruti Technical Services (MTS), a dubious subsidiary of Maruti. Sonia signed on the dotted line entitling her to a monthly salary, 1 per cent commission on net profits, house and travel expenses, car, driver, etc. However, none of these perks was directly passed on to her. Sonia was unaware of the larger, legal dimensions but when Rajiv came to know that MTS was posing as a consultancy service and had taken ten lakh rupees from Maruti, which was struggling to survive in spite of generous contributions from public sector banks, he was livid. Angrily, he asked Sonia, 'How could you do this?!'

A commission of inquiry headed by Justice A.C. Gupta probed the issue and submitted its report in 1978 during the Janata Party regime. The commission concluded, '[I]t is a fact known to all concerned that Shrimati Sonia Gandhi was a foreign national. In view of the provisions of the foreign exchange regulation act of 1973, which had come into force on 1 January 1974, she could neither hold shares of any Indian company nor hold any office of profit in such company from the date the act came into force without the prior approval of the Reserve Bank of India. Ultimately, she tendered her resignation on 21 January 1975.'[5]

The issue resurfaced when Rajiv took over as the Prime Minister. Rajiv, refuting the charge, made it clear that his wife never drew a monthly salary of Rs 2500 or visited the Maruti office or factory.[6]

After her defeat in the elections of 1977, Indira was forced to vacate the Prime Minister's house and move to 12 Willingdon Crescent with both daughters-in-law, grandchildren, attendants and dogs. It was in this smaller house that Sonia really became closer to Indira. She did not keep an ayah for Rahul and Priyanka and began cooking both meals of the day. Indira was extremely wary of keeping a cook as the old one had died and she suspected that the new government would try and poison her family. Sonia was spotted picking up vegetables at Khan Market, a shopping area favoured by diplomats and bureaucrats. She began growing broccoli in the vegetable patch behind the house. Indira, facing challenges from various quarters, would not leave an opportunity to praise Sonia. The preferential treatment of Sonia upset Maneka, who was also trying to help out mother-in-law with the feisty *Surya* magazine, among other things. Maneka wondered why Sonia was treated as special just because she could buy groceries and cook.

Indira's family friends, ranging from Pupul Jayakar to Mohsina Kidwai, attribute a number of factors why Indira had a preference for Sonia over Maneka. 'In many ways, she was much more Indian than an average Indian girl,' Mohsina Kidwai recalled. 'Indiraji always admired her for her good eye for handicrafts, handloom and antiques. She short-listed and selected the menu for dinners. When Frontier Gandhi, Khan Abdul Ghaffar Khan, visited India in connection with Gandhi centenary celebrations, Sonia was Indiraji's personal emissary looking after his one meal a day, food, etc.'[7]

Indira's return to Parliament in 1978 from the Chikmagalur parliamentary seat in southern Karnakata—where she won by a massive margin—marked a turning point. Incidentally, the seat was vacated by H.D. Deve Gowda, who later would head a rag-tag coalition as Prime Minister in 1996-97. The Chikmagalur victory restored the confidence of the family. For both Sonia and Maneka, life at 12 Willingdon Crescent was a lively experience of an Indian joint family with its share of skirmishes and happy moments. Maneka and Sonia temporarily became friends when Maneka was expecting Feroze Varun. The elder sister-in-law took care of her food, giving her vital tips and spending a lot of time with her until the baby was born in March 1980.

Maneka was very fond of 12 Willingdon Crescent. It was here that she began to fully understand Sanjay and what he was trying to accomplish. The man was in a hurry to transform India into a modern nation state. Maneka was convinced that Sanjay was grossly misunderstood. A lot of the mess that was created by Congresswallahs during the Emergency was quietly passed on to Sanjay, she felt. Likewise, the media, suffering from Emergency excesses, held him accountable for crimes that he had not committed, as she expressed repeatedly in interviews.[8]

Maneka's attachment to 12 Willingdon Crescent was so intense that she made an attempt to move in there in 2001 as a minister in the Vajpayee government. The government forced a private trust headed by Sonia in memory of Sanjay to move out of the government premises that it had been occupying for more than a decade. Maneka, who had little or no sympathy for the trust for its open association with Sonia and the Congress, made no efforts to stall the eviction. Instead she made a bid to wangle the ministerial bungalow on grounds of her emotional links with the house. But the house was already taken over by one E. Punnuswamy, a Pattali Makkal Katchi (PMK) MP from Tamil Nadu, who bluntly refused to move out. Maneka was disappointed, especially with the urban development minister, Jagmohan, who ignored her plea. The office-bearers of the Sanjay Gandhi Memorial Trust blamed her for inaction and belittlement of Sanjay's memory. 'As [a] Union minister in [the government], she should have resisted. It was one among a few institutions in memory of Sanjay,' said Captain Parveen Davar, secretary of the trust. Maneka's camp denied the charge, saying she had no sympathy with a trust that had become a dumping ground for out-of-work Congress politicians. The trust was finally shifted to a small room at 24 Akbar Road.

Sonia and Rajiv were away in Italy when Sanjay died in an air crash while practising loops in his Pitts S-2A aircraft over Safdarjung Airport on 23 June 1980. A chartered aircraft was sent to Rome to fetch them. On the way, it picked up Maneka's mother, Amteshwar, sister Ambika, Congress leader V.C. Shukla and industrialist Swraj Paul from London. Shukla and Paul kept telling Amteshwar that she should try to keep the two families together and rally round Rajiv. Amteshwar was too grieved to apply her mind to this aspect. However, within days the Anand family, which had risen from being a decisively middle-class army family to one with political clout during the Sanjay era, was once again viewed with suspicion and distrust. A section of

Congress leaders who had suffered during the Sanjay era began a campaign saying that the Anand family wanted Indira to draft Maneka in politics. The whisper campaign had its impact.

In any case, Sanjay's death had changed everything. Indira was a broken person. Sometimes she would hold herself responsible for Sanjay's death; sometimes she would blame the young widow. In her wavering mood, she began putting pressure on Rajiv to give up flying completely, fearing for his life. Rajiv was in no mood to oblige his mother, but he agreed to take leave to be at her side.

Word was soon out that Rajiv would emerge as Sanjay's successor. It came as a rude shock to Maneka, as Indira had promised to make her her personal secretary. Maneka wondered how Indira could draft a political novice like Rajiv. After all, on numerous occasions Indira herself had described Rajiv as an apolitical person.

Indira's close circle, ranging from Pupul Jayakar, Dhirendra Brahmachari and R.K. Dhawan to writer Khushwant Singh, was sharply divided on the issue of Sanjay's successor. Some media persons who had easy access to Indira and Maneka's family began lobbying for a political role for Maneka. Indira was undecided.

Sonia opposed Maneka's entry. Although she was not keen for Rajiv to become a political player, she viewed Maneka as an unpredictable and ambitious person. According to Pupul Jayakar, 'At first Indira understood Maneka's despair. She was anxious to find something that would occupy Maneka's time and in a compassionate gesture to the young widow, suggested to Maneka to become her secretary and travel with her. This upset Sonia. Letters were exchanged between Sonia and Indira, and Indira, realizing the need for Rajiv and family, withdrew the offer.'[9]

Sonia may have blocked Maneka's entry in politics, but she was equally opposed to Rajiv stepping into Sanjay's shoes. At one juncture, she even threatened to walk out of his life if he were to join politics. Sonia recalls that she 'fought like a tigress' for the sake of Rajiv and the children but most of all for 'our freedom—that simple human right that we had so carefully and consistently preserved.'[10]

Sonia, however, slowly gave in, realizing that both Rajiv and Indira needed each other in the political arena. 'I understood Rajiv's duty to her. At the same time, I was angry and resentful towards a system, which, as I saw it, demanded him as a sacrificial lamb. It would crush and destroy him—of that I was absolutely certain.' For Rajiv, his decision was reminiscent of his mother explaining why she had to become housekeeper to Jawaharlal Nehru: 'It was not really a choice . . . there was nobody else to do that. I felt that there was a void and I could not see anyone else filling it; there was in a sense an inevitability about it.'[11]

Sonia has never clarified why she vehemently opposed Maneka's entry into politics. Sources close to Sonia said she felt Maneka's inexperience and haughty behaviour would become a liability for Indira. Sonia was also said to be extremely wary of the Anand family, particularly of Amteshwar Anand.

The exit of Maneka from the Indira household witnessed many turns and twists, an ideal script for any saas-bahu serial. Indira's so-called perfect bahu, who cooked food, bought groceries, helped Indira choose the right sarees, raised children and showed no inclination towards politics and politicking, strangely made no attempt to be a peacemaker. Some of Sonia's friends said that her conduct must also be seen in a human context. After all, she too was a bahu and had to protect her turf. Her assessment of Maneka's potential threat and personal bias may have prevented her from acting decisively.[12]

Maneka, however, does not hold her responsible. According to her, Indira and other members of the family changed their attitude once Sanjay died: 'I realized that I was nothing but Maneka to them.'[13]

Maneka began working on an independent line in her effort to enter politics. She had the support of some influential friends of Sanjay who had benefited immensely under him, but many backed out when Maneka told them she was planning to go against Indira. Suddenly Maneka discovered that except for Akbar 'Dumpy' Ahmad, known for his fiery speeches and outspoken behaviour, virtually everyone else had changed loyalties. Dumpy, who loved dogs and the good things in life, stayed on, working round the clock to float the Sanjay Vichar Manch, a quasi-political outfit. Indira was livid and plainly told Maneka to leave Safdarjung Road if she wished to run a political organization.

Although a political novice, Maneka played her cards well, dictating the timing of her exit from the Indira household. At the time, Indira was in London with Sonia while Rajiv was busy learning the ropes of politics and governance from a select band of academicians, bureaucrats and technocrats.

Indira returned from London on the morning of 28 March 1982. Family watchers said the Prime Minister was in a foul mood, so much so that she did not even return Maneka's greeting. Soon Indira stormed barefoot into Maneka's room in the company of two witnesses, Dhirendra Brahmachari and R.K. Dhawan, ordering her to leave her residence. Maneka first exhibited innocence, wondering why she was being given marching orders. When Indira referred to her Sanjay Vichar Manch speech, Maneka said she had cleared it. This infuriated Indira further. They exchanged heated words, and Indira told her to leave without any belongings.

The debate went on for long and finally at 1 a.m., she began walking out of the house. For the dozens of media persons, including the correspondents of major foreign news agencies like Reuters, AFP and BBC, it was an opportunity of a lifetime. 'There was Indira, shouting, hair dishevelled, and Maneka, sobbing in a low voice. I have watched hundreds of Hindi films and soap operas but nothing like that. It was so real,' said a photographer who captured the entire episode on film.

Indira's two daughters-in-law are still at loggerheads. Sonia refuses to comment on Maneka, but Sanjay's widow is not so diplomatic. She is known to make acerbic remarks about her sister-in-law—on her political style and way of functioning, even personal comments. Speaking on Doordarshan, Maneka said, 'It is true that she is a foreigner. But more than that, she has never done any social work and does not have any training. We are not born politicians, but you learn, study, and most important, you feel that something should be done.'[14]

The rivalry between the two took a piquant turn when Maneka, who had won as an independent from Pilibhit in western UP, became a minister in the National Democratic Alliance (NDA) government headed by Atal Behari Vajpayee in 1999.

In a subsequent reshuffle she was appointed minister for culture, a position which gave her supervision over various family trusts headed by Sonia. Maneka ordered a probe into alleged financial irregularities in some of these trusts and questioned the trust deed of the Indira Gandhi National Centre for the Arts (IGNCA). The pace at which she started looking into these institutions upset many people. In an abrupt move, she was taken out of the ministry and moved to the more innocuous department of statistics. Maneka held Sonia responsible for her exit.

The publication of *Indira: The Life of Indira Nehru Gandhi* by Katherine Frank provided further ground for discord. Maneka alleged that the older bahu of Indira was instrumental in the inclusion of hoary tales involving Sanjay in the book. She claimed that Sonia and the Congress party were trying to project Sanjay in a poor light and show Sonia, Priyanka and Rahul as the true inheritors of the Nehru–Gandhi legacy. Frank had met Sonia while conducting research for the book and acknowledged Sonia's support in terms of granting access to family letters and photographs.

When the book came out, some Congress leaders felt portions of it showed Sanjay and Indira in a negative way, but aide and adviser on literary matters K. Natwar Singh and party spokesman Jaipal Reddy advised Sonia against issuing any statement or demanding a ban. Maneka acted quickly against some statements in the book and won an out-of-court defamation suit in England. Maneka quickly asserted that it was Varun's sense of outrage against Frank that prompted her to file charges against the author.

Maneka is dismissive about her failure to inherit the legacy of the family. According to her, the whole idea of linking the Congress with the Nehru–Gandhi legacy is incorrect. 'The legacy lies in carrying out the ideals set by the family,' she says, asserting that it does not matter to her that it is Sonia who is accruing the political benefits of belonging to the dynasty.

While the young Gandhis were reluctant to attack one another in public, K. Natwar Singh launched a no-holds-barred verbal assault on Maneka. The Sonia camp was quick to remind the nation about the circumstances and the manner in which Maneka made common cause with Indira's detractors, eventually accepting the post of a junior minister in the BJP-led coalition.

FIVE

THE PRIME MINISTER'S WIFE

Even as Indira's aides were planning Maneka's exit from the Prime Minister's house, Rajiv was being groomed for politics. A suite of rooms was readied at 1 Safdarjung Road and made accessible from a separate entrance on 1 Akbar Road. Here Rajiv was given a private secretary, Vincent George, who was drawn from the AICC secretarial pool.

Vijay Dhar, whose father, D.P. Dhar, had been among Indira's inner circle of advisers, began preparing the pilot for his new role, and by November 1980, Rajiv's office became an alternative durbar. Industrialists, scientists, scholars and senior Indian Administrative Service (IAS) officers unhappy with their ministers started queuing up. In many cases, Rajiv began by saying, 'I'll tell Mummy' or he would himself telephone a minister or a high official and order him to speed up a laggard file so as to get closure on a project. It was at this juncture that Rajiv first came in contact with the likes of hotelier Lalit Suri, chubby Italian pointman Ottavio Quattrocchi and Satish Sharma, a buddy from his flying days. Soon Arun Singh, a fellow Doon school alumni and now a corporate executive, replaced Dhar as adviser.

Rajiv's entry into politics made an impact on Sonia. She had already given up western dress and she rescinded her Italian citizenship in 1983. She began accompanying Rajiv on political tours, where she was told to smile, wave and demurely walk behind him. She confined herself to concentrating on Rajiv's parliamentary constituency of Amethi, prodding Sharma to take action on the many complaints and requests sent by constituents.

Rajiv was in the habit of sharing everything with Sonia. He would be up late nights, enthusiastically telling her the finer points of Indian history and how advancements in science and technology could transform Indian society. Slowly Sonia started taking interest, sharing Rajiv's vision of India.

Alongside, after Sanjay's death Indira became extremely religious, and in Sonia, she found a willing partner to share her beliefs. As Indira began keeping Monday fasts, Sonia too joined her. Indira then switched over to Tuesday and Sonia followed. While Sonia says little about her faith except that she would like to be cremated in accordance with Hindu rites, she admits keeping fasts, attributing the habit to Indira. 'I followed her . . . Mummy used to say you should sacrifice something you like very much for God. Everyone likes food, so I offer one day's food to God.'[1]

The worsening situation in Punjab, as militants unleashed a violent struggle that took a daily toll of lives, led to Operation Blue Star in June 1984 to evict Sant Bhindranwale and his followers from the Golden Temple in Amritsar. The operation achieved the immediate aim of removing Sant Bhindranwale from the scene, but the Sikh community was incensed at the destruction caused to its holiest shrine. The fallout had a disastrous impact on Indira. She was convinced that her life was in danger. On several occasions she called her grandson Rahul to tell him not to cry if anything happened to her and gave detailed instructions about her cremation. As if she had a premonition, on that fateful morning of 31 October 1984, Indira would just not let go of Priyanka as she readied for school. She hugged her tightly and reminded Rahul of her instruction.

Sonia had just finished washing her hair when she heard what she thought were crackers bursting nearby. Then she heard the maid crying. Sonia rushed outside shouting, 'Mummy, oh my God, Mummy,' picked up Indira and cradled her head in her lap. She didn't stop to tidy herself before getting into the Ambassador to accompany her to hospital. At 2.20 p.m., Indira was officially declared dead. Rajiv was in West Bengal and heard the news en route as he flew back to Delhi.

As soon as Rajiv reached Delhi, P.C. Alexander, principal secretary to Indira, and other trusted aides told him that the Cabinet and the Congress party wanted him to be the Prime Minister.

Alexander said he had to make a determined bid to tear Rajiv away from Sonia at the All India Institute of Medical Sciences (AIIMS). Sonia was pleading with Rajiv not to consent, but Rajiv believed that it was his duty to do so.

It took Sonia many months to recover after Indira's assassination. She lost about fifteen pounds in two months, and her asthma attacks became more frequent. The two dimples that were the most attractive attributes of a laughing Sonia became a rarity.

As Prime Minister's wife, Sonia's photographs depicted her as an inscrutable person, constantly tense, aloof and cold. Rajiv's critics were quick to brand her as a power behind the throne. Someone described her as Noor Jahan of Turin while others described her as a Sphinx, the mythical Greek monster with a woman's head and lion's body who waited outside Thebes, asking travellers a riddle and killing them when they failed to answer it.

During Rajiv's tenure as Prime Minister (1984-89), Sonia attempted to keep away from politics and lead a normal life. Her social circle consisted of a small group of European and Indian friends. The highlight of each week was the Sunday brunch, when these friends— mostly business persons and junior diplomats—would gather at 5 Race Course Road and chatter delightedly in French, Spanish or Italian. Quattrocchi was one of the friends present at the Sunday brunch. Another permanent fixture was Nadia, Sonia's sister, who is married to a Spanish diplomat, José Valdemoro, then posted in New Delhi. Some of these Sunday meals were Indian and served in thalis. Often Sonia exhibited her culinary skills by cooking lasagna and prawns in hot garlic sauce, which became a rage among friends.

When Rajiv was Prime Minister, there was a strict demarcation between 7 Race Course Road and the adjoining 5 Race Course Road that served as his office and residence respectively. No one, including such close associates as Indian Foreign Service (IFS) officer Mani Shankar Aiyar and senior IAS officer Wajahat Habibullah, who were in the Prime Minister's Office (PMO), and close associates like Sam Pitroda and P. Chidambaram, were allowed inside Rajiv's family quarters. Both Mani and Habibullah had studied with Rajiv in Doon school but their proximity-cum-friendship was not enough to have easy access to the Sonia household.

Access was limited to a handful of personal friends like Suman and Manjulika Dubey, Jaya and Amitabh Bachchan, Arun and Nina Singh, Mohan and Nirmal Thadani, Michael and Usha Albuquerque, Sunita and Ramesh Kohli, Ottavio and Maria Quattrocchi, Satish and Sterre Sharma, and a few others. Dubey, an outstanding journalist, remained a close Rajiv associate all along. His wife, Manjulika, assisted Sonia with her book, *Rajiv*.

Sonia's day started at 6 a.m. with bed tea. The family would be at the breakfast table at 8.30 a.m. Once Rajiv left, Sonia would scan the newspapers, attend to household details. Usually, between 11 a.m. and 12.30 p.m., she would go shopping or to exhibitions. When Rajiv was away, her evening schedule included watching movies on video.[2]

During this phase, each of her gestures came under close public scrutiny. Soon word started going round that Sonia's collection of sarees, sandals, shahtoosh and jamewar shawls and artefacts put her in the same league as Imelda Marcos.

Sonia's close friends explain this by saying that her collection of sarees consisted largely of gifts received by Indira that were passed on to her. When Sonia took over as the Congress president, she started a practice of donating sarees to AICC karamcharis. Sources said she received more than 1000 sarees in 1999 as gifts from Tamil Nadu, Karnataka, Kerala, Andhra Pradesh, Pondicherry and other states. Year after year, the collection kept growing.

According to Sharad Pawar, there was 'saree diplomacy' in the Congress. Just before raising the banner of revolt against Sonia in May 1999, Sharad alleged that Arjun Singh's wife, Saroj, aka Rani Sahiba, used to pick Chanderi sarees for Sonia. 'It helped to strike a rapport between the two families,' Pawar said.[3]

Sonia's friends do not deny her interest in Tanjore miniature paintings and other objets d'art, but they say that Sonia does not have much by way of a personal collection. According to them, when Indira was Prime Minister, most of these items were purchased by the gift committee that Sonia headed and were presented to visiting dignitaries.

Moreover, there were family traditions involved. In the Nehru–Gandhi family, it was important to invest in ivory pieces and paintings. Maneka, acknowledged that point saying, 'In this family, each one of us is judged by what we want and how we get it. I do not believe in that method and I do not believe in what they want . . . . That is where the irreconcilable difference lies . . . I don't hate them. I just find them venal. It is one of the sins that I cannot forget.'[4]

Sonia was extremely particular about her appearance, taking care to call in her personal beautician and spend time on her grooming. Over the years, her beauticians have changed with the likes of Shahnaz Hussain, a beauty consultant often called the czarina of herbal-based beauty treatment, offering consultation and useful tips. At one juncture, Hussain acted as a go-between Sonia and Mayawati, the powerful leader of the BSP and chief minister of UP, her two high-profile clients. Sonia attended Mayawati's birthday party in February 1999. The BSP supremo, who has a strong base among Dalits, returned the gesture, her party voting against the Vajpayee government and helping bring it down in April 1999.

Things were moving smoothly for Sonia and Rajiv till 16 April 1987 when a Swedish radio station made a startling disclosure, the reverberations of which haven't died down even now. It broadcast details of bribes that, it alleged, had been paid to Indian politicians to clinch the $600 million Bofors gun deal. The contract was the biggest export order ever won by Sweden and the pleased Bofors Managing Director, Martin Ardbo, had hoisted the Indian flag at the company's works at Karlskoga.

One immediate fallout of the broadcast was that Quattrocchi, whose name cropped up in the deal, was dropped from the elite group at the Prime Minister's residence. With him, European business and diplomatic friends drifted away, and the Sunday brunches with their continental fare and thali lunch vanished.

Suddenly, Rajiv's government was under scrutiny, and Sonia found herself a target. In each deal that the Rajiv government signed, an Italian connection was probed. When Rajiv dropped Arun Singh as defence minister, the gossip mills began working overtime. The two Doon school buddies reportedly fell out over Bofors as Singh favoured cancellation of the deal once the charges of a kickback gained credence, but Rajiv overruled him saying this would lower the country's image among international arms manufacturuers.

Sonia and Arun's wife Nina used to be on the best of terms in the 1980s, when Arun used to look after the Amethi parliamentary seat, a dusty principality in Awadh region of Uttar Pradesh whose only claim to fame is its tag as the seat won by Sanjay, Rajiv and now Sonia. Nina would accompany Sonia to Amethi to distribute medical supplies and undertake other welfare activities. The women were regularly seen together travelling from village to village. They would listen to the people's grievances and tell them about women's emancipation and family planning. Sonia used to avoid making political speeches, restricting herself to ask them to vote for Rajiv. 'Patiji ko vote dijiye' (vote for my husband) was one of her favourite sentences. She would giggle after finishing it, much to the amusement of the people of Amethi, who were extremely fond of her.

Arun Singh has never spoken about why he fell out with Rajiv. He left Delhi, settled in a remote farmhouse in Kumaon Hills of Uttaranchal, and staged a comeback many years later, in 2001, to accept a low-profile but important assignment in the defence ministry.

Rajiv also became conscious of the spotlight on Sonia and tried some damage control. He had not realized that except for Lal Bahadur Shastri, previous Prime Ministers were either widowers or widows. The Indian masses and media were not equipped to deal with a glamour couple like the Kennedys or the Blairs. His projecting himself as a good family man got him the image of a henpecked husband. Even Congress leaders dissatisfied with Rajiv found Sonia a soft target.

When Rajiv was in power, his lifestyle came under close scrutiny. His love for designer shoes, fast cars and expensive items became hot subjects of discussions and debate. In New Delhi, for the first time the Prime Minister was seen driving himself, and this in a swanky Mercedes-Benz gifted by Jordan's King Hussein. Mani Shankar Aiyar, a foreign-service bureaucrat-turned-politician, had another explanation for why people, particularly media persons, considered Rajiv a yuppie. 'Perhaps they do not like to see a man born with a silver spoon in his mouth turn it into gold,' he said.

Rajiv also drew criticism for his cherished annual holidays, when he used to pursue his interest in photography and wildlife. Much before he entered politics, Rajiv and Sonia used to regularly vacation in Italy and India. During Christmas and New Year, the entire family, including Sonia's mother, her sisters and their husbands, used to get together. The practice continued when Rajiv became Prime Minister. Sonia's mother and sisters went to Kanha National Park in Madhya Pradesh in 1985 with Rajiv, Sonia, Priyanka and Rahul. Next year, it was Ranthambore, where reigning film actress Sridevi performed before a select audience. The media lapped up the event. In a poor country, the chief executive was not expected to have a good time.

Rajiv was unmindful of the criticism. He ignored advice and continued to live his life the way he liked to. In December 1987 the destination was Lakshadweep. The Bofors scandal, meanwhile, was gathering force. By the time Rajiv realized that the tide was turning against him, it was too late.

Besides being apolitical, Sonia was also media shy and hated being photographed. Pictures with Rajiv at public functions show her looking tense and stern. Family friends say it had to do with Sonia's lingering fears for Rajiv's life. 'She just could not relax. We told her to project herself as the smiling, charming person that she indeed was. But whenever she faced the camera, tension would show all over her face. We soon gave up,' said a media manager associated with Rajiv who is now part of the Congress.[5]

Rajiv Gandhi's defeat in 1989 was a blessing of sorts for Sonia and the children. As leader of the Opposition, Rajiv had much more time for them. For Sonia, the disappointment of defeat vanished quickly upon seeing Rajiv savour simple, everyday pleasures again. There were uninterrupted meals. 'Sitting . . . in tranquillity, we would occasionally watch a video film together, listen to music,' she said.[6] Rajiv was also not too disheartened by the defeat. He told a music-loving friend from outside the political arena, 'Finally some peace for me. I can now just sit and listen to music with the children. I want to resume my interest in amateur radio.'

However, political developments quickly began drawing Rajiv's full attention. 'He was a changed man,' recalled Ahmad Patel, a party leader from Gujarat close to Rajiv. 'He wanted to identify with the common man. For months, there was no air conditioner at 10 Janpath,' he said.[7] Rajiv then embarked upon a sadbhavna yatra, travelling by train through western UP to Lucknow braving the heat in ordinary class. The gesture made an impact, and he began drawing huge crowds.

During this period, as Rajiv and Sonia found time to be together, he began sharing his views on political issues with her. Sonia listened attentively and often offered advice. Rajiv admired her photographic memory and her sharp ability to judge those around him.

During the 1991 elections, Rajiv drew up a list of party candidates who needed financial help. When he died in the midst of electioneering, his grieving widow sent funds to them. It was a gesture that touched them deeply. Former AICC spokesman Chandulal Chandrakar, for instance, once refused to obey the party line during the Narasimha Rao regime when he was expected to distance himself from 10 Janpath. Chandrakar had no regrets. He said that he would never turn against the family, narrating how he got ten lakh rupees when he needed the money most. 'Rajivji had died, and I was in the middle of elections. I had no hope from any quarter till I received a note that said that in accordance with Rajivji's wishes, the money was being given to me,' Chandrakar recalled.[8] Unfortunately, Chandrakar did not live long enough to see the emergence of Sonia as a politician.

Sonia's and Rajiv's twenty-third wedding anniversary fell on 25 February 1991. The couple had a quiet dinner in a restaurant in Tehran. A week before that Sonia was in Amethi when Rajiv decided to launch a diplomatic initiative to end the Gulf War. Rajiv was extremely keen to take Sonia along. A special aircraft was sent to fetch her. 'He was extremely edgy as there was some delay in Sonia's arrival. She got only a few hours to pack her bags but managed to accompany Rajiv,' a Rajiv associate said.

Rajiv visited Amethi for the last time in April 1991, and Sonia was with him. Rajiv told his constituents, 'It may not be possible for me to come [again]. But Sonia will be there to look after you.'

SIX

A TUG OF WAR

When P.V. Narasimha Rao took over as Prime Minister in 1991 at the age of seventy-one, little was known about him in spite of his decades of experience in public life, as chief minister of Andhra Pradesh and Union minister for external affairs, human resource development, and home and finance, among other portfolios. His long stint in Delhi had made him a sort of outsider in his native state of Andhra Pradesh. But in Delhi, he had many friends and admirers. Indira was extremely fond of him, giving him key assignments in spite of the stiff opposition from many towering state leaders like M. Chenna Reddy, Brahmanand Reddy and Vijay Bhaskar Reddy. He was one of the few to have access to her residence. After Indira, Rajiv too found much to admire in him, including his low-key style of functioning and his ability to defuse even the most volatile situation.

Many Congress stalwarts saw him as a harmless sort of person, a stopgap arrangement, and a man who was on the verge of retirement. The reading of Arjun Singh's and Sharad Pawar's camps was that the old man would not survive for long, and they would soon be stepping into his shoes.

For Sonia, Rao was a bit of an unknown quantity. She saw him, as did others, as learned and wise, and a loyal and highly respected senior leader of the party. Their earlier meetings, when he used to come to meet Indira, did not go beyond exchanging namaste. Upon Indira's

A TUG OF WAR

death, Rajiv had requested Rao and Mohsina Kidwai to lead the funeral procession. Thus when Sonia learnt that Rao had been chosen to lead the party, she did not oppose his candidature—which could be seen as an approval of his appointment. She was, in any case, hardly in a frame of mind to ponder over such an issue. Sources close to her, however, maintain that she would have expressed reservations had the party picked Sharad Pawar as its leader.[1]

Both Sonia and Rao were reticent persons, and when he took over as Prime Minister, the two hardly spoke to each other, preferring to deal with Wajahat Habibullah and Ramu Damodaran. Habibullah, an IAS officer of the 1967 batch from the Jammu and Kashmir cadre, was drafted as the chief executive of the Rajiv Gandhi Foundation (RGF), headed by Sonia, while Damodaran was private secretary to Rao. The Narasimha Rao government's decision to loan a senior officer like Habibullah was a departure from government rules and procedures, and it was made as a special gesture towards Sonia, who was heading the foundation.

Between them, Habibullah and Damodaran helped prevent many skirmishes between Rajiv's widow and Rao that were engineered by senior party leaders for their own political ends. However, when Habibullah left for his home cadre as the divisional commissioner of Srinagar in 1994 and subsequently Damodaran was sent to the United Nations, relations between Rao and Sonia began to deteriorate.

Rao had started off on the right foot. Within days of taking over as Prime Minister, he made a gesture that was appreciated by Sonia. He was appointed as a trustee of the Rajiv Gandhi Foundation. There was a tussle as to where the first RGF meeting should take place. Sonia was keen to have it at 10 Janpath, but some persons close to Rao raised the issue of protocol. Habibullah and Damodaran saved the situation when the latter communicated Sonia's request to Rao that she was in no mental condition to visit 7 Race Course Road since it used to be Rajiv's office. Sensitive to her feelings, he called up Sonia saying that he would be coming over to 10 Janpath. However, in Congress circles, the PM's gesture was misconstrued as paying obeisance. The RGF meetings continued at Sonia's residence till another trustee, Dr

Shankar Dayal Sharma, became the President. They were then held at Rashtrapati Bhavan.

The first budget of the new government was presented by Dr Manmohan Singh, Rao's surprise choice as finance minister to sort out the country's economic mess. Dr Singh, a brilliant academician and economic guru who had also been governor of the Reserve Bank, embarked on massive economic restructuring. His was a landmark budget that introduced measures to privatize the economy and structural reforms and included, as a special gesture, a Rs 100 crore grant for the RGF. The Opposition quickly made an issue of how a private trust was being given hard-earned taxpayer's money. All hell broke loose. Sonia, Priyanka, Rahul and Amitabh Bachchan, all members of the RGF, were aghast. Some of Rao's ministerial colleagues blamed the Prime Minister for embarrassing Sonia. The Rao camp retaliated, pointing a finger at the shouting brigade, a band of self-proclaimed Rajiv loyalists, for the fiasco.

The shouting brigade was an influential group of Rajya Sabha members consisting mostly of first-timers who had been hand-picked by Rajiv and comprising Suresh Pachauri, Ratnakar Pandey, S.S. Ahluwalia and Baba Mishra; their only claim to fame was that they had the ability to pounce on anyone who dared to speak against Rajiv or Sonia in 1991. The group had tried hard to prevail upon Sonia to take over the party leadership. At one juncture, Sonia got so tired of their antics and statements that she denied them an audience. Pandey, for instance, kept telling the world that he had taught her Hindi, though Sonia had actually learned the language at Hindi Institute in Green Park. On another occasion, he said he would offer his skin if Sonia wished to wear shoes made of it. Ahluwalia began embarking on an annual yatra collecting holy water from all the rivers and carrying it to Sriperumbudur. Yet Ahluwalia, known for his sense of timing, eventually gave up on Sonia and joined hands with Narasimha Rao, becoming a junior minister, and then shifted loyalty to join the BJP. By 2002-2003, he was the BJP's favourite spokesman to attack Sonia on major TV networks!

Whatever the reason for the grant, the move boomeranged.

Withdrawing it would only worsen the embarrassment. Rao asked Dr Manmohan Singh to clarify the government position to Sonia. Dr Singh called on Sonia, but as he sat facing her, he could not muster the courage to come to the point. He kept speaking in general terms till tea was served. Finally he began slowly, apologizing, saying that he had no intention of embarrassing her or belittling the cherished memory of Rajiv, and then going on to explain the government's dilemma. The grant was withdrawn after Sonia wrote a letter to Rao. It said, 'While we thank you personally and your colleagues for this most generous gesture, it would be best if the government instead identified suitable projects and programmes and fund them directly and thus honour the memory of my husband.'[2]

After the row over the RGF grant settled down, another controversy arose, this time involving Sonia's private secretary, Vincent George. The Congress was to select party nominees for the Rajya Sabha from Karnataka, and some senior party leaders ganged up against Margaret Alva, who was seeking an unprecedented fourth successive term. They propped up George's name, though he actually hails from Kerala. (For the Rajya Sabha seat, the candidate should be a resident of the state from where he is contesting, but it is a convention that is often flouted.) Rao was hesitant to clear George's name, though almost all the party bigwigs, particularly K. Karunakaran and Arjun Singh, were keen that he be nominated. There was no word from Sonia either in favour of or against George. As Rao was leaving for Russia, he called on Sonia to inquire if she wanted George to be in the Upper House. Sonia made it clear that if the party wanted to give a ticket to George, the decision should be based on merit and in keeping with political considerations. Rao understood the point. When the list of candidates was faxed from abroad, George had been denied a ticket.[3] Instead, Margaret Alva's name was on the list.

To many, this issue was a major factor in the distrust that characterized the relationship between 10 Janpath and 7 Race Course Road over the next four years. Sonia's private secretary, it was claimed, became hostile towards Rao. The theory went that George was singularly responsible for widening the wedge between the two, and he had a role to play in the events that finally led to the split of the party.

Disgruntled leaders and party activists unhappy with the Narasimha Rao regime began to be given audience to Sonia. George would call up MPs saying that Sonia was free to meet them between 5 and 7 p.m. on particular days. The message to their mind was clear— they were welcome to air their grievances to her. Congressmen readily obliged George, and the queues outside 10 Janpath were never small.

To the outside world, the importance of Vincent George was never fully understood. His role was either exaggerated as that of some kind of super boss or downgraded to that of a petty clerk. The truth was different. For ten long years, between 1991 and 2001, when he was finally sidelined, George had the distinction of having constant access to Sonia. He was in charge of arranging meetings—be they with senior leaders or grassroots workers, industry and other bigwigs or supporters from the villages—and tracking down party leaders. His supporters even today boast of 'George sahib' being able to find any party leader within half an hour—a distinction that no one in the party could match. He was loyal, hard working and efficient, and he never exceeded his brief. Unlike R.K. Dhawan and M.L. Fotedar, George was unfortunate not to have been given a political position as a reward for his sincerity.

Narasimha Rao's detractors, including Arjun Singh, K. Karunakaran, M.L. Fotedar, K. Natwar Singh, K.N. Singh and Sheila Dikshit, moved closer to George. An effort was made to keep conveying to Sonia that all was not well under the new government, be it in respect of the Ayodhya dispute, the economic reforms, which were seen in many quarters as being anti-poor, or the tardy probe into the Rajiv Gandhi assassination case. Sonia may have had her own view on all these issues, but George's role was significant. He facilitated the access of a large number of Congress leaders and MPs who wished to drive home the same point to her—that the Congress would lose its character if she did not intervene. The private secretary, it was said, missed no opportunity in forwarding press reports and other titbits to Sonia that Rao was systematically trying to undermine the Nehru– Gandhi legacy.

The Prime Minister could sense the deterioration in relations with 10 Janpath, but for reasons best known to him, he made no attempt to develop a personal rapport with Sonia, preferring to depend upon the Damodaran–Habibullah channel, which ended by early 1994.

In September 1991, the Election Commission announced by-elections for the Amethi Lok Sabha seat that was represented by Rajiv Gandhi. The shouting brigade, now renamed the Sonia brigade, swung into action. The likes of Ratnakar Pandey, S.S. Ahluwalia and Suresh Pachauri were back in action openly asking the Prime Minister to call on Sonia and persuade her to contest from Amethi as Rajiv's successor.

There was a renewed 'Sonia lao' (draft Sonia) campaign. This time, Sonia lost patience. Acting on the advice of Rahul and Priyanka, the family decided to go on a tour of Europe and America. The loyalists were stunned, but those who knew her well sympathized with her predicament. Priyanka was most upset with the campaign. One day, she told the RGF trustees, 'What do they (the Congressmen) think? Should we keep sacrificing our lives? We have had enough of politics.'[4]

When Rao heard of Sonia's travel plans, he immediately called on her. The meeting lasted for an hour. Sonia made it clear that she had no intention to contest Amethi. He said that there was a view in the party that Captain Satish Sharma, who used to look after Amethi when Rajiv was Prime Minister, should be given the party ticket. Sonia's response to this was the same as when the issue of giving a ticket to Vincent George had been raised—that a ticket to Captain Sharma should be given on merit, in keeping with political considerations. Captain Sharma was given the ticket, but the impression that went round was that Sonia had recommended him. His own statements corroborated this view. Taking a leaf from the Ramayana, he said like Bharat, he was keeping the seat secure for Bhaujai (sister-in-law). He succeeded in convincing the Amethi electorate that his candidature had Sonia's blessings and that she would soon be contesting the polls to look after Amethi.

Sonia exhibited her political colours, perhaps for the first time, when the Babri Masjid was demolished on 6 December 1992. She overruled P. Chidambaram and other members of the RGF by having the foundation issue a hard-hitting statement condemning the act. Chidambaram and others were of the view that the foundation was an apolitical trust; as such, there was no need to make a comment on a political issue. Sonia summarily rejected the argument. She pointed out that Rajiv and other members of the Nehru–Gandhi family were closely identified with the country's secular fabric, and if the RGF failed to express its sense of outrage, she would be betraying their legacy. The statement Sonia issued as chairperson of the foundation indicted the Narasimha Rao government too. The Prime Minister, also a trustee of the foundation, had to swallow the reprimand.

Sonia's stand on the Babri Masjid demolition rang alarm bells across the political spectrum. Those close to Rao took it as a confirmation that the lady at 10 Janpath was indeed biding time for a more active political role. His detractors were delighted, for they sensed this too. Rao, battling on many fronts, once again made little effort to clarify his government's position to Sonia and the misunderstanding only grew further.

Not everyone in the Narasimha Rao camp was sitting idle. Prior to the Babri demolition, Congressmen, particularly from north India, were upset over talk in party circles that the days of the family were over. Rao was dubbed as Chanakya, the legendary practitioner of statecraft in the Mauryan Empire, and a reluctant revolutionary. He was being compared with Jawaharlal Nehru in terms of his scholarship and conduct as a statesman. Like Nehru, he was seen as a man who understood the intricacies of international affairs and was guided by a profound commitment to the task of nation building. If Nehru was the father of the planned economy, Rao was the father of the new economic policy that would put India on par with other developed nations. Some political commentators compared him to Lal Bahadur Shastri in trying to take India on a new path. Like him, however, they said, he was not being allowed to grow, simply because he did not belong to the family.

In 1994, an independent TV producer prepared a capsule on the Congress campaign for the assembly elections. The presentation was made to Rao and his close associates, but it was rejected on the grounds that it focused on the party's glorious past, starting with Nehru and going on to glorify Indira and Rajiv. Hours later the producer was given an audience with Sonia to narrate how he was discouraged from highlighting the family's contribution.

Rao, who was just short of a majority in the Lok Sabha, initially played his cards well. There were unconfirmed reports of the Chanakya trying to get tacit support from the likes of Chandra Shekhar, V.P. Singh, Ramakrishna Hegde—people known for their antipathy to the family—and the Left, promising to end dynasty rule. In private conversations, the Prime Minister reportedly told Atal Behari Vajpayee of the opposition Bharatiya Janata Party (BJP), with whom he had an excellent rapport, that the option before the Opposition was limited—back him or bring back the dynasty it always opposed. To many Congress leaders, particularly those from the south, Rao was a symbol of the aspirations of the rank and file. On other occasions, the Narasimha Rao camp tried to play the Brahminical card, emphasizing to leaders like Vajpayee that in the post-Mandal era, he would check the rise of the Bahujan Samaj Party and other caste-based political outfits.

Rao's parliamentary affairs minister, a canny politician from the tribal-dominated areas of undivided Madhya Pradesh and a key player in the Sanjay Gandhi era, Vidya Charan Shukla, also added fuel to fire. Shukla, who had deserted Rajiv in the late 1980s, along with V.P. Singh and Arun Nehru, who held the parliamentary affairs charge, told the Lok Sabha that the controversial Bofors papers were on the way. The anti-Narasimha Rao group in the Congress ran to 10 Janpath accusing Rao of trying to browbeat Sonia. Bofors was a red flag to Sonia. Arjun Singh, Madhavrao Scindia and Natwar Singh wondered why Rao was not disciplining Shukla. 'Do we take it that there is no difference between the Rao regime and V.P. Singh?' they asked. V.P. Singh had been Rajiv's foremost critic on the Bofors issue. Locked up in Swiss vaults, the Bofors papers never came, but Sonia did not take kindly to the oblique threat.

In the beginning, Rao called on Sonia on the eve of every Cabinet reshuffle, but he discontinued the practice after his advisers told him that it was seen as a sign of weakness and projected her as some sort of extra-constitutional authority. In any case, he and Sonia were hardly discussing politics when they met, not to mention ministry formation exercises! The conversation would, after the exchange of pleasantries, invariably revolve around the studies of Rahul and Priyanka, the life and times of Indira and Rajiv, and generalities such as the weather.

Rao's less than frequent visits to 10 Janpath became a subject of intense discussion among Congressmen. Many leaders who used to view 10 Janpath as a shortcut to success and patronage started avoiding George and Sonia, preferring to associate themselves with Rao. As a reaction, some Congressmen from Uttar Pradesh, Bihar and Madhya Pradesh increased their visits to 10 Janpath, as they were unable to get into the Narasimha Rao camp.

All through this period, Sonia remained indifferent to politics. She was happy to receive various foreign dignitaries who called on her, oblivious to the rumblings in the Ministry of External Affairs. Some officials in South Block—which houses the external affairs ministry—raised the issue of protocol, wondering why dignitaries like Yasser Arafat, Nelson Mandela and King Hussein should call on a person who was not holding any public office. Rao overruled such objections. As long as these leaders had no reservations about visiting her, the government should not needlessly raise the issue of protocol. Suddenly, however, in 1995, South Block intervened. Sonia was told that Prince Abdullah of Jordan would not call on her. Instead, she would have to go and meet him. Sonia asked some foreign policy experts if it was unusual for foreign dignitaries to call on her. Almost all of them said that if the dignitary so wished, there was nothing improper in such a meeting. Congressmen felt such a directive could not have come without the knowledge of the PMO, as the ministry and the PMO work in close tandem.

The differences with the Narasimha Rao government notwithstanding, there were no qualms about accepting government generosity to the foundation. There was an unofficial rule that all projects belonging to the RGF should be cleared on a priority basis.

Union ministries such as those for social welfare, the environment, rural development, human resource development, as also the department of culture, cleared virtually every RGF project. Sitaram Kesri, who was heading the social welfare ministry under Rao, was a frequent visitor at 10 Janpath. 'Koi khidmat, koi sewa? (Any favour, any service?),' he would intone as he entered. Arjun Singh and later Madhavrao Scindia were ministers for human resource development. They too had given standing instructions to their officials that all RGF projects should be cleared quickly. Similarly, the Congress governments such as those of Digvijay Singh in Madhya Pradesh, Bhajan Lal in Haryana, J.B. Patnaik in Orissa and S.C. Jameer in Nagaland were extremely helpful where the RGF was concerned.

The government patronage of the RGF continued well after Narasimha Rao. The two United Front governments that followed, headed by H.D. Deve Gowda and Inder Kumar Gujral respectively, were also favourable to the RGF, but the foundation began losing support when the Vajpayee government came to power in 1998. According to some close family friends and senior Congress leaders, Sonia's decision to enter politics was greatly influenced by this factor too. She realized that without her active role in politics, the Nehru–Gandhi legacy perpetuated by various trusts would not last long.

Sources close to Rao said that during his tenure as Prime Minister, he was always willing to oblige her but a section of the party worked overtime to create misunderstanding between the two. They said that Rao was even prepared to accommodate those raising the Sonia bogey, namely Captain Satish Sharma, Suresh Pachauri and S.S. Ahluwalia, who were drafted in the Union council of ministers. But in the absence of any clear indication from Sonia, Rao was unable to make out who was close to her.

For example, veteran Congress leader Narain Dutt Tiwari, who later headed the breakaway Congress group with Arjun Singh, failed to get into the Prime Minister's camp as Rao felt that would anger Sonia.

In Rao's assessment, 10 Janpath disliked Tiwari on account of his not-so-pleasant relations with Rajiv. As mentioned, Rajiv had disliked

Tiwari's independence and his refusal to withdraw his nomination from the Naini Tal parliamentary seat in the 1991 general elections. To Rajiv, it was an act of defiance that smacked of rebellion. Those around Rajiv had convinced him that Tiwari was emerging as a threat and was contemplating a leadership challenge after the 1991 polls.

But after Rajiv's assassination and the elections which Tiwari lost that same year, the four-time Uttar Pradesh chief minister changed tactics, projecting himself as a Rajiv loyalist. He managed to get an appointment with Sonia, during which he emotionally denied that he had had any ambition to challenge Rajiv's leadership. Sonia did not react to Tiwari's new role and listened to him attentively. Word reached Rao that Tiwari was playing games. No concession was granted to Tiwari who was also trying to get into the CWC as Rao continued to sideline him. The Tiwari camp thereupon began to allege a sinister design in ignoring leaders from Uttar Pradesh. As long as the Congress failed to revive the party in the Hindi heartland, there would be no threat to Rao's leadership, went the argument. Once again, the lack of communication between Sonia and Rao allowed more misunderstandings to crop up. He never bothered to ask Sonia if she had any serious reservation about Tiwari.

The probe into Rajiv's assassination also created distance between Sonia and Rao. Apart from Sonia, Rahul and Priyanka were extremely keen that the guilty should be punished soon, but the court process required time. The Verma Commission of inquiry gave its report on the lapses that led to Rajiv's assassination, but many recommendations were not followed up. The Jain Commission of Inquiry, headed by a high court judge, Justice (Retd) Milap Chand Jain, probing the conspiracy angle, went on and on, summoning endless witnesses, to the point that the inquiry became absurd. Several conspiracy theories were presented and dismissed. Some blamed the LTTE, others said it was the handiwork of Khalistanis. Yet another group blamed it on the Israelis and the CIA. However, there was no clarity as to whether the assassination was a group or an individual effort. There were also allegations that a political clique inside India was responsible for the assassination. The media lapped up the various theories propounded in the small conference room in the Vigyan Bhavan annexe till everyone got tired of the speculation.

Priyanka regularly attended the Verma and Jain Commission hearings at Vigyan Bhavan. From the Congress side, Arjun Singh would not miss a chance to attend and sit through the long proceedings. His presence was not without political significance, but the point remained that the Narasimha Rao government itself appeared casual about the trial.

Rao deputed senior minister P. Chidambaram, who was a trustee of the RGF, to monitor the Rajiv assassination probe. Chidambaram was expected to constantly brief Sonia and her children, but this did not work out once developments in Tamil Nadu politics led to his joining the Tamil Maanila Congress (TMC), a breakaway Congress group which parted company with Rao on the eve of the 1996 elections. The TMC went on to join hands with the DMK in the state, which was seen as being sympathetic towards the LTTE, a group viewed as responsible for masterminding the assassination. In 2002 the TMC finally returned to the parent organization under Sonia. Paradoxically, Chidambaram, who continued to be a trustee of the RGF, did not return, preferring to run a smaller party whose influence did not cross his Sivaganga parliamentary seat on the southern tip of the country.

From 1991 to 1996, a section of party leaders, particularly those from north India, never missed an opportunity to knock at her door. They always got a hearing. Sonia seldom spoke, but her willingness to hear out all those unhappy with the Prime Minister was indication enough to these visitors that she did not approve of his style of functioning.

Arjun Singh was the first to sense that. Having tried other manoeuvres, Singh and a band of Congress leaders zeroed in on a strategy to make Sonia 'liberate' the Congress. Lacing Nehruvian principles of secularism, plurality, non-alignment and left-of-centre economics with realpolitik, Arjun Singh, M.L. Fotedar, Narain Dutt Tiwari and others not only succeeded in creating more distance between Rao and Sonia but also managed to deal a deadly blow to Rao that finally resulted in the defeat of the Congress in the 1996 general elections.

Singh also raised the bogey of the one-man, one-post issue within the Congress. In the Congress there was a tradition from the time of Nehru that the two top posts—those of leader of the party and Prime Minister—were clubbed together, making Nehru, Indira and Rajiv all-powerful. Singh's game plan was to force Rao to leave the party post and thereby curtail his powers, but he refused to oblige.

In 1994 Singh tried to force a vote in an AICC session at Surajkund on the one-man, one-post issue, but the Narasimha Rao camp carried the day with a resolution that in the case of the Prime Minister, there should be an exception. The resolution was adopted by voice vote. For the first time, Haryana policemen manned an AICC session, masquerading as Sewa Dal workers. When former hockey Olympian, party MP Aslam Sher Khan, and a handful of partymen marched towards the dais to register their protest, they were badly manhandled. In the melée that followed, one policeman in Sewa Dal uniform was seen holding a senior leader by the testicles, threatening him with dire consequences! The dissidents were intimidated by the use of brute force and surrendered tamely.[5]

The event took place on the first day of the two-day party session. Arjun Singh was sitting on the podium watching the drama. At the main entrance, about twenty AICC delegates led by Aslam Sher Khan, Ajit Jogi (who later became chief minister of Chhattisgarh), Dileep Singh Bhuria, K.N. Singh, Sheila Dikshit and others sat on a dharna demanding inner-party democracy. Sher Khan was sporting a white skull cap underlining the fact that Muslims were unhappy with Rao over the events leading to the demolition of the Babri Masjid. When the session began to adopt the resolution by voice vote, Sher Khan, Bhuria and Jogi began protesting, marching towards the dais and eliciting the policemen's reaction.

What was Sonia Gandhi's role in these behind-the-scenes manoeuvrings? Was she party to or aware of what happened at the Surajkund AICC meet? According to senior party leaders, she was very much in the know and had sympathy for the dissidents. However, she was unwilling to come out in the open as she had no desire to head a breakaway Congress group. This line of argument was made clear to the dissidents opposed to Rao. More by body language than a specific commitment, she had indicated that she was not happy at the way the Narasimha Rao regime was functioning and that she wanted the dissidents to go on with their campaign.

The Singh–Tiwari faction finally parted ways from Rao. Arjun Singh resigned as Rao's human resource development minister on 25 December 1994. He was in a hurry to do something. As for Tiwari, he was not holding any important post and his supporters were getting restless.

In the Rao–Singh tug of war Rao gained an upper hand when the dissidents deserted the Singh camp by 1995 and came back to him. He succeeded in securing a majority in Parliament owing to defections from the Janata Dal. Finally the dissidents came out in the open for a final showdown on 19 May 1995 at Talkatora Stadium.

There was high drama throughout the day. The convention began at 9 a.m., and within hours it became clear that the party was heading for a split. The tone and tenor of the speeches were so critical of the Prime Minister that they would have embarrassed even the BJP and the Left! Rao was accused, among other things, of the Babri demolition, mortgaging the nation's economic sovereignty, compromising on the Nehruvian principle of non-aligment in international affairs and belittling the legacy of Rajiv Gandhi, besides being a covert agent of the right-wing Rashtriya Swayamsevak Sangh (RSS).

By afternoon, the leaders called on Sonia to inform her that tempers were running high and that she should do something. A nervous Sonia could not bring herself to talk to Rao. She instead chose K. Karunakaran to speak to him to prevent a split. Karunakaran, known for his direct manner, called on Rao, but the latter was unwilling to concede much. He had intelligence reports about the language used by his fellow partymen at the convention. 'How do you expect me to make concessions?' Rao asked. Karunakaran dropped Sonia's name, saying that she wanted him to 'do something'. Rao wearily agreed to look into 'some aspects' of Arjun Singh's agenda, but it was a case of too little, too late.[6]

The rebels were running out of patience. In the evening, they gathered again at 10 Janpath and told Sonia about Rao's offer. 'Madam, we will be lynched. Pani sir se uncha ho gaya hai (things are beyond repair),' they told her. Sonia kept silent. It was a choice of becoming a footnote in history or betraying some loyal soldiers. The hard calculation that followed in her mind was based upon pragmatic considerations. The rebels were politely told to do what they felt like. The unspoken message was, 'I am with you but the time is not most appropriate.'

Sonia has never commented about what actually happened in May 1995. However, when she took over as the Congress chief in 1998, there were numerous instances when she accorded preferential treatment to those who had left the party during the Narasimha Rao regime and ignored those who had actively sided with Rao. The practice continued till 2001 when the 'T' (the breakaway group was called Congress T—the T standing for Tiwari) charge began to bite, and she quietly began distancing herself from them. The T-brand loyalists sulked, but they could not protest too much, as now they had nowhere to go.

All along Sonia has denied the charge that she had any role in the 19 May split. However, although she may not have had a direct hand in the split, there is a view that she encouraged all those who were opposed to Rao. Throughout the Narasimha Rao regime, 10 Janpath served as an alternative power centre or a listening post against him. From 1994 to 1996, senior ministers in his Cabinet even avoided visiting Sonia fearing that it would go against them.

In the intra-party feud between Rao and Singh, therefore, Sonia was far from being neutral. Her supporters said that whenever she made an effort to keep the party united, the Narasimha Rao camp attached 'political motives' to her efforts. 'She was cultivating a band of loyal soldiers in Arjun Singh, Natwar Singh, M.L. Fotedar, Narain Dutt Tiwari, Mohsina Kidwai, Sheila Dikshit and others. Years later, many of these leaders became part of her coterie and AICC office-bearers. In retrospect, I cannot say that her hands were clean,' said a party leader who had stayed on with Rao.[7]

Leaders like Ajit Jogi and Digvijay Singh, who did not go to Arjun Singh's party, said they had tried hard to ascertain Sonia's mindset but could not gauge it. 'Had she told me I would not have stayed for a moment with the Rao Congress,' Jogi said, recalling the day he, along with a handful of MPs, had gone to seek her guidance. 'She heard us out but did not say you go this way or that way. So we stayed on where we were,' Jogi said. Digvijay too got the same impression. 'Diggy Raja' was an important player. Had he sided with Arjun Singh, the breakaway group would have posed a more formidable challenge to Rao.[8]

For many political commentators, Sonia was playing politics without risking anything. In this sense, the breakaway group was taken for a ride. They all along kept thinking that Sonia would bless them. There was talk that Sonia would attend the convention, but she failed to turn up.

Congressmen have a finely honed survival instinct. A majority of them stayed on with Rao as he was the Prime Minister, but on 14 March 1998, no one sided with Sitaram Kesri when he was unceremoniously thrown out as the Congress president. The crucial difference between Rao of 1995 and Kesri of 1998 was that Rao could dole out goodies as the Prime Minister, while Kesri had little to offer as the party president.

Subsequent events too substantiated the view that Sonia had some role to play in the intra-party feud. In 1997 she told Kesri to take back the breakaway group led by Arjun Singh and Tiwari. Kesri was reluctant as he was nursing a grudge against Singh, but Sonia forced his hand by asking him the date on which the merger would take place. A sulking Kesri paved the way for rapprochement, but he refused to greet them. It was left to AICC spokesman Vithal Gadgil to announce the homecoming of Singh, Tiwari and others.

It was not as if the Rao camp was not playing politics. When the elections drew closer, his managers did the unthinkable—opening a Pandora's box called the Jain hawala case. It was a desperate act by Rao to win people's support. There were grave charges of corruption against his government and some of his family members. The Muslims were determined to teach him a lesson on account of the Babri Masjid demolition and both the Right and the Left represented by the BJP and the Communist Party of India–Marxist (CPM) respectively were gunning for him. Acting on the advice of the director of the Central Bureau of Investigation (CBI), Vijay Rama Rao, who hailed from Andhra Pradesh, Rao ordered an inquiry into the alleged payoffs to a galaxy of political leaders and ministers that included Lal Krishna Advani, Sharad Yadav, Arjun Singh, Narain Dutt Tiwari, P. Shiv Shankar as also his own party leaders namely Madhavrao Scindia, Buta Singh, Bhajan Lal, Vidya Charan Shukla, Kamal Nath and Motilal Vora, besides some top bureaucrats. The hawala case was based on diary entries made by two Jain brothers hailing from Madhya Pradesh who had allegedly bribed several top politicians in return for favours. The entries carried the names of these leaders and the amounts, running into several lakhs, paid to them.

The hawala probe sent shock waves across party lines. It was the first time in the history of India that so many political leaders were booked under the Prevention of Corruption Act. There was a violent reaction. Madhavrao Scindia termed it as a political conspiracy, while Arjun Singh and Tiwari, who were out of the Congress, said it was a political vendetta. But the plight of Vidya Charan Shukla and Kamal Nath was unique. They, like many others, had stood by Rao through thick and thin.

The Chanakya was unfazed. 'Let the law take its course,' he said, generously accepting a plea that all those figuring in the scandal be given a chance to put up a proxy candidate, which could be wife, son, or daughter, to contest the elections while they were embroiled in the case. The suggestion was considered ridiculous, but some actually availed it. Some wanted to field their mistresses! This proposal was vetoed by Rao. Scindia left the Congress in a huff, and till his death, in an air crash in September 2001, he continued to have a profound dislike for Narasimha Rao.

The hawala battle lines were quickly drawn. Politicians framed in the scam decided to come together and 'fix' Narasimha Rao. At an informal level, these leaders remained in close touch with each other.

'Anyone but him,' said a top BJP leader while discussing the Madhya Pradesh Lok Sabha scene with a Congress leader in 1996. The Congress leader was in complete agreement. 'Not Rao. Please make sure that even a dozen MPs do not win from our state,' he said, elaborating upon the caste factors and resources that would influence the results.

The Congress tally from undivided MP (Chhattisgarh wasn't formed then) got stuck at ten out of forty Lok Sabha seats whereas the Narasimha Rao camp was hoping to get about thirty seats. There were similar stories from other states where Congress leaders worked out a tacit understanding with the BJP and regional leaders to defeat the official nominee. At the eleventh hour, Rao realized the futility of raking up the hawala case. After the defeat, Vijay Rama Rao was shunted out from the CBI and Delhi. But the man under whose tenure the CBI was called the 'Congress Bureau of Investigation' was much smarter than people thought him to be. He quickly changed sides and joined the Telugu Desam Party to become a minister in the Chandrababu Naidu government. Mercifully, Naidu assigned him road development, keeping him away from home, intelligence or surveillance departments.

Years later, many close aides of Narasimha Rao who had defended the hawala charge sheet admitted it was a Himalayan blunder. The hawala charges did not stick in court as the judges considered the accusations, mainly in the form of diary entries, abbreviated names and incomplete figures of political pay-offs, non-admissible as evidence.

On 24 August 1995 Sonia decided to go public against the Narasimha Rao regime. The occasion was the anniversary of Rajiv's birthday, and the venue was Amethi, where Sonia expressed her deep sense of anguish over the delay in the assassination trial while addressing a large gathering.

'Sonia, save the country,' the crowd chanted as she, her head covered demurely by her saree, slowly climbed the steps to the rostrum closely followed by Priyanka. Sonia was nervous and hesitant, but Priyanka was a picture of confidence, waving back at the multitude below.

'Mummy, look at the crowds, don't you think you should wave back?' she said, tapping her mother's shoulder.

In her seven-minute speech, Rajiv's widow asked Amethi's citizens to share her vedna (pain) at the delay. She said if a probe into the assassination of a former Prime Minister could take so much time without making much headway, what would be the plight of ordinary citizens seeking justice? 'You people can understand my feelings,' she said in fluent Hindi, thumping the lectern as she complained about the slow progress of the probe. She may have been lamenting the slow pace of the judicial system in the country, but coming from Sonia at a time when the ruling Congress party was torn by factionalism, the criticism was seen as a thinly veiled attack on the Prime Minister himself.

Her insinuations became a little more obvious when she declared that the principles of former Prime Ministers—Rajiv, his mother Indira Gandhi and grandfather Jawaharlal Nehru—were being put to the test. 'There is divisiveness all around,' Sonia said in comments that were interpreted as another jab at the Narasimha Rao leadership. Then, apparently referring to the family, Sonia added: 'This is the time when we should follow the example set by those leaders for whom the nation stands above everything else.'[9]

Barring Madhya Pradesh chief minister Digvijay Singh and party MP Suresh Pachauri who defied the informal word to stay away from Amethi, Congressmen did not come out to support Sonia. To Sonia, this came as a rude jolt. The so-called family loyalists opposed to Rao were quick to tell her that they had warned her. They averred that if she stayed out of politics, the nation would forget her and the legacy of the Nehru–Gandhi family. To some, it was an important political lesson for Sonia, who began seeing merit in the argument.

Rao summoned his advisers to review the situation, but he was told not to worry. S.S. Ahluwalia, who was made minister in the government, was asked to snub Arjun Singh, who had said that it was a matter of shame for all Congressmen that Rajiv's widow was forced to make such remarks. Ahluwalia, no longer part of the Sonia brigade, said, 'Why should we put our heads down in shame? It is a matter of shame for those who have left the Congress.'[10]

Sonia's outburst at Amethi would have created far more political turmoil had it not been for developments in Andhra Pradesh, where Chandrababu Naidu scored over mentor and father-in-law N.T. Rama Rao to emerge as a major player in the national political arena. It was not a coincidence that he upset Sonia's plans in August 1995. He continued to do so in the 1998 and 1999 general elections by siding with Vajpayee.

The Congress defeat in the 1996 general elections came as no surprise to Sonia. She had received ample feedback from all over the country that the party would not reach the 200 seats mark in the elections. Soon after the polls, the breakaway group called on her, asking her to take over and formally declare the Tiwari Congress as the real Congress, but once again, she remained noncommittal.

Within days of the election defeat, it became clear that Rao would not be able to run the party. He was all-powerful and important as long as he was the Prime Minister, but running an organization was altogether a different game. Sonia was watching developments, keeping an eye on both the Narasimha Rao and Sharad Pawar camps. Pawar was developing close links with the newly created United Front. Sonia had no objection to H.D. Deve Gowda, a powerful backward leader in his home state of Karnataka who was propelled onto the national stage by the United Front's need for a consensus candidate, becoming Prime Minister, as long as Rama Krishna Hegde was kept out. Hegde, who had been a chief minister of Karnataka, had never tried to hide his opposition to dynasty or his antipathy towards the Nehru–Gandhi family. In fact, Hegde was about to leave the Janata Dal—where he didn't get along with Gowda—and join the Congress during the Kesri era, but 10 Janpath vetoed his return. Hegde was perceived as too independent, and his lifelong opposition to dynasty rule became the biggest obstacle to his return to the Congress. Kesri was upset with Sonia for blocking Hegde's return, but he did not go public. 'Kya batain, hum Madam ki ichha ke khilaf nahin ja sakte (I cannot go against the wishes of Madam),' he said.[11]

Sonia refused to have a say in Rao's successor, but she was stunned when she heard the news that Kesri would replace Rao. To many in 10 Janpath, it was Rao's way of seeking revenge from the Congress that first promoted him to the prime ministership and later bluntly forced him to resign as the leader of the party. 'There was nothing meritorious in Kesri except that he was an insignificant backward from Bihar where the party was a big zero. Rao thought he would manipulate Kesri, run the party by proxy or destroy the party by putting in an unworthy person,' a Congress Working Committee member said.

Sonia always had a liking for Kesri even though she used to get constant feedback that he was bad-mouthing her. In Sonia's presence, Kesri always flashed his proximity to Indira and projected himself as a loyalist. But Sonia judged Kesri from the feedback she received from Indira, which was not quite favourable. Given a choice, she would have opted for A.K. Antony as Rao's successor, but to many in the Congress the development could have blocked her own prospects. In that sense, Sonia's move to stay away from Rao's successor paid rich dividends. Antony withdrew from the fray against Kesri and reportedly told his associates that he would not be a good Congressman on taking stand on issues such as Bofors.

When Kesri was unceremoniously removed as AICC chief in March 1998, Sonia retained him as a special invitee in the CWC—a courtesy that was not extended to Rao. Unlike Kesri, the Sonia camp always viewed Rao as some sort of threat, as someone capable of staging a comeback. Initially, Sonia was toying with the idea of drafting Rao as a CWC invitee, but she developed cold feet when everyone in the party and in her family cautioned her against it.

Even Rao's Cabinet colleagues, who had stoutly defended him in the Babri case, told Sonia that Muslims would punish the Congress if he were included. Some leaders, projecting themselves as friends of Rao, said the old man was himself not interested. 'If you need his counsel, we will go and get it. He is one of us,' a senior leader said. Sonia continued to send Natwar Singh, Dr Manmohan Singh and Pranab Mukherjee to seek Rao's opinion on major foreign affairs and economic issues. She called on him when he was booked in the Jharkhand Mukti Morcha (JMM) bribery case, in which the JMM's

MPs were apparently 'lured' to vote for the government in a crucial vote of confidence in 1993. Sonia also asked the AICC's legal cell to extend all help in the JMM case. But given the legal cell's calibre, the Chanakya was wise enough to quickly say a polite thank you and opt for a professional set of lawyers.

Relations between Rao and Sonia could never be termed as good. Whenever the two leaders came together, something happened that widened the wedge. In 2001 when Sonia took complete charge of the party, after defeating Prasada in the organizational elections, she invited him to attend the Bangalore plenary. The former Prime Minister was seen sitting on the dais going through resolutions, giving suggestions and raising hands whenever any resolution was put to the vote. To partymen, it was a good sign that the man who ran a minority government for five successful years was advising Sonia.

But the warmth between the two vanished fast when he chose to appear before the Constitution Review Panel headed by his old friend, Justice (Retd) M.N. Venkatchaliah. To Sonia, it was a hostile act. According to her, the panel set up by the Vajpayee regime had a hidden agenda to recommend that persons of foreign origins should not be allowed to hold high office—that of the President, Prime Minister and Vice President, among a few others. She asked close associates why Rao chose to become party to a panel whose sole aim appeared to be to debar her from holding high office. She first thought of asking Mukherjee, Natwar Singh or Dr Singh to meet Rao to inquire what prompted him to go before the panel but decided otherwise. Within days of his appearance, she directed all party chief ministers, CWC members, Congress MLAs, MPs and other functionaries not to appear before the commission. It was a snub to Rao, and a caution to other partymen too.

Rao sensed Sonia's discomfort and decided to clear the confusion. True to his style, the Chanakya did not approach Sonia directly. Instead he told Mukherjee that he had done nothing wrong in appearing before the commission. According to Rao, he went and met Venkatachaliah to clear Indira's name in the context of the accession of Sikkim. Rao reportedly told the committee that it was entirely wrong to consider that Indira had played havoc with constitutional provisions while inducting Sikkim as an Indian state. Pranab conveyed Rao's feelings to Sonia, who quickly gave him a clean chit saying that she always held him in high regard as Indira had great respect for him!

Throughout his tenure as the party chief and Prime Minister, Narasimha Rao avoided a head-on confrontation with Sonia. After he demitted office, he stayed away from internal politics, though his name was dragged in each time there was a leadership tussle in the party. A number of lightweight leaders like Matang Singh, Bhuvnesh Chaturvedi and Maninderjit Singh Bitta who had come into the limelight during Rao's premiership tried to use their connection with him against Sonia. Matang Singh, a contractor from Assam, excelled in politicking and had become a minister in the PMO in 1995. While he was a manipulator par excellence, Rao also drafted the low-key Chaturvedi, a journalist-turned-politician from Rajasthan. Bitta was head of the Indian Youth Congress. He specialized in gathering crowds at short notice to hold public demonstrations. In the Sonia Congress, Matang Singh, Chaturvedi and Bitta lost whatever clout they had. Matang was expelled, Bitta remained a dissident, and Chaturvedi was seldom seen or heard.

But the former Prime Minister gave no indication that these individuals had his blessings. His apolitical role was more evident when he refused to support his key manager, Jitendra Prasada, who contested against Sonia for the AICC president's post in November 2000.

Prasada, a suave backroom manager for Narasimha Rao from 1991 to 1996, became a victim of palace intrigue when he was forced to take on Sonia in the party polls. Marginalized in the Sonia Congress, Prasada was initially teaming up with Rajesh Pilot to start a low-key rebellion in the guise of inner-party democracy. The real motive of the exercise was to check Arjun Singh and Madhavrao Scindia, who were calling the shots in the Sonia regime. Some disgruntled party leaders from Orissa, the North-East and Uttar Pradesh along with those outside the Congress who felt threatened by the rise of Sonia quickly began supporting the Prasada–Pilot team.

But these equations changed dramatically with the death of Pilot in a road accident in June 2000. Pilot, who was popular with the middle class, had established a good name for his politically correct stances, clean image and efficiency. Hailing from a modest Gujjar family of western Uttar Pradesh, Rajeshwar Prasad, as he was originally called, joined the Indian Air Force and liked flying so much that he changed his name to Rajesh Pilot. The squadron leader-turned-politician regularly won from the Dausa Lok Sabha seat in Rajasthan where he did not have the advantage of state domicile.

In a political career spread over fifteen years, Pilot loved to take on the high and mighty and enjoyed the media attention. He was an efficient minister under Rajiv but after the Babri demolition in 1993, he began to score political points against the likes of Arjun Singh, Sharad Pawar, Madhavrao Scindia and Kamal Nath. On 25 February 1993, when the BJP organized a demonstration near Parliament, Pilot, as a junior minister in the internal security ministry, made unprecedented bandobast to thwart any threat to mosques in the area. Coming as it did soon after the Babri demolition, there were apprehensions the demonstration could turn violent, but the day passed peacefully. Pilot boasted that had he been in charge of security on 6 December 1992, instead of his senior S.B. Chavan, in the internal security ministry, the mosque would not have been demolished.

Pilot then turned on the heat on godman Chandraswami who was perceived to be close to Rao. A tantrik, Chandraswami had powerful friends like international arms dealer Adnan Khashoggi, the Sultan of Brunei, and Margaret Thatcher, and equally well-placed enemies. In 1995 Chandraswami was wanted in connection with a series of cases, but nobody could act against him due to his high connections. Pilot got him arrested. It was more than a coincidence that in the subsequent Cabinet reshuffle, Pilot was shunted out of internal security to look after forests and environment.

On 14 June 2000, as he drove a jeep at breakneck speed from Dausa to Jaipur to catch a flight to Delhi, he overtook his own escort vehicle at a blind spot and collided with a state transport bus. The man who was always in a hurry left behind a thousand and one unfulfilled ambitions. One of them was to take on Sonia in the Congress organizational polls scheduled in November 2000.

In Pilot's absence, all eyes turned to Jitendra Prasada. Prasada, however, lacked the vibrant, clean image that could generate mass support. Jitty Bhai, as Prasada was fondly called, loved his food, drink and poetry. Coming from a distinguished family in the princely state of Shahjahanpur, Prasada's manners were those of a Lucknowi nawab—he had in fact studied at Lucknow's Colvin Taluqdar College which was once exlusively meant for wards of nawabs and court officers, or taluqdars. He took pride in his family's ties with India's most famous poet, Rabindranath Tagore. Prasada cut his political teeth under Rajiv from 1985 to 1989 when he served as Congress general secretary and Rajiv's political secretary. Prasada retained the prize post when Rao became all-important between 1991 and 1996. Under Rao, the Brahmin from Uttar Pradesh had his task cut out for him. He was expected to keep leaders like Arjun Singh, Narain Dutt Tiwari, Mohsina Kidwai and Sheila Dikshit under check. Prasada did that with all the resources at his command, but in the process, the Congress lost its roots in Uttar Pradesh, the state which mattered most in the country's politics due to its sheer size and population. Once the Congress lost its control over those eighty-five parliamentary seats in the 545-member Lok Sabha, it could never get a clear majority to form a government of its own at the national level.

Prasada, however, miscalculated the political situation while taking on Sonia. Prasada had no illusions about his prospects of defeating Sonia in an election that was tilted heavily in her favour. The entire election machinery was in her hands, including that of picking poll observers and returning officers. Prasada believed that Sonia would ask him to withdraw from the fray and reward him with a senior position in the party.

Leaders like Natwar Singh and Ahmad Patel, who were projecting themselves as peacemakers, cemented this line of thinking. But some leaders in the Sonia camp, namely Arjun Singh and Vincent George, had other plans. These leaders argued that the tag of elected party chief would go a long way in consolidating Sonia's position in the

Congress. At the eleventh hour, they forced Prasada's hands, refusing to concede an inch. Prasada had no option but to take on Sonia.

All AICC functionaries were asked to drum up support for Sonia. In Bhopal, Hyderabad, Jaipur and a few other places where Jitty Bhai toured as part of his campaigning, he was greeted with locked doors at the Pradesh Congress Committee (PCC) offices and black flags. A tense Prasada looked for a way out. Meanwhile, the peacemakers shuttled between his house and 10 Janpath, claiming to be working on some formula that was non-existent.

As the date for withdrawal of names drew nearer, Jitty Bhai waited in vain for a call from 10 Janpath offering a face-saving, last-minute withdrawal. Humiliated and marginalized, Jitty Bhai realized that his gambit had failed. Accompanied by a handful of leaders from Uttar Pradesh, Prasada filed his nomination papers and was humbled in the party polls as Sonia went on to get nearly 99 per cent of the votes. The peacemakers and many of those who had encouraged Prasada to teach Sonia a lesson were nowhere in sight. Prasada did not recover from the trauma of defeat. A few months later, he suffered a brain haemorrhage and died. The man who knew so much about palace intrigue became one of its worst victims.

SEVEN

EDUCATING SONIA

The Nehru–Gandhis follow several Kashmiri, Parsi and Hindu traditions, but a curious one is the manner in which they educate their wards. After Jawaharlal Nehru, his great-granddaughter Priyanka was the first graduate in the family. Indira was a good student, but she could not complete her formal education. Nehru was acutely conscious of this, so he made a concerted effort to enlighten her on history, culture, literature, science, technology, religion and a range of other subjects. By the time she became Prime Minister, her level of knowledge was higher than that of the average graduate or even a post-graduate.

While educating her, Nehru may not have envisaged dynasty rule, but he did have an overwhelming desire to train Indira in a different manner. He had scant regard for the existing education system, including that of public schools and convents. In one of his letters, Nehru wrote to Indira what he expected from her. To prepare her for the future, he 'wrote piles and piles of historical and other letters' to her to gently train her mind in 'that wider understanding of life and events that is essential for any big work'.[1]

Unfortunately, Indira could not give her sons the kind of attention her father had given to her. She was preoccupied with managing the Nehru household and her troubled marriage, and consequently her children performed badly in academics. Asked to comment on his stay in Cambridge where he had gone to do a degree in mechanical engineering at Trinity College, Rajiv would laugh and say, 'Oh, I simply flunked!'[2]

After Sanjay's death, Indira began grooming Rajiv for a greater political role. Belatedly, she made conscious efforts to enlighten him on the finer aspects of polity and governance. Since Indira did not have Nehru's skills, she sought the services of experts drawn from various fields to specially train Rajiv.

Rajiv met daily with the likes of missile man A.P.J. Abdul Kalam, scientist Professor Yashpal, agriculture expert M.S. Swaminathan, economist A.M. Khusro and experts drawn from other fields.

These interactions were found to be useful by both sides. Rajiv got tremendous insight into issues facing the nation in all spheres, while the experts had the satisfaction of conveying their views to Indira through Rajiv.

Later Indira drafted Rajiv's cousin Arun Nehru, a high-flying corporate executive known for his aggressive style of functioning, to serve as Rajiv's assistant. Nehru, nicknamed Appu (baby elephant) on account of his weight, had a way of looking at things that was alien to the political culture of the Congress. He believed in winning at all costs. Behind the polished manner and the fondness for the good things of life was a hard taskmaster who intensely disliked failure.

For Rajiv's friends, the two-year learning period was responsible for Rajiv's focus on modernization and many innovative ideas such as a village-based governance system (panchayati raj). Rajiv wanted to have a three-tier system so that villagers would not have to travel hundreds of miles to state headquarters for smaller projects like sinking wells. His other pet subject was the thrust on computerization and information technology. Rajiv, much ahead of other politicians in the country, could sense its impending relevance to a country like India. He was laughed at by Sitaram Kesri and others for relying on computerization of votes, but Rajiv ignored the criticism to focus on time-bound technology missions, initiating electoral reforms, lowering the age to vote, introducing an anti-defection law, offering political solution to insurgency in the North-East and instituting economic reforms. These were seminal ideas which would change the face of

India. Panchayati raj, for instance, was a giant step forward that brought governance to the grass-roots level in addition to bringing women into the mainstream, as a third of the seats were reserved for them in the village councils. Great strides were made in communications to link up the country through an accessible telephone system, the full impact coming a few years later with the boom in telecommunications in the country.

Observers viewed Rajiv's brush with these ideas as a mixed bag. As a modern man, Rajiv brought in a whiff of fresh air, but his inexperience and excessive reliance on a close circle of friends often compounded the complex problems and the bigger issues involved. Nevertheless, even his worst critics acknowledged that he was maturing into a seasoned politician at the time of his death.

Rajiv's death brought Sonia into sharp public focus. The alacrity with which the Congress Working Committee offered her the party leadership and a possibility of leading the nation rattled the Indian intelligentsia. People wondered if she was really capable of leading millions. At that juncture, Sonia's grief was far too intense for her to ponder the question, but with the passage of time, she and others began to reconsider her leadership potential.

The change was evident three years after Rajiv's death. When senior Congress leaders considered to be loyal to the 'family' pleaded with her to discipline Narasimha Rao or play an active role in politics, the housewife did air her doubts, wondering aloud how she would overcome linguistic and cultural barriers to enter an arena where anything and everything is under intense public scrutiny. The supporters brushed aside such apprehensions saying one need not be a born leader. Everything can be arranged, you can be groomed easily, they said, and pointed at the Congress's reservoir of talent. 'Your family has favoured so many over the decades. Can they not teach you a few things?' said a leader from Uttar Pradesh.

Acutely aware of her many shortcomings, Sonia began the exercise of educating herself the moment she firmed up her mind to join politics. Some of her critics said that the idea of setting up the Rajiv Gandhi Foundation, where an array of experts was summoned on a regular basis, was a first step in that direction. Congressmen vehemently deny the charge. According to them, till at least three years after Rajiv's death, Sonia had no plans to enter politics. 'It was when she saw the collapse of the party and the rise of the BJP that she decided to do her bit to save the nation from the clutches of communalism and fascism,' said a senior CWC member. He said that the idea behind the Rajiv Gandhi Foundation was a much broader one than merely to fill her in on subjects of contemporary importance.

Sonia had watched Indira and Rajiv tackle the most difficult issues facing the nation, but this was not enough, as Sonia used to avoid taking interest in matters of governance unless drawn into discussion by them. Indira used to respect her sense of aloofness, except in the last six months of her life when she began sharing a lot of things with a bahu who had become like a daughter to her.

In Rajiv's case too, he would seek Sonia's counsel often. It was an open secret that Sonia was party to Rajiv's decision to join politics even though she had strong reservations initially. Congress circles acknowledge that in 1989, when Rajiv suffered defeat in the general elections and there was talk that the former Prime Minister would buy a one-way ticket to Italy, Sonia strongly favoured that he stay on in politics.[3]

The stamp of the Nehru–Gandhi family legacy was evident when she finally took over as the party chief in 1998. She took many decisions based on what she had learnt from her mother-in-law and her husband. But what was most remarkable was that she consciously avoided making the mistakes that had proved costly to both Indira and Rajiv. Among them was her decision not to disturb chief ministers of the Congress-ruled states. It was a significant departure from the Indira–Rajiv days, when chief ministers were changed as frequently as three to four times in a five-year term.

Sonia's critics said that political compulsions forced her not to act against the chief ministers. Unlike Indira and Rajiv, they said, Sonia was not the Prime Minister and lacked the mandate to play musical chairs in the states. But Congress chief ministers were delighted to have a party boss who backed them to the hilt. They were given a free hand to do what they liked.

In the first two years, Sonia removed just one chief minister, Janki Ballabh Patnaik. The Orissa chief minister was replaced in 1999 following the murder of Christian missionary Graham Staines. What upset Sonia most was Patnaik's near endorsement of the Hindutva hardliners' justification of 'disciplining Christian missionaries' and the demand for a nationwide debate on religious conversions.[4] She also had a nagging doubt of his loyalty, suspecting him of being hand-in-glove with Narasimha Rao and others of the old guard.

Patnaik, however, represented a powerful lobby within the Congress. The old guard was not happy at the summary way in which she removed the chief minister. Subsequent events in Orissa politics didn't reflect favourably on her when the new chief minister, Gridhar Gomang, specially chosen by her, failed to provide relief and rehabilitation after a super cyclone caused heavy devastation in coastal Orissa. She corrected the wrong the following year when she made him state party unit chief after the party's crushing defeat in the assembly polls in 2000. The Congress lost the assembly polls bagging just 10 out of 137 assembly seats.

Sonia quickly learnt the lessons from Orissa. She took a principled decision not to disturb chief ministers and directed all AICC general secretaries to keep them in good humour. Dissident activities against Digvijay Singh, Sheila Dikshit, S.M. Krishna, Vilasrao Deshmukh (Deshmukh was finally removed in January 2003 when the state party leaders and alliance partner Nationalist Congress Party asked for his exit) and other Congress chief ministers died a natural death when Sonia made it clear that she was in no mood to hear campaigns to remove a chief minister. Her policy of least interference in the day-to-day functioning of fifteen Congress-ruled states made her immensely popular among the chief ministers. This was a clear departure from Indira's and Rajiv's style of functioning, in which the chief minister's office was a game of musical chairs. If Congress chief ministers like Vasantdada Patil of Maharashtra, M.Chenna Reddy of Andhra Pradesh or Veerendra Patil of Karnataka resisted, they were dubbed dissidents and isolated within the party. People like Digvijay Singh, Ajit Jogi and

S.M. Krishna seldom had problems with Delhi under Sonia. As a result these chief ministers always had a good word to say about her, even in their off-the-record conversations. It also put an end to the counterplots, such as those in the Tirupati and Baramati conclaves where senior leaders and chief ministers had met secretly to plot the downfall of Rajiv and Narasimha Rao respectively.

When she took over as the Congress chief, there was a certain unease between her and Sharad Pawar. Though Pawar concurred with the party's decision to request Sonia to save the Congress, he later candidly admitted that he was never comfortable with her. Their conversations never lasted long and even that short duration was punctuated by long pauses. After revolting against her on the ground of her foreign origins, Pawar said that Sonia would never openly speak to him, but a CWC member who had tried hard to bring about a rapprochement between Pawar and Sonia said the same thing about him: 'We encouraged him to have an open, heart-to-heart discussion with the Congress president, but he would just not open up.'[5]

Pawar's detractors alleged that the Maratha leader was not speaking freely because he was thinking of toppling her. Pawar had an informal poll survey done, which concluded that if he raised the banner of revolt against Sonia on the ground of her origins, he would be a second Lokmanya Tilak, the freedom fighter from Maharashtra who took the cause of independence to the people. The actual findings of the survey were never made public.[6]

The process of hands-on education began when she started interacting with experts on a regular basis during the last days of the Narasimha Rao regime in 1996. First, even those close to her failed to see a pattern in the exercise, but increasingly it became clear that her interactions with the likes of historian Romila Thapar, sociologist Zoya Hasan, jurist P.N. Bhagwati, former Intelligence Bureau chief M.K. Narayanan, and political scientist Rajiv Bhargava had a purpose to them.

Others whom she began to consult once Sitaram Kesri emerged as head of the Congress, were economist Y.K. Alagh, pollster Yogendra Yadav, foreign policy expert J.N. Dixit, L.M. Singhvi (Singhvi later joined the BJP but his son, Manu Abhishek Singhvi, joined Sonia's think tank) Natwar Singh and Pranab Mukherjee. She found Mukherjee an interesting talker and told associates that she found him to be an authority on a range of subjects. He also had a fund of anecdotes to spice up his analysis of various issues. Sonia loved his accounts of how Indira used to manage to solve many tricky problems.

While none of these experts was willing to come on record to describe these interactions, many privately said that they were impressed by Sonia's interest, eagerness and attentiveness. One significant aspect was that Sonia hardly gave her view on any issue, whether it be Ayodhya or economic reform. She would jot down points, and at most she would paraphrase a remark to check if she had understood correctly. In that sense, the teachers were unanimous that Sonia was a good student.[7]

Sonia continues the practice of taking copious notes, even in the CWC meetings. For many party leaders, it is a little unsettling. 'It is as if she may confront us at a later date if we change our stand,' a CWC member said.

After March 1998, when she formally took over as the Congress president, the interaction with the intelligentsia became regular and organized. The party drew a list of about fifty experts on subjects ranging from electoral reforms and delimitation exercise of Parliament and assembly constituencies, to foreign policy, Indian history and the history of the Indian National Congress. In addition, Congress leaders like Salman Khurshid, an authority on constitutional law, economic expert Jairam Ramesh, foreign service expert Mani Shankar Aiyar and politician Margaret Alva (who had a lot of hands-on experience in administration and gender-related issues) began giving notes on important issues pertaining to the nation. Each time you met her, you were supposed to make a presentation. Charts, diagrams and paradigms would help. 'If you go with a problem, you should offer a solution too. That is the survival kit in the Congress when you are dealing with the party chief,' said an associate who had served as a close aide to Indira and Rajiv Gandhi.

While Sonia was a good student, there were minor mistakes that seldom went out of 10 Janpath or the party headquarters at 24 Akbar Road. For instance, in 1997-98, the party decided to set up a panel under Ghulam Nabi Azad to celebrate fifty years of independence. In that connection, the birth anniversary of Bhagat Singh was observed, and Sonia was invited to pay floral tribute to the freedom fighter. A note on his life and times was passed on to her. Sonia had rehearsed a small speech but did not deliver it. The mystery was soon solved. Apparently, the speech had constantly referred to Bhagat Singh as Sardar Bhagat Singh, and Sonia got confused seeing Bhagat Singh's picture minus turban but wearing his trademark hat. In that brief moment of decision, she decided to avoid making a speech lest it be misunderstood. Privately, party leaders had a good laugh about it.

There was another incident when Madhavrao Scindia introduced an influential caste leader to Sonia. The person concerned was an important leader in Uttar Pradesh who had cut his political teeth in the Samajwadi Party and the Bharatiya Janata Party. He had a sharp, analytical mind, and he gave her some expert insights into caste equations in Uttar Pradesh. Sonia, however, did not think much of the emphasis on caste in UP and spoke her mind. She went on to state that as head of the Congress, she wished to downplay caste considerations. The UP leader quickly got up saying he would come again when the AICC chief had a better idea of how important caste equations were in UP politics.

There was another significant aspect of Sonia's education that did not go unnoticed. Over days, weeks and months, Sonia developed some grasp of the issues of the day and began giving short speeches. On economic matters, however, she avoided articulating her point of view. While she listened patiently to discussions on the economic problems facing India, she refrained from offering prescriptions. Initially, she seemed favourable to the left-of-centre approach on economic issues, but in 2001 she veered round to supporting reforms to the hilt.

On the economy, Dr Manmohan Singh emerged as her key tutor. He had been supporting the left-of-centre approach but went on to become the architect of the Indian model of fiscal reforms taking the country out of the economic crisis of 1991. His influence on her was so strong that she refused to heed left-wing leaders like A.K. Antony, Mani Shankar Aiyar, Arjun Singh and a number of others favouring a middle path. To many Congress leaders, this was worrying.

Sonia's trust of Dr Singh led to speculation in the Congress that the AICC chief was projecting him as the party's prime ministerial candidate. But leaders like Digvijay Singh and Ajit Jogi firmly believed that Sonia alone would be candidate for PM. Some believed that Sonia had a genuine liking for Dr Singh, who was known for his clean image. For the traditional dhoti-kurta-clad Congressman, however, he represented the elite. When Madhavrao Scindia was alive, his supporters were also wary of him, considering him a challenger to the number two slot in the party.

Sonia tried to master Hindi from various sources before taking the plunge into politics. After her marriage, she began learning Hindi at home. Indira arranged for a tutor from the Hindi Institute at Green Park to teach her to read and write in the Devanagri script, and slowly she developed a liking for the language. Her teacher found her a good learner who seldom missed her homework.

'I had no choice so I learnt it,' Sonia said, pointing at the tradition of speaking only in Hindi at the dinner table since the time of Motilal Nehru.[8] No one, including the head of the family, was permitted to break the tradition. It is one custom that is still practised at 10 Janpath. In the first few months that Sonia began to speak in Hindi, Sanjay would laugh each time she made a mistake, but Indira and Rajiv would quickly reprimand him and help Sonia. Sonia took Sanjay's remarks sportingly. In 1980, a few days before his death, she managed to correct *his* Hindi. Everyone present had a good laugh. Sonia also made it a point to try to speak to all her Indian friends in Hindi. Now she initiates a conversation in Hindi with all those who hail from the Hindi heartland and speaks in English to those who come from across the Vindhyas.

Once she was elected to Parliament, the process of educating Sonia gained momentum with partymen vying to take up the assignment. The party's former chief whip in the Lok Sabha, Professor P.J. Kurian, who had lost the election, took it upon himself to brief Sonia about parliamentary conventions and customs. Also assisting her were Madhavrao Scindia, Shivraj Patil, Makhan Lal Fotedar, Margaret Alva, Prithviraj Chavan, Salman Khurshid, Arjun Singh, P.M. Sayeed, Mani Shankar Aiyar, Girja Vyas and Pawan Bansal.

Sources close to Sonia said that her first few months in Parliament were most testing. There were five hundred pairs of eyes watching her every movement. The press gallery, special gallery, visitor's gallery, diplomatic gallery were all packed too. There were at least a dozen eager beavers among the Congress benches itching to give unsolicited advice. Worse, trusted hands like Vincent George and Pulak Chatterjee, Sonia's private secretary as leader of the Opposition to the rank of joint secretary, a bright 1968 IAS officer from Uttar Pradesh cadre, could not be of any help once she was inside the Lok Sabha. As a Sonia aide said, 'Madam is a reticent person and she hated the intense public glare. She did not want to give the impression that Congress leaders were helping her. There used to be intense relief each time Parliament got adjourned.'[9]

Sonia was aware of the prevailing tension in the Congress Parliamentary Party but saw little reason to panic. She told her associates that she needed time, recalling how Rajiv could not make a speech during his first year of Parliament (1981-82).

Slowly, she began picking up the ropes. She made her first speech as a member of the Lok Sabha on 29 October 1999, though she had spoken there on five occasions before to felicitate the Speaker and Deputy Speaker, second motions of their election and announce her resignation from the Bellary Lok Sabha seat. Sonia had won from both Amethi and Bellary, but according to the law she could keep just one seat. Bellary, an industrial town in Karnataka, gave Sonia a mandate in spite of spirited efforts by the BJP's Sushma Swaraj who had taken pains to learn Kannada. There was constant media speculation that she would humble Sonia. But a day before campaigning ended, Priyanka arrived, and the entire township was out to see and hear her.

Sushma did not wait for the verdict to be out. She knew she had lost.

For her speech, Sonia came prepared with reams of paper printed in bold 30-point type with just a couple of sentences written on each sheet. Sonia began speaking amid catcalls, but Speaker G.M.C. Balayogi was extremely considerate. At the back of his mind was his own experience as he too had faced a communication problem when he was appointed Lok Sabha Speaker in 1998. (He was from Andhra Pradesh and not very fluent in Hindi.)

With this presentation, Sonia passed the litmus test. She began by taking a dig at the Vajpayee regime for attributing the ongoing economic reforms to the Congress. Sonia said, 'I congratulate the government for having read the Congress manifesto in great detail.' The House then saw an emotional Sonia criticize the government's handling of the Bofors issue. She was furious because the CBI had just filed a charge sheet naming Rajiv as the prime suspect in the case. She said that the 'government has been selective and its action is purely political vendetta'. While the Bofors investigation must go on, she said, 'What we cannot tolerate, however, is framing of a man who is innocent and who is not here to defend himself.'

The forceful plea did not work as the government expressed its helplessness in removing Rajiv's name from the Bofors charge sheet. The issue continued to agitate Sonia and Congress MPs. However, her speech made an instant impact on the party MPs. The MPs saw a Sonia who was not hesitant to talk about the Bofors investigation, despite its sensitivity. The memories of a smiling and youthful Rajiv resurfaced. They accepted Sonia as their leader despite perceived shortcomings.

Initially, her role as leader of the Opposition left a lot to be desired. Congress MPs were used to be being led from the front, but with Sonia around, it was left to Madhavrao Scindia, Priyaranjan Das Munshi, Mani Shankar Aiyar, Shivraj Patil and Jaipal Reddy to take on the government. Sonia made elaborate arrangements to decide about the issues of the day. She formed a number of party panels such as a political affairs committee, a legislative affairs panel and a research and reference committee, but very soon they began functioning at cross-purposes and relegating the Congress Parliamentary Party executive into the background. In the course of 2001-2002, very many issues came up, such as the Tehelka exposé, in which a web site released footage of some defence officials and ruling coalition party functionaries accepting bribes, the Unit Trust of India (UTI) scandal, in which investors saw their savings whittled away, and the failed Agra summit between Prime Minister Vajpayee and President Pervez Musharraf of Pakistan. The Congress, however, failed to exploit them.

The Tehelka exposé in 2001 by itself was calculated to throw the entire political spectrum into an uproar, alleging as it did corruption at high levels in defence deals. The UTI scam too was an emotive issue as it affected the fortunes of millions of small investors.

Having acquired the status of leader of the Opposition, Sonia was expected to interact with her political adversaries like Mulayam Singh Yadav, Chandra Shekhar, Sharad Pawar, Mayawati, P.A. Sangma and others. As she was shy and reluctant to approach them directly, there was a lack of coordination and functional relationship within the Opposition ranks. Samjawadi Party leaders Mulayam Singh Yadav and Amar Singh began openly discrediting her over her failure to take the Opposition along. Sonia sought the help of Jaipal Reddy and CPM leaders Harkishen Singh Surjeet and Somnath Chatterjee to deal with Mulayam Singh while the Congress's deputy leader, Madhavrao Scindia, and chief whip Priyaranjan Das Munshi were assigned the task of interacting with Mayawati, Pawar and Ajit Singh, son of former Prime Minister Charan Singh who had inherited his father's farmer constituency, and others.

In the first few months, the system appeared sketchy, and there was constant one-upmanship between the Congress and the Samajwadi Party on issues such as Ayodhya which showed the Opposition in extremely poor light. Sonia tried hard to build bridges with Mulayam Singh through Jaipal, Laloo Prasad and Surjeet, but her efforts failed as he always perceived her as a threat. Unlike Pawar or the BJP's then parliamentary affairs minister Pramod Mahajan, he never underestimated Sonia's strength given her surname. Privately, he consistently maintained that the threat to him in UP was not so much from the BJP or the BSP but from the Congress. 'The BJP helps us stay in contention. The Congress can eat up our base,' he once told a party MP who had gone favouring a rapprochement with a secular Congress to keep the BJP at bay.[10]

As both the Congress and the Samajwadi Party were vying for the non-BJP secular space, the two parties could not come together. Each time Mulayam Singh or Sonia suffered a poll debacle, there were calls for realignment of secular forces. On his part, Mulayam Singh kept his options open. He sided with the Vajpayee regime supporting the American war against terrorism resulting in bombing of Afghanistan when the Congress chose to criticize the government. He had a pointman in Amar Singh, a former Congressman who excelled in cutting deals and making friends with influential industrial houses. When the BJP formed a formidable alliance with the BSP in Uttar Pradesh in 2002-2003, he sought the services of a prominent industrial house to bring the Samajwadi Party and the Congress together.

Among the Opposition leaders, Sonia enjoyed a special rapport with Harkishen Singh Surjeet and Jyoti Basu, the aristocratic CPM leader from West Bengal who holds the distinction of being the country's longest serving chief minister. When Pawar and Sangma raised the foreign origins issue in 1999, Sonia called on Surjeet unannounced. The veteran communist leader was delighted to receive her at his Teen Murti Lane residence. In the absence of an air conditioner, Sonia began sweating profusely. Surjeet said apologetically, 'I have just one air conditioner that is in my bedroom. You are like my daughter and in case you do not mind, we can sit there.' The two moved there, but the cane chair which Sonia was offered was ripped. Sonia quietly slipped in a cushion and sat on it while Surjeet began recalling how Indira had faced a stiff challenge from the old guard in 1969 and she had checkmated them. The CPM leader said he would give two mantras to her that would keep her afloat in the worst crisis. 'Beti, remember, India is essentially a poor country, so do not get carried away by the propaganda of the benefits of reforms. The Congress has survived because it has always stood by the poor. For the sake of the nation, never ever give up on the pro-poor tilt,' he said. The other mantra was to stay away from communal forces. 'There might be a temptation to get into power. Always resist such a thing. Our experience of 1989 [when the Left supported a non-Congress government headed by V.P. Singh which was also backed by the BJP] has been extremely bitter. So never ever join hands with communal forces. After all, what is India without the poor and secularism?' he asked. Sonia could not have agreed more. To her, the old man's words were indeed guru mantras.

Inside Parliament, Sonia, lacking in experience and confidence, became a soft target of the treasury benches. But each time she was challenged or humiliated by the ruling coalition, she prepared to get even. According to family sources, Sonia used to tell her children that her political opponents did not know the stuff she was made of. When Prime Minister Vajpayee taunted the Congress on the party's stand on the nuclear deterrence issue, Sonia kept quiet, causing acute embarrassment to her own benches.

Afterwards she summoned experts on strategic studies, defence and nuclear issues, including those who were not part of the Congress think tank, understood the nuances and went back to Parliament to speak on the subject. Her speech included a reminder of the earlier occasion when she had failed to answer the Prime Minister's query. Speaking in the Lok Sabha on 12 March 2001, a somewhat more confident Sonia asked Vajpayee, 'Even on the nuclear doctrine, is there a clarity of vision? Last session, the honourable Prime Minister raised a laugh by challenging me to tell him what the Congress's policy was on the nuclear deterrent. I do not begrudge the Prime Minister that laugh, for he is, after all, one of the wittiest parliamentarians in the last fifty years! But sir, we regard national security as far too important an issue to be settled by banter on the floor of the House. So let me throw the question back to the Prime Minister. What is the NDA government's nuclear doctrine? For the last eighteen months, the recommendations of the National Security Advisory Board have been gathering dust. The three little words, "minimum credible deterrent", do not amount to a policy. They have to be fleshed out; they have to be spelt out as a policy. When that is done, as a responsible Opposition we would react to it and if possible, shall lend support. But how can we, sir, lend support now? How can we support a policy that, as far as we know, does not exist?'

By March 2002, Sonia began crossing swords with the Prime Minister. Her body language too bespoke a more assured person. On 26 March 2002, when the two Houses met for a joint sitting to discuss the controversial Prevention of Terrorism Ordinance, Sonia alleged that Vajpayee was pushing the ordinance under pressure from the Sangh Parivar.

Vajpayee was offended. A belligerent Vajpayee went all out against Sonia questioning her tone and tenor. Congress MPs were left stunned. They had an idea that the leader of the Opposition and the Prime Minister had not been on the best of terms for many months, but the verbal assault in the Central Hall of Parliament left many around Sonia speechless. They said there was nothing in her speech that could have warranted such harsh remarks.

Some Congress leaders saw it as Vajpayee's calculated move to go on the offensive. Rattled by the events in Gujarat and Ayodhya, Vajpayee had chosen to assert his supremacy in a televised debate, they said. The Prime Minister tried to debunk Sonia's premise that he was pushing through the anti-terrorism bill under pressure from the Sangh Parivar, a view that had gained currency in Delhi's political circles. Vajpayee was also upset that many MPs, particularly those belonging to the Left, had accused him of acting under pressure from the US.

In his short but acrimonious intervention, Vajpayee was quick to point out that it was a Congress Prime Minister (P.V. Narasimha Rao) who had called off a nuclear test at the last moment under pressure from a foreign power. He also reminded the nation that he had turned down President Clinton's invitation to visit the US at the height of the Kargil conflict in 1999 when the Pakistani Prime Minister Nawaz Sharif had already reached there.

On another occasion, during the motion of thanks to the President's address, Vajpayee had objected to Sonia's description of the Gujarat riots in 2002 as genocide. The Prime Minister had cautioned her against using strong words, pointing to possible international ramifications.

At the personal level, too, there is little rapport between the leader of the House and the leader of the Opposition. Vajpayee and Sonia seldom exchange greetings, preferring to deal with each other through bureaucrats and letters.

Congress leaders said Vajpayee's strategy to pin down Sonia was a result of the growing clout of the main Opposition party, particularly after its victory in three more states. By 2002 the Congress had gained power in fourteen states and Union territories that covered more than half the country. These were Madhya Pradesh, Chhattisgarh, Maharashtra, Rajasthan, Delhi, Punjab, Uttaranchal, Kerala, Karnataka, Pondicherry, Nagaland, Arunachal Pradesh, Manipur and Assam. In addition, the Congress swept the Delhi municipal polls in March 2002 winning three-fourths of the seats. In such a scenario, Vajpayee was under pressure to take on the Congress, they said.

The Vajpayee–Sonia showdown had a sideshow too. Veteran leader Arjun Singh rushed to Sonia's rescue when Vajpayee said of the Congress president, 'Who is she to put me in the dock?' Singh's brief point of order may not have been forceful, but in the context of intra-party affairs, it underlined his importance and his equation with 10 Janpath. Arjun was most vocal and in the forefront of the protest when Vajpayee decided to take on Sonia.

Sonia's determination to learn was widely appreciated in the Congress. Party MP Girja Vyas said, 'There is a fighter in her and that is a very good thing.' Sonia created a huge body called the political affairs committee and began chairing meetings each morning when Parliament was in session. Initially, there were too many conflicting views, but soon Sonia picked experts in various fields who would have a final say on the matter. For instance, Dr Manmohan Singh, Pranab Mukherjee and Jairam Ramesh handled economic matters. Foreign policy matters were largely left to K. Natwar Singh and R.L. Bhatia, who was minister of state for external affairs under Narasimha Rao. Mani Shankar Aiyar and Salman Khurshid were also asked to contribute, but if there was a conflict between Natwar Singh and

Aiyar, she would back the former.

On secularism, Ayodhya and the saffronization of education, she looked to Arjun Singh and Rajya Sabha party backbenchers Eduardo Faleiro and K.M. Khan, AICC secretary Janardhan Dwivedi and non-political entities like Zoya Hasan and Romila Thapar. Legal aspects were assigned to former law minister H.R. Bhardwaj, Kapil Sibal and Shiv Shankar. Dr Manmohan Singh, Madhavrao Scindia, Priyaranjan Das Munshi and Pulak Chatterjee were pressed into action to deal with the government, and at the informal level, Maharashtra leader Murli Deora, Natwar Singh and Jairam Ramesh were given the task of speaking to friendly persons in the government to break impasses and get things done.

There were reports that Natwar Singh used his old friendship with Brajesh Mishra to ensure that Sonia was given the chance to address the United Nation's General Assembly on AIDS/HIV in June 2001, much to the chagrin of the Union health minister, C.P. Thakur, who was leader of the delegation. Natwar Singh was also credited with arranging meetings with Vice President Dick Cheney and other higher-ups in the Bush administration during her first visit to the US as leader of the Opposition in 2001. Sonia's elevation was part of a deal in return for her move to drop Vajpayee's name from a memorandum submitted to then President K.R. Narayanan demanding the Prime Minister's resignation in the wake of the Tehelka exposé.

The US visit was a milestone in Sonia's political career, enhancing her confidence by several notches. She was relieved to note that everyone spoke from a prepared text, as if speaking extempore indicated a lack of seriousness. She interacted freely with one and all, displaying her sense of humour and personal charm. The Indian community in the US was delighted, finding her a quick-witted, intelligent person.

Sonia's successful US visit created a stir in the government and the BJP. There were many red faces including that of BJP MP Dina Nath Mishra, editor of the book Sonia 'The Unknown', which levelled many non-serious and bizarre charges against her. Ironically, it was Mishra's party that sent Sonia as a representative of one billion persons to the UN AIDS conference in June 2001. She carried the day with dignity, underlining that although in domestic politics her party had differences with the BJP and the NDA, there was complete consensus on issues such as tackling poverty and disease and on stabilizing the population.[11]

Sonia's style of functioning became a subject of intense discussion in Congress circles. Within days of taking over as party president, Sonia made it clear that the party would be given a corporate touch. She appointed Sangma to submit a report on its functioning. The task force report of 1998 had some interesting suggestions, such as a boardroom-type seating arrangement for the CWC members. Sangma was of the view that in the television era, sitting Indian-style on the floor resting against bolsters and cushions did not project the Congress as a twenty-first century political party. He was also against the mandatory dress code of khadi and the provision that completely debars Congress activists from dealing in alcohol. Sonia had a good mind to implement these recommendations on grounds of pragmatism, but before she could act, Sangma walked out of the Congress forcing her to put the path-breaking report in cold storage. A copy of the report is currently lying in an outhouse of 24 Akbar Road.

In another effort to introduce a corporate culture in the party, in February 2000 Sonia set up departments for science and technology, environment, human rights, Other Backward Castes (OBCs), minorities, policy, planning and coordination, communications, public relations, media and information, foreign affairs, economy, law and so on, creating 144 posts in the AICC to man these, but party leaders entrusted with the task of running these departments largely remained indifferent. Each departmental head insisted upon getting secretarial staff, fax, telephone and a room, but once the infrastructure was provided to them, they hardly attended office.

Having failed to introduce a corporate culture, Sonia tried to streamline the party's style of functioning. It started with an attempt to carry everyone along, holding monthly CWC meetings and allowing free and frank discussions, but slowly the democratization process gave way to the long-ingrained coterie culture. Though Sonia contested the charge, the AICC chief remained dependent on a select band of advisers. In a bid to ward off criticism, she shuffled around with the coterie, but leaders like Arjun Singh, Natwar Singh and private secretary Vincent George continued to have a say in all decision making.

Party leaders said Sonia may have lacked Rajiv's warmth, but she was not indifferent like Narasimha Rao. She tried to maintain a certain distance, drawing a distinction between her public and personal life. She made it clear, for example, that Sunday would be her day off, unless there was an emergency. For many Congress leaders, including chief ministers, it was a shock of sorts. Digvijay Singh used to visit Delhi on weekends, but his requests for appointments remained unattended on Sunday, and so he began to call on her on Saturday evenings. In party meetings, there was no scope for loose talk and personal attacks. Mobile phones were to be switched off. She insisted on attendance, making it mandatory for all office-bearers to inform her office in advance about their tour programmes.

Sonia usually came prepared to party meetings and expected others to do the same. There was a meeting of the chief ministers of Congress-ruled states where the Delhi chief minister Sheila Dikshit, and her then Maharashtra counterpart, Vilasrao Deshmukh, got to see another side of Sonia. Both chief ministers had come rather unprepared and failed to give convincing replies about schemes for scheduled castes, scheduled tribes and minorities. Sonia was quick to reprimand them. 'You should have come prepared. What is the point of holding such meetings if chief ministers do not come prepared?'

Accountability was another area that gained currency under Sonia. As party president, Sonia gave a free hand to all office-bearers, but if they faltered, she moved swiftly to punish them. Veteran leader Pranab Mukherjee was sacked as AICC general secretary when he mishandled party affairs in Haryana by aligning with a tottering Bansi Lal government. Lal, who was defence minister in the Indira government during the Emergency (1975-77), was heading a state government in Haryana when many of his regional party Haryana Vikas Party MLAs began to desert him. Lal, a veteran of many political battles, panicked. He tapped some of his old contacts in the Congress to bail him out. The tide, however, had turned against him. The Congress stepped in but could not prevent the fall of his government. Lal's archrival, Om Prakash Chautala, formed an alternative government and called for fresh polls. In these, the Congress lost the state where it had a fair chance of winning before the Lal fiasco.

Pranab later had a thousand and one explanations, but the AICC chief was not convinced. In consideration of Mukherjee's seniority, he was allowed to tender his resignation owning 'moral responsibility'. The Haryana episode served as a warning of sorts for Congress bigwigs. They realized that if a leader like Mukherjee could be asked to go, they were also vulnerable.

Ghulam Nabi Azad become another victim of Sonia's accountability mantra. An assertive Sonia suddenly dropped Azad as general secretary on 27 March 2002 and gave him a punishing assignment as chief of the Jammu and Kashmir Congress, a unit that was virtually defunct in the violence-ridden state. Azad had earned the dubious distinction of being a 'rootless wonder' because he had no support base in his home state. He once contested the assembly polls from Kishtwar but lost miserably.

Azad had dominated the AICC for more than a decade. As AICC general secretary, he claimed to have looked after party affairs of twenty-four states. In scattered tenures, he had the distinction of occupying various rooms at 24 Akbar Road. He had first been spotted by Indira, who drafted him in the Youth Congress. He soon came in touch with Sanjay, who took him under his wing. Azad did not look back. He went on to head the Youth Congress and the Sewa Dal and then became party general secretary. The young man turned out to be an excellent weathercock, having a knack of being in the right spot at the right time. When Rajiv began having problems with Vishwanath Pratap Singh, Azad quickly offered his services, resigning from a ministerial assignment to take up party work. When Narasimha Rao faced a challenge from Arjun Singh, Azad decided to take on the thakur. In an incredible admission, Azad claimed that he had spent more than 1000 hours with Rajiv in private, implying that there was none other who could boast of such proximity to Rajiv!

Once Narasimha Rao was shown the door, Azad became a favourite bhatija (nephew) of 'Chacha' Sitaram Kesri. Until Sharad Pawar decided to throw a leadership challenge to the ailing AICC chief. Azad was in a fix as he was deeply indebted to Pawar. The gratitude stemmed from reasons ranging from Pawar ensuring his victory in the 1984 Lok Sabha elections from Vashim in Maharashtra to mobilizing resources for the Rajya Sabha polls. As Azad dithered and pleaded sick, Kesri became restless over his defiance. The cosy relations between chacha and bhatija took a dive. Till his death, Kesri continued to speak ill of him, but Azad was unmindful. He had found a new mentor in Sonia and bridged his differences with Arjun Singh.

Under Sonia, Azad increased his clout considerably. He was put in charge of party affairs in Karnataka and Kerala in 2001. The Congress won elections in both states. His camp began circulating reports that he had a magic touch, that he was a lucky mascot for the party. He was not a ghulam (slave) but azad (independent). Others said he was indispensable. The talk reached Sonia, and she began looking more closely at his style of functioning. Soon after, the general secretary burnt his fingers in Kerala when he failed to strike a balance between chief minister A.K. Antony and his archrival K. Karunakaran. When, in February 2002, the party won elections in the Himalayan state of Uttaranchal, Azad made an abortive bid to prop up trade union leader Harish Rawat as the new chief minister of the state. The elected MLAs opted for veteran leader Narain Dutt Tiwari. The MLAs complained to Sonia that Azad was thrusting his choice on them.

Azad ran out of luck in March 2002 and paid the price for the party's drubbing in the Uttar Pradesh polls. He was AICC general secretary in charge of the state. Sources said Sonia discarded him because of his proximity to the Samajwadi Party led by Mulayam Singh Yadav. There were allegations backed by statistics that said the Congress performed badly in places where the Samajwadi Party had won comfortably. The insinuation was that he had tried to work out a deal with Mulayam Singh without taking permission from the high command. The Congress forfeited deposits in as many as 325 out of

403 assembly seats. In the Afzalgarh constituency in Bijnore district, the party finished a distant eleventh, much behind many independents and non-serious players!

Azad's exit, however, surprised many in the party. Senior leaders took it as a sign of Sonia acting independently, dumping her reliance on the coterie.

As the J&K Congress unit chief, Azad faced an uphill task. The JKPCC president was expected to revitalize the party and take on the firmly entrenched National Conference. The problem was that he was perceived to be close to the party's chief, Farooq Abdullah, their friendship dating back to his election to the Rajya Sabha five-and-a-half years before, when the National Conference donated its surplus votes to see him through.

However, with a slice of luck, Azad proved his detractors wrong in Jammu and Kashmir. The outcome of the assembly polls in November 2002 surprised everyone, including Azad, as the party did exceedingly well, finishing second behind the National Conference. The arithmetic was such that a Congress government under Azad became a possibility but Sonia, aware of Azad's limitations, accorded primacy to the mandate in the Kashmir valley where a regional party under a former Congress leader, Mufti Mohammad Sayeed, had been successful. Sonia overruled the twenty-odd MLAs and crowned Sayeed. Incidentally, Sayeed was among the few Congressmen who had left the party after Sonia had taken over as chief in 1998.

Sonia's sensitivity to the feelings of the people in the state earned her respect. Her decision was dubbed statesman-like. Azad did not protest too much realizing that he was getting a berth in the Rajya Sabha and important assignments in the party. Sayeed and the Congress worked out an elaborate arrangement as part of a common minimum programme for the state.

The Congress under Sonia gave high priority to some of the thorny issues that were hanging fire for years. Successive party leaderships had failed to take drastic action on the issue of reservation for women in party posts, allocation of tickets and party funding. In this arena, Sonia deserves credit for displaying leadership qualities while tiding over the storm within the Congress and enforcing measures that she felt were necessary. The regional satraps and vested interests who thought she could be manipulated were in for a shock. Sonia got the Congress the distinction of being the first political party that gave 33 per cent quota to women at all levels of the party hierarchy. Overruling the majority sentiment, she got sweeping amendments through in the Congress constitution.

On the application side, there were genuine problems in getting one-third of women nominees at block and district levels of the party. However, she kept a strict vigil, and whenever she got an opportunity, she filled party posts with women nominees. Under Sonia, the Congress became the first national-level party to support a controversial women's reservation bill that sought to reserve one-third of parliamentary and assembly seats for women. The bill failed to get through the Lok Sabha, but it found a powerful advocate in Sonia. In successive Lok Sabhas, Sonia made it a point to embarrass the ruling coalition by raking up the issue of quota for women. In this respect, she won many admirers across party lines.

On 10 June 2001, the Congress under Sonia became the first all-white party. Chanting a new mantra of integrity, accountability and transparency, the country's oldest political party pledged to accept monetary donations only through cheques. As was the 33 per cent quota for women, the sweeping changes in the way the party was funded was a personal triumph for her. She managed to push through the path-breaking reforms in this murky area, overruling sceptics within the CWC who expressed doubts about the feasibility of cheque payments. But the AICC chief remained unfazed. Sonia said the Congress was prepared to clean up the entire system, but it was for the government to take the initiative to bring about electoral reforms. In her view, the Congress is game on state funding of polls, recommended by two all-party parliamentary panels headed by Dinesh Goswami and Indrajit Gupta, both outstanding parliamentarians who are now dead.

On rough calculation, the Congress's annual expenses (without election expenses) run to about Rs 10 crores, which are raised through all sorts of means, including those which cannot be shown in audit. Sonia said she wanted to change all that. In her scheme of things, everyone who is someone in the party would have to pay to fill the coffers. The party decided to raise a Rs 50 crore corpus by 2003 by asking its eleven lakh active workers to pay Rs 100 a year. For Pradesh Congress Committee delegates, the amount was Rs 300 a year and for members of the All India Congress Committee it was Rs 600. MPs, MLAs, ministers, chief ministers, as also chairpersons of district boards, autonomous bodies, municipal corporations and other panels had to contribute one month's salary.

Sonia also thought of some novel methods of raising funds. Those seeking party tickets for elections were asked to pay Rs 5000 for assembly seats and Rs 10,000 for Lok Sabha tickets. In case they failed to get the ticket, the money was non-refundable. Likewise, corporates and captains of industry were encouraged to make payments by cheque in accordance with existing rules in the Companies Act. The party recommended that the ceiling under section 293(A) of the Companies Act of 1956 should be enhanced. The various chambers of commerce welcomed the clean-up resolution. Individuals like Ratan Tata, chairman of the Tatas, who have been advocating the need for transparency and accountability, hailed Sonia's move. Sonia appeared pleased and told aides that party funding was one area where she wanted to do a lot.

Another ambition is to make the Congress a party of the best and the brightest. Unless the party provides a conducive atmosphere for the entry of such individuals, the credibility of politicians will not be restored, she feels.

While Sonia succeeded on some fronts, her public image of an apolitical, reluctant politician was a result of her own creation. She took the plunge into politics but remained morbidly afraid of the media. Her party colleagues perpetuated the fear. The AICC chief restricted herself to giving the occasional sound bite to private TV networks.

Sonia tried to interact more with the media but her advisers, including senior party functionaries, scuttled the move. These leaders told Sonia that both Indira and Rajiv had suffered from media witch-hunting. For a long time, Sonia firmly believed that the media was nursing a grudge against her. Each day 10 Janpath was flooded with requests for interviews, but she turned them down waiting for a suitable moment.

One such occasion seemed to present itself when the television news channel CNN collaborated with *Time* magazine, and their team decided to fly down to Delhi in 2001. At the last moment, the interview was cancelled as someone advised Sonia to give her first interview to an Indian publication. She short-listed the large circulation Hindi daily *Punjab Kesri* (recommended by Priyanka Gandhi) and *The Times of India*, but other newspaper barons threw a fit. The Italian media stationed in New Delhi thought meeting Sonia would be easier for them, but they were in for a shock too, for they were curtly told to get in touch with Ajit Jogi and V.N. Gadgil.

A number of well-meaning persons suggested to Sonia that she have a full-time media adviser or consultant who could help her stay in touch with the media. Sonia was keen to have the services of H.Y. Sharda Prasad, former information adviser to Indira, and Suman Dubey, but both politely declined. A number of retired journalists, journalists-turned politicians and TV personalities were keen, but sometimes Sonia did not consider them suitable or lobbying and counter-lobbying within the Congress prevented such an appointment. Ultimately, the move was shelved.

Sonia's inexperience too played a role in her mishandling of the media. In 1998, some months after she took over as party president, she decided to meet those covering the Congress individually. The interaction was supposed to be one-on-one and strictly off the record. She insisted on seeing the list of journalists who were to call on her and asked for the resumés of these individuals. To make matters worse, the AICC's media department began calling up scribes asking them to hand over their CVs if they wished to see the AICC chief. The request created a good deal of merriment till Sonia herself withdrew the demand.

EIGHT

SONIA TAKES OVER THE CONGRESS

It was in the third week of December 1997 that Sonia Gandhi first indicated her willingness to take a more active role in politics. She chose Madhya Pradesh chief minister Digvijay 'Diggy Raja' Singh to break the news. He had called on her complaining against the Congress chief Sitaram Kesri. For him and many other party leaders, Kesri was more of a liability than an asset. The old man who avoided contesting direct elections had no vision or mass appeal. For him, the route to success was simple—plea, petition and manipulation. Behind a simple Gandhian profile, Kesri was a shrewd politician with a knack of being on the winning side. He had cut many deals and annoyed many partymen. Kesri had survived for decades, but once he took over as the Congress chief, his flaws as a leader became glaringly obvious.

Singh did not mince words in saying that under Kesri the Congress was heading towards disaster. As long as Kesri was head of the Congress, the party would not even get 100 seats in the Lok Sabha polls that were announced for January 1998.

Sonia attentively heard Singh's formulation and then casually asked, 'What will happen if I campaign for the Congress?' He could not believe his ears. 'Madam, that would electrify our rank and file. We will sweep the polls!' He could visualize Sonia addressing mammoth public meetings in his state. To him, it was a reminder of the heady days of Rajiv in 1984 that marked Singh's debut in the Lok Sabha. He could hardly forget how Rajiv had made him Congress unit chief of Madhya Pradesh in 1987 although he lacked experience. Rajiv had sounded him for the coveted post, and Singh blurted it out to his mentor Arjun Singh who, in turn, quickly approached Rajiv offering his services for the job! Rajiv summoned Digvijay wondering how Arjun came to know about a private conversation between them. 'It was an important political lesson for me,' he later recalled, admitting that Rajiv's trust in him made him a 10 Janpath loyalist for ever.

Digvijay Singh was not alone in labelling Kesri a liability for the Congress or in being a beneficiary of the benevolent acts of the Nehru–Gandhi family. By December 1997, barring a handful of Kesri loyalists, virtually everyone had turned against him. Ahmad Patel, Kamal Nath, Vayalar Ravi, Ashok Gehlot and dozens of Young Turks frequently met Sonia to remind her of her historic responsibility to save the nation from fascist forces. As a member of the great family, she could not escape her responsibilities, Patel told her. 'Millions of party workers are willing to die for you. How can you allow the collapse of the Congress before your eyes,' Gehlot said, pointing at the large-scale desertions in the party. Aslam Sher Khan, Mani Shankar Aiyar, Suresh Kalmadi, Buta Singh and P.R. Kumarmangalam were some of the prominent leaders who had left the party. Kumarmangalam died soon thereafter, but one by one, Aiyar, Buta and Kalmadi returned to the parent organization once Sonia took over as AICC chief.

The old guard of the Congress was also at work. Fed up with Kesri's antics, leaders like K. Karunakaran, Arjun Singh, A.K. Antony, Jitendra Prasada, Vijay Bhaskar Reddy, V.N. Gadgil and Madhav Sinh Solanki kept exerting pressure on Sonia to intervene. Arjun Singh and Prasada, who had masterminded the collapse of the I.K. Gujral government on the basis of the Jain Commission report, gently reminded her of the need to reciprocate the feelings of the Congress workers who could not tolerate the presence of two DMK ministers in a government supported by the Congress.

The moral pressure of the Rajiv assassination probe was, in fact, a turning point. It was one issue that could make the family overcome its reluctance to take an active role in politics. Arjun Singh was the first to identify the weak spot months after Rao took over as the Prime Minister in 1991. He began attending virtually all the sittings of the Verma and Jain commission hearings, sending details of the proceedings to 10 Janpath. At first they got no response. Rahul and Priyanka were also regularly seen at the Vigyan Bhavan annexe where the hearings were taking place. But Singh's bid to strike rapport with them did not succeed, since the Gandhi children remained aloof from Congress politicians.

The sum and substance of Arjun's campaign was that unless Sonia took a more active political role, the Rajiv assassination probe would not make any headway, and the real culprits of the dastardly act and the key conspirators might even get away. A secondary part of his campaign was that the Rao government had a sinister design in scuttling the probe—a charge that gained momentum when Arjun Singh resigned from the Rao government in December 1994. Many Congress leaders also felt that Sonia was not convinced that the LTTE was solely responsible for Rajiv's assassination. She was of the view that the LTTE may have been a willing agent for other agencies involved in that dastardly act.

Arjun Singh's detractor Jitendra Prasada used the same ploy to get even with Kesri, which resulted in the downfall of the Gujral government. Like Singh, Prasada hired a battery of lawyers to examine the bulky Jain Commission report, picking instances that seemed to link the DMK with the LTTE.

Amidst these behind-the-scenes deliberations, Sonia too had began putting aside her contempt for politics. Events in the past few years had altered her thinking. The betrayal of Narasimha Rao, the tardy progress in the Rajiv assassination probe, the ever-declining fortunes of the Congress and all-round attack on the Nehru–Gandhi legacy weighed heavily in favour of testing the uncertain waters of politics. If the Congress were to disintegrate, would not she be held responsible?

In the next forty-eight hours, she tried to probe Rahul and Priyanka's mind. Predictably, Rahul became agitated. 'Let us not get into the mess,' was his advice. Priyanka, however, was thoughtful. 'Mama, let us see,' was her response. The family met again at dinner that night. Various pros and cons were discussed and Rahul reluctantly gave up. 'Mama, I will leave work and be with you in all public meetings,' he offered. The family then tentatively decided that Sonia would make the announcement around Christmas so that she could campaign for the Congress in the general elections.

It was at this juncture that Sonia fell out with Amitabh Bachchan. Bachchan was completely against Sonia entering politics. He described Congress leaders as vultures who wanted to cash in on the Nehru–Gandhi family's appeal to serve their political ends. For the first time in thirty years, he and Sonia were not on the same wavelength. While Sonia saw some merit in what Amit was saying, she stayed with her decision.

That choice marked a painful parting between the two families. Bachchan began distancing himself from 10 Janpath, feeling let down, and he was quietly dropped as a trustee of the Rajiv Gandhi Foundation. Years later when Bachchan invited Sonia to the premiere of his son Abhishek's first film, *Refugee*, Sonia declined the invitation pointing out that as the Congress president she could not go to a five-star hotel! A few days later, however, she was spotted in a five-star hotel at a party thrown by Congress leader Subbi Rami Reddy.

Meanwhile, blissfully unaware of the developments at 10 Janpath, 'Chacha' Sitaram Kesri was busy trying to build a band of loyalists for himself. Kesri knew that the party MPs were unhappy over the manner in which he pulled down the United Front governments of H.D. Deve Gowda and I.K. Gujral. His relations with 10 Janpath had taken a beating over his reluctance to bring down Gujral's government over the Jain Commission report. Kesri was bitter that Arjun Singh and Prasada had succeeded in projecting him as a villain in Sonia's eyes. He tried to patch things up and paid several visits to her, but he failed to gauge her mood. 'There was something in her eyes that made me uneasy, but I had no idea that she was going to take the plunge or dump me so unceremoniously,' Kesri later told his friends in the media, blaming Singh and Prasada for spoiling his otherwise 'excellent rapport' with her.

After all, as welfare minister between 1991 and 1996, Kesri had given standing orders to his ministry officials to clear all projects of the RGF on priority basis. With Sonia as head of the RGF, Kesri thought that his gesture would keep him in her good books. Kesri's logic was simple. A lot of money under his ministry earmarked for nongovernmental organizations (NGOs) was going unused or disappearing into the hands of unscrupulous elements. Kesri thought he was killing two birds with one stone. 'Sarkari paisa hain. Agar Indira ke parivar ke paas ja raha hai to kya boorai hai (It is government money. Even if it is going to Indira's family, I see no harm),' Kesri told some journalists.[1]

Kesri had severe limitations as the president of the Congress. Leaders from the south and the North-East had a problem communicating with him, and partymen from the north never accepted Kesri as their leader due to caste considerations! After all, the Congress had retained its upper-caste character in Uttar Pradesh, Bihar, Madhya Pradesh, Rajasthan, Punjab and elsewhere. Kesri also made his dislike for the north Indian Brahmins and thakurs obvious. He was open about forging a grand alliance with the likes of Laloo Prasad Yadav, Kanshi Ram and Mulayam Singh Yadav. His views unnerved a large section of upper-caste leaders from the Hindi heartland who were already struggling to survive, losing successive Lok Sabha polls with huge margins. Kesri's promise to 'Mandalize' the Congress made them sit up, as they were now about to lose their position within the organization too.

Kesri, who came from a modest background and had no formal education, also began priding himself as a commoner who was elected by the party rank and file. Though everyone within the Congress and outside it viewed the organizational polls that concluded in Calcutta in September 1997 as farcical, Kesri took the compliment of elected AICC chief too seriously. His commoner reference was taken as a sign of defiance towards Sonia and the Nehru–Gandhi family. To make matters worse, between Kesri and 10 Janpath, a handful of former MPs systematically began passing on bits of information and gossip to Vincent George exaggerating what Kesri was saying about Sonia and her loyalists. One leader from Madhya Pradesh told George, 'He says he will finish off the Nehru–Gandhi family,' and quoted Kesri as saying, 'The days of rajas and maharajas are over. Foreigners must go back. I have fought thousands of angrez and what is a petty Italian!'

Many of these hangers-on used to attend Kesri's late-night court held in his bedroom. He was a widower and even middle-rung party leaders had free access to his house. Adjacent to the bedroom was a smaller ante-room that was used for serious political deliberations. The bedroom reeked of alcohol and smoke, while the conversation revolved around politics, gossip and sex. Kesri's court used to have an amazing mix of people. Freeloaders, intellectuals and moneybags attended while Chacha sat on his bed with a glass of milk and medicines lined up on the side table. 'Take some cold milk? It is good for the stomach,' Kesri would tell anyone willing to listen. He would then scratch himself vigorously and offer cherries to his dog Ruchi and pass them on to the gathering.

The veteran leader was himself a great storyteller and gossip, with a view on virtually everything. 'Ek baat bata deten hain (Let me tell you something),' he would start. The tale he loved to tell was how Rajendra Babu (Dr Rajendra Prasad, the first President) had a great liking for him. Prasad had visited Danapur and spotted the young freedom fighter in him. 'I went to jail several times,' Kesri would recount, exposing his back to show the spots where he received lashes from the 'lal pagris', as the lathi-wielding Raj police in Bihar were called.

Kesri's detractors had a different story, claiming that young Kesri was booked under hoarding charges during the Second World War. Kesri's take on this was that the British used to deliberately come up with charges such as this to malign freedom fighters.

Sometimes Kesri would speak of how Subhash Chandra Bose was greater than Jawaharlal Nehru. 'I was part of the Forward Bloc and Netaji's team in Calcutta,' he would say, closing his eyes. He would ruminate on how India would have been different if Gandhiji had not made a mistake in picking Nehru instead of Bose. The non-violent pacifist would give way to the radical Kesri. 'We have a slave mentality. We have not got freedom after shedding blood. The non-violent method made us impotent. Had Subhash been around, the country would have been different,' Kesri would say, propagating a theory that the Nehru-led, Delhi-centric Congress consciously suppressed leadership from Bengal. 'From Bose to Mamata Banerjee, it is the same story of suppression and injustice,' Kesri would tell a flabbergasted audience that was left wondering how Bose could be compared to Banerjee.[2]

In the same breath, he recalled his proximity to some Bollywood actresses and how he used to borrow money from former AICC chief Dev Kanta Borooah to visit Bombay! The courtiers would delightfully chip in: 'One day an actress came to see Kesriji when I was present. She said, "Main aap ke pass chhoti see aas le kar aayi hun (I have come to you seeking a small favour)." I felt like telling her—please don't lie. You do not have a chhoti ass!' The bawdy joke drew hysterical laughter from all quarters including Kesri.

On 28 December 1997 Sonia chose to go public about her intention to join politics. It was a sleepy afternoon when beat regulars gathered at 24 Akbar Road for a routine press conference. Kesri too wanted to share a word with journalists in a post-briefing informal chat.

He reached the party headquarters at 2.30 p.m., but an hour before the scheduled press meet at 4 p.m., a small note from 10 Janpath ruined his mood. A lowly functionary, Tom Vaddakan,[3] ran through a small passage between 10 Janpath and 24 Akbar Road carrying an announcement from Vincent George that said Sonia would campaign for the Congress in the general elections.

Initially Vaddakan was not allowed to pass Sonia's message to Kesri. The guard outside Kesri's room would not let him in. 'It is important and if you do not let me in, you will lose your job,' an irritated Vaddakan said, but the guard was unfazed. 'Sahib does not want to be disturbed,' he said matter-of-factly. Suddenly, Tom saw Harish Khare, a journalist from the *Hindu* who had an appointment with Kesri. 'Sir, please pass

this on to him. It is from 10 Janpath and the guard is not letting me in.'
Khare took the note and gave it to Kesri.

Kesri's face fell the moment he finished reading it. He struggled to
respond, mumbling to himself, 'Sub kuch khatam. Wo aa rahi hai (It
is all over. She is coming).' Kesri then broke the news to Khare.
Interestingly, Kesri did not address the briefing to make the
announcement, notwithstanding his scores of public statements
requesting Sonia to help out the party. It was left to V.N. Gadgil to
make the announcement to the world.

It was a surprising gesture from Kesri not to hog the limelight that
day. After all, when Madhavrao Scindia and S. Bangarappa, former
Karnataka chief minister, returned to the parent organization, Kesri
was there to receive them in the AICC portico and escort them to the
briefing room before making a formal announcement. Sources close
to Kesri later admitted that the old man was keen to welcome Sonia
but decided against it. He was reminded of the designs of his detractors
like Arjun Singh and Jitendra Prasada who were using 10 Janpath to
dislodge him. Kesri also realized that it was not befitting of an elected
AICC chief to be seen as playing second fiddle to Sonia.

When the news of Kesri's defiance reached 10 Janpath, Sonia began
wondering if she had taken the correct course. She suddenly realized
that her entry would not be as smooth as projected by Digvijay Singh,
Arjun Singh, Kamal Nath and others. Her mind raced back to a
statement made by a close family friend who had vehemently opposed
her decision to enter public life. 'I have been a Congress MP. I know
the party too well. It is a snake-pit. You will soon realize that the most
trusted persons can turn against you.' The prediction turned out to be
true on several occasions. In Sonia's own words, 'I have no regret that
I joined politics. But yes, it pained me when I saw people who had
repeatedly requested me to take the plunge level baseless allegations
against me and leave the party.' The reference was to P.A. Sangma,
Tariq Anwar and Sharad Pawar in May 1999.

Sonia shrugged off the idea of withdrawing her move. She foresaw
a dismal future for the Congress if she did not join the party. The
AICC treasurer, Ahmad Patel, helped her articulate these ideas in a

presentation produced with the aid of a professional agency. It said that the Congress would disintegrate into several factions and the BJP would gain strength and undermine the country's secular fabric. The inference was clear—join the Congress and you will have millions of party workers willing to die for the honour of the family.

Sonia was not unaware of the points made by the presentation. As the slides played out the scenario, Sonia firmed up her mind. 'I am a fighter, and I will overcome the handicaps,' she told herself. In the back of her mind was the sequence of events that resulted in the fall of the Gujral government over the Jain Commission report. Years later, Sonia told some family friends that destiny ensured a political role for her. 'I was dead opposed to it. In fact, in 1991 I was shocked and considered Congressmen extremely insensitive when the CWC passed a resolution asking me to take over as the party chief. Seven years after, I just could not resist,' she admitted.[4]

The choice of 28 December 1997 was not without significance. It was the 112th anniversary of the Indian National Congress. The general elections were announced and the Congress state election committees, central election committee and other important bodies that allot tickets to aspirants were to meet on 3 and 4 January 1998. As the Congress president, Kesri had a final say, but Sonia's arrival spoilt everything. In the meetings that took place, Kesri was reduced to a puppet. Each day, general secretary Oscar Fernandes would bring a file from 10 Janpath that was reportedly sent by Vincent George, and Kesri was expected to clear all the names. Kesri suspected that Arjun Singh was acting in concert with George and that the duo was keeping Sonia in the dark, but the old man could never muster the courage to complain against George, though he met Sonia a number of times. Each time he said that proper persons were not getting party tickets, Sonia would say, 'Kesriji, please consult Arjun Singhji and Madhavrao!'

The New Year brought chaos. The Kesri camp was busy projecting it as the 'year of Kesri' while Sonia's managers were finalizing venues for her debut and consulting astrologers. On 11 January 1998, Sriperumbudur became the venue of her first public meeting. Requests from prospective candidates pleading that Sonia should touch their constituency flooded 10 Janpath. She was seen as their passport to success.

Vincent George suddenly became extremely busy. Helping him were dozens of loyal workers who were experts in a range of subjects, Congress history and culture among them. It was an elite band of experts that used to help Rajiv. A place's historical importance, link to Indira and Rajiv, and caste and religious considerations were some of the factors that were taken into account in chalking out Sonia's itinerary. After all, she was 'Indira II' in the making. She first needed to regain the confidence of the traditional vote bank—the poor, tribals and weaker sections, the Muslims and other minorities.

As Congressmen made a beeline for 10 Janpath, there was a sharp decline in the number of visitors at Kesri's 7 Purana Qila Road residence. Only the usual hanger-ons remained. Each day Kesri was confronted with more bad news. For among the points Sonia made in her speeches was that all was not well with the Congress. She made it clear that she would not confine herself to campaigning for the party but would continue to play an active role in politics even after the elections.[5]

For the first time in the history of the Congress, the party president was kept away from campaigning. None of the states, including his own state Bihar, sought Kesri's services. The old man tried to visit Jalandhar, but the aircraft had to turn around while flying over Ambala as Kesri developed a breathing problem in the unpressurized cabin. Azad later said that he remained extremely tense till the aircraft landed at Palam. 'I was seriously worried about Chacha's health. He appeared in acute pain, almost choking.'[6]

The outcome of the elections to the twelfth Lok Sabha came as a shock to the Congress. In the back-breaking campaign that saw Sonia address 130-odd meetings, the Congress's final tally read 142. Besides handing over the family borough of Amethi to the BJP, she could not save two of her most trusted lieutenants, Arjun Singh and Narain Dutt Tiwari, who lost in Hoshangabad (Madhya Pradesh) and Naini Tal (then in Uttar Pradesh). But her managers quickly put the blame on Kesri, who had not stepped out of his house. They said that owing to organizational weaknesses, the party failed to cash in on Sonia's charisma. She accepted the argument and agreed to take direct control of the party, insisting, however, that Kesri step down gracefully and invite her to take over. Chacha was in no mood to oblige her.

Restless CWC members began holding conclaves to work out plans on how to install Sonia. The task was left to Kesri's two favourite 'nephews'—Ahmad Patel and Azad—to sound him out about retiring gracefully. But Kesri laughed off the proposal. 'You have been sent by Arjun Singh and George. It cannot be Soniaji's words. If she wants me out, let her say so,' Chacha said.

Sharad Pawar too joined the 'Kesri hatao' campaign. He was getting feedback from Mumbai and the corporate world that said that as long as Kesri was head of the party, the industrial houses would not support it. Pawar teamed up with Prasada and A.K. Antony, and later Pranab Mukherjee joined in. Every week the senior leaders would meet in small groups to review the situation. Invariably Pawar would favour a 'surgical operation', but Mukherjee and Antony would seek more time.

Sensing trouble, the Kesri camp launched a counter-offensive. The first casualties were the CWC meetings that had to be convened by the party chief. Kesri was advised not to call the CWC as it might ask him to step down. Kesri was convinced that the party constitution gave him ultimate powers and that as long as he was the elected chief, nobody would dare to remove him.

The CWC finally met on 5 March 1998 to assess the party's poor performance in the general elections. The outcome of the meeting was significant on two counts. First, it asked Sonia to play a more direct and meaningful role and requested her to help the party elect the new leader of the CPP, a post that Kesri occupied. Kesri was upset with Mukherjee and Pawar, and he later told Tariq Anwar, 'If Sharad thinks he can become CPP leader, tell him to forget it. Soniaji will never let it happen.' Kesri was proved right for soon after Sonia took over, she got herself elected as the CPP leader though she was not a member of Parliament. The CPP constitution was amended to state that any party leader was free to get elected to its parliamentary body even if he/she was not a member of either House![7]

After the Ahmad–Azad mission failed, three senior leaders, Dr Manmohan Singh, Pranab Mukherjee and A.K. Antony, approached Kesri. The trio acknowledged Kesri's services but told him that a change of guard was in the interest of the party. Antony said Sonia was willing to take over. Surrounded by senior colleagues, Kesri was at a loss for words. He said, 'If you wise persons feel that I am coming in the way of reviving the party, I will step down. But I will have a word with Madam.' The leaders thought their mission was successful, but Kesri cleverly used the opportunity to buy more time. He began sounding out CWC members, and much to his dismay, he realized that except for Tariq Anwar, all of them had switched sides.

Kesri then called on Sonia declaring that he was willing to step down as the party chief if she was going to take over from him. Much to his horror, Sonia gently asked him, 'When?' The old man was crestfallen. He could not take on Sonia. After all, it was Indira Gandhi who made him AICC treasurer. The bravado of being elected AICC chief was nowhere in sight. Kesri promised to hold a press conference to make the formal announcement. For once, he kept his word and did not share his intention even with his close associates. These included some prominent journalists who were his political advisers.

On 9 March, Kesri announced his resignation, but within minutes he changed his mind. Kesri claimed that he had merely stated his intention to step down, though all the major newspapers quoted him as saying that he had resigned. Chacha's coterie chided him for handing over power to Sonia on a platter. Kesri rephrased his comments claiming that he would place his resignation before the AICC general body meeting, which has over 1000 delegates, so as to seek their approval. 'They have elected me, and I will seek their permission,' he told the press. But nobody took the statement seriously. Azad, Patel, Arjun Singh and other CWC members quickly called on Sonia, taking credit for the success.

Over the next few days, Kesri went on giving interviews that he had not resigned and that the leadership issue would be settled by the

AICC. Number 10 Janpath summoned loyal CWC members seeking an explanation. 'Oh, Chacha is upset over adverse publicity. He is a rustic fellow,' a CWC member told Sonia, as he boasted that he would set everything in order. 'I have consulted astrologers who say 14 March is an auspicious day to take over,' he said, but Sonia only nodded warily.

Antony, Mukherjee and Dr Singh again called on Kesri, but the old man was in a bad mood this time. 'You wanted me to resign. I have done it,' he said bluntly, even refusing to offer a cup of tea to them. Pranab cleared his throat and asked, 'When should the CWC meet?' That remark infuriated Kesri who shot back, 'It is up to me to decide.' The trio faithfully reported the incident to Sonia.

George spoke to Prasada wondering why Kesri was creating hurdles in Sonia's way. Prasada assured him that Chacha would be 'fixed soon'. A day before the coup, on 14 March, he hosted a lunch at which all CWC members except for the Orissa chief minister, J.B. Patnaik, and his Mizo counterpart, Lalthanhawla, were present. Thirteen CWC members gathered at Pranab's house at 9.30 a.m. to draft a strongly worded resolution that asked Kesri to immediately convene a CWC meet to end the uncertainty in the wake of his decision to resign as the party chief. It said that Kesri's gesture had bewildered party workers all over the country and he should step down in Sonia's favour. Pranab discovered a provision in the Congress constitution that supposedly empowered the CWC to take drastic action under very special circumstances. Party leaders later admitted that the provision did not specifically say it had powers to remove an elected party president.

The manoeuvring reached its nadir on the fateful day. As soon as the CWC met at 11 a.m., Kesri began protesting over the minutes of the meeting. He became hysterical when Pranab thanked him for his services as the party chief and moved a resolution asking Sonia to take over. Chacha adjourned the meeting within eight minutes and retired to his office adjacent to the hall where the CWC was meeting at 24 Akbar Road. No amount of persuasion from Dr Singh, Mukherjee, Antony and Patel changed his mind. Those in favour of change had anticipated it all. At 11.20 Prasada, the vice president of the party, took the chair signalling Pranab to move the resolution formally to invite Sonia to take over. The lone Kesri loyalist, Tariq Anwar, followed his leader, refusing to be party to 'the unconstitutional and unprecedented measures' that were being adopted by the CWC. He staged a walkout.

The remaining CWC members then rushed to 10 Janpath. At about noon, the committee formally handed over the chair to her. Kesri's nameplate was quickly removed and thrown into the dustbin and a sparkling black-and-white plaque bearing Sonia's name was fixed outside the Congress president's office well ahead of her arrival at the party headquarters. Sonia came to Akbar Road at 5.30 to chair the CWC meet and take over as the party chief. She looked bright and confident for the occasion, but she was not pleased about the circumstances in which she was taking over. 'It would have been a lot better if everything had gone smoothly,' she told a party functionary, while admitting that Kesri would not have vacated the seat voluntarily.

As soon as the CWC meeting was over, she called on Kesri, describing him as a 'great leader'. Kesri was once again in a dilemma. 'It was gracious of her to have visited me when friends and colleagues deserted me. However, I failed to communicate the sense of betrayal. I was her host and she was my guest,' he said. Sonia also announced that Kesri's team of office-bearers would remain unchanged.[8]

Kesri died a disturbed and disillusioned man. He could not reconcile himself to his unceremonious ouster. Left without friends, in his last days, Kesri tried to jump onto Mamata Banerjee's bandwagon, but the Trinamul chief had little to offer. Disappointed, Kesri began lauding Feroze Varun, Sanjay and Maneka's son, as a potential challenger to Sonia and Priyanka, but before he could mobilize support for the young Gandhi, he fell in the bathroom. The seemingly small injury led to complications, for which he had to be hospitalized. There was much that he wanted to say, but he suffered an asthma attack and then slid into coma. In the public eye, he died a loyalist, carrying his secrets with him.

NINE

THE FAVOURED FEW

One accusation that has been constantly made against Sonia is that she is surrounded by a small coterie that influences the entire decision-making process. Some call them advisers, others cronies, while the bitter ones simply describe them as the cabal.

Ironically, the coterie charge is levelled by the faithful and dissidents alike. Whenever something goes wrong, loyalists blame her advisers. Sonia's detractors say that she is tutored by a group of party leaders who lack mass support and have a vested interest in keeping the name of the family alive.

Sonia is acutely aware of the charges. At first, she took them as an indictment of her style of functioning. However, over time, she began to view the criticism as a professional hazard. The Congress president tried to erase the charge by expanding her group of advisers, but this did not help. Soon reports had it that Sonia had several coteries, her A team, B team and so on!

Others mocked Sonia saying she was applying the Hindu concept of division of work in her own way—leaders like Pranab Mukherjee, Natwar Singh, Dr Manmohan Singh, Ghulam Nabi Azad, Ambika Soni and Ahmad Patel were treated like Brahmins who did little work but got rewarded handsomely. This group, considered Sonia's A team, consists of people who have not necessarily done well in elections. Leaders like Mukherjee, for instance, who has been with the party and close to the family for some four decades, barring a brief period in exile, has never contested a Lok Sabha election. Dr Manmohan Singh contested the prestigious South Delhi seat in 1999 but lost by a wide margin. Nor have Ambika Soni and Patel had luck in direct elections. Azad won once from Vashim in Maharashtra, which is not his home state.

The second group consisting of Kshatriyas—the likes of Digvijay Singh, Ashok Gehlot, S.M. Krishna and A.K. Antony—are people who have fought and won many electoral battles. The Kshatriyas are viewed with suspicion as being ambitious and are kept away from Delhi. The leadership avails itself of their services in times of crisis.

The third group of leaders, the Vaishyas, include Motilal Vora, AICC treasurer from 2001 to 2003 after stints as chief minister, Union minister and governor, R.K. Dhawan, M.L. Fotedar, Murli Deora, and Captain Satish Sharma. Sonia uses their services for specific purposes. These leaders are important without being accorded front-rank status.

The remaining ones are foot soldiers who man the party but do not have much say in the decision-making processes.

For many political analysts, the coterie charge has more than a grain of truth. Even before Sonia joined politics, former Prime Minister P.V. Narasimha Rao viewed dissident leader Arjun Singh as a mole. Singh did not mind the accusation and made political capital out of it. Even as Narasimha Rao went on to lose his political authority in 1995 and 1996 because of various scams, the list of Sonia loyalists swelled. The 1995 split in the Congress formalized a select band of party leaders consisting of Narain Dutt Tiwari, Arjun Singh, Mohsina Kidwai, M.L. Fotedar, Natwar Singh and Sheila Dikshit as Sonia loyalists. Except for Tiwari, others got the distinction of being part of Sonia's coterie when she took over as Congress chief, and they were subsequently given prized posts in the party.

Sonia's reliance upon and comfort level with the erstwhile Tiwari Congress leaders resulted in a deep-rooted insecurity among the majority of Congress leaders. Many openly began saying that loyalty to the party had no premium. The anti-Congress parties also lapped up the coterie charge, alleging that Sonia was 'guided' by Arjun Singh,

onia with her mother-in-law, Indira Gandhi, with whom she had a warm relationship.

Sonia and Rajiv Gandhi with Pope John Paul II during the papal stay at Rashtrapati Bhavan in 1986. Sonia was raised in a conservative Catholic family.

Sonia with Prime Minister P.V. Narasimha Rao in 1991. He was chosen to lead the party afte
Rajiv's death.

Sanjay and Maneka Gandhi, Sonia's
brother- and sister-in-law. Sanjay died
in an air crash on 23 June 1980.

Vincent George, originally Rajiv's private secretary, became Sonia's after her husband's death.

Ghulam Nabi Azad, Congress party leader and a strong political supporter of Rajiv and Sonia.

When Sitaram Kesri was unceremoniously removed as AICC chief in March 1998, Sonia retained him as a special invitee in the CWC—a courtesy not extended to Narasimha Rao.

Arjun Singh encouraged Sonia to play a role in politics after Rajiv's death.

Rajesh Pilot opposed Sonia for the AICC president's post in November 2000 and teamed up with Jitendra Prasada to start a low-key rebellion in the guise of inner-party democracy.

Sharad Pawar, a major player from Maharashtra.

onia with her children, Priyanka and Rahul, at Teen Murti Bhavan in 1996.

onia and Hillary Rodham Clinton (two seats to her left) at Mother Teresa's funeral in Kolkata in 1997. Priyanka Gandhi is seated behind Sonia.

Sonia as president of the Congress party in 2000, a year which tested her as a leader.

Sonia at a meeting in Guwahati with the chief ministers of the Congress-ruled states in April 2002. With her is author Rasheed Kidwai (right) and Kamal Nath, AICC General Secretary (left).

Sonia as leader of the opposition at an all-party meeting in New Delhi. Seated with her are the Prime Minister, Atal Behari Vajpayee (far right) and Pramod Mahajan, earlier the minister for parliamentary affairs.

One of Sonia's areas of focus has been party organization. Here she is seen with Arjun Singh at the National Convention of District Chief Organizers in New Delhi in 2002.

M.L. Fotedar, Vincent George and Natwar Singh.

Rattled by this criticism, Sonia made moves to show that she was an independent leader who was not reliant on a coterie. Arjun Singh was denied a Rajya Sabha ticket in 1998. At her first interaction with the media at Rajya Sabha Deputy Speaker Najma Heptullah's residence in April 1998, Sonia plainly said it was a mistake to field defeated candidates in the Upper House, thus making it clear that Singh would not be brought into the Rajya Sabha.

Singh was near Sonia when she made this announcement, but his face remained devoid of emotion as he heard her remark. For many Congress leaders, however, Sonia's statement lacked sensitivity. Here was a man who had fought her proxy battle with Narasimha Rao. It was he who had kept the 'Sonia factor' alive for seven long years after Rajiv's assassination. He had also sacrificed his political career to propagate the cause of the family, spurning lucrative offers from the Narasimha Rao camp. For instance, in 1993 he was offered the post of external affairs minister, a position which would have legitimized him as number two in the Narasimha Rao regime.

Singh swallowed the public humiliation without making a fuss. Soon after he was summoned to 10 Janpath where the leadership made it clear that it meant no offence. Singh was elated at Sonia's gracious gesture. After a gap of two years, Sonia finally brought him into the Rajya Sabha in 2001. He says he has no regrets in politics, and he continues to offer advice to the party leadership whenever his services are sought, though poor health curtailed his role in Congress affairs in 2002-2003. Yet with this public humiliation, his reputation as Sonia's Man Friday was somewhat eclipsed. The only consolation to the man who thought himself destined to be the Prime Minister was the elevation of his son Rahul to number two in the Digvijay Singh ministry in Madhya Pradesh.

Even his worst critics acknowledge Arjun Singh's political acumen, sense of timing and his ability to turn the tables. The former Madhya Pradesh chief minister had the satisfaction of beating all his opponents, from Narasimha Rao to Kesri to Pawar to Prasada. 'Arjun may have lost many battles during the Rao–Kesri era, but he won the ultimate war. The stand taken during 1992-96 was vindicated,' said one of his lieutenants. Narasimha Rao had the ultimate indignity of being thrown out as Congress chief. Kesri met with a similar fate. Pawar left the Congress to try and chart a new path. Prasada fought Sonia for the party presidentship and was routed.

One of the key decisions that Sonia took after taking over as Congress chief was to project economic reforms guru Dr Manmohan Singh as a figurehead. It was a brilliant strategy because if there was one person in the Congress who drew nationwide respect and admiration, it was undoubtedly Dr Singh. True, he hadn't won an election, but Sonia had come across evidence of the role of some senior Congress leaders in ensuring his defeat from the South Delhi Lok Sabha seat in 1999, possibly because they perceived him as a threat to their own position in the party hierarchy. A victory in the election would have further entrenched his position.

Soon he became an eyesore for the traditional topiwallahs, who viewed the technocrat with suspicion. A committee headed by A.K. Antony that investigated the poll debacle concluded that Dr Singh's reforms led to the downfall of the party and resulted in the Congress's worst-ever performance. Sonia did not agree with the conclusion. Disregarding the Antony panel, she went on to appoint him as leader of the Opposition in Rajya Sabha. The move caused heartburn for some, for they saw the move as a virtual crowning of Singh as number two in the party.

The reforms man, however, slipped from the number two slot primarily because he was uncomfortable dealing with traditional Congressmen, who had little or no awareness of the changing global situation and latest trends in economic thinking. At party fora, Singh hated the idea of being grilled by people who had no knowledge of the fundamentals of economics. His skirmishes with Congress leaders left him a disillusioned man. At one juncture, he even toyed with the idea of quitting to take up academics and track two diplomacy, but Sonia persuaded him to stay on, promising to defend his policies.

Under Sonia, senior Congress leaders divided themselves into two camps. While Tiwari, Singh, Fotedar, Dikshit and Kidwai flaunted the loyalty card, Sharad Pawar (till he remained in the Congress, that is, till May 1999), Rajesh Pilot, Jitendra Prasada, Madhavrao Scindia and P.A. Sangma started projecting themselves as principled dissident leaders.

Driven by personal ambition, Pawar, Pilot, Prasada and later Scindia started considering whether the party, floundering under a Nehru–Gandhi, would not do better under their leadership.[1] For they realized that Sonia would not be able to deliver them power anytime soon. For these seasoned Congressmen, the problem was that they had got hold of an election-winning machine with a famous name, but upon finding that it was not performing, they got desperate to try something else. There were no emotions involved.

It was in sharp contrast to the mood on 28 December 1997, when they all had sung in unison: 'We've got a belated Christmas gift. Soniaji has agreed to campaign for the party.' Party president Sitaram Kesari had said that he felt mentally relieved and glibly reiterated his old thesis that the Congress had weakened whenever the party moved away from the Nehru–Gandhi family.[2]

The Congress party's spokesman, V.N. Gadgil, had said that Sonia Gandhi's decision to campaign would make 'a world of difference' in the 1998 general elections. 'Her decision has enthused, inspired and electrified Congress workers all over the country,' Gadgil said while giving a political discourse on how Sonia's mere presence in Indira's house had trained her in politics and how her concern for the poor was genuine.[3]

However, by 2000, Gadgil, who had predicted the return of the Congress on the national scene under Sonia, was a disillusioned man. Or as he used to say, initially he was disillusioned, 'but now I have no illusions'.[4] Joining him in the whisper campaign were Pilot and Prasada, who now saw Sonia as autocratic and domineering. Sonia was hurt when she heard what some of her close associates were saying, but soon she realized that it was exactly why many key players had discarded Narasimha Rao and Kesri as dead wood.

Gadgil suddenly discovered a mediocre leader in Sonia and reasoned: 'To expect a person to perform beyond his capacity is unfair to that person, and he is bound to fail.' Days before his death, Gadgil's other theory was that Sonia had started alienating India's overwhelming Hindu majority.[5]

The loyalists launched a counteroffensive, reminding partymen that many of these dissidents did not have a Lok Sabha constituency of their own. Some others did not even have enough support from MLAs in their home states to get elected to the Rajya Sabha. Others had become national figures overnight simply because of their repeated exposure on TV.

The big question that Pawar, Prasada, Pilot, Scindia and Gadgil did not answer was why they had not recognized the inabilities of Rajiv's foreign-born widow beforehand. If the team of wizards recruited the wrong person for the key job, shouldn't they all be held accountable?

According to Sonia, the charge of keeping a coterie and encouraging palace politics was an old one and lacked punch. Even when the Nehru–Gandhi family was not at the helm of the Congress affairs and control went into the hands of Narasimha Rao and Kesri, the operative style remained the same. Her opponents avoided admitting that they had used the same tactics to worm their way into first the palace and then the kitchen cabinet.

Sonia had reason to be bitter with those levelling the coterie charge. After all, they were the same ones who had urged her for seven years to take charge of the party. Moreover, their record showed that they had no taste for collective leadership or for democratization of the party in the real sense of the term.

Some of Sonia's supporters went further, asking if the dissidents were well versed with the geographical or political map of the whole of India. Most of them were regional satraps and did not look beyond their home states, home districts or even Lok Sabha constituencies. If none of the experienced leaders, with several decades of honing their skills in the rough and tumble of Congress politics, could acquire Indira's sense of timing, how could Sonia, by virtue of being just her daughter-in-law, be expected to possess that, a Sonia loyalist from Uttar Pradesh argued.

But what worried many Congressmen most was Sonia's problems

in managing some of the political crises. For instance, between 1998 and 2003, each time the Congress failed to do well in Uttar Pradesh and faced a split (it kept losing its support base), Sonia tried to gloss over the setback, making little effort to revive the party. She kept playing musical chairs with the state Congress chief's post. First Prasada was removed and Tiwari was appointed. Then Salman Khurshid was appointed. Sri Prakash Jaiswal replaced Khurshid, but Sonia remained dissatisfied and brought in Arun Kumar Singh 'Munna', a little-known political entity. His appointment invited criticism from a leading Hindi daily, the *Hindustan*. In a headline, it sarcastically pointed out, 'Hindustan ki tammana, Uttar Pradesh mein Munna' (Desiring [power in] India and bringing in Munna in Uttar Pradesh!). In April 2003, Sonia experimented with the UP Congress leadership again, replacing 'Munna' with another Rajput leader, Jagdambika Pal. Pal had deserted the Congress in 1997 to help the BJP form a government in UP, a move that gave him the reputation of being an opportunist.

The party's situation in UP was all the more important since it was the Congress's stronghold till 1989. Once it lost the support base in UP, the Congress fortunes began to decline at the national level as well. From 1991 to 1996, the Congress had five MPs. The 1996-98 figure slipped to three. In 1999 it rose to ten but subsequent assembly polls showed that the Congress was on the decline.

Often leaks were made insinuating that either Rahul or Priyanka would be joining the Congress to boost its performance in UP. But after some time, even Congressmen stopped getting enthusasitic about this prospect.

In Congress circles, Sonia was, however, seen as a good person who seldom interfered in the functioning of the party and the government, hated the idea of pitting one against another and took up the cause of several politically correct issues such as gender sensitivity, women's empowerment and health and education.

At first, some of her decisions boomeranged. Among the most contentious ones was her decison to back Laloo Prasad Yadav in caste-ridden Bihar in 1999. Sonia chose to support him against the wishes of the majority of Congressmen in the state and outside it. Yadav, who made no bones about projecting himself as a champion of intermediate castes in Bihar, had become unpopular with the upper castes, who traditionally backed the Congress in India's second largest and politically significant state of Bihar with forty seats in Parliament.

Laloo Prasad was also an accused in a multi-crore scam in which Central and state money earmarked for animal fodder was siphoned off. His whimsical style of functioning and the increasing corruption during his governance made him unpopular among the middle class, which was further upset by the way he propped up his wife, Rabri Devi, as chief minister when he was debarred from continuing in the post in 1999.

Digvijay Singh claimed that Sonia herself was averse to the idea of supporting him, but she caved under pressure from the Left parties and a section of the Congress who influenced her. They persuaded her that if she did not support him and keep the BJP at bay, her secular credentials would be tarnished. Reluctantly, Sonia gave the nod. Within days of Rabri Devi taking over as the chief minister, there was a series of bloody caste massacres in Bihar. Support to the couple was then openly challenged by Pilot and Prasada in the CWC meetings.

At 24 Akbar Road, Bihar leaders were seething with anger, saying that by supporting Laloo Prasad and Rabri Devi, Sonia had exposed herself for what she was—just another unscrupulous politician, ready to back Laloo for her own political compulsions.

Once Sonia backed him, the gloves were off. Pilot made it a habit of briefing the media on how he opposed the alliance with Laloo Prasad's party, the Rashtriya Janata Dal, in the CWC, but AICC general secretary Mohsina Kidwai denied this, saying Pilot always maintained that he was with the majority decision. The majority view was that the Congress should bail out Rabri Devi to keep communal forces (that is, the BJP and Samata Party) at bay.

Then came the Haryana fiasco. An extremely unpopular government headed by Bansi Lal in Haryana was on the verge of losing support after the BJP decided to pull out of the alliance. Bansi Lal, a powerful leader during the Sanjay Gandhi era, sent an SOS. Once again, acting on the advice of the coterie, Sonia decided to bail out a tottering Bansi Lal government. The government did not survive long as assembly polls were called. The Congress suffered a rout. All the ministers and MLAs belonging to the Bansi Lal regime lost badly. Pranab Mukherjee, who was then AICC general secretary in charge of Haryana, had to step down, much against his wishes.

Before resigning, Mukherjee made a feeble attempt to justify the Haryana fiasco by giving a laughable explanation that the Congress did not want political instability in a sensitive border state. When a scribe pointed out that Haryana was not a border state as none of its districts touch Pakistan, Nepal, China, Bhutan or any other neighbouring country, Pranab attributed it to his wrong sense of geography, saying that when he studied geography, Haryana was part of greater Punjab having borders with Pakistan!

Arjun Singh's and Pranab Mukherjee's names also figured among those having a soft corner for Bansi Lal. These leaders were said to have influenced Sonia. Soon the Sonia coterie consisting of Arjun Singh, M.L. Fotedar, Pranab Mukherjee and Vincent George became the favourite target of the media and disgruntled party leaders. Once Mukherjee resigned, the focus shifted to George. Many felt George had become 'too big'. He was projected as Sonia's eyes and ears and a formidable member of the coterie around her, courted by some CWC members and chief ministers of party-ruled states.

Unfortunately for the coterie, the years 1999 and 2000 were not good for Sonia as Congress president. There were a series of bad decisions. The most glaring one was Sonia's sound bite to TV channels outside Rashtrapati Bhavan in May 1999, when the Vajpayee government had lost the majority in the Lok Sabha but the Congress was not in a position to form an alternative government. Sonia had been invited by President K.R. Narayanan, and after meeting him, she told TV channels, 'We have 272' (a figure needed to prove majority in parliament). She failed to get that magic number as many smaller groups opposed to the BJP, namely the Samajwadi Party, the Revolutionary Socialist Party (RSP) and the Forward Bloc, refused to support her as Prime Minister on grounds of her foreign origins. Perhaps what Sonia meant to say was that a majority of MPs were against the BJP, so an alternative government was possible. But her choice of words was dubbed a great lie by her detractors.

There was a series of meetings, telephone calls and informal interaction with other Opposition leaders before Sonia made that claim. As they discussed the situation at AICC headquarters, khadi topis firmly in place, Congress leaders dreamt of getting back to power. Some began to wonder if Pawar would get the industry portfolio as finance would go to Dr Singh, while Scindia and Arjun Singh would fight over the home ministry and Mukherjee would opt for either the external affairs or defence ministry. Someone picked up a pencil and started writing the names of senior leaders along with their likely portfolios. Tea arrived and a leader from Maharashtra shouted, 'Kuch meetha bhi hona chahiye! (Should not there be some sweets!).' There was a sense of expectancy, and the mood was extremely upbeat.

Arjun Singh, Dr Manmohan Singh, Natwar Singh, Pranab Mukherjee and others who were holding crucial talks with Harkishen Singh Surjeeet, Laloo Prasad Yadav, Mayawati, and others had given verbal assurance that Sonia would have their support. In fact, they had almost tutored her to make the claim before the media.

Sonia's coterie was so confident of getting support from the unpredictable, left-of-centre Samajawadi Party chief Mulayam Singh Yadav and some others that they were even heard saying, 'Where will they go?' Their calculation was that secular parties like the Samajwadi Party, RSP and Forward Bloc would not join hands with the BJP and its allies. Since a majority of the Lok Sabha MPs did not want to face another general election so soon after the last one, Sonia's advisers were reasonably confident that she would become Prime Minister.

Against this background, the coterie advised her to make the 272-seat claim so that an alternative government could be put in place quickly. The episode highlighted Sonia's lack of experience in the political arena and her dependence on her close circle of advisers.

There were several crucial mistakes in the entire episode. The Congressmen, in their zeal to come into power, failed to see the return of an old paradigm—the coming together of former socialists who had once fought jointly against Indira. The old campaigner George Fernandes was back in action asking erstwhile friends like Mulayam Singh and others if they had forgotten what Jayaprakash Narayan suffered during the Emergency. The campaign was also reportedly laced with other goodies, such as helping out friendly industrialists embroiled in disputes with the government.

The 272-seat episode and the Bihar and Haryana fiascos made Congressmen restless. They could not blame Sonia, so they began targetting the people around her. The coterie charge, however, lost its bite when Sonia bagged 99 per cent of the votes for party leadership in November 2000.

Vincent George was finally marginalized when he was booked in 2001 in a disproportionate assets case. When the news hit the headlines, Sonia could not ask him to leave. She told Jaipal Reddy, the party spokesman, not to run him down or defend him. However, she used his short leave from 10 Janpath to shift his office from her ante-room to the executive quarters. No one replaced George in that room. It was instead converted into a waiting lounge for VVIPs.

Soon after her election, Sonia tried to promote another set of people who got the coterie tag. It consisted of Ambika Soni, Ahmad Patel, Jairam Ramesh, Mukul Wasnik and Pulak Chatterjee, the senior IAS officer attached as private secretary to Sonia in her role as leader of the Opposition, but the new coterie lacked the political stature of Arjun Singh, Fotedar, Natwar Singh and George.

Sonia's choice of Ambika Soni was interesting. Like Mukherjee and Azad, Soni lacked a support base, but she was articulate and had a good understanding of organizational matters. Moreover, unlike Arjun Singh, none of the senior leaders viewed her as a threat. Soni was not part of the erstwhile Tiwari Congress, which saved Sonia from the charge that she was promoting those who had rebelled against Narasimha Rao.

The Arjun Singh camp was particularly disappointed. The noises emanating from the Arjun Singh camp about 'Madam' being surrounded by sycophants created minor ripples in the party. Coming from him, the comments had to be taken note of. His supporters came up with an illustrative story of their own. The story went like this. Laila, having heard that her beloved Majnu was wandering about in the streets hungry, sent her maid with some milk. A greedy beggar, his eye on the milk, started shouting, 'Hai Laila,' pretending to be Majnu. On hearing that the actual Majnu's condition had deteriorated further, Laila sent out her maid again, substituting the milk with a bowl of blood. This time, the beggar pointed to the real Majnu, saying, "Hum doodh wale Majnu hai, khoon wala woh raha" (I am the Majnu for the milk, the one for blood is over there). The tale was apparently narrated to Sonia, in the hope that it would help her decide who were her genuine loyalists. Sonia responded positively appointing Arjun as key policy planner for the party's Shimla brain storming session in July 2003. But Arjun Singh's supporters were not particularly delighted. Shouldn't the milk of kindness flow before the blood? they wondered. The battles for supremacy among various camps continue.

Sonia, however, went on to make many enemies both in Arjun Singh's camp and among those close to George. Several unsigned letters circulated in the Congress to remind Congressmen of Soni's past, including her testimony before the Shah Commission of Inquiry against Indira. But she continued to enjoy Sonia's confidence. In turn, she developed her own coterie, promoting the likes of Jairam Ramesh, Salman Khurshid, Shelja and other light-weight state-level politicians. She achieved limited success in getting some of these persons appointed to key posts. Jairam Ramesh and Khurshid provided her vital inputs on political and economic matters, which in turn enhanced her stature before Sonia as a person who had all the facts and figures available with her when required.

A wiser Sonia began to put in place a set of checks and balances. If she received complaints about one general secretary, she would appoint someone else as a observer, getting vital feedback from other quarters. The strategy worked in allegations of corruption. There have also been allegations that chief ministers of the Congress-ruled states keep the party functionaries happy by offering them money and other allurements. Image-conscious Sonia tried to put an end to these practices but achieved limited success.

TEN

SONIA'S FAITH

The question of faith is a curious one to ask, especially in a country as secular and diverse as India. It should, normally, be of little significance—an intrusion into the private life of an individual, if anything.

Yet, for millions of Congress workers, the issue of Sonia's faith is of paramount importance. Is she a practising Christian? Does she subscribe to the Hindu faith in accordance with the Nehru–Gandhi family tradition? Does she have equal respect for all faiths? In their view, the answers to these questions have a crucial bearing on their fortunes. In a Hindu-majority India, they argue, it would be impossible for Sonia as a Christian to become the Prime Minister. However, the task would be a lot easier if she was identified with the majority faith, they conclude. Even senior Congress leaders, chief ministers of Congress-ruled states and members of the Congress Working Committee subscribe to this line of thinking.

Conscious of these factors, Sonia, from the very beginning of her political life in 1998, refused to be drawn into the controversy surrounding her faith. In fact, critics are convinced that political compulsions have drawn her more closely to Hinduism than she or her family would have liked. In the absence of any clear indication of her true faith, the uncharitable view has been allowed to gain currency. It is not that many persons, including the author, have not tried to probe her mind on this aspect, but she refuses to comment. Nor do any of those close to her. The issue is simply not open to discussion.

She was brought up as a regular churchgoer in Orbassano and as a firm believer in family values. While aspiring for the big things in life, she was not willing to compromise on principles. Her father's strong influence and the discipline he imposed helped. Stephano Maino, who died in 1988, was extremely worried about Sonia, especially after Indira's assassination and reports of the rise of religious fundamentalism in India. Stephano constantly told his friends that while he was extremely pleased with son-in-law Rajiv, he was wary of the spotlight being on Sonia.

The old man did not have to face the death of his son-in-law or see his daughter's entry into politics, which he would have certainly opposed. Her mother reportedly called Sonia to urge her to return to Italy after Rajiv's assassination. The suggestion enraged Sonia so much that she abruptly snapped the line. Hours later, Sonia called back to tell her that there was no going back—India was her country. It was a similarly determined Sonia who had taken a lead in advising Rajiv to stay on in politics after his 1989 defeat. The rout had shattered him, and he was toying with the idea of leaving politics to resume his career as a commercial pilot.

In her Cambridge days, when she was dating Rajiv, Sonia rarely attended Sunday service, though the church served as their meeting place occasionally. Nor has she been regular in India, though she seldom misses Christmas Mass.

During the 1999 general elections when the Sangh Parivar launched a nation-wide campaign for a Ram Rajya versus 'Rome' Rajya on grounds of her foreign origins and Christian faith, the Roman Catholic Association in India took the unprecedented step of denying that Sonia was a practising Catholic.

After Sonia and Rajiv's marriage, Indira is widely believed to have had a great influence on Sonia in matters of faith and religion. In the months preceding her death, Sonia used be an attentive listener when Indira shared some of her innermost thoughts about her vision of God, life after death, karma and so on. Moreover, Sonia voluntarily accompanied Indira whenever she interacted with noted religious leaders from various parts of the country. Indira was so fond of her that she would invariably ask godmen to bless her daughter-in-law.

Indira became deeply religious after the death of Sanjay. She gave standing instructions to her personal staff to grant audience to all godmen. Her key political aides like R.K. Dhawan used to bring maulvis, gurus, babas and munis on a regular basis. One maulvi, Maulana Jamil Illyasi of New Delhi's Kasturba Gandhi Road mosque, was credited with predicting rather accurately Indira's return to power in 1980. Illyasi demanded a visit to Indira's bedroom, an unusual request that was granted. The maulvi quickly placed a ganda or charm instructing Indira to avail his services after her victory. Indira won the 1980 parliamentary polls and Dhawan reminded her about the maulvi's words, but somehow he was not given an appointment.

However, the maulvi was called in after Sanjay's death and he attributed the tragedy to the powerful ganda placed inside Indira's bedroom. He was quickly ushered in to rectify matters. Illaysi then asked Indira to perform namaaz! The Prime Minister was puzzled. She said she did not know how to offer namaaz. Illyasi said it was not a problem. 'Simply follow what I do,' he said and Indira obliged.[1]

Rajiv also discussed his beliefs with Sonia. In the early days of their marriage, he told her that he and Sanjay were not brought up to follow any particular faith. In the years after marriage, Sonia adopted a similar course of not following any particular religion but having faith in all. She accompanied him whenever he visited any place of worship. Her head covered with her pallu, she would even bend down and touch the feet of godmen. She was with Rajiv when he called on Devraha baba on the eve of the 1989 elections. The baba used to live on a wooden platform resting on stilts six feet above the ground, ostensibly to avoid human vibrations! His way of blessing was also unique: he would kick a devotee. Sonia was spared this blessing from the ageless guru. Rajiv and Sonia then went to Ambaji temple in Gujarat. It was her second visit to Ambaji since Indira had taken her there in 1979 when she was about to embark on the do-or-die election of 1979-80. Ambaji had then blessed Indira, who returned to power, but Rajiv was not as lucky when he tried to repeat his mother's feat in

1989. After the defeat, Rajiv's devotional visits came under criticism on the ground that they alienated Muslims. Sonia herself missed no opportunity in sending a chadar (sheet) to Khawaja Garib Nawaz's shrine in Ajmer at the annual Urs.

During the 1998 general election campaign, Sonia, as the Congress president, paid her respects at the Tirupati Temple in Andhra Pradesh, abode of Lord Venkateshwara. The AICC chief skirted the core issue of her faith by refusing to sign the register kept for non-Hindus to declare their faith in Lord Venkateshwara. A functionary of the Tirupati Tirumala Devasthanams (TTD) rushed to Sonia's rescue, pointing out that as a daughter-in-law of Indira, she was following the religion of her husband and mother-in-law. Though he stopped short of stating that she was a Hindu, her supporters, including the former chairman of the TTD, Subbi Rami Reddy, managed to arrange darshan. Sonia got Balaji's blessings without declaring herself a Hindu.[2]

The episode evoked a sharp reaction from the Sangh Parivar. The Vishwa Hindu Parishad (VHP) vice president, Acharya Giriraj Kishore, lashed out at Sonia for her refusal to sign the visitor's register at the TTD. He said that by not affirming her faith in the Hindu religion before entering the shrine, she had violated tradition and offended Hindu society. He also alleged that she had forcibly entered the shrine and accused the temple management of succumbing to pressure. However, the acharya had no comment to offer when he was told that Sonia's bête noire, Chandrababu Naidu, who had clout as the chief minister of Andhra Pradesh, did not come in the way of a devotee seeking Balaji's blessings and was dismissive about the whole episode.

The head priest asked Sonia to follow C.K. Jaffer Sharief, the Congress minister who had visited Tirupati and signed the register. Sonia's managers worked overtime to ensure that she had her way. Until twenty-four hours before the darshan, every Andhra Congress leader gave the impression that Sonia would fulfil all the formalities, including signing the declaration. But the change took place in the night when the temple authorities had a long meeting with Congress leaders about her impending visit. During the negotiations, TTD officials advised that Sonia should sign the declaration, as is the practice, but two senior Congress leaders, Subbi Rami Reddy and Y.S. Rajshekhar Reddy, argued that there was no need for her to do so, as it would amount to admitting that Sonia is not a Hindu. Later, TTD executive officer I.V. Subba Rao said that those who accompanied her pointed out that since her marriage to Rajiv Gandhi in 1968, she had been following the Nehru–Gandhi (implying Hindu) tradition and, therefore, the declaration was not warranted.

In her zeal to win over the majority community Sonia even flirted with the Congress ideology that had placed secularism as a cornerstone of Indian polity. Soon after her Tirupati visit, the CWC passed a resolution affirming that 'Hinduism is the most effective guarantor of secularism in India.' It was an unusual declaration, aimed at depriving the BJP of its Hindutva USP. An influential section of the Congress, however, was not convinced. A CWC member laughed off the logic of being one-up on the BJP. 'The BJP still has an edge over us. They said it first.'

In fact, Sonia's rightward tilt began five months after she took over as the party chief. It began during the Panchmarhi conclave of the AICC in September 1998, when Sonia visited the Mahadev Temple near Panchmarhi. The right-wing leaders of the party were delighted. Veteran leader V.N. Gadgil was quick to call on Sonia to congratulate her on the Congress's emphasis on the primacy of Hinduism. Gadgil, however, lamented the fact her visit to the temple was not as widely publicized as it should have been. Sonia gave him no reply, but she took note of what he was saying—it was essential for her to be seen as being comfortable with her adopted country's traditions and ethos.[3]

After the Mahadev visit, Sonia rushed off to the Brahma temple at Pushkar, this time ensuring that the visit was properly highlighted by the media. Next, she went to the Ramakrishna Mission in New Delhi on 12 January 1999. It was at this mission in New Delhi that Sonia really found peace. While some of her visits to religious shrines were aimed at cementing her link with Hinduism, the mission was a preferred destination whenever she felt hurt or low. When the BJP and the Sangh Parivar raised the origins issue, Sonia sought refuge at the mission, spending a day with Swami Gokulananda Maharaj there. As the Ramakrishna Mission is widely respected all over the country— its admirers including the Hindutva protagonist Dr Murli Manohar Joshi—her association with it succeeded in taking some of the sting out of the BJP campaign. Swami Gokulananda quickly gave a clean chit to Sonia saying she was as much an Indian as anyone else. The swami said Sonia was leading a disciplined life and he saw nothing wrong in her foreign origins.[4]

Even as Sonia moved closer to Hinduism, anti-Christian violence gained momentum in parts of India, as if there was a correlation between the two. In Gujarat, there were large-scale attacks on missionaries. Her aides were quick to realize that some fundamentalist elements were trying to provoke her and get her embroiled in a debate on conversions. While some senior party leaders issued statements accusing the Sangh Parivar of stepping up attacks on Christians for their support to the Congress, Sonia was singing a different tune. She gave an address at the Ramakrishna Mission in which she eulogized Swami Vivekananda and rejected a narrowly focused Hinduism: 'India is secular primarily because Hinduism, both as a philosophy and as a way of life, has been based on what our ancients said: Truth is one, the wise pursue it variously.'[5]

P.A. Sangma, who raked up the foreign origins issue in May 1999 and left the party along with Sharad Pawar, was, paradoxically, a key player in projecting Sonia as a Hindu. On 13 January 1999, four months before Sangma dramatically revised his views about Sonia, the former Lok Sabha Speaker made a statement that Sonia was not a practising Christian. Sangma's remark sent shock waves, as Sonia had never allowed anyone to speak on her behalf on the subject of her faith. She had kept quiet even when the Roman Catholic Association of India had declared that she was not a practising Christian. Congressmen assumed that Sangma's comments on her personal beliefs had her sanction.

By May 1999 Sangma, however, began to sing a different tune. He lamented Sonia's alleged bid to distance herself from Christianity, wondering why was she being so self-conscious about her faith. The inference was that Sonia was distancing herself from her faith to gain public acceptability as a future Prime Minister. With each passing day, Sangma tried to sell the line that he had revolted against power-hungry Sonia. He told a group of Christian leaders and close associates that he fell out with Sonia when she refused to take on the Sangh Parivar regarding the attacks on Christians in Gujarat and elsewhere. Sonia was reportedly lukewarm to the idea of going all-out on the issue. Sonia's stand was blasphemous for Sangma. 'Why should one be apologetic about one's faith? I am proud to be Christian, as I am proud to be an Indian. In fact, I owe everything to the church,' Sangma told a journalist, recalling that he had been raised by an Italian priest. He then went on to speak bitterly about Sonia's naïvete in mixing politics with religion.[6]

Sangma's critics in the Congress, however, dismiss his premises. They point at his January remark in defence of Sonia that she was not a 'practising Christian'. As a senior Congress leader put it, 'For "practising" Sangma, religion is to be used selectively. If he felt that Sonia was being self-conscious about her faith, why did not he go public? It is an afterthought.' Many Congress leaders said Sangma's revolt against Sonia was a product of his political ambitions which had gained strength once he became Lok Sabha Speaker. When Sitaram Kesri was party chief and Sangma was Lok Sabha Speaker, Sangma used to share his vision with journalists. 'What the Congress needs is a dynamic leader who commands the respect of the Indian middle class,' he would say. The dynamic leader to whom he referred was apparently himself. Unfortunately, his vision was not shared by a bulk of the CWC members.

The CWC met on 16 January 1999, and Arjun Singh moved a resolution endorsing Sonia's remarks at the Ramakrishna Mission that India was secular essentially on account of Hinduism. It once again highlighted the 'Sangma syndrome' of speaking in different voices at different times. After all, it was Arjun Singh who had led the battle against Narasimha Rao for compromising the secular credentials of the Congress. The Singh camp, however, insisted that there was a world of difference between Sonia's approach to Hinduism and Narasimha Rao's focus on Hindutva. Strongly supported by Gadgil and others, Singh's associates said that in the Indian context, secularism should not be seen as negating religion. Rather, it should be viewed as as a tenet under which each faith has equal opportunity to prosper.[7]

The question of Sonia's faith proved a troublesome one much before she joined politics too, and at times it had a bearing on the political and even diplomatic sphere. When Sonia accompanied Rajiv to Kathmandu in 1989, the visit was billed as a mega event as Rajiv was expected to streamline relations with Nepal, the lone Hindu kingdom in the world. Rajiv and King Birendra got along well till the Indian premier decided to visit the historic Pashupatinath Temple. As at Tirupati and Puri, non-Hindus are debarred from entering the holy premises. Rajiv insisted upon taking Sonia, but the priests were in no mood to oblige and King Birendra expressed his inability to veto the representatives of God. There was also talk that King Birendra's wife, Queen Aishwarya, who had some influence over the temple trust, took a strong position not to let Sonia in.

Rajiv reportedly took it as a personal affront, thinking that it was the King's way of snubbing him. He returned without paying his respects at Pashupatinath. And as to the relations between the two countries, far from an improvement, they deteriorated after the visit. There was an economic blockade all along the porous Indo-Nepalese border that hurt Nepal badly. Outrage grew against India and the king came under immense pressure from anti-monarchy forces. A truce was declared after K. Natwar Singh, then foreign secretary, sneaked into Nepal to have secret negotiations with the king.

The Sangh Parivar had its own theory of the Nepal episode. According to Dina Nath Mishra, journalist turned BJP MP, Rajiv, at the behest of Sonia, had demanded the release of some sixty Christian missionaries, whom the king had jailed for proselytization, forbidden by law in Nepal. When King Birendra refused on the ground that it was an internal matter of Nepal, Rajiv got annoyed and slapped the trade embargo![8]

The question of her faith continued to hound Sonia. In January 2001 the president of the Congress party decided to take a holy dip at Allahabad during the Kumbh Mela, an occasion of high religious significance. Sonia chose to make a twin statement by taking the holy dip at Triveni on 22 January 2001, trying to hush up the row about her origins and showcasing a liberal-moderate alternative to the Sangh's brand of Hindutva.

A 10 Janpath insider said Sonia had long been scouting for ways to silence her Italian-origins ruckus and grabbed the Kumbh opportunity to do so. 'She was itching to make that statement. She was tired of the RSS's campaign over her religious beliefs,' an AICC official close to Sonia said.

Sonia took the decision on the holy dip in consultation with Digvijay Singh, M.L. Fotedar and Suresh Pachauri. They also set up talks with the Dwarkapeeth Shankaracharya, Swami Swaroopanand, an old friend of the Congress who was willing to extend a helping hand against the VHP.

Sonia aides said while she was for keeping her religion private, she had been forced to rethink by the RSS's perpetual onslaught. Party leaders also recalled a will she made in 1983 that expressed her wish to be cremated according to Hindu rites. At that time there were no signs of Rajiv becoming Prime Minister, not to mention a political role for Sonia. 'It is, therefore, absolutely uncharitable to attach political motives to Sonia's zeal for Hindu rites and customs,' a family friend said.

The Congress chief also flashed the correct signals in the run-up to the 2002 Uttar Pradesh assembly elections, deftly overturning charges that she lacked aggressiveness by crossing swords with the Sangh and robbing it of its monopoly on Hinduism. Congressmen were once again delighted. 'The real impact will be in rural India. Pictures of Sonia Gandhi taking a dip, performing Ganga puja, Ganpati puja, Kul Devta puja and Triveni puja will neutralize the RSS's jan jagran abhiyan (mass contact programme) that has been harping on her foreign origins and make a difference in public perception,' a Congress spin doctor said.[9]

In August 2001, she decided to inaugurate the Ganesh Utsav celebrations at Pune. Her visit, masterminded by Suresh Kalmadi and Maharashtra Pradesh Congress Committee chief Govind Rao Adik to snub Sonia-baiter Sharad Pawar on his home ground was a roaring success. Here again Sonia played her religious card to the hilt offering aarti and performing puja to Lord Ganesha. Ganesha's blessings were important to Sonia, of course, as they are supposed to bring good fortune, something that was desperately needed by Sonia and the Congress, but it was also significant that it was in Pune that Lokmanya Tilak used the Ganesh festival to turn the freedom struggle into a mass movement. On the political side, archrival Sharad Pawar was left fuming. In a single stroke, Sonia had stolen the march in his bastion. Pune neighbours Baramati, Pawar's stronghold, and the annual Ganesh Utsav used to be his show.

Politics apart, family friends and 10 Janpath insiders said while she respected godmen and representatives of various faiths, she was not a devotee or disciple of anyone. Unlike Indira, she consciously avoided getting too close to any godman. Instead, Sonia identified a select band of party leaders—Arjun Singh, Ahmad Patel, Digvijay Singh, M.L. Fotedar, Girja Vyas, Suresh Pachauri, Mabel Rebello, Ajit Jogi and P.J. Kurian among them—who served as 'contact persons' with various religious leaders. Some leaders reportedly organized yagnas such as a 'manokamna yagna' to fulfil ambition and the less pleasant 'mahamurtanjya yagna' supposedly to harm one's political rivals. But on her part, Sonia extended no patronage to such events.

In February 2002, Sonia finally mustered the courage to take on the Hindutva forces on the contentious Ram temple issue. The Congress president shared a platform with three Shankaracharyas at Dighauri in Madhya Pradesh to take an independent line on the Ayodhya dispute.

The conclave, a brainchild of the Madhya Pradesh chief minister Digvijay Singh, was aimed at breaking the VHP's hegemony over the Ram temple movement. Singh had roped in the highly respected Shankaracharya of Kanchi Kamakoti Peeth, Swami Jayendra Saraswati; his Puri counterpart, Swami Nishchalananda; and the

Shankaracharya of Dwarka, Swami Swaroopananda. The fourth Shankaracharya, who heads the Sharada Peeth in Karnataka, is not a prominent player.

In Sonia's scheme of things, if the court ruled in favour of a Ram temple at the disputed site in Ayodhya, the Ramalaya Trust, headed by Swami Swaroopananda, should be in charge of its construction instead of the Vishwa Hindu Parishad.

The Dighauri Dharma Sansad also tried to resolve the Ayodhya dispute through a peaceful consensus after consulting Muslim religious leaders. However, prominent Muslim leaders and organizations involved with the Babri dispute declined to attend the meet.

Sonia and Digvijay Singh were not disappointed by the Muslim leaders' guarded reaction. Their first priority was to court tolerant Hindus who are not comfortable with the VHP's aggressive Hindutva agenda. The Dighauri Dharma Sansad's timing was significant, for it coincided with the VHP's uneasy relations with the BJP-led government amid reports of a division within the VHP on the temple movement.

Sonia's visit caused considerable uneasiness in the Congress and the BJP. Some CWC members cautioned her against taking part, but she countered the argument by asserting that the party should not shy away from taking a stand on the vexed issue. She told them that she decided to play an active role in the debate after realizing that the Congress would continue to be irrelevant in Uttar Pradesh till it took a firm stand on Ayodhya. 'We are saying that we will abide by the court verdict. We are also saying that in case the majority community gets the legal mandate to construct the temple, the Ramalaya trust should build the temple instead of the VHP,' a top Congress functionary said.

Prime Minister Vajpayee reacted angrily to her proximity with the Shankaracharyas. Speaking in the Lok Sabha on the vote of thanks to the Presidential address, he wondered why he was being criticized for holding parleys with the VHP sants when Sonia had bowed before the Shankaracharyas. 'If she takes Shankaracharya's blessings, why should I be deprived from getting blessed by Mahant Ramchandra

Paramhans?' he queried.

Sonia still ties around her wrist a red thread given to her by a Hindu priest. She has great faith in that red thread, believing that it protects her from all evil. Each time there is a family occasion, Sonia summons the family pandit from Banaras to perform religious rites. When Priyanka's son, Rehan, was born, Sonia called for the pandit who performed elaborate pujas and namkaran. Naming Priyanka's son proved to be a hard decision and for a month there was no consensus among the baby's paternal and maternal kin and everyone began to call him Baba.

Finally a decision was left to Grandma Sonia, who suggested a name starting with the letter 'R' in memory of Rajiv. Priyanka suggested Rehan, a Parsi name, to reestablish the family's links with Feroze Gandhi's faith. Sonia readily agreed and the final name reads Rehan Rajiv Gandhi Vadra. A horoscope was prepared that predicted fame and fortune but not a political role for the sixth generation Gandhi. Priyanka and Sonia were relieved, but no one in the Congress believes the prediction.

ELEVEN

THE NEW GENERATION

'Ellorum Congressikku vote podungal (All of you vote for the Congress).' That was the only sentence Priyanka Gandhi uttered, but it seemed to drive the crowd wild.[1]

Sriperumbudur was supposed to mark Sonia Gandhi's political debut. But on 11 January 1998, Priyanka completely overshadowed her. Priyanka's red and orange sari was brighter than Sonia's green and maroon—and so was her smile. In sharp contrast to a nervous and hesitant Sonia, Priyanka was confident, effusive and comfortable with the crowd.

Congress circles across the country were elated. They had two crowd pullers instead of one. While Priyanka's appeal appeared wider, Congressmen were careful not to play up this point. The wiser among them were quick to declare: 'Congress will not have leadership problems for the next fifty years. Sonia will lead the party for at least twenty years and then we will have Priyanka.'[2]

The effect of the Sriperumbudur success was so intense that the Karnataka Pradesh Congress Committee plastered Bangalore with posters and banners welcoming the mother–daughter duo for their second public meeting scheduled a week after the Sriperumbudur one. But the huge crowd at the National College grounds in the city was disappointed when the AICC functionary, H. Hanumanthappa, announced that Priyanka could not come as she was not well.

Sources at 10 Janpath said Priyanka had herself opted out. She did not want to rival Sonia. The young Gandhi was upset over media reports that had began to compare her with her mother. When Hanumanthappa and others tried to reason with her, she said, 'I am not entering politics, so why do you want to create the hype?'[3]

Priyanka said this with good reason. It was eleven months since she had got married to Robert Vadra. Besides the adjustments necessitated by her marriage, at 10 Janpath too Priyanka had many responsibilities. With Rahul away in Britain, she was Sonia's closest aide. When Sonia drove down to Rashtrapati Bhavan in 1999 to inform a stunned K.R. Narayanan that she and her children wanted to plead for mercy for Nalini Murugan, who was condemned to death for her part in Rajiv's assassination, the poignant appeal was said to be Priyanka's brainchild. Sonia's case before the President hinged on one argument: another child should not be orphaned. Murugan, one of the four awaiting execution in a Tamil Nadu jail for their role in the assassination, should be spared to raise her eight-year-old daughter.

Sources said the decision to seek clemency was taken after a painful discussion among Sonia, Priyanka and Rahul. 'Let no child suffer the miseries of being orphaned by an act of state,' a Congress leader quoted Priyanka as saying to Sonia and Rahul. They were in agreement with her.

Murugan had married her husband, also convicted in the assassination and facing death by hanging, while in jail. In captivity, she gave birth to a girl, now an eight-year-old living in Australia. The girl used to visit her parents in jail every fortnight for half an hour, but following Sonia's appeal, the girl left the country with Nalini Murugan and her paternal grandparents.

The family had given up hope of Nalini Murugan being spared. According to Congress sources, an executioner had even begun oiling the iron trapdoors of the gallows in Vellore Jail, where she was lodged. The Tamil Nadu governor had turned down the mercy plea of the Murugans and their two accomplices.

Priyanka brought up the subject with her mother after reading a newspaper report about Nalini Murugan waiting for the execution, a family friend said. Sonia, Priyanka and Rahul felt the execution would not bring them any solace. Rahul added that the gesture might bring into focus the futility of terrorist acts that lead to death and destruction.

It was not for the first time that Priyanka and Rahul had influenced Sonia to take a difficult decision. Even as children, they were encouraged to air their views freely. Both Rajiv and Sonia valued their point of view. Rajiv was in fact extremely proud of the way he and Sonia had brought up the children. 'We are more of a friend' was how he used to proudly describe his relations with Priyanka and Rahul.[4]

It was Priyanka and Rahul who assisted Sonia in making up her mind to join politics. Many Congress leaders said that Sonia began nursing political ambitions two years after Rajiv's assassination, but she did not reveal them till Priyanka and Rahul started encouraging her to take a more active political role. The children were against her entering politics until 1994, when they realized that the family had no option. They reached this conclusion in separate ways.

Rahul noticed a drop in attendance at 10 Janpath and felt that the Narasimha Rao regime was systematically undermining the family's role—and its legacy of tolerance—in national politics.

The second and more important factor that influenced Rahul was the rise of the BJP on the national political scene. To Rahul, the party stood for everything the family opposed. The family was collectively convinced that it had to fight the BJP as it was bent upon destroying whatever good was achieved from Nehru to Rajiv. Contrary to popular belief, it was Rahul's persuasion that influenced Sonia more than Priyanka's. Rahul offered to quit his job in London to help her, a gesture that deeply moved Sonia.

Priyanka too was influenced, albeit from different quarters. Her in-laws made no bones that they wanted a political role for their daughter-in-law. Priyanka's sister-in-law, Michelle, and brother-in-law, Richard, openly declared that Priyanka would one day become Prime Minister of the country—a statement that did not meet with approval at 10 Janpath.

Priyanka first came in touch with Robert Vadra in 1986, when she was fifteen. There was little in common between the two except for their love for dogs, music and dancing. The simple friendship developed into a relationship. The two were finally spotted together at fashion designer Ashish Soni's show in Delhi in 1993, and the next day, the newspapers had the picture of Priyanka in a sleeveless black T-shirt with Vadra.

As a teenager, Priyanka had encountered many suitors belonging to the rich and famous category. However, she doubted their sincerity as most of them were either in awe of her or sought to brag about their friendship. Priyanka was most upset with the son of a Union minister who later joined the BJP. What was a simple friendship was projected as a matrimonial alliance till Priyanka snapped all ties with him. The acrimony severed family ties going back three generations.

On the day of Priyanka's wedding, two bridegrooms arrived at 10 Janpath claiming that she was married to them! One was Ramkrishan Gowd, who even petitioned a court to restrain Priyanka from marrying Vadra. Surprisingly, the court did not reject Gowd's petition outright, although he had earlier made a similar claim about film actresses Sridevi and Jaya Prada. The other bridegroom was mentally unbalanced. There was also a lecturer in Jawaharlal Nehru University (JNU) who used to write love letters to Priyanka. During the Narasimha Rao government he was reportedly called to a police station one day and roughed up by the Delhi police. The 'treatment' evoked condemnation from the JNU community.

Many were surprised by Priyanka's choice. Vadra, son of a brassware magnate from Moradabad, 150 kilometres north-east of Delhi, had kept a low profile till the world came to know about the marriage on 18 February 1997. Sonia reportedly had reservations about Priyanka marrying him as he had not gone to college after completing his A-levels from the British School. Moreover, some members of the Vadra family had strong RSS links, having donated their property and wealth to the Sangh.[5]

However, Priyanka saw little merit in Sonia's criticism and threatened to have a court wedding. Family friends and Rahul finally succeeded in prevailing upon Sonia to accept the Vadras. To many family friends, Priyanka's move to marry Robert was a continuation of a family tradition. According to them, there was little in common between Jawaharlal Nehru and Kamla, Indira and Feroze, Sanjay and Maneka, and indeed Rajiv and Sonia. By Sonia's own admission, 'our families could not have been more different'.[6]

Priyanka's wedding was a grand event. The civil marriage took place at 10 Janpath on the morning of 18 February 1997. Only close family members of the Gandhis and Vadras were invited. In the evening, a barat consisting of twenty cars reached the house from the Vadras' New Friends Colony residence. Sonia, Rahul, Gautam Kaul, Vincent George and Naresh Katju received the guests at the gate amid the melodious notes of the shehnai. Rahul performed kanyadan while the family priest, Iqbal Kishan Reu, performed the rites.

Priyanka looked beautiful in Indira's favourite silk temple saree with a pink and red border supplemented by floral and gold jewellery and an almost transparent veil. She wore little make-up. A beaming Sonia wore a burgundy and gold Paithani silk saree, and Rahul sported a pink turban and black Nehru jacket.

The guest list became a subject for discussion in society circles. Because it was an extremely restricted list, receiving an invitation to the marriage carried a great deal of prestige. Many Congress stalwarts were not even invited. Prominent among those present at the wedding were Sitaram Kesri, B.K. Nehru, Mohammad Yunus, Captain Satish Sharma, Feroze Varun Gandhi, Amitabh Bachchan, Sonia's sisters and mother, the President, and the Prime Minister. An assortment of Kashmiri, Mughlai and Continental food prepared by Hilton (later renamed the Inter-Continental) chefs was served. The Vadras gave a reception at the Oberoi on the following day. Once again, bride Priyanka stole the limelight with her seedha pallu purple and pink saree. The groom wore an Ashish Soni-designed black classic suit. The guests were served wedding cake and high tea.

Within months of the marriage, Sonia developed a great liking for her son-in-law, but she continued to maintain her distance from the Vadras. As the Congress president, she gave clear instructions to all AICC functionaries and 10 Janpath officials not to extend favours to the family.

In January 2002, Sonia went public cautioning the party leaders not to have anything to do with the Vadras. The directive to Congress chief ministers, state unit bosses and senior leaders came shortly after Robert issued a public notice snapping ties with his family. Sonia's action was unusual, to say the least, as she was known to guard the family's privacy zealously. 'The whole world knows that Sonia is a reticent person and intensely dislikes anyone misusing the family name. It was not that the Vadras were not warned. But there were just too many instances, forcing Robert to take a drastic step,' a family friend said.[7]

Sources at 10 Janpath said Sonia took the step after receiving complaints that the Vadras had been using their Gandhi connection to help out people seeking various favours. When Salman Khurshid was the Uttar Pradesh chief, Richard Vadra had allegedly called him up and recommended the names of party officials from Moradabad. Another Vadra family member approached a prominent educational society chairman with a visiting card that it was claimed said 'in-law of Priyanka Gandhi'. Party leaders said there were numerous instances of the Vadras having approached VIPs and chief ministers, one of whom had recently gone to Sonia for advice. 'We were told to be careful with them. We knew something was amiss,' a CWC member said.

Sonia is believed to have told her son-in-law that such allegations brought disrepute to the party and lowered the prestige of the family. They also gave her political adversaries a tool to malign her during the campaign for the Uttar Pradesh assembly elections that were held in February 2002.

Before issuing his public notice, Robert had many heated arguments with his father and brother. The public notice was drafted by Robert's advocate Arun Bhardwaj, the son of former law minister Hansraj Bhardwaj and a close associate of Captain Satish Sharma. The notice, published on 3 January 2002, read:

It has been brought to the notice of my client that some persons, including Rajinder Vadra, resident of C-7, Amar Colony, and Richard Vadra, resident of Basant Vihar colony, Civil Lines,

Moradabad, UP are misrepresenting to the public that they are working for on behalf of my client and allegedly promising jobs and other favours in return for money.

Even though Rajinder Vadra and Richard Vadra are relatives of my client but they have no access to my client. Public at large is hereby put to notice that my client has not authorized Rajinder Vadra and Richard Vadra and anybody else to work for him or to use his name in any manner and make such misrepresentation to anybody. Such misrepresentations are without the knowledge and consent of my client.[8]

Rajinder Vadra was outraged. He quickly accused Sonia of engineering a split among the Vadras by snatching away his son. Domestic quarrels, defamation suits and legal notices soon became public. Congressmen from Uttar Pradesh, however, took it as a sign of Priyanka preparing to take a plunge into politics at a later stage. They said the legal notice was aimed at protecting Priyanka from coming under a cloud due to her in-laws.

Rajinder Vadra consulted senior lawyers to file a defamation suit against the Gandhis and a section of the media for causing disrepute to the family. He denied any financial irregularity and said that Robert did not consult him before issuing the notice.[9]

Family friends said relations among the Vadras had worsened so much that family elders were unwilling to act as peacemakers. Many members of the Vadra family rallied round Rajinder and Richard. They wondered why Priyanka did not visit Moradabad more frequently. Many close relatives of the Vadras said they did not have easy access to either 10 Janpath or Priyanka's 35 Lodhi Estate residence.

Robert Vadra runs Artex, a company that deals in costume jewellery in bone, wood, plastic and black metal. He constantly travels to the US, Europe and Australia. Priyanka too has an interest in designing costume jewellery and often accompanies him.

While Priyanka had her way in finding her life partner, Rahul had to go through many upheavals. As a teenager in Delhi's social circles, he was constantly linked to Amitabh Bachchan's daughter Shweta, who finally married into the Nanda family, of the Escorts group. Some consider this as the point where family ties between the Bachchans and the Gandhis ended, but family friends suspect some other developments that spoilt the relations.

Whatever the reason, both Amitabh and Sonia seemed to be suffering from a deep sense of hurt. Amit, as Sonia fondly called him, was her first friend in India. She used to tie rakhi on him, and after Rajiv's death, he was a pillar of strength for the entire family. In fact, Rahul and Priyanka used to call him mamun (maternal uncle). Priyanka has told friends that she greatly misses mamun Bachchan.

But one thing seemed clear. The Gandhis fell out with only one branch of the Bachchans. After all, Rahul continued to be close to the London-based Ajitabh, aka Bunty, and Ramola Bachchan, spending weekends with them.

Rahul's name is constantly linked with a Venezuelan girl, Jonita. She is said to be working in Madrid in a department store and is in frequent touch with Rahul. The two met through Sonia's elder sister Nadia and seem to be greatly in love. She was Rahul's guest when the first dawn of the new millennium broke over Kachal in the Andaman Islands.

The issue of Rahul's marriage has become the subject of political debate for all the wrong reasons. A section of the Congress feels the entry of another foreigner in 10 Janpath would not be politically beneficial for the party. Some leaders even went to the extent of looking for a suitable match, short-listing north Indian Brahmin girls for Rahul, but he refused to see them.

As Sonia says, since childhood, both Priyanka and Rahul have been groomed to take their own decisions, be it in academics, politics or marriage. 'They are capable of deciding about their future,' Sonia said while fielding a series of questions on the possibility of Rahul or Priyanka entering politics.[10] Sonia stressed that for the time being they were not inclined. Congressmen liked the ring of 'for the time being'. Perhaps Sonia consciously avoided ruling out a political role for her children altogether. On another occasion, she said, 'Inki ichha par hai (It is for them to decide).'[11]

As she returned from campaigning in Bellary on the night of 3 September 1999, Priyanka talked with the author under the watchful eyes of Sonia. Her mood kept changing from sunny to grim, from introspective to chirpy, according to the subject. She spoke about politics, 'Mama', and Sushma Swaraj on the two-hour trip. She neither silenced nor strengthened the buzz about her joining electoral politics, choosing instead to say that contesting is not something that is inherited but deserved. When I asked why her husband was not travelling with her, Priyanka said with a grin, 'My hubby has no interest in politics.' She even fielded questions on having turned vegetarian two years ago. It was her personal decision, she said.[12]

Priyanka showed her political colours during the September 1999 election campaign. While Sonia was busy campaigning elsewhere in the country, she focused on the Amethi, Sultanpur and Rae Bareli parliamentary seats, a cluster in central Uttar Pradesh that has the distinction of sending Indira, Rajiv, Sanjay and Sonia to Parliament. In Amethi she had no difficulty in becoming the darling of the masses. The villagers saw in her an uncanny resemblance to Indira.

Priyanka's moment of glory came in Rae Bareli when she alone demolished her uncle, Arun Nehru, pitted against family retainer Captain Satish Sharma. Nehru, a BJP nominee, was forging ahead till Priyanka decided to chip in. Addressing a rally in Rae Bareli, Priyanka delivered a brutal putdown in chaste Hindi, 'Mujhe aap se ek shikayat hai. Mere pita ke mantri-mandal mein rehte hue jisne gaddari ki, bhai ki peeth mein chura mara, jawab dijiye, aise aadmi ko aap ne yahan ghusne kaise diya? Unki yahan aane ki himmat kaise hui? (I have a complaint. A man who was a traitor in my father's Cabinet, who stabbed him in the back, answer me, how did you let this man in here? How did he have the guts to come here?).'

As her stunned audience listened, she went on, 'Yahan aane se pehle maine apni maa se baat ki thi. Maa ne kaha kisi ki burai mat karna. Magar main jawan hoon, dil ki baat aap se na kahun to kisse kahun? (I spoke to my mother before coming here. She told me not to speak badly of anyone. But I am young, and if I cannot say what is in my heart to you, then to whom else can I speak?).'

She was equally harsh on the BJP. Reminding her audience of her grandmother Indira's role in the constituency—'yeh Indiraji ki karmbhoomi hai'—she questioned the BJP's record in respect of development and the quality of its governance. They had done nothing for Rae Bareli, and wouldn't either, she said before going on to recommend Captain Satish Sharma, 'Yeh mere parivar ke hain. Aap jante hain ki inke aane se yahan vikas hoga (He is from my family. You know he will develop the constituency).'

The young Gandhi's remarks were so fierce that Prime Minister Vajpayee failed to counter them when he visited Rae Bareli a day later. In his typical style, Vajpayee took a dig at Priyanka saying that he was 'scared' to visit Rae Bareli as it was someone else's 'ilaka' (territory). The Prime Minister then went on to blast the dynasty claiming their days were over. But it was too late. The voters of Rae Bareli had made up their mind. The verdict spoke loud and clear. Nehru was trounced. He could only manage a fourth spot and forfeited his security deposit.

Two senior BJP leaders, Uma Bharti and Sushma Swaraj, privately admitted that Priyanka had tremendous appeal. Swaraj perhaps spoke from her own experience, as she was confident about winning the Bellary seat against Sonia—until Priyanka arrived on the scene. Much before the votes were cast, Swaraj knew the verdict.

Interestingly, whenever a question is asked about Priyanka's political role, Sonia consciously adds Rahul's name. In private conversations too, she accords equal importance to the possibility of Rahul's entry in politics, though Congressmen overwhelmingly favour Priyanka and periodically ask Sonia to draft her into the Youth Congress. Not once has any senior leader of the Youth Congress passed a resolution demanding Rahul's induction. But from all accounts, Rahul continues to be Sonia's favourite.

Rahul was born on 19 June 1970. Sonia had suffered a miscarriage and was doubly cautious this time, taking a good deal of rest. The period saw family members in different roles. Indira, in spite of her pressing engagements as Prime Minister, played her role as would-be grandma rather well, having at least one meal a day with Sonia. Sonia has wholly acknowledged Sanjay's concern and the time he spent with her, particularly when Rajiv was away on official duty. Rajiv was, of course, extremely caring, particularly after Rahul's birth. He would get up at midnight, clean and change Rahul before and after his feed, and carry him till he fell asleep.

Indira named Rahul. According to Sonia, Indira actually wanted to name Rajiv as Rahul. She had written a letter to Nehru three weeks after Rajiv was born suggesting the name but was overruled. This time, Indira had her way.

Indira again had her way in naming Priyanka. She was born days after the end of the Indo-Pak war in December 1971. Sheikh Mujib-ur-Rahman, who was travelling from Pakistan to Dhaka via New Delhi to lead the newly freed Bangladesh, got a chance to see infant Priyanka.

Unlike Indira, Rahul and Priyanka had a carefree childhood full of attention, fun and foreign travel. Sonia and Rajiv tried to be strict parents, but Indira would go out of the way to save the grandchildren from a scolding. For instance, Rajiv used to insist on the children finishing their food, and Indira would eat from their plates to save them from getting any kind of punishment. Whenever Rajiv scolded the children, Indira would take them to her room and pacify them.

Rahul and Priyanka were sent to the Junior Modern School on Humayun Road before being admitted to Doon School and Welhams respectively. The period from 1977 to 1979 was difficult for the children, for they were often teased in their respective schools. Rajiv was extremely sensitive about it and wrote to them saying, 'Sometimes you will read all sorts of things in the papers about dadi, mama or about me but you should not worry. You might even find that some in the school tease you about it but you will know that most of these things are not true . . . You must learn to be able to face such provocations . . . to rise above all these irritants, and not to let them bother you.'[13]

Soon safety considerations brought them to Delhi. Rahul was admitted to St. Columba's, and Priyanka was in the adjoining Convent of Jesus and Mary. But security considerations following the increase in militancy in Punjab and the assassination of Indira forced them to leave the schools. Thus the last day Rahul and Priyanka attended school was 31 October 1984.

During Rajiv's prime ministership, the children were virtually under house arrest, though private tutors used to visit them regularly. Private tuition, no matter how good, was a poor substitute for school. Priyanka scored better and got into Jesus and Mary College on merit, but Rahul had to go through the sports quota in St Stephen's College.

Rahul's induction in St Stephen's created a stir. On the first day the new boy swept through the portals of the college in a convoy of armoured vehicles. Rahul stepped out of a white, bullet-proof Ambassador, stood still and then heaved a sigh of relief, as if he was back where he belonged. The National Student Union of India (NSUI), the youth wing of the Congress party, did its bit, parading boys and girls wearing T-shirts that said, 'Rahul, we are with you.'

At the college, Rahul was treated like any other fachta (fresher). Sportingly, Rahul agreed to be ragged, accepting the part of a tennis ball and being bounced back and forth in a long rally between two senior girls wearing micro minis—clothes that the college principal, Dr J.H. Hala, said people of a bygone generation would not be seen dead in.

Rahul was admitted to read history in the reputed college where every year only a lucky 370-odd students are selected from the thousands who apply.

The trouble was that Rahul had managed just 61 per cent in his board exams, and he was admitted to the college on the basis of sports quota (a relaxation of 10 per cent marks) on grounds that he was an accomplished shooter. As soon as the news was out, the Opposition and the media quickly termed it as an act of favouritism alleging irregularities in Rahul's admission. Some senior alumni came to his defence. Suman Dubey, a family friend and then an official in the information ministry, was one who was genuinely impressed by Rahul's prowess with the pistol. 'How many boys under 19 have won eight medals at national level?' he asked.[14]

According to Rahul's certificates, he had secured fourth spot in the thirty-second national shooting competition held in Delhi from 26 December 1988 to 5 January 1999. He had finished fourth in centre fire pistol 25 M (Indian rule) men's (civilian) individual event with an impressive score of 271 out of a possible 300, which means that he had got more than 90 per cent of his targets. According to Rahul's coach, Dr Rajpal, his performance was much better than that of then additional commissioner of police B.S. Brar and many IPS officers who had participated in the event.[15]

Prior to this, Rahul had bagged eight medals in the Delhi shooting competition on the Tughlakabad ranges. Rahul also won support from unexpected quarters when Ajit Singh's daughter, Depti, herself a shooter, said, 'Rahul is an excellent shooter and if he concentrates more, he can shape into a national star.'[16] Ajit was then Janata Dal secretary general and a bitter critic of Rajiv Gandhi.

According to university guidelines, any outstanding sportsman (who has secured a place in a national championship) is entitled to get admission provided he or she has secured more than 40 per cent marks in the class XII examination. The college authorities, defending the admission, pointed out that two footballers admitted that year had in fact secured less marks than Rahul. Rajkumar Clement and S.K. Chakroverty, who were part of the college's physical education department, said the college had the distinction of having many international shooters on its rolls—Karni Singh, Mansher Singh, Randhir Singh, Harisimran Sandhu and P.S. Bedi. The controversy settled once B. Adityan and Randhir Singh of the Indian Olympic Association verified the authenticity of Rahul's certificate and Dr Rajpal's challenge to prove the documents false remained uncontested.[17]

Rahul, however, did not stay long in St Stephen's and went to Harvard to pursue a course in bank securities. He later took up a job in London.

In 2000, a new controversy about the Gandhi heirs arose when

Sanjay's son, Feroze Varun, began talking about politics. Varun, who turned twenty that year, was embroiled in an argument at Sanjay's samadhi on his father's death anniversary on 23 June. His objection arose when the police stopped him for frisking as part of security arrangements. Varun accused Delhi chief minister Sheila Dikshit of turning a blind eye when he was subjected to the security drill. The Indian Youth Congress president, Randeep Singh Surjewala, was credited with rushing to Varun's rescue and touching his feet. The event created a stir in the Congress. An explanation was sought and Surjewala quickly gave a medical certificate saying that he was running a 104-degree temperature that day so it could not have been him.[18]

Varun then gave a series of interviews, both on and off the record, saying things that greatly upset Sonia and her children. Sitaram Kesri was sulking, and from his deathbed he declared Varun as a 'true Gandhi'. Kesri went on to add, 'I may not be around but the boy will excel in politics. He is a scholar and the first graduate from Nehru–Gandhi family since Nehru.' Kesri's dig at Sonia, Rajiv and Indira was, however, inaccurate as Priyanka had passed her undergraduate psychology exams much ahead of Varun. And, according to Priyanka, Rahul has completed his M.Phil from the University of Cambridge. Kesri made these observations soon after a function where Varun's collection of poetry was released.

The acrimony between the two branches of the Nehru–Gandhi family soon began to percolate down to the next generation with Maneka's son preparing for a political role and the Congress projecting Rahul and Priyanka as the true inheritors of the family's legacy.

Varun, who was fond of Priyanka, seemed like a changed man. The London School of Economics student was last seen at 10 Janpath in February 1997 for Priyanka's wedding. In private conversations, Varun said things that quickly reached Priyanka and greatly infuriated her. Even birthday greetings and the occasional telephone call ceased between the two. This was in sharp contrast to the period when Indira was alive and Varun visited the Gandhi household once a week. The practice was stopped after Indira's assassination. However, when Rajiv was Prime Minister and Varun was staying with his mother, there used to be occasional visits. Maneka had no objection to these. As she told *Probe* magazine in 1988, 'I would certainly encourage the children meeting each other, because whatever our differences may be in this generation, I do not think they should be carried over to the next generation.'[19]

In the following years, the social contact between the cousins was further restricted. Rajiv claimed the restriction was from Maneka's side. 'We used to ask him to come. She used to send him over. But that seems to have been stopped now. Not from our side. From their side.'

Congress leaders even now are wary of speaking about Varun, but they keep a close tab on his movements. Some Congressmen privately admitted that Varun's entry into politics ahead of Priyanka might wean away some disgruntled sections of the party, though Varun's campaign for candidates put up by his mother in the Pilibhit region during the Uttar Pradesh assembly polls in 2002 did not succeed—none of the candidates put up by Maneka won a seat.

The unending saga of the Nehru–Gandhi family feud has one important message. Be it Priyanka, Rahul or Varun, Congress leaders have absolute faith in them. A housewife, a bank securities agent or a recent graduate is still seen as their best bet to turn their fortunes. The three Gandhis are considered to be born leaders, charismatic and capable of deciding the destiny of millions. The BJP is equally interested in them, but for altogether different reasons. According to BJP ideologue S. Gurumurthy, the issue of foreign origins applies to Rahul and Priyanka too, so they should be rejected on the same grounds.

Gurumurthy cites Italian nationality laws to substantiate his argument. Under Italian law, Rahul and Priyanka are citizens of Italy by birth as they are born to an Italian mother, he says. Gurumurthy also quoted Article 13 of the Italian constitution that allows all citizens to resume Italian citizenship at all times. A 1992 amendment also provides for dual citizenship for Italian citizens, which is applicable to Rahul and Priyanka. 'Sonia has a guarantee of permanent Italian citizenship as safety net, to be resumed at will, at all times. Rahul and Priyanka are born citizens of Italy. The Indian citizenship laws do not contradict Italian laws from conferring a suspended citizenship on Sonia and citizenship by birth to Rahul and Priyanka,' Gurumurthy asserts.[20]

The Congress and 10 Janpath have not contradicted Gurumurthy's contentions. Senior party leaders said Gurumurthy's formulations were academic, even if true, and had no relevance. 'The fact is that Priyanka and Rahul are cent per cent Indians and have acceptability as Indians throughout the country. These charges would not stick,' said a CWC member.

In fact, Congressmen seem mentally prepared to accept the leadership of the Nehru–Gandhi family for many generations to come. An example of family loyalty can be found in Karunakaran. He is the oldest AICC delegate. Since 1937 'the leader', as Karunakaran is popularly called in Kerala, has witnessed the rise of five generations of Nehru–Gandhis. In 1937, when Karunakaran attended an AICC session for the first time, it was eight years since Jawaharlal Nehru had taken over from his father, Motilal Nehru, as the Congress president. Jawaharlal's long stint till 1964 saw Karunakaran emerge as a state-level leader pitted against legendary Marxists like E.M.S. Namboodiripad.

Karunakaran's big day was when Indira took over as Congress supremo after a brief interregnum filled in by Lal Bahadur Shastri (1964-66). The Indira years saw him become chief minister, and leave and come back to the coveted post. Karunakaran was in Indira's good books but more importantly Sanjay took a liking for him. If the son was kept in good humour, the mother would not have any complaint. Riding on this simple survival kit, Karunakaran's writ continued to run in the state even after Sanjay and Indira died. For him, Rajiv was equally towering and understanding.

The problem arose when a lesser mortal, namely Narasimha Rao, took over as the Prime Minister and Congress president. Karunakaran suddenly realized his seniority in the party and wondered why Narasimha Rao should lord over him.

Along with Arjun Singh, he too changed track during the period 1991-96, but he was careful not to sacrifice too much. He continued to be a minister in the Narasimha Rao government while periodically paying his respects to an apolitical entity called 'Madam Sonia Gandhi'.

It was Karunakaran's experience and wisdom that prompted him to visit Priyanka's house, ostensibly to condole the death of her sister-in-law, Michelle Vadra, in 2001, and in the process have a darshan of young Rehan. Like millions of Congress workers, Karunakaran is convinced that one day Priyanka will lead the Indian National Congress. His prompt decision to bow before infant Rehan was a lesson to his son, Murlidharan, who was accompanying him to the 35 Lodhi Estate residence of Priyanka.

Karunakaran is not in a minority in recognizing the importance of Priyanka and Rahul. At the Rajiv Gandhi assassination trial at Vigyan Bhavan, many Congress leaders used to attend just in case they got a chance to do a namaste to Priyanka or Rahul. Even Jaipal Reddy rushed to a cricket match at Nehru stadium on 4 November 2001 when he heard that Rahul and Robert had come to play a friendly match between 10 Janpath and the media, though for a good part of his life he had remained a bitter critic of the dynasty.

TWELVE

THE REBELS

Everyone was growing restless, anxious to catch up with India's World Cup cricket opener against South Africa in England. The 15 May 1999 CWC meeting was supposed to be a brief one, where everyone was in hurry to finalize the list of candidates for the Goa assembly polls and discuss the Rajiv assassination case as well as poll alliances, so that cricket enthusiasts could return to their television sets as early as possible. Sitting on spotless white sheets, then Sharad Pawar smiled and P.A. Sangma stood up. The rebellion in the Congress had begun, signalled by the mighty Maratha, executed by the diminutive samurai with a swish of his razor-sharp tongue, and watched by Sonia and the rest of her stunned council.

As recounted by those present at the meeting, Sangma slowly built a case for how the BJP campaign against Sonia's foreign origins was seeping deep down to even remote villages. Then came the unkindest cut. 'We know very little about you, about your parents,' Sangma told her.

Those present claim that Sonia was shocked by Sangma's bluntness, who was drafted into the CWC as her nominee. The third signatory, Sitaram Kesri's protégé Tariq Anwar, too, had survived in the CWC even after his mentor's departure, courtesy of Sonia.

Then the man she had made leader of the Opposition (until Sonia herself became a Lok Sabha member in September 1999) picked up from where Sangma left off. With opening remarks as deceptive as the smile signal, Pawar said Sonia Gandhi had done a great job as the party chief. 'You brought unity in the party and revamped the organization. However, the Congress has not succeeded in answering the BJP's campaign about your foreign origins. Let us take a serious note of it.'

The lady from Orbassano was confronting a crisis that was much more grave than the one her husband had faced a decade ago when he faced corruption charges in the Bofors gun deal or the ones her mother-in-law faced, in 1969, when she had to witness a split in the Congress, and in 1977 when she had to face a humiliating electoral defeat. Suddenly the reality dawned upon Sonia: she continued to be a loner in what she had thought to be her own 'parivar'.

Sangma went on, 'When people ask us why the Congress has failed to get a qualified Indian among [India's] 980 million citizens as its prime ministerial candidate, we have no answer. I think they are right,' he said.

Perhaps Amitabh Bachchan was right when he said Congressmen were merely using the Nehru–Gandhi family to stay in power, Sonia wondered. After all, it was these leaders who had pleaded with her to take the reins of the Congress and 'liberate' the party from Sitaram Kesri.

After Sangma had finished his speech, Rajesh Pilot tried to see some merit in what Pawar and Sangma had said. Pilot, however, did not join the rebels' rank, favouring the newly elected MPs to address the leadership issue. At that juncture, R.K. Dhawan lost his cool. He rubbished the Sharad–Sangma theory and said, 'Bhai, you seem to be taking up the BJP-RSS agenda.'

Dhawan had barely finished when the CWC members saw Sonia get up and begin walking out of the room. As Ghulam Nabi Azad, Ahmad Patel, Mohsina Kidwai, K. Karunakaran, Vijay Bhaskar Reddy, Jitendra Prasada and Sitaram Kesri looked on uncomfortably, not knowing what to do, Arjun Singh suddenly got up and ran behind her, not waiting to even put on his shoes. Sonia kept walking, her footsteps loud in the silence. Suddenly she turned around to see Singh, barefoot, hands folded. He did not say anything—he did not need to.

The folded hands conveyed both a request for her to stay on and remorse, his own and that of a large section of party workers.

Singh's gesture was a measure of the stakes involved. It was he who had mastermind the 'draft Sonia campaign'. If she were to walk out of the party, it would be the end of all his dreams, ranging from his desire to see the Congress staging a comeback in national politics to his personal ambition for high office.

A CWC member said the incident was a chilling reminder of 1977, when Indira received a letter with a similar message—challenging Indira's authority as she had lost the confidence of the party and the people—from Jagjivan Ram at a CWC meeting. 'Sonia Gandhi considers her mother-in-law to be her role model. She now has to fight and prove herself like Indira Gandhi,' he added. Sonia, however, had no illusions about herself. When some CWC members approached her asking to her to fight back like Indira Gandhi, Sonia retorted in uncharacteristic manner, 'I am not the daughter of Jawaharlal Nehru!'[1]

Ironically, it was Sonia herself who raised the issue of the BJP's campaign against her foreign origins, asserting she would fight till the end. Sitting next to Pawar, Dhawan told her comfortingly: 'Madam, you are not alone in this battle. We are all with you.'

Once Sonia walked away, the CWC meeting ended on an abrupt note with Arjun Singh drafting a resolution that attacked the BJP's campaign against Sonia. Pawar and Sangma were unfazed. While leaving, they told Pranab Mukherjee that it was their last CWC meeting.

Just after the meeting, when Mukherjee, Scindia and others were pretending to concentrate on the list of nominees for Goa, Sonia received the letter from the trio that read like a charge sheet against her. Sonia did not bother to read it. Vincent George called up senior leaders including Arjun Singh, Pranab Mukherjee and Dr Manmohan Singh to formulate a response.

Arjun Singh took charge to deal with the crisis. The veteran warhorse quickly branded Pawar, Sangma and Anwar present-day 'Mir Jafars' for their 'betrayal'. He told party leaders that Pawar had lived up to his reputation for ruthlessness by attacking Sonia when she was most vulnerable. It was Singh, as vice president of the party, who had used his influence to convince a reluctant Rajiv to bring back Pawar in the Congress in 1985.

Pawar's critics point out that shortly after Rajiv's death, he was one of the signatories to the long list of Congress leaders demanding Sonia Gandhi take charge of the party. She had then flatly refused to do so. Again, in 1997, when the Congress plotters quietly staged a coup and Sonia Gandhi took over from Kesri, Pawar was an active player.

In fact, a few days before taking on Sonia on the foreigner issue, Pawar was given the key responsibility of acquiring signatures from probable allies soon after the fall of the Vajpayee government. The letter had made it clear that Sonia would be the prime ministerial candidate. Pawar was also entrusted with the crucial job of stitching up alliances in other states. He was in Chennai only a few days before the rebellion for talks with the Anna Dravida Munnetra Kazhagam (ADMK) chief, Jayalalitha. He was to be in Chennai the day after the CWC meet.

To many, the revolt had been brewing for some months. Beneath the professional veneer, Pawar and Sonia Gandhi never seemed to get along with each other. She preferred to maintain a distance, keeping in mind Rajiv's opinion that Pawar was a good leader but not one to be trusted.

Pawar was not new either to performing sudden somersaults or going against someone whom he had supported. Early in his career, in 1978, he had brought down a Congress government in Maharashtra headed by Vasantdada Patil. According to V.N. Gadgil, Pawar defended Patil in the assembly during the no-confidence motion and, after finishing the speech, went straight to the governor withdrawing support for Patil.[2]

Pawar told his confidants in February 1999 that the Congress was now revolving around 20 Canning Lane, where Arjun Singh then lived. But Singh was not his target. It appeared later to Sonia that Pawar was unwilling to play Singh's role as the second-in-command. In May 1999, Pawar was fifty-eight and knew fully well that if Sonia took charge, his prospects of securing the prime job in the country would disappear.

In Pawar's scheme of things, revolt against Sonia was based upon a scenario that no political party or group would get majority in the thirteenth Lok Sabha. Former Prime Minister Chandra Shekhar, Samajwadi Party leader Mulayam Singh Yadav and Samata Party leader George Fernandes were said to be his close associates who convinced him to make a bid for the Prime Minister's post. The logic was simple—as long as Sonia was Congress chief, regional satraps like Chandrababu Naidu, Mayawati, Mulayam Singh Yadav, Mamata Banerjee and Jayalalitha would not back her for the top job. Pawar, on the other hand, was confident of running a coalition. The 1999 general elections gave a clear mandate to the BJP and its allies. What was worse for Pawar was that in his home turf of Maharashta, he finished behind the Congress in the state assembly polls—the Congress got seventy-six seats while Pawar's group bagged fifty-eight.

When Sonia reached home after leaving the CWC meet, she could only think of calling Priyanka. They did not speak much, but Priyanka realized that she was deeply upset. Rahul too was in Delhi, and the three got together. Rahul was furious and told Sonia to leave politics for good. Priyanka too favoured Rahul's line. Priyanka picked up a pen and drafted a letter. Sonia and Rahul made a few amendments. The letter was addressed to Pranab Mukherjee, who was the general secretary and had chaired the CWC meeting in Sonia's absence.[3]

The CWC met again to discuss the Pawar–Sangma–Anwar letter, but the trio did not show up. Sangma rushed off to the USA where his son was getting a degree while Anwar and Pawar insisted on Sangma's presence. The loyalists, however, were unwilling to make any concessions. They pointed at emergency provisions of the party constitution that made it clear that the CWC can be convened at any time with all those present in the capital.

As partymen raised slogans hailing Sonia and condemning Pawar—'Sangma, Tariq aur Pawar, inko maro jute char'—(beat up Sangma, Tariq and Pawar with shoes) a sombre Congress president arrived to attend the meeting. However, she excused herself soon after, saying she would prefer to stay away as she would be the subject of the meeting.

Soon after her departure, Vincent George arrived carrying her resignation letter. The letter was dated 15 May, the day the trio fired the salvo. The big news was out. Sonia had quit as Congress president, fifteen months after she took over.

The letter said:

At this morning's meeting of Congress Working Committee, certain of my colleagues expressed views to the effect that my having been born elsewhere is a liability to the Congress party. I am pained by their lack of confidence in my ability to act in the best interest of the party and the country.

In these circumstances, my sense of loyalty to the party and duty to my country compelled me to tender my resignation from the post of party president.

Though born in a foreign land, I chose India as my country. I am Indian and shall remain so till my last breath.

India is my motherland, dearer to me than my own life. I came into the service of Congress party, knowing that it is the only party capable of providing India with a stable, secular, progressive and independent government. That belief remains unshakeable.

I came into the service of the party not for a position or power but because the party faced a challenge to its very existence and I could not stand idly by. I do not intend to do so now.

I have been privileged to receive the love and affection of ordinary Congressmen and women from all over the country and I will continue to serve the party as a loyal and active member to the best of my ability.

Signed,
Sonia Gandhi

The CWC unanimously rejected her resignation. When CWC members called on her to plead that she review the decision, she said she was deeply upset by the staggering display of xenophobia surrounding her origins. She said she had decided to step down as soon as she received the trio's letter on Saturday. Sources close to her said that the AICC chief was deeply upset over the fact that no one tried to cut short Sangma and Pawar when they spoke so harshly. 'It was the silence of the lambs in the CWC that upset her most,' said a close aide.

Family friends said Sonia was pained at the growing attacks on Christians since she took over as party chief. In fact, she had wondered in conversations with several people, including Sangma, if there was a link between her political role and the onslaught. She had also been disturbed by the BJP's consistent attacks on her origins, but she appeared determined to fight as long as the party was behind her.

What she did not expect was a personal attack by her own partymen. For many days to come, Sonia kept asking them where she went wrong and why senior leaders like Pawar and Sangma took such an extreme step. 'She did not want the issue of her foreign origins to come in the way of Congress prospects,' a party leader said.

The timing of Pawar's revolt crippled the Congress. Dates for the general elections were going to be announced and the party was facing assembly polls in Goa. Even senior leaders were groping in the dark on the daunting issue of succession if they failed to persuade Sonia to return. The campaign for general elections was about to take off and the CWC was unwilling to choose a new leader midstream who could not only hold the party together but also run a credible campaign. In their heart of hearts, every CWC member knew that the Congress did not have such a leader, much less one who could run a victorious campaign.

Once again Arjun Singh and Vincent George took charge. Akbar Road was flooded with Congressmen of all hues and shades shouting 'Sonia lao, desh bachao.' First the chief ministers of Congress-ruled states called on her. Digvijay Singh said they would all resign en masse. 'We have become chief ministers thanks to you. What is the

point in continuing if you are not around'?[4] Then came all the state
unit chiefs. Thousands of ordinary party workers got access to 10
Janpath. Some women broke down asking Sonia to reconsider. An
elderly Muslim asked Sonia if she had thought about the plight of
minorities in a BJP-run government. 'You do not want to fight for us?'
he asked.

The road outside 10 Janpath was blocked for days. There were
dozens of stalls of state leaders sitting on dharna throughout the day
and night, refusing to go unless Sonia reconsidered. When Rahul was
returning from a visit with a friend, he was mobbed by partymen
requesting him to persuade Sonia to withdraw her resignation. A
rethink began between Rahul and Priyanka—perhaps it was wrong to
doubt partymen's sincerity. The trio of Pawar–Sangma–Anwar might
only represent a small minority.

Sonia's critics were also taken aback by the sudden burst of emotion
and solidarity. Pawar was quick to realize that his plan had
boomeranged. Sonia was getting a renewed mandate from partymen.
Instead of weakening her, their onslaught had made her stronger.
Pawar's private secretary was seen hovering around 10 Janpath. Each
day the news was depressing for Pawar. While it is true some sections
of the crowd were mobilized, a large number of them were there out of
genuine admiration and respect for Sonia.

Each day CWC members met Sonia individually to plead with
her and office-bearers of front organizations of the party issued appeals.
The loyalists began regrouping in a bid to crush the Pawar-led revolt.
The first priority was to prevent any kind of split. Two CWC members,
Rajesh Pilot and Jitendra Prasada, who were seen to be soft on the trio,
were quick to issue statements assuring full support to Sonia. Sensing
the mood in the party, others like J.B. Patnaik, Santosh Mohan Deb
and Sitaram Kesri, who were perceived as being close to Pawar, snapped
all ties with his group.

On 16 May, the party leadership decided to convene an emergency
CWC meeting at 4 p.m. Pawar had already informed CWC member
Oscar Fernandes that he would not attend the meeting. In case a
decision was taken against the observations made in the letter, he

should be considered a dissenter, Pawar added. Sangma would not be present either, as he was en route to the US. Anwar came up with the curious reason that he would not attend the meeting unless Pawar and Sangma were present.

Theoretically, the Congress leadership had a number of options. It could expel the rebels, a line of action pushed by Arjun Singh. The trio's demand could be rejected through a vote in the CWC, loaded with Sonia loyalists, and then action taken. The rebels could be persuaded to withdraw the letter and leave the leadership issue to newly elected MPs. As a last resort, Sonia could voluntarily make an offer not to hold any public office.

But these options existed only on paper. Most Congressmen were unanimous that no leader other than Sonia could keep them united and win them votes. The rebels had no place in the party; they would have to go.

In the absence of Sonia, the CWC summarily expelled the Sonia-challengers from the primary membership of the party for six years by a majority vote, setting the stage for a split. Significantly, the CWC's decision was not unanimous, with senior leader A.K. Antony registering a note of dissent. Emphasizing the need for unity, Antony objected on procedural grounds, saying the party should first slap a show-cause notice on the dissidents and suspend them before taking any extreme step.

Only Antony could afford to suggest this. The loyalists could not dub him as a rebel given his high standing and clean image in the party. In his brief intervention, Antony said, 'Let us first suspend them. Give them a chance to explain their conduct.' But he was overruled by other CWC members, especially hawks like Arjun Singh, Vijay Bhaskar Reddy and Pranab Mukherjee, who chaired the meeting.

Afterwards, Sitaram Kesri, Rajesh Pilot, Jitendra Prasada and Ahmad Patel said they too favoured a step-by-step approach to deal with the rebels. But they did not say this in the meeting, tamely abiding by the majority view in keeping with the mood of party workers who wanted stringent action.

There were dramatic scenes at the Congress headquarters where an agitated crowd manhandled Kesri, tearing his clothes and damaging his car before the CWC meeting. The veteran leader had to return home to change his clothes. Kesri, who was a special invitee to the CWC, was targetted because of his proximity to Tariq Anwar. Prasada and Pilot were also roughed up over their alleged sympathy for the dissidents. Sonia was quick to disapprove of the action. She called up Kesri and apologized on behalf of the party workers and instructed the Congress general secretaries to restrain supporters.

The AICC general secretary, Oscar Fernandes, immediately conveyed the CWC decision to Sonia, but she remained unmoved. The leaders then decided to convene an emergency session of the AICC to ratify the CWC's decision and exert pressure on Sonia to rescind her resignation.

The CWC members had met several times during the day before formally gathering to iron out their differences on how to tackle the rebels. Antony, Ahmad and Pilot argued that the party should follow procedure as laid down in the party constitution. Mukherjee, Reddy and Singh countered that the CWC had the powers to waive these rules. 'It is in keeping with the party constitution and precedents,' Mukherjee said.

Justifying the expulsions, Mukherjee said Pawar, Sangma and Anwar had violated party discipline by not abiding by the majority decision of Sunday's CWC meeting that rejected their demand. The trio wanted the election manifesto to include a clause that the party would bring in a constitutional amendment to bar Indians of foreign origins from occupying high office. Mukherjee said the issue had no political logic. 'Who should be the Prime Minister is an issue which should be decided by the voters who elect the MPs,' he added. The CWC members alleged the rebels had deliberately taken up an issue that was raked up by the BJP. 'They have joined hands with the communal and fascist forces,' they said.

Sonia may have rejected the CWC's plea to take back her resignation, but Priyanka and Rahul now felt that she should persevere. Sonia too was convinced that she should stay on. Ambika Soni, Ahmad Patel and Natwar Singh told her that her exit would strengthen Pawar.

'Do you want to do that?' asked one leader. Family friends said the Priyanka factor too forced Sonia to reconsider. In Sonia's assessment, her exit in 1999 would have adversely affected the prospects of Priyanka or even Rahul taking up politics.

As the days passed, Congressmen became more confident that Sonia would stay on. Ajit Jogi, who was Congress spokesman, pointed out that Sonia had not resigned as chairperson of the Congress Parliamentary Party. She had also agreed to campaign for the party in the Goa assembly polls scheduled for June 1999.

A triumphant Pranab Mukherjee announced Sonia Gandhi's return at a hastily summoned press conference, saying: 'We told Soniaji that she was indispensable and she has withdrawn her resignation.' He quickly lit his pipe—always a reliable barometer of his mood—as a sign that everything was back to normal in the party. Thus, Sonia agreed to preside over the AICC session that was initially called to deal with the crisis triggered by her resignation. Party leaders said Sonia decided to take back her resignation the night before the AICC session because she was told by leaders that they were expecting trouble if she did not preside over the meeting. In a show of helplessness and loyalty, senior CWC members admitted they had even failed to resolve elementary issues such as who should hoist the flag and who should preside over the AICC in her absence.

A week after she returned to the helm, giving her followers renewed hope and to her detractors another chance to dub her as power-hungry and manipulative. The BJP said it was the 'end of Sonia Gandhi's theatricals', while expelled leader Sharad Pawar said, 'It was only expected. The resignation and withdrawal were aimed at diverting attention from basic issues raised by us. The entire show seen in the past few days seems to have been stage-managed.'[5]

The drama had indeed about ended when the CWC met in the evening and passed a resolution requesting her to withdraw her resignation. As if on cue, Sonia responded positively to the appeal. Party leaders said once they got the feeling that she was willing to attend the AICC meeting, they stepped up pressure on her to announce the decision immediately.

Having regained control over the party and reconciled to the idea of staying in politics, Sonia decided to go on the offensive. She dared her opponents to take the issue of her foreign origins to the people and made it clear that she was in the race for the prime ministership. 'The people of India will give a fitting reply to those questioning my patriotism . . . As far as the issue of prime ministership is concerned, the Congress Parliamentary Party (CPP) will decide it,' she said.[6] Since Sonia continued to be chairperson of the CPP, her statement left no room for doubt on the issue.

Sonia took up the challenge of her adversaries and declared she was as much an Indian as anyone else. 'Meri hindustaniat par shak karne walon ko main jawab nahin doongee. Is desh ki janata degi. Munh tod jawab degi,' she said. She told Congress delegates: 'Yeh desh mere jivan ke pal pal mein shamil raha. Main suhagin yahan bani, maa yahan bani, main widhwa apki ankhon ke samne hui. Is desh ki sabse mahan putri Indiraji ne apni saans meri bahon mein todi.'[7] In essence, those who doubted her patriotism would get a befitting reply not only from her but also from the people. India was an ineluctable part of her life; she was married here, became a mother here and was widowed here. Indira died in her arms.

The impact of the speech was instant. Many AICC delegates were seen wiping tears. Sonia herself sought to explain the circumstances leading to her resignation by accusing Pawar and other expelled leaders of being hand-in-glove with the BJP and wondering how they could raise the issue of her origins when they themselves had come with folded hands to ask her to take over the Congress leadership. 'Now the same set of people is trying to sow the seeds of doubt in the minds of my countrymen. They have joined hands with the forces against which I came to fight,' she said.

The Congress chief said she had quit a week ago with a 'heavy heart' but had decided to come back because 'the party has given me new assurance and hope'. After refusing to enter politics for seven years, she had not come to grab power, but to 'save the party from disintegration and the country from being overrun by communal forces'. That fight, she asserted, would continue. 'I will not let you down. What has happened in the past nine days should give us inspiration for a new beginning,' she said.

In an echo of Congress chief Dev Kanta Borooah's famous Emergency-era slogan of 'Indira is India, India is Indira,' the thundering cry at Talkatora stadium was: 'Sonia is the Congress, the Congress is Sonia.'

The party may not have emerged stronger from the resignation drama but Sonia certainly had. The party was now more subservient to her than before. Indira had drawn fawning loyalty by dint of her proven ability to deliver power. Sonia did it with no track record and the mere offer of half a hope. That showed much about the state of her partymen. 'Can you imagine this session without Sonia Gandhi?' remarked one of them, as the helmswoman arrived to thunderous ovation. 'There would not have been one. No Sonia, no session, no Sonia, no party.'

And if Sonia unleashed the whip briefly, it was only to ensure there was no detritus of dissent staining her crown any more. 'Those who want to walk with me should do so with their heads and their hearts,' she said, very much the headmistress at an assembly of spanked schoolboys. 'Those who have even an iota of uncertainty are free to chart their own course.'

She left none in doubt about the position she was taking. 'I want a Congress that would be prepared to go along with me and be prepared to die for the principles I have decided to follow.'[8]

Well aware that there still were elements in the CWC quibbling about her Italian lineage, Sonia moved quick and hard to terminate the debate with her blunt take-it-or-leave-it approach. The party took it without demur.

The issue of her foreign origins was closed within the Congress. Sonia probably should thank Sharad Pawar for putting an end to what was hitherto a difficult to address whisper campaign. He opened the lid on it; Sonia grabbed the chance to shut it tight.

From Talkatora onwards, the re-empowered leader stamped her authority harder and controlled dissent more harshly. The CWC collectively turned more loyal, its members vying with one another to be counted among her supporters.

The AICC session was no more than the inauguration of the new Congress durbar, purged of the black sheep. Arrayed in the new durbar were the courtiers paying obeisance to the new empress. If only, she would deliver them an empire.

THIRTEEN

THE CONTROVERSIES

Sonia is not new to controversies; she had to face many before she took over as the Congress party chief. The difference was that after 1998, the hullabaloo about her foreign origins, citizenship, close relatives, Bofors, Ottavio Quattrocchi and family trusts suddenly gained momentum—a sort of premium that she was expected to pay for her new role as a politician.

For millions of Congress workers, the issue of Sonia's foreign origins did not occur till she formally took over as the Congress president on 14 March 1998. They were only too glad to get a powerful and charismatic leader. As an Uttar Pradesh Congress Committee member reacted when news of her taking charge reached Lucknow, 'We have found a Sachin Tendulkar now!'[1] The reference was to India's ace cricketer.

The euphoria of Sonia's formal entry into the Congress in 1998 was so high that many party leaders, including CWC members, felt that the Congress was within striking distance of power. The assembly poll results in Madhya Pradesh, Rajasthan and Delhi reinforced the belief. By December 1998 Sonia was ahead of even Vajpayee as prime ministerial candidate in a survey conducted by *India Today*.[2]

Sonia's opposition was taken off guard. The exit of the Vajpayee government in April 1999 rattled the BJP and its allies so much that the top leadership went into a huddle wondering how to cope with her rising appeal.

There was considerable debate within the BJP and the Sangh Parivar. Finally the parivar had its say in deciding that it would rake up Sonia's foreign origins issue. Vajpayee and other BJP leaders were uncomfortable fearing that the move could boomerang. On the other hand, L.K. Advani and Pramod Mahajan were confident of obtaining political advantage from it.

There was a series of meetings of the top brass of the BJP and the Sangh Parivar. A crack team consisting of Govindacharya, S. Gurumurthy and Parez Chand was formed to focus on Sonia Gandhi in all respects. Govindacharya is a BJP ideologue, while Gurumurthy and Parez are part of the Swadeshi Jagran Manch, an RSS-allied organization that focuses on economic issues and policy. Govindacharya was quick to spot her most vulnerable point. 'The lady has spent thirty-six years out of fifty-three years as an Italian. Let us make that an issue.'[3] The political machinery got cracking, preparing talking points, while legal experts began poring over citizenship laws.

The Sangh decided to launch its attack on Sonia through the VHP on grounds that it was a social issue, so that if the assault failed, the political repercussions would be minimized.

The BJP's campaign zeroed in on the following points:

(a) Why did she not apply for Indian citizenship soon after her marriage with Rajiv Gandhi in 1968? She voluntarily chose to register herself as a foreigner for fifteen years under the foreigners Act spread into three 5-year duration permits. By 1973, she was eligible to become an Indian citizen. In 1978, she again sought extension. Finally, she took up Indian citizenship on 30 April 1983, a time when Rajiv Gandhi had given up flying and become Indira's political heir.

(b) Sonia continued to be a dual citizen. Italy did not require her to surrender her Italian passport as she automatically retains her original citizenship. Sonia had renounced her Italian citizenship but the fundamental principle in the Italian constitution is such that the domicile of every Italian is inviolable.

(c) Sonia will be constantly faced with a conflict of interest. Every person has emotional attachment to the land of his or her birth. Only a natural born citizen can truly love his/her country. In the case of her becoming the Prime Minister, could not there be a clash of interest?

(d) Some of the service rules applicable to defence personnel who occupy positions of lesser importance than the Prime Minister. For instance, the rules frown upon marriages with foreign spouses because of the possibility of sensitive official secrets consciously or unconsciously leaking out. The rationale is that there are certain positions where a nation cannot take the slightest risk; there is the risk of divided allegiance, even if citizenship is formally renounced.

The BJP campaign also highlighted Sonia's failure to delete her name from the electoral roles in 1980 when she was still a foreign national. The BJP claimed that Sonia chose to become an Indian citizen when a family member questioning the presence of a foreigner in the Prime Minister's house filed a case in court.

According to the BJP, there was also a question of international reciprocity—a cardinal international relationship in respect of law of citizenship—that was missing between India and Italy. To drive home the point, BJP leaders quoted Rai Singh, who served in the Indian embassy in Rome in the 1950s, as saying,

It may be recalled that in the mid-1950s Italian film director Roberto Rossellini, during his visit to India, fell in love with Bengali film actress Sonali, who eventually eloped with him to Rome, leaving behind her husband and children.

In Italy, Sonali married Rossellini and as his legal wife, she acquired Italian citizenship after duly renouncing her Indian citizenship. However, years later, in the 1960s, when she wanted to stand for an elective office at the municipal level, she was told that she was not entitled to do so under Italian law. Sonali approached the Indian embassy in Rome. After informal and discreet inquiries, I learnt that there was no reciprocal protocol treaty or law as such between India and Italy. Hence no help could be rendered to Sonali despite her being Italian citizen of Indian origins.

The revolt within the Congress over Sonia's foreign origins came as a blessing to the BJP and the Sangh. Dattopant Thengari, leader of the Sangh-affiliated Bharatiya Mazdoor Sangh (BMS), got in touch with rebel leader P. A. Sangma. The friendship between the two dates back to the time when Sangma was Union labour minister and in close touch with Thengari and other trade union leaders. A loose understanding was arrived at that attacks on Sonia would be coordinated and followed up with simultaneous press conferences and so forth.

However, the political components in the BJP were also itching to take on Sonia. Pramod Mahajan, BJP strategist, jumped the gun, launching a rather personalized attack on the AICC chief that embarrassed the BJP. He quickly disowned some rather tasteless references in the attack, and the party told him to lie low. Congress campaign managers were quick to link Mahajan's references with his disregard for women. The Left parties and many women organizations opposed to the BJP rushed to Sonia's rescue terming Mahajan's remarks as unwarranted. Sonia's association with many religious organizations, such as the Ramakrishna Mission, also helped to blunt the Sangh attack.

The BJP's campaign against Sonia failed to gain momentum as the Congress's legal experts pointed out there was nothing in law that could be held against Sonia. Even the hardline BJP leader L.K. Advani admitted that Sonia's citizenship was in order. Ram Jethmalani, one of India's most prominent lawyers, who served as Union law minister in the Vajpayee government, strongly opposed a constitutional amendment to debar Sonia from holding high public office. He argued, 'We cannot change laws to neutralize a single person by creating in her way a legal disability anew. It will be more honourable to fight on her existing disabilities which are many and formidable.'[4] Subramanian Swamy, who also filed several petitions against Sonia, too admitted that legally there was nothing against Sonia. Swamy, however, said Sonia's Indian citizenship should be withdrawn on the basis of his allegations against her.

Regarding fears of conflict of interest and concerns that she would be handling sensitive documents, Congress leaders said these were mere apprehensions, as Sonia was yet to become Prime Minister. A Congress leader said, 'It indicates their psyche and deep-rooted fear against Sonia. After all, if she is so full of disabilities, why worry so much about her?'

The BJP also highlighted the observations made by B. Raman, former head of the Intelligence Bureau, who wrote an article in the *Statesman* in 1999 claiming that Rajiv had associated with Sonia's Italian brother-in-law to push through a training project to seek security expertise from Italy. Like other BJP leaders, Raman based his arguments on the premise that Sonia's appointment as the Prime Minister may bring conflict of interest while ordering sensitive intelligence operations in Italy and other European countries.[5]

Soon a major paradox developed in the debate over Sonia Gandhi's foreign origins. Her detractors were virtually unanimous that her birth in faraway Orbassano was some sort of threat to national security and sovereignty. Privately many of these leaders even accused her of being a sleeper—planted by international forces hostile to India—to become active when the time came to strike.

At the same time, Sonia's detractors charged her with sticking to her Italian citizenship till the very last moment—from 1968 to 1983— till it became binding on her to renounce it. Sonia's desire to clutch on to her Italian citizenship was presented as a sign of lesser affection for India and of a wish to flee to her homeland in case of politically adverse circumstances. Gurumurthy and others who designed the campaign against Sonia repeatedly said that during the 1971 war and the Emergency, Sonia had left the country or sought refuge in embassies.[6]

The question that remained unexplained was that if she was a sleeper, why would she wait fifteen years to take up Indian citizenship, a step that could have made her a serious political player much before 1998?

Sources close to Sonia maintained that of all the allegations, the ones relating to her foreign origins hurt the most. Each time this issue was raked up, Sonia felt uncomfortable, almost regretting her decision to join politics. She tried to counter the campaign by making it a point to say 'India is my motherland', or use a similar phrase, in all her major speeches during 1999. Addressing a rally in Goa in May 1999, Sonia said, 'I will live and die for my motherland.' To which Gurumurthy's rejoinder was, 'Had she made the statement not in May 1999 but in April 1983, her motherland would have been different . . . Not India, which was then not her motherland but only her mother-in-law's land.'

Sonia's detractors brought Sangma forward to keep the foreign origins issue going. Sangma was drafted in a government-sponsored Constitution review panel headed by retired Supreme Court Chief Justice M.N. Venkatchaliah. Ostensibly the objective of the panel was to look at the functioning of the Constitution without touching on its basic structure. A number of legal experts close to the BJP were inducted in the panel that was supposed to conduct an apolitical exercise. But Sangma's appointment raised many eyebrows. The former Lok Sabha Speaker made no bones about his intentions. From day one, Sangma declared that the panel would look into the possibility of debarring persons of foreign origins from holding high public office, namely those of Prime Minister, President, Vice President and a few others, such as Chief Election Commissioner. The Congress quickly announced that it would boycott the panel.

In the panel's first meeting Sangma moved a paper on this subject. Justice Venkatchaliah did not approve. He wanted the review panel to undertake an academic exercise rather than a political one. Sangma was unmoved. A bitter tug of war followed. Venkatchaliah made it clear that individual, specific issues would not be allowed to dominate. Sangma met Prime Minister Vajpayee and threatened to quit the panel. The government swung into action prevailing upon both Venkatchaliah and Sangma to stay on. Once again political manoeuvring ensured that the issue of foreign origins was kept alive just in case Sonia got any closer to power. But Sangma felt disenchanted over the government's reluctance to end Sonia's political career. In March 2002, he resigned in a huff.

In 1999 when Sonia failed to form an alternative government after the fall of the Vajpayee government, she made another enemy, Dr Subramanian Swamy, who had this far been her self-proclaimed admirer and 'personal friend'. He was the one who brought Sonia close to the ADMK leader, J. Jayalalitha, in March 1999 at a tea party held in Ashok Hotel that brought down the Vajpayee regime.

The party was arranged by Swamy who called Jayalalitha, Sonia and several other opposition leaders. Sonia was reluctant to go, and a number of party leaders advised her against it. But the coterie around her convinced her to go and break the ice with Jayalalitha, who wanted to meet Sonia at a neutral venue. Known for being whimsical and imperious, she had refused to call on Sonia. Sonia responded similarly.

The tea served at the Ashok was a fresh brew from Darjeeling and created a stir in Delhi's political circles. Jayalalitha offered Sonia a shawl acknowledging her as a leader. Sonia recipocated the gesture recalling how Rajiv used to talk about her as a trusted friend and well-wisher of the family. Host Swamy intervened, wondering why the Congress and the ADMK did not team up to throw out the communal and corrupt NDA regime at the Centre. Jayalalitha said she was willing if the Congress took the lead. Sonia said that she was in agreement but would need her party's nod. Swamy began to distribute sweets and a photo session featuring the two leaders started.

The Swamy–Sonia relations took a nosedive when he wrote a book on the conspiracies behind the assassination of Rajiv and presented the first copy to Sonia. Swamy called on Sonia several times. As he sat on the olive-green sofa in 10 Janpath's drawing room, Swamy advised Sonia to remove Arjun Singh from her 'coterie' and claimed that Rajiv had preferred Swamy as Prime Minister in 1990 instead of Chandra Shekhar. Sonia was amused by Swamy's claim but refused to read the book, let alone act against Arjun Singh. When Sonia was asked about Swamy's charges against Singh, she said smiling, 'You know what Swamy is all about.'[7]

Swamy is not known to be half-hearted either in his friendships or in his enmities. He placed Sonia on top of his list of enemies, relegating others like Jayalalitha, Ramakrishna Hegde, Chandra Shekhar and Vajpayee to lower positions.

He then made multiple allegations against the Gandhis. His first charge was that Sonia, Rahul and other family members received money from the KGB (the former Soviet secret service that is now called the Federal Intelligence Service[FIS]). According to Swamy, Sonia kept the money in Swiss accounts. He also accused her of being soft towards the LTTE. (An assumption based upon Sonia's mercy plea to President K.R. Narayanan seeking commutation of the sentence on Nalini Murugan in the Rajiv assassination case).

Swamy also charged Sonia's parents and sisters with benefiting from the sale of Indian artefacts and antiques in letters to Minister of State for Personnel Vasundhara Raje, who was looking after the CBI. The minister forwarded the 'routine letter' to the CBI for necessary action. The development stalled Parliament for many days with Congress MPs alleging political vendetta and Swamy promptly informing the media that his allegations had been referred to the CBI. The stalemate continued for several days during the second half of the budget session of Parliament in 2001 until Prime Minister Vajpayee personally assured members that no action was being taken against the leader of the Opposition. Vajpayee admitted that he had routinely said the charges would be looked into. The CBI, he added, had not launched a formal inquiry or even a preliminary inquiry, as the CBI calls inquiries where it does not register a First Information Report (FIR). Government sources, however, said that Swamy's charges were not 'dismissed'. One Union minister hostile to Sonia said, 'It may come in handy for us in difficult times!' hinting at the possibility of the Vajpayee regime raking up the subject at some other juncture.

But a determined Swamy shot off another letter to Vasundhara Raje demanding that an FIR should be registered against Sonia for 'carrying out a procedurally correct investigation'. He also threatened that 'any lethargy on behalf of the CBI would invite a high court monitoring of the investigation', hinting that he would go to the courts.

It was a full-scale attack on Sonia and Rahul, as well as Sonia's mother and sister Anushka, who live in Italy. The Vajpayee government, which had earlier assured the House that it would not act against Sonia, relished Swamy's charges as they provided a diversion to its own troubles on the exposures made by Tehelka.com on arms deals.

For a government reeling under the charges of various scams resulting in the loss of crores of rupees, Swamy provided the BJP a handy stick to put the Congress on the defensive. But the government also had faced trouble from Swamy. Among other things, Swamy had repeatedly accused Vajpayee of being a British collaborator during the Quit India movement.

A defensive Sonia camp termed Swamy's charges as 'baseless and malicious allegations without having an iota of truth' and said they were not worth a reaction. Congress leaders close to Sonia told party MPs that Swamy was frustrated that the Congress had not helped him to become an MP and this was his revenge. They said the so-called KGB documents were forgeries made in the US as part of the 'psychological warfare against independent-minded leaders of the non-aligned countries'.

According to government sources, the CBI was expected to make discreet inquiries in Russia (where FIS archives are located), the US (Swamy claims the archives are available in Harvard University), Italy and India. A CBI official admitted that it could be a wild goose chase consuming several months. The CBI sources also indicated the agency would keep the pot bubbling, especially as the steam was hurting the government of the day's enemy number one.[8]

Sonia had her first brush with controversy on 25 January 1973 when an extraordinary meeting of Maruti shareholders appointed her as director of Maruti Technical Services Pvt. Ltd. The other director was Sanjay Gandhi.

Sonia claimed she was completely ignorant about the whole exercise as she merely signed on the dotted line. She did not get a chance to share details with Rajiv as he was away. However, when Rajiv came to know, he immediately told her to withdraw from the Maruti boards.[9]

During the Janata regime, a commission of inquiry headed by

Justice A.C. Gupta quoted S.M. Rege, secretary to Maruti Ltd, as saying that Sonia knew she was a foreign national. The commission observed that the shares held by her were in contravention of Foreign Exchange Regulation Act (FERA) of 1973 and therefore 'ab initio void'.[10]

The proximity to Sanjay again got her in trouble when Indira's detractors rocked Parliament in 1974 questioning Sonia's appointment as insurance agent of two companies—Oriental Insurance and General Insurance—which raised funds for fledgling Maruti companies. Once again, much of the criticism revolved around her foreign national status that violated FERA provisions. The insurance companies refused to confirm or deny the Sonia link, and no one in the Congress is willing to talk about the insurance episode.

Along with the issue of her foreign origins, the Bofors controversy and her alleged proximity to Italian businessman Ottavio Quattrocchi, suspected of having been a conduit for kickbacks in the Bofors case, caused Sonia a great deal of trouble and continue to haunt her. Sonia first remained silent hoping that the twin issues would die down. She then began speaking about it, focusing on the failure of successive governments to nab the alleged recipients of the gun-purchase kickbacks. She repeatedly quoted Rajiv that none of his family members were involved in getting bribes. But far from dying down, Bofors and the Q-connection continue to be potent issues against Sonia and the Congress.

Many years later, the Bofors scandal shows no signs of going away. Rajiv Gandhi's advisers had told him that Bofors was a middle-class preoccupation that would have no impact on the country at large. The same logic was dished out to Sonia when she took over as Congress chief. But each time elections are held, the Bofors issue flares up from nowhere. In 2000 the Vajpayee government finally filed a charge sheet thirteen years after the allegations hit the headlines, but it generated its own share of controversy because it named Rajiv among the accused. Angry Congressmen stopped the Lok Sabha from functioning for several days.

By today's standards, the total amount involved in the Bofors kickbacks—Rs 64 crores—looks like peanuts. Successive scams that came to light during the Narasimha Rao, Gujral, Deve Gowda and Vajpayee regimes involve hundreds of crores. For example, any of the accused in the Harshad Mehta securities scam made more money in a fortnight than the whole money involved in the Bofors case. So why is it that Bofors exercises such a hold over the national imagination? Why is it the scandal won't go away? According to senior journalist Vir Sanghvi, Bofors became an issue because it involved a man who was perceived to be Mr Clean. When Mr Clean tried to become Mr Cover-up, he created more outrage.[11] Secondly, the issue was about national security and defence. But then, even the worst critics of Rajiv accept that, on technical counts, the Bofors gun was second to none, and it proved as much when it was deployed during the 1999 Kargil war.

Now that so much has been discovered in the Bofors kickbacks, one wonders why Rajiv would have compromised so much, paying a huge political price. Either the Congress had taken the commission so Rajiv could never admit it completely, or Quattrocchi was involved, goes the conjecture. Even if Quattrocchi had been operating in an individual capacity, any revelation that suggested an Italian connection would have severely compromised Rajiv. Sonia would have been the subject of the attack and it is unlikely that he would have been able to tolerate that level of personal assault, so Rajiv kept mum, is the surmise.

Ottavio Quattrocchi was a close family friend of the Gandhis. He came to India as a chartered accountant in Chennai in the 1970s for an Italian multinational company and soon shifted his base to Delhi as a representative of the Milan-based Snamprogetti. The affable Italian was a man about town who moved in and out of Indira's residence. In Italy he had no direct family or professional links with the Maino family.

Quattrocchi did not have much influence till Rajiv became Prime Minister and began liberalizing the economy. One minister in the Rajiv government, Ramchandra Rath, officially complained against him for exerting pressure and walking into his ministerial chambers without permission, etc. Rath was dropped in the next round of Cabinet expansion. Though there was no proof that this had gone against him, till date, Rath firmly believes that the 'discourtesy shown to Quattrocchi' was responsible for his ouster.[12]

Another account says that Quattrocchi's wife, Maria, was part of Sonia's inner circle. The ladies club, which included Sterre Satish Sharma and Nina Arun Singh, ostensibly had nothing to do with politics, but many suspected that these powerful ladies had a say in the decision-making process.

Coincidence or not, Snamprogetti began receiving prized contracts from 1985 onwards. The company generously rewarded Quattrocchi, who rose to become regional director for the entire South-east Asian operations. Snamprogetti, however, had nothing to do with Bofors. The company clarified it was not aware of Quattrocchi's alleged other activities in India, maintaining that he was their full-time representative in India. Quattrocchi retired from the company in 1996 and is presently stationed in Kuala Lumpur as a consultant. The CBI has sought his extradition to prosecute him in the Bofors case.

Sonia Gandhi has refused to discuss her alleged links with Quattrocchi. When the question was raised during the release of the 1999 election manifesto, she said, 'The CBI has said he is a suspect. But we have never seen the papers naming him in the deal. They should show the papers establishing that he is guilty.'[13]

Sources close to Sonia accused her opponents of using Quattrocchi to tarnish her image. She is prepared to accept that he was a family friend but strongly refutes the charge that she, her husband or mother-in-law ever favoured him in any business deal.

Quattrocchi too tried to give a clean chit to Sonia, a move that boomeranged and embarrassed Sonia within the Congress. He said, 'She is innocent. As far as I am concerned it [Bofors] is a politically motivated case. My only fault was that I was a friend of Rajiv and Sonia Gandhi.' He has denied any wrongdoing.[14]

Sonia's stint in politics brought the spotlight on several family trusts that she now manages. Her estranged sister-in-law, Maneka Gandhi, deeply resented Sonia's grip over these trusts, including the one set up in memory of Sanjay. The NDA government painstakingly collected material and made an issue about the functioning of these trusts and the money generated. For instance, Jaya Jaitley, president of the Samata Party, a constituent of the ruling alliance, questioned the issue of copyrights and the royalty going to Sonia and her children. According to her, it was strange that Sonia and her family members were getting royalty from the speeches and writings of Jawaharlal Nehru, Indira and Rajiv when the government's Publications Division holds the copyright of the Prime Minister's speeches. She said that when the Nehru Memorial Trust published his letters to chief ministers among the selected works of Nehru, the royalty again went to the family.

There are other issues involving Sonia which are controversial. For instance, Teen Murti House is government-owned property, yet it houses private trusts such as the Nehru Memorial Fund, the Nehru Cambridge Trust and the Kamla Nehru Trust, which runs a hospital in Allahabad. Sonia heads all these. Likewise, the Rajiv Gandhi Foundation is located at Jawahar Bhawan on Dr Rajendra Prasad Road, but Jawahar Bhawan was supposed to be the Congress party headquarters, and all party MPs in the 1980s donated a month's salary to raise funds for it. Much before Sonia formally took up politics, as Jawahar Bhawan trust chairperson, she leased the building to the Rajiv Gandhi Foundation, which she directs.

Maneka was divested of the charge of ministry of culture on the eve of the inauguration of the Indira Gandhi National Centre for the Arts (IGNCA) complex on 18 November 2001. There was talk of a deal between the government and the leader of the Opposition, i.e., Sonia. Maneka sulked and privately attributed her removal to her decision to order a probe against Sonia in connection with alleged irregularities in the centre's functioning when Sonia was chairperson. The Vajpayee regime and the Congress deny the charge. Before Maneka's charges, Sonia had fought a protracted battle to control the IGNCA, but an equally determined BJP regime forced her to step down as life president.

The IGNCA was set up in 1987 as a tribute to Indira Gandhi. A corpus fund of Rs 50 crores, a grant of Rs 100 crores and twenty-one acres of prime land in Delhi's central vista was allotted to it. The land alone was considered to be worth hundreds of crores of rupees. In addition, fifteen duplex flats in Asiad Village (worth about a crore each) and a battery of government officials on deputation were granted to the centre. The original deed provided for the trustees to hold office for a period of ten years, and the President of India was appointed visitor to review the centre's functioning. After Rajiv's death, the Narasimha Rao regime made Sonia its chairperson.

By May 1995, the relations between the Narasimha Rao regime and 10 Janpath had hit an all-time low. The IGNCA trustees made crucial changes in the deed making the chairperson (Sonia) life president and appointed P.V. Narasimha Rao, former President R. Venkatraman, H.Y. Sharda Prasad, Pupul Jayakar and Kapila Vatsayan as life members. The Union human resource development minister, Madhavrao Scindia, approved the deed without consulting the Cabinet or other departments. Those in the know said that both Rao and Scindia were fully aware of the implications, but the government thought the move would help restore the functional relationship between Rao and Sonia.

Pupul Jayakar quickly withdrew from the panel. The old associate of Indira said, 'Indira would be shuddering in her grave if she knew what was happening in her name!'[15] There were many red faces in the government. Sonia wondered why she was included without prior consent. As part of the damage limitation exercise, Dr Manmohan Singh was drafted in her place.

When the BJP-led coalition took over in 1999, Dr Murli Manohar Joshi took the charge of cleansing the IGNCA. The government insisted on the centre opening its books for the Comptroller and Auditor General (CAG). By the time Sonia was removed and Maneka took charge of the ministry, he ordered the CBI to probe into instances of malfunctioning and several acts of omission and commission.

Sonia lost control over the centre badly. Her coterie had ill advised her making her believe that the government would not be able to dislodge trustees. But successive court battles ensured that the government had its way. P.V. Narasimha Rao and L.M. Singhvi were saved further embarrassment when Sonia stepped down as life president. But the government's bid to restore the status quo ante proved so difficult that a Union minister remarked, 'It was more difficult than throwing out Pakistani intruders in Kargil!'[16]

The controversy over the Rs 100 crore donation to the Rajiv Gandhi Foundation has been dealt with in chapter six. Among all family trusts, the RGF's performance was the best till Sonia joined politics. By early 2001, the high-profile foundation was in complete disarray due to Sonia's preoccupation with her new responsibilities and the foundation's lack of official patronage and paucity of funds.

The RGF, set up in 1991, began functioning as a think tank to provide inputs for policy research. It hosted a number of international leaders and luminaries such as Margaret Thatcher, Hillary Rodham Clinton, Nelson Mandela, Edward Said, John Kenneth Galbraith, Professor Amartya Sen and Dr Mahboob-ul-Haque.

But by 2001 the RGF gatherings lost the glamour and seriousness that they used to generate earlier. Trust functionaries said they were finding it difficult to rope in international statesmen as the personal links with the Nehru–Gandhi family were getting weaker with the Congress being out of power for almost a decade. For instance, they said, the new leaderships in Great Britain, Germany, France, the US, Japan and West Asia had very little personal rapport with the Congress leadership, which was not the case a decade ago. As a result, the RGF had to route all invitations to foreign dignitaries through the ministry of external affairs. The ministry, RGF sources said, did not take a lead in such matters.

India's former ambassador to the US, Abid Hussain, left the RGF in a huff when Sonia took over as Congress party chief. Sources close to him said he did not want to be part of a foundation whose chairperson had become a political player.

Mainly, however, the decline of the RGF had to do with Sonia's preoccupation with politics. She stopped visiting the foundation's office and conducted meetings from her residence. The RGF trust consisted of some well-known names like P. Chidambaram, Suman Dubey, M.S. Swaminathan, Montek Singh Ahluwalia, Dr Manmohan

Singh, R.P. Goenka, Y.K. Alagh and Sridath Ramphal, but it met just once a year. Moreover, the foundation curtailed many of its popular programmes such as its innovative hospital on wheels, a train that used to stop at stations in rural areas providing sophisticated free medical care to those unable to travel long distances.

Another area of disappointment under Sonia's leadership was the fate of newspapers that were founded by Jawaharlal Nehru. Neglect was responsible for closure of the *National Herald* in Lucknow, a prominent English daily founded by Nehru in 1937. The newpaper had had many illustrious editors, Feroze Gandhi and M. Chalapati Rau among them, and had played a significant role in the freedom struggle. Later the group started a quality Urdu daily, *Quami Awaz*, and a Hindi daily, *Nav Jeevan*, published from New Delhi and Lucknow. The publication ran into financial difficulties in the 1980s, and its Lucknow editions were suspended in the early 1990s.

Employees working for the newspaper group had great hope that these publications would be revived under Sonia, but this hope was belied. In November 2001 Sonia appointed Narain Dutt Tiwari as chairman of Associated Journals Ltd., the holding company, but Tiwari failed to do much before he went off as chief minister of Uttaranchal. Sonia then appointed Motilal Vora, the AICC treasurer, as chairman of the group, but he found little time to devote to the paper and availed the services of his brother, Govind Vora, but the Voras have not been able to revive the paper either.

Today, the Sanjay Gandhi Memorial Trust and the Kamla Nehru Trust are in an organizational and fiscal morass. Unlike the plush premises of the RGF at Jawahar Bhawan, the Sanjay Trust is functioning from one six-by-nine outhouse at 24 Akbar Road. The trust that boasts of trustees such as Tiwari, Rameshwar Thakur and Sonia has not conducted any major activity for years owing to lack of funds. The Sanjay Gandhi Memorial Hospital situated in Gaurigunj in Amethi is run by the trust but is plagued with problems, periodic strikes and non-payment of salaries to its employees among them.

Once Sonia joined politics in 1998, her spin doctors tried hard to put a lid on various controversies surrounding the Congress chief.

They prepared a point-by-point rebuttal to often-repeated charges against her and posted them on the Internet. The state units made copies in regional languages and distributed these to the rank and file. The overseas Congress also spread the rebuttal around to silence her critics, mainly Non-Resident Indians. Sample some of these in a question-answer form:

- Sonia Gandhi cannot win any elections for the Congress party after the foreigner issue has been raised.

  REPLY: The foreigner issue had been raised when major states had gone to polls in the recent past. Yet Sonia Gandhi won the elections for the Congress.

- Sonia's sister, Nadia Valdemoro, reached New Delhi, after Vajpayee government fell in April 1999, to be by her side amidst reports that she might soon become India's Prime Minister.

  REPLY: What's wrong with two sisters sharing their joys and sorrows?

- Should Sonia Gandhi become Prime Minister, her relatives in Italy would be fully entitled to round-the-clock protection by the Black Cat commandos at the Indian taxpayer's expense.

  REPLY: The Indian government does not provide protection to relatives/family members of VIPs or VVIPs when they live abroad. The same rule was applied to Rahul Gandhi when he was in London. The same rule will also be applied to Sonia Gandhi's family in Italy.

- Do we need another round of 'Civilizing'? Is any Basu, any Mulayam, born in the heat and dust of India preferable to the 'Senora' as our leader?

  REPLY: Definitely Sonia has got much better virtues and qualities than many. Basu is too old for the PM's post and he himself is supporting Sonia Gandhi.

- No other country's constitution allows a foreign-born citizen to become its chief executive. The Indian Constitution should be amended to bar foreign-born persons.

REPLY: The framers of the Constitution clearly did not forbid a foreign-born citizen from becoming Prime Minister. Why should the law be changed for the sake of a person who is liked by millions of Indians? The Constitution gives equal rights to all citizens, as its main theme is Article 14, which gives the Right to Equality. Any constitutional amendment in that direction would be a mockery of Article 14.

- It is an insult to a country of 980 million that the Congress cannot find one India-born person to project as PM. Not any ABC can become Prime Minister of India.

REPLY: Since Sonia is an Indian citizen and belongs to the most respected and loved Indian family, she cannot be treated as a foreigner just because of her skin colour or accent. She is part of the Indian mainstream and has more Indianness than many leaders whose wives and children aspire for American green cards. She has chosen to stay in India despite constant threats to her and her children's lives.

- As a foreign-born citizen who has extensive family links abroad, she can be a security risk as pressure can be brought on her to act against national interests.

REPLY: There is not a single instance when she has acted against national interest. The track record of some of the recent Prime Ministers has been dubious, especially as they indulged in secret negotiations on India's nuclear status without taking the country into confidence. Many of the accusers have children working for multinationals and foreign governments abroad through whom pressure can be brought and has come.

- She became a voter much before she became a citizen. This was a fraud on the electoral system.

REPLY: Sonia never enrolled herself as a voter when she was not a citizen. The enrolment might have happened because the door-to-door enumerator was checking on residents of each house. She also voted for the first time after becoming a citizen.

- She has no knowledge of Indian life, culture and ethos. She has led a sheltered life and has not worked through the ranks of political parties.

REPLY: She has imbibed Indian ethos and culture. Otherwise how can she be acceptable to so many people in all parts of the country? Her political instincts are correct. She is heading the most experienced political party in the world and she believes in collective functioning of the party and the government.

- She has two passports, Indian and Italian. She has even used the Italian passport after becoming an Indian citizen.

REPLY: She voluntarily gave up Italian citizenship in 1983 and also surrendered her passport. She has always travelled on an Indian passport ever since she became an Indian citizen. There are records in government files to prove that she has only an Indian passport.[17]

FOURTEEN

SONIA THE LEADER

Sonia's stint as Congress president has seen her weather many highs and lows. After a flying start came massive disappointment, but by 2002 the AICC chief stabilized her position proving her critics wrong that her only claim to fame was the Gandhi surname. Just as things were looking up for the so-called Prime Minister in waiting, the outcome of the Gujarat assembly polls posed a big question mark over her future. The return of aggressive Hindutva at the centre stage of Indian polity made her look vulnerable.

Regardless of electoral prospects, however, opponents and well-wishers alike agree that Sonia has introduced a new style of functioning in her party. Though not a reformist, she succeeded in bringing about some change. Slowly, behind the scenes, she changed the Congress work culture. The old style Congressman adjusted, sometimes clumsily, to a more corporate style of operation and tried to be gender-sensitive and relatively clean in the party's fiscal matters.

While Sonia missed no opportunity in projecting herself along the lines of her role models Indira and Rajiv, her own distinct style emerged. She introduced what Jairam Ramesh called a Japanese style of decision-making based on three steps—consulting the maximum number of persons, formulating a policy and then carrying the party along.[1]

Congressmen got to see a new Sonia. Her growing confidence, however, caught many leaders off guard. West Bengal's once powerful leader A.B.A. Ghani Khan Chowdhury became her first victim. Months before the 2000 assembly polls in Bengal, Chowdhury, holding charge of the West Bengal Pradesh Congress Committee (WBPCC) unit, raised the bogey of a mahajot (grand alliance) with rebel Congress leader Mamata Banerjee, who had joined hands with the BJP at the Centre to defeat the ruling Left alliance in Bengal. Sonia was reluctant to join hands with Mamata, but Chowdhury led a relentless campaign, almost raising a revolt against Sonia.

Closer to the assembly polls, he became lukewarm to the idea of mahajot as Mamata demanded bulk of assembly seats. Sonia, keen to create fissures in the BJP-led coalitions, extended a hand of friendship to Mamata's Trinamul Congress. Chowdhury panicked. He rushed to Sonia to wax on the virtues of going it alone. Sonia heard him out. In her lap was a red folder. As Chowdhury finished speaking and gulped a noisy sip of tea, Sonia said, 'But Barkat da, a few weeks before you were saying something different. I have all your statements, press clippings and papers in this folder. They say that without Mamata, the Congress would draw a big zero in Bengal.' The old man shuffled uncomfortably. There was silence till Chowdhury sought permission to leave. The moment Chowdhury was out of her living room, he hissed, 'Tini netri hoye gechhen! (She has become a leader!)'[2]

The Bengal election results were a disappointment for Sonia. The mahajot experiment failed miserably, and Chowdhury tendered his resignation as WBPCC chief. The division between the Congress and the breakaway Trinamul Congress at the grass-roots level was so intense that it precluded any alliance. Sonia addressed the problem. She was convinced that senior party leader Pranab Mukherjee was responsible for events leading to Mamata's exit from the party, which destroyed the West Bengal Congress. Pranab was summoned and given the task of reviving the post-polls party network in Bengal.

The Bengali bhadralok was taken aback. The former economics professor was well tuned to Delhi and happy as the party's chief whip in Rajya Sabha. But the orders were final. 'You are going to Bengal as you know so much about state politics,' Sonia told him, perhaps with some irony. From day one, a reluctant Pranab sought to quit the job.

In a year and a half, he met Sonia six times with an identical request—give the charge to someone else so that he could focus more on parliamentary work. Sonia always smiled and said he was doing a wonderful job as a parliamentarian and equally so as WBPCC chief. Pranab's agony continued. Among other things, the WBPCC had few resources and the annual expense on running state and district Congress committees alone exceeded Rs 15 lakh.

After Chowdhury and Pranab, Ghulam Nabi Azad became her next victim. Azad's downfall came close on the heels of the party's electoral successes in Uttaranchal, Punjab and Manipur assembly polls in February 2002 and coincided with its landslide victory in the Municipal Corporation of Delhi. Much to the astonishment of party veterans, Sonia started cracking the whip. In a rare show of authority, she transferred Azad, who was the AICC general secretary, to Jammu and Kashmir as Pradesh Congress Committee (JKPCC) president.

Azad hated the new assignment till the party emerged as a major player in the J & K assembly polls in October 2002, with Azad in the running as chief ministerial nominee. In March 2002 he had fought against going there, refusing to take charge of the JKPCC office in Srinagar citing security and health reasons. The kingmaker of J&K could not reconcile to the idea that he would be asked to do the job of a PCC chief. After all, since the 1970s, the rootless wonder had held several important government and organizational posts in the Delhi durbar.

Sonia, however, was determined to send Azad to Srinagar and with good reason. For years Azad had had an iron grip over the JKPCC. Sitting in Delhi, he would interfere even in appointments of district Congress units by operating through his trusted man, Peerzada Mohammed Sayeed. Successive PCC chiefs, AICC general secretaries and state party leaders had resented Azad's rule by proxy. When Azad finally called on her murmuring that his wife, Shamim, was worried about his security, Sonia said, 'You have so much interest in J&K Congress, so you might as well run it. Our party workers and leaders in the state are braving militancy. We will speak to the Prime Minister to take up the issue of security.' The matter was closed.

Azad's abrupt shifting indicated a growing confidence in her leadership qualities. Moreover, it was a political message to the people of J&K that the Congress was taking the state assembly polls seriously. But Congressmen were unsure. After all, the PCC office at Srinagar had remained shut for many years. Azad's predecessor, Mohammad Shafi Qureshi, had, in fact, resigned when he was asked to stay put in Srinagar.

But once Sonia's gamble in the state paid off, Azad changed his view. At a CWC meeting soon after the party emerged as the second largest in the polls, Azad said, 'Soniaji had the farsightedness which obviously I lacked. She is the leader, she is a visionary, we are lesser mortals and I have no shame in admitting it.'[3] Azad's adulation set the tone for the rest of the CWC meeting when Arjun Singh, R.K. Dhawan, Mohsina Kidwai and Ambika Soni credited Sonia with achieving what Narasimha Rao had failed—winning back the confidence of the majority community (namely Hindus) in the region, where the party trounced the BJP. They collectively said there was no reason why the verdict could not be repeated elsewhere in the country. Natwar Singh chipped in saying what the Congressmen needed to do was to blindly follow 'Madam'.[4]

The government-formation process in J&K also saw Sonia show her political wisdom. At a hurriedly convened CWC meeting on 11 October 2002, Sonia made it clear that in her scheme of things, there was no inevitability of a Congress-led government as the AICC chief had an open mind on the choice of the new chief minister given the larger issues involved in the troubled state.

The initial euphoria to increase the Congress tally from fourteen to fifteen party-ruled states evaporated. Sonia's 'statesman-like' approach baffled some CWC members while it surprised many in the Vajpayee regime.

Sources close to Sonia claimed that she did not have much difficulty in arriving at a decision. True to her preference for the Japanese style of decision-making, she first sought the views of her close associates. The CWC members then made up their mind in favour of People's Democratic Party (PDP) leader Mufti Mohammed Sayeed, and the decision was carried with ease. Of course, Sayeed's argument that a chief minister of J&K hailing from the Muslim-majority valley would be better equipped to deal with separatists convinced her to opt for him.

During Mufti's forty-five-minute meeting with Sonia, the country's former internal security minister made a strong case for representation from the Valley. Sayeed told Sonia that the Kashmiri people had great expectations after voting out the National Conference. He underlined the primacy of the Valley in finding a peaceful solution to the situation in Kashmir. Sayeed kept recalling his long association with Indira and Rajiv and how the two leaders had a dream of putting an end to violence. Sayeed said that at his advanced stage of life, he wished to contribute something for lasting peace.[5]

Sonia smiled occasionally, and while Sayeed went on enlisting the Congress's secular credentials and contribution in J&K, she could not help asking him why he left the parent organization if it was so good. A sheepish Sayeed quickly attributed his move to a communication gap and admitted his own naivety in leaving the Congress four years ago. The canny politician sought to regain some ground, saying that in politics nothing was certain, thereby hinting at the possibility of the return of PDP to the Congress in future. Sonia, having scored the point, said, 'Let us talk about present rather than the past or the future.'

The confidence gained by Sonia following the string of electoral successes had manifested itself at the time of nomination of party candidates for the Rajya Sabha elections. She sidelined powerful regional satraps and chief ministers such as Digvijay Singh, S.M. Krishna, Tarun Gogoi, Ajit Jogi and Vilasrao Deshmukh in her choice of candidates from their states but made them accept her nominees.

Sonia's confidence was on display too in the way she attacked Prime Minister Vajpayee during the debate on the Prevention of Terrorism Ordinance (POTO) in the joint session of Parliament on 26 March 2002. She was a picture of confidence. Her speech was strong enough to provoke Vajpayee into making an unusual intervention, turning the entire debate into a Sonia vs. Vajpayee battle. She began by describing the legislation as an 'instrument of suppression' which would be used by the government to suppress 'political opponents, religious minorities, ethnic groups, weaker sections and trade unions'. She said the constitutional provision of holding a joint session of Parliament was resorted to by the government in order to 'further an agenda of divisiveness . . . to achieve its narrow and controversial end', and not to 'celebrate a consensus on a measure of national importance'.

Sonia cited examples of how the government could misuse the legislation. In this context she cited the way in which the Gujarat government used its provisions selectively against minorities. She reminded the Prime Minister of his duty to 'protect the welfare of the people of India' and wanted to know whether he 'will be submissive and succumb to the internal pressure of his party and its sister organizations'. She concluded her speech with a warning to the Prime Minister: 'Your moment of reckoning has come.'

The speech stung Vajpayee. In his response, he dealt solely with the Congress chief's speech, leaving out the topic of the debate. The gloves were off. Vajpayee launched a frontal attack, saying that she had no right to remind him that his moment of reckoning had come or to talk about the internal politics of his party or the Sangh Parivar.

For political observers, Sonia's speech stood out against that of the Prime Minister. Hers was a passionate appeal to Vajpayee not to let political considerations bring into existence a draconian piece of legislation that had the potential to violate basic human rights, especially at a time when the polity was divided owing to the Gujarat communal riots and the Ayodhya agitation. In contrast, the Prime Minister's speech lacked substance. It was a personal attack and had a laudatory tone about his own long stint in Parliament, which did not go down well with many seasoned parliamentarians like Chandra Shekhar, Somnath Chatterjee and Jaipal Reddy.[6]

Sonia's leadership qualities, her confidence and practice of allowing all shades of opinions to have a say worked well in intraparty affairs where Congressmen were used to the imperious conduct of Indira. Critics of her style remain. BJP's Arun Jaitley said, 'You cannot have her as a Prime Minister whose comprehension and understanding is constantly under doubt.'[7] Some of the leaders ideologically closer to the Congress too found fault with Sonia's reliance on prepared text. Samajwadi Party leader Mulayam Singh Yadav and Janata Dal ideologue Surendra Mohan questioned her competence, wondering why she seldom spoke in all-party meetings convened on important issues. Mohan said, 'It is strange that she constantly writes to the Prime Minister on policy matters but seldom speaks at all-party meets.'[8]

But there was one uniform admission. The Sonia of 2002 was remarkably different from that of 1998. 1n 1998 many may have viewed Sonia as a supreme saviour—a person who saved the Congress from certain death under the clumsy leadership of Sitaram Kesri—but outside the Congress, she was almost written off as a housewife whose only claim to fame was her Gandhi connection.

Two years down the line, even the most optimistic ones in the Congress were having second thoughts. Did we take a right decision in inviting her to lead the party? they wondered. Family loyalists like Jitendra Prasada, V.N. Gadgil and regional satraps like the former maharaja of Gwalior, Madhavrao Scindia, led the pack telling partymen that she was good but not good enough. The coterie charge that the Congress president had no mind of her own and that she was constantly guided by a group of senior party leaders refused to go away. The Congress's worst-ever performance in the 1999 general elections seemed to confirm their doubts.

By 2000, the fence-sitters gathered again planning to organize another coup. A meeting was arranged. Prasada told the ambitious Rajesh Pilot to lead from the front. Maratha leader Sharad Pawar, now out of the Congress, signalled a go-ahead. Karunakaran assured support from the south. At least five members of the CWC promised to come out at the right time, and former Prime Minister Narasimha Rao's name was once again invoked. Though he never formally pledged support to this group of power seekers, his blessings were taken for granted.

Several rounds of lunch and dinner followed, but somehow the game plan was never finalized. The old debate over who should take over after Sonia was shunted out came as the biggest obstacle. Some were in favour of a tried-and-tested Rao, while Pilot made it clear that he alone would lead the anti-Sonia front. Prasada offered a compromise. He suggested a collective leadership, saying Sonia should first be challenged in the organizational polls. He said that Pilot should contest Sonia while declaring himself as a standby candidate. A legal expert who was present in one such meeting declared himself as a challenger to Sonia, saying that if nobody came forward, he would contest. Prasada was not amused and told the first-time Rajya Sabha MP not to be in a hurry. 'Arre bhai, you are not in some bar council where you can score some brownie points in contesting against Ram Jethmalani,' he said.[9]

The Sonia camp got wind of the discussions. She quickly summoned her loyal supporters. Natwar Singh volunteered to go to the other camp. However, the career diplomat was not taken seriously by Prasada who told Natwar, 'Kya milne julne mein koi pabandi hai? Aap log to har jagah conspiracy dekhte hain. (Is there a bar on meeting among ourselves? You people keep seeing a conspiracy angle in everything).' Natwar reported the response to Sonia.[10]

Three more leaders were pressed into action. Digvijay Singh met Prasada with the ostensible purpose of discussing that all was not well in the party. Ahmad Patel offered his services and R.K. Dhawan too joined in, though nobody specifically asked him to do so.

Patel was viewed with suspicion, but he convinced Prasada that he was not happy with the state of affairs in the party. Dhawan restored the channel of communication with those claiming to be loyal to Narasimha Rao. Sonia started getting constant feedback. She was alarmed to note that the dissent was much deeper than she had realized. She decided to meet the disgruntled party leaders to tide over the leadership challenge.

With both sides bracing for a showdown, a tragedy occurred that summarily altered the course of the intraparty feud. This was the death of Rajesh Pilot. With it, the dissident activities died down. Prasada tried hard to replace Pilot, but he lacked credibility and a mass base.

Sonia's record as a leader is one laced with failures and success. She may have done exceedingly well in some areas, but lack of perspective and a killer instinct continue to be her biggest drawbacks. Take for example the Tehelka exposé into murky defence deals that had all the ingredients to topple the Vajpayee regime. As with the Bofors scandal, the sensitive and often emotive issue of national security was interlinked with Tehelka.

But the way she and her party handled the Tehelka case, it became a classic case of one step forward and two steps backwards. The party was upbeat at Bangalore where the eighty-first session of the AICC was held against the backdrop of the Tehelka revelations and the Opposition outcry in Parliament. There was also great demand for the resignation of the Vajpayee-led NDA government. The Congress had finally positioned itself politically and ideologically in such a manner that it could work out an alliance with other Opposition parties including the Left. But did all this add up to a strategic perspective? Sonia gave a clarion call to 'liberate the country from the shackles of the shameful, corrupt and communal NDA government' and promised to restore to the party its past glory.[11]

But once back in Delhi, the lack of perspective became evident when the much-touted action plan for an agitation against the government had only the Congress as the main player and excluded the other Opposition parties. The Left, Samajwadi Party and other non-NDA parties were upset and wondered why they were left out if the plan was intended to achieve the immediate objective of liberating the country from NDA rule. The Congress could have given a greater impetus to the plan had it been more broad-based, they argued. Sonia could have opted for a joint Opposition movement. The interests of realpolitik would have been served better that way. In any case, the Congress plan set too much hope on events unfolding to its benefit and its ability to launch a mass agitation. The net result was that the action plan never really took off among the masses.

A senior Congress leader said what the Tehelka action plan showed was that the dominant sections of the party leadership, including Sonia, did not have a real understanding of how to go about forging a coalition at the national level. Paradoxically, the need for this sort of arrangement, as opposed to the Congress's own theory of one-party rule, was acknowledged at the Bangalore plenary.

But the big blow came from Gujarat. It was a sunny afternoon in New Delhi on 15 December 2002 when Sonia began to read a note summing up the state election results. As her eyes moved down the page, the worry lines on her forehead deepened. The paper in front of her, submitted by Congress general secretary in charge of Gujarat Kamal Nath, read as follows:

The Congress did not win a single seat within a 100-km radius of Godhra, where a coach of the Sabarmati Express was set ablaze on 27 February, killing 58.

Out of 65 seats that fell in areas affected by the riots, the BJP won 53. At Sayajigunj in the heart of Vadodara, the Congress had won the assembly by-election on 24 February by over 20,000 votes. Now, it lost by over 90,000 votes.

In Sabarmati, the Congress had won by 22,000 votes 15 months ago. Now party heavyweight and former deputy chief minister Narhari Amin was trounced by over 70,000 votes.

In seats farther from Godhra, the Congress posted comfortable victories. Ironically, despite a strong Hindutva wave, the Congress won in the temple towns of Somnath, Dwarka and Ambaji.

Wherever there were 25,000 or more Muslim voters, the Congress nominees generally lost as part of 'profound polarization' on communal lines.

The Congress lost all seats bordering Madhya Pradesh, which is headed for elections next year. The Congress's KHAM (Kshatriya-Harijan-Adivasi-Muslim) combination failed to take off as Kshatriyas—the community its state chief Shankersinh Vaghela belongs to—ensured the defeat of his son Mahendrasinh. The silent Hindutva wave transcended Patel, Kshatriya and other caste combinations.

The Congress fared badly in all tribal seats, taking a hit in the

entire stretch from Chhota Udaipur, Panchmahal and Dahod up
to Vadodara.

The party lost seats even where there was no dispute over ticket
distribution. The defeat of MP Dinsha Patel, Narhari Amin,
Sidhartha Patel and Naresh Raval was a proof.[12]

The message from Nath's note on the Gujarat results thus went
beyond the boundaries of the state. If 'Modi-ization' spread to
neighbouring Madhya Pradesh, Rajasthan and Maharashtra, Sonia
had no recipe to tackle it. The Congress president telephoned party
chief ministers, asking them to be more vigilant. 'We have a challenge
before us,' she said.

For Sonia's managers, the biggest problem was how to prevent the
Gujarat-model from being replicated in poll-bound states mostly ruled
by the Congress. In terms of numbers in the Lok Sabha, the Congress
has a daunting task, as it is a spent force in Uttar Pradesh, Bihar,
Bengal and Tamil Nadu.

Indicating the post-Gujarat mood that prevailed in the party, a
senior CWC member said: 'The trouble is that we know what the
problem is, but we do not know the solution.'

For Congressmen, Gujarat posed a bigger question: whether their
Prime Minister-in-waiting will make it in Delhi in the near future. At
the party headquarters, the unanimous view was that after the Gujarat
verdict, politics would not be the same in the country. Some of Sonia's
managers fear that if Hindutva forces gain currency at the national
level, partymen could start viewing her as a liability. The favourable
verdicts of fourteen states suddenly started looking insignificant and
once again, Sonia began to look vulnerable.

Perhaps it was a combination of these factors that prompted Sonia
to skip lunch on 15 December 2002, the day the Gujarat results came
out. She did not see any visitors till 4 p.m.

Soon the knives were out in the Congress over the party's strategy
to focus blatantly on majority votes during the assembly polls. While
it posed no threat to Sonia's leadership or her unassailable position
within the party, under attack was the troika of Young Turks—Kamal

Nath, Ambika Soni and Ahmad Patel—who were key members in formulating the Gujarat strategy.

Soon after the Gujarat polls, CWC members advised Sonia to pick up the threads from Panchmarhi, where she had promised to restore the party's lost glory and make the Congress a party of the best and brightest. Some suggested that the party should try to get back breakaway factions like Sharad Pawar's Nationalist Congress Party and Mamata Banerjee's Trinamul Congress on the lines of the merger of Tamil Maanila Congress in Tamil Nadu.

Others said the Congress would be able to derive advantage from the return of these breakaway factions only if it showed the capability to propel both itself and its newfound allies to power in the states as well as in the Centre. As a senior CWC member pointed out, ultimately all the questions boiled down to gaining power, which alone would fulfil the larger objective of regaining past glory.[13]

Soon after the Gujarat elections, assembly polls were held in Himachal Pradesh. The BJP, buoyed by the Gujarat results, brought in Hindutva hardliner Narendra Modi for campaigning, but anti-incumbency and deep factionalism proved fatal for the ruling BJP. The Himachal victory somewhat restored Sonia's confidence. After all, Himachal had more than 96 per cent of Hindu population and if it could not be swayed by Modi's rhetoric, there was still hope for the Sonia-led Congress.

Sonia decided to go on the offensive. She summoned a meeting of the Congress chief ministers at Srinagar where no national leader had dared to hold a political conclave in nearly two decades. The Srinagar meet was a roaring success in terms of Sonia's public image even as the Vajpayee regime privately lamented it, saying it stretched the security arrangements in the troubled state. The message from Srinagar was clear—the Congress under Sonia has a pan-Indian identity.

A month later, the Congress president sought to assert her leadership once again, convening a brain-storming session of the party think tank at Shimla. As Sonia sat through protracted debates on the need for coalition, sipping jasmine tea, the think tank made two critical formulations—the Congress is ready for a broad-based secular alliance, a rainbow coalition of 'like-mined parties'. The second part of the formulation was a personal triumph for Sonia. It said as and when such a coalition becomes operational, Sonia would head it.

The Shimla resolve made waves discomforting her political opponents like Sharad Pawar and Mulayam Singh Yadav. Political exigencies in Maharashtra and Uttar Pradesh were such that these mercurial regional satraps were desperately seeking Congress support. Pawar and Mulayam began to look for cover, saying it was premature to discuss the leadership issue. Pawar said it was not necessary that the biggest group should head such a coalition. Mulayam went a step further saying Sonia's foreign origin was no longer an issue.

For the first time, Sonia tried to clear some doubts surrounding her leadership. In her presidential address, Sonia told party delegates that as party chief she independently takes all crucial decisions. The remark was unusual from a reticent person like Sonia but her close advisers said she decided to go public to scotch gossip that she was guided by a coterie.

Thus, the effort to attain power at the Centre was indeed a test of Sonia's leadership qualities. Her actions in the last few years have shown that despite having the support of the rank and file, she has been overly cautious with regard to the many groups in the party.

Political commentators like Kanti Bajpai and Mahesh Rangarajan are convinced that Sonia is here to stay. Recalling his interactions on foreign policy issues with Sonia, Bajpai said, 'She seems prepared to listen to all sorts of voices,' adding that earlier she gave away little. But by 2002, her body language showed quickness of response and a candidness in stating her own views even if it meant disagreeing with you.[14] Rangarajan said that Sonia's biggest problem was that she was a general of a shrunken army that had to battle on many fronts before hoping to win the war. Giving some concrete examples, Rangarajan said, 'It remains to be seen how she wins over the great Indian middle class without alienating the poorer sections of society. How will she win back Dalits and farmers who have moved away from the Congress?'[15]

Others are not so assured of her future success. Another noted political commentator, Saeed Naqvi, is unsure about Sonia's ability to reach 7 Race Course Road. 'We really do not know what she stands for. All we know is secrecy and a coterie,' he lamented. Sociologist Dipankar Gupta said Sonia's problem was that she was neither a run-of-the-mill neta nor a visionary. Yet he thinks that if she succeeds in bringing all the secular forces on one side, she can surmount her opponents.

Certainly her victory in many state polls and the enthusiasm she has generated in the Congress ranks offer her an opportunity to consolidate her position in the party and move towards 7 Race Course Road.

Even as the debate about Sonia Gandhi's leadership skills and inexperience continued, she sprang a surprise that turned out to be a major personal triumph for her. Two days after attending a 'unity conclave' of opposition parties at CPM MP Somnath Chatterjee's residence where she relished hilsa fish, Sonia decided to move a no-confidence motion against Prime Minister Atal Bihari Vajpayee.

The motion moved on 18 August 2003 indicted the Vajpayee regime on several counts ranging from corruption to anarchy. It was predictably defeated, given the Opposition strength in Parliament. What it did succeed in doing, however, was to pitch her as an alternative leader to Vajpayee. Here was the leader of the Opposition leading from the front, mixing aggression with wit, no longer the first-time MP who struggled with words as she took the oath as member of Parliament. The message was clear: any future collaboration with other non-NDA partners would have to be under her leadership.

FIFTEEN

LOOKING TO THE FUTURE

S onia talks, off and on, of beginning at the beginning, that is, what she said when she took over as Congress president.

It signals a journey back in time to the days she publicly proclaimed rebuilding the Congress as her political goal. She lost her way at a tea party on 29 March 1999, but since then, she has tried to pick up the thread. Leaning back on a sofa, part of the three-piece seating arrangement that is the first island near the door in the vast drawing room of the heavily guarded 10 Janpath, Sonia chooses her words carefully, brow creased in deliberation.

A picture of her mother-in-law adorns the spotless white wall of the drawing room, sharing the space with portraits of Mahatma Gandhi, Jawaharlal Nehru and Rajiv. Sonia is promising people-oriented policies, words that have fallen into disgrace through overuse since the 'garibi hatao' slogan of the 1970s. She tries to lift them out of the quicksand of poll-time politics. The Congress, she says, will make a sincere attempt to pass on the benefits of development to the poor, if voted to power.

Sonia does not sell dreams too hard. She seems optimistic of being able to implement all-round development, in areas including education, greater gender sensivity, availability of clean drinking water, environmental awareness and social welfare. These are major problems befitting the agenda of a party like the Congress. For example, more than 2,00,000 villages across the country do not have clean drinking water. Nearly a third of the country's population has no access to basic literacy. Sonia says these basic issues need to be addressed again, referring to her speeches outside and inside Parliament and asserting that raising these issues should not be dismissed as rhetoric.

She stills admits to entering politics with reluctance, but does not voice any regrets—having just felt the sting of a campaign over her foreign origins that resulted in the exit of Sharad Pawar and P.A. Sangma from the party.

It was said in those dark days of May 1999 that she had again withdrawn into her shell, that Priyanka was her sole companion. Will she now accompany her mother on the election trail? Uttar Pradesh partymen have been asking for her. Sonia listens to questions intently, bending forward, hands folded neatly in her lap.

The mother will neither encourage nor discourage. Priyanka will have to decide for herself. Her upbringing should have equipped her to take independent decisions. Sonia smiles at the subtle suggestion. Shouldn't she have been insistent rather than letting Priyanka make up her mind? After all, she confesses to being in the hunt for a new breed of party member—middle class, educated and interested in a political career.

That takes her back to the beginning, to when she took over as party president in March 1998 in Panchmarhi. The resolution taken there announced boldly that the Congress wanted to be a party of the 'best and brightest'.[1]

It is not clear how it will return to the roots. The Congress did begin with the kind of people she professes to be seeking. But she claims to have discovered the other half of the whole that the Congress once was—faceless workers who are not in the party to be ministers.

As the Congress party chief, Sonia has learnt many lessons. One of them is her antipathy towards coalitions. Sonia viewed even positive signals from her adversaries, like Mulayam Singh Yadav and Sharad Pawar, as part of a carefully crafted strategy that went beyond floor coordination in Parliament. Close associates like Digvijay Singh said that Sonia had very sharp political instincts, claiming that she was opposed to the idea of joining hands with Laloo Prasad Yadav in Bihar, reeling under misgovernance, but gave in after the Congress Working Committee members forced her to back Laloo after the 2000 assembly polls.

In her assessment, the third front protagonists envisaged a leading role for themselves on the premise that in the composition of a new Lok Sabha, the Congress would be in no position to stake a claim without their participation. The second part of their argument was based on the assumption that inexperienced Sonia would be too reluctant to head any rainbow coalition.

But the AICC chief has different plans. Having burnt her fingers in May 1999, when she failed to stitch together a coalition after the fall of the Vajpayee regime, Sonia is circumspect about joining hands with the 'third front' to keep 'communal forces' at bay.

Roping in Mamata's Trinamul Congress was near impossible on two counts. First, the bitterness of the Bengal polls was still fresh and more important, Mamata's outfit cannot be anywhere near the Left. Instead of joining the secular front, Sonia focused on Punjab, Uttaranchal and Manipur, weaning these states from the BJP and the NDA partners.

According to Sonia, the Vajpayee government should continue till 2004, when general elections will be held. In the meantime she hopes to shape up as a mature politician and go to the voters on the development plank, showcasing the states where the Congress is in power as models of good governance. Sonia believes that time alone would convince the voters that coalitions are not ideal for kick-starting growth and all-round development.

The AICC chief made it clear that she has no magic wand to bring the Congress back to Raisina Hill. Many Congress leaders were of the view that the logic of Sonia's entry in politics was a revival of the party in Uttar Pradesh, Bihar, Tamil Nadu and Bengal that account for more than 200 Lok Sabha seats. Sonia admitted her failure to bring back the good old days of the party in these four states. But sources close to her maintain that it was beyond her individual capacity to revive the Congress in a state like Uttar Pradesh when the entire organizational network had collapsed and the state leadership was packed with political has-beens.

Fourteen top Congress leaders from UP, holding key posts in the CWC, Central Election Committee and Uttar Pradesh Congress Committee (UPCC), have their permanent residence in Delhi or in adjoining Noida, which falls in UP. Each of them wants to get into a party panel but declined to contest assembly or Lok Sabha polls. The infighting in the UPCC was so intense that Sonia was flooded with requests for change of leadership before UPCC chief Sri Prakash Jaiswal could take charge at Lucknow's Mall Avenue office in 2001! In many districts, party offices remained intact but signboards changed. Instead of the UPCC, they read Bahujan Samaj Party, Loktantrik Party, Apna Dal, Samajwadi Party and Bharatiya Janata Party.

Uttar Pradesh had witnessed a slight shift in 1999 when the Congress bagged ten Lok Sabha seats and its vote percentage crossed the single digit mark to 18 per cent. But soon it was back to square one. Veterans blamed Sonia's political inexperience. She preferred Salman Khurshid to Rajesh Pilot as state Congress chief, but Khurshid stayed on in Delhi and opened the battle on too many fronts. His move to target Mulayam Singh Yadav (with Sonia's blessings) boomeranged. On the one hand, Khurshid projected himself as a Muslim leader, and on the other he tried, albeit unsuccessfully, to project Yadav as some sort of betrayer of the Muslim cause. The Muslims of UP were not prepared to buy that argument, even if they had some sympathy for Sonia and faith in her credentials. Once again the party fell between two stools in the caste and religious divide in the state.

For some inexplicable reason, Sonia stayed away from Uttar Pradesh for long gaps. There were numerous proposals that she should hold CWC meetings at Allahabad and interact with workers. She planned to travel by road and train, but largely the plan remained on paper. Once she visited eastern UP by the Vaishali Express, intermingling with journalists and locals, and told Sanjeev Sinha of *Indian Express* that she would be undertaking such tours more often, but it did not happen.[2] Sometimes the move was shelved on grounds of security, at other times it was called off as one faction of the UPCC did not relish the prospect of Sonia visiting strongholds of the other faction.

Sonia's failure to revive UP put intense pressure on the entry of Priyanka in politics. According to Sonia, there is not a single state leader who has not demanded Priyanka directly or indirectly. UP Congressmen are unanimous that Priyanka alone can shore up the party's prospects. After all, Priyanka was solely responsible for the shocking defeat of Arun Nehru. Many believe that her sustained campaign would demolish the likes of Mulayam, Mayawati and Rajnath Singh. Women candidates who enjoy mass support and have their ear to the ground, like Uma Bharti and Sushma Swaraj, have recognized Priyanka's power. Giving generous compliments, Bharti said that Priyanka could be a one-time wonder in defeating the BJP in UP![3]

The call to draft Priyanka ranged from fielding her in the assembly to making her the Youth Congress chief. But Sonia remained unfazed. Priyanka herself remained reluctant. She gave birth to Rehan on 29 August 2000 and devoted the next year entirely to him. Priyanka even curtailed her periodic visits to Amethi, which greatly annoyed party sympathizers. The news of her second pregnancy in February 2002 sealed all speculation about her immediate entry in politics. A hopeless show in February 2002 in UP and a subsequent split in January 2003 have contributed to Sonia's worries. In UP, for instance, the Congress forfeited deposits in as many as 325 out of 403 assembly seats.[4]

While there was a general consensus that Priyanka would be a great source of strength for the Congress, some have advised Sonia against her entry, pointing out that she may emerge as a power centre.

Initially, the whole argument amused Sonia. The mother could never think in terms of a daughter emerging as a challenger at any stage. Slowly, however, a realization set in that it would be more prudent to save Priyanka for the time being and bring her in closer to the general elections, where Sonia and the Congress would be waging a decisive war against political opponents.

In Bihar, Sonia ran out of ideas when her party collectively decided to play second fiddle to Laloo Prasad Yadav's Rashtriya Janata Dal (RJD). The decision to join the government of Rabri Devi, wife of Laloo Prasad, was not an easy one for Sonia and the CWC given the casteist profile of Laloo and the RJD and the corruption charges against the RJD leadership. However, Sonia decided to go along with the majority view when the state leadership caved in. She was also convinced by the argument that communalism was the greater enemy and so the fight against corruption was put on the backburner.

Not everyone in the Congress was happy with this decision. Rajesh Pilot and Jitendra Prasada raised muted criticism but went along with the majority view. Sonia was puzzled by some senior leaders who chose to speak for the alliance in the CWC meetings but gave different statements in the press. She, however, decided not to make an issue of it, simply directing Oscar Fernandes to record their views as stated in the CWC meetings. This documentation gave her leverage whenever some leaders tried to take a different line.

While dealing with Bihar, Sonia was appalled by the sorry state of affairs. She wondered how P.V. Narasimha Rao and Sitaram Kesri permitted so much drift, nepotism and corruption in the Bihar Pradesh Congress Committee (BPCC). Unlike UP, where she saw a ray of hope, Bihar was seen as a lost cause as Bihar Congress leaders were seen as being unwilling to put in the requisite effort. Most state leaders had already worked out some tacit understanding with Yadav. Many were allegedly on his 'payroll'. Under these circumstances, Sonia chose the simple route of 'consolidating secular fabric'—a high-sounding formulation that left many Congressmen somewhat baffled.[5]

She conveyed a similar helplessness while dealing with Tamil Nadu. As in UP and Bihar, the Congress had lost its support base there. There were several constituencies where the number of primary and active Congress workers exceeded the number of votes pulled by a Congress candidate! While in Bihar many Congress leaders had become 'parasites' dependent on Yadav's largesse, in Tamil Nadu, many senior leaders had struck individual deals with Jayalalitha. When she mooted the idea of going it alone in Tamil Nadu, there were virtually no takers either in the Tamil Nadu Congress Committee (TNCC) or in the CWC.

Sonia had difficulty in striking a rapport with Jayalalitha. She found her to be too imperious and temperamental. Much before she entered politics, Sonia had learnt a great deal about Jayalalitha from Rajiv. She was aware that he accorded special importance to her, such as driving down to Poes Garden (her residence) even when he was Prime Minister.

Sonia had reliable reports that Jayalalitha held her in low esteem. The ADMK supremo was said to feel that Sonia lacked political tact and experience. Sonia then decided to deal with Jayalalitha through an intermediary. She first chose Karunakaran, but Jayalalitha rejected him saying he was unreliable. Arjun Singh was on good terms with the ADMK chief, but Sonia felt that if he were used the coterie charge that Singh, Fotedar, Natwar Singh and George were manipulating her would gain currency.

She then fielded Sharad Pawar, who proved to be too smart. In 1999 while Sonia waited with bated breath about the outcome of the seat-sharing formula between the Congress and the ADMK, Pawar and Jayalalitha were plotting a coup. Within days of Pawar's return from Chennai, he dropped the bombshell, challenging Sonia's ability to be Prime Minister on the ground of her foreign origins. Though Sonia does not say anything about Jayalalitha's role, many leaders close to her suspected Jayalalitha of encouraging Pawar to dislodge Sonia and take the reins of the Congress party.

Dr Manmohan Singh replaced Pawar. But the good doctor was too apolitical for Jayalalitha's taste. Pranab Mukherjee abruptly replaced Dr Singh. An industrial house reportedly tried to bring them together, but Jayalalitha missed no opportunity in showing the Congress in poor light. On one occasion, when the haggling over seats reached its nadir, Jayalalitha wanted to know the names of the constituencies sought by Pranab. The leader from Bengal fumbled, and Jayalalitha smiled triumphantly. She also humiliated the state Congress leadership by refusing to meet TNCC office-bearers accompanying Pranab.

The Jayalalitha–Sonia ego clash came out in the open when the ADMK chief publicly snubbed her, refusing to share the dais at a meeting in Vallipuram in Tamil Nadu during the 1999 election campaign. Sonia waited in vain while Jayalalitha's secretary furnished a lame excuse that she was running behind schedule.

In 2001 when political exigencies forced Jayalalitha and Sonia to come together, the AICC chief came up with a novel idea of dealing with a third party. The breakaway Congress leader G.K. Moopanar served as a go-between. Harkishen Singh Surjeet, the CPM general secretary and a strong votary of consolidation of secular forces, suggested Moopanar's name. Moopanar conducted the negotiations honestly, briefing Sonia on a daily basis. Finally, Jayalalitha doled out fifteen assembly seats for the Congress, which was too little, but Moopanar convinced Sonia to accept the share, promising to merge his breakaway group with the parent organization. After elections, Moopanar met Sonia a few times preparing grounds for the merger, but he did not live long enough to see that happen.

Moopanar had a special standing at 10 Janpath. He was a sort of exception in the sense that Sonia's doors were always open for him even though he was heading a breakaway group. For Sonia, he was a powerful regional satrap, an expert in southern politics. He was so dependable that when he left the Congress, Narasimha Rao could not resist asking for him while short-listing the party candidates for Andhra Pradesh during the 1996 general elections. R.K. Dhawan, who was sitting next to Narasimha Rao in the Congress Central Election Committee meeting, gently reminded him that Moopanar was no longer in the party.

For Sonia, too, Moopanar was one man on whom Rajiv and Indira used to count heavily. Moopanar was never hesitant to give advice to Sonia on national and regional issues, and she greatly valued his comments. In their conversations, Moopanar invariably disarmed her by expressing his desire for merger and then enlisting the problems within his Tamil Maanila Congress that had to do with P. Chidambaram's stiff opposition to returning to the Congress. Interestingly, Chidambaram continued to be a trustee of the Rajiv Gandhi Foundation in spite of his political differences. It was an example of how Sonia kept political and non-political issues separate.

West Bengal posed a different set of problems for Sonia. Unlike Bihar, Tamil Nadu and Uttar Pradesh, the organizational set-up and support base in the state had remained somewhat intact, but once again, political exigencies forced Sonia's hands and the defeat of the mahajot (Congress–Trinamul alliance) in the 2001 assembly polls pushed the party back to square one.

Sonia faced a major political dilemma that went beyond West Bengal. It was about the need for a broad-based front against the Left to drive them out of Writers Building. But such a front had to have the BJP, a political outcaste in the Hindi heartland. Mamata Banerjee and the Congress's own Ghani Khan Chowdhury insisted on the BJP's inclusion on the grounds that it was not perceived as communal there in the way it is perceived to be in UP, MP, Gujarat, Maharashtra, etc. They argued that unless the entire anti-Left vote bank was organized and brought under one umbrella, the CPM led-coalition would stay on.

But the argument had no takers in Delhi where almost the entire CWC rejected the theory without ado. Arjun Singh, Ghulam Nabi Azad and others argued that it would be suicidal and a blot on the Congress's secular credentials if it were seen to be inching closer to the BJP. A.K. Antony and Karunakaran too issued an ultimatum as they were also facing assembly polls in Kerala. Sonia was told that the party would lose its unique selling proposition as one party that had never joined hands with communal forces. Sonia saw great merit in the argument and at the cost of losing West Bengal, she forced Banerjee's hands too. A number of party leaders left the Congress because of the alliance.

Sonia said that she had no regret about her determined refusal to join hands with the BJP, directly or indirectly. For thousands of party workers who had lost their life, been beaten up and suffered humiliation, the fight against communalism was too important an issue. Instead of reviving the party and holding street demonstrations, the AICC chief continued with Pranab Mukherjee as West Bengal Pradesh Congress Committee chief, who openly said his heart was not in the job.

The Congress leaders backed the Sonia line in Bengal, but they wondered if the Left would reciprocate the gesture in backing the Congress for its bid at the Centre. They said that the Left would raise the bogey of third-front rule even if it were numerically inferior to the Congress. A majority of Congress leaders are extremely wary of joining hands with the non-BJP opposition. The Congress is one political party that has a pan-Indian identity. In Andhra Pradesh, it is at loggerheads with Chandrababu Naidu's Telugu Desam Party (TDP). In Bengal, Kerala and Tripura, the Left is its main opponent. In Orissa, the Congress and the Biju Janata Dal (BJD) are the main rivals while in the entire North-East, it is a contender for power pitted against regional parties. So, like the BJP, it does not have the luxury of zero presence in the east or south. The question that constantly limits Sonia's room for manoeuvre while considering setting up an alternative front against the BJP-led NDA is that the Congress has no political space to share with the likes of the Akali Dal, BJD, TDP, DMK, Asom Gana Parishad (AGP), Shiv Sena and other regional players.

A number of academic and political discussions have failed to offer a solution. In Panchmarhi, the party collectively decided on going it alone—ekla chalo re. Leaders recalled the glorious past and unanimously pleaded to bring back the good old days. However, once in Delhi, political compulsions forced them to join hands with Laloo and the RJD to keep the communal forces at bay in Bihar, and tie up with Jayalalitha to check the rise of the BJP in Tamil Nadu. The point was hotly debated by the Antony committee report that probed the causes of defeat in the 1998 general elections.

On her part, Sonia says she been trying to infuse fresh blood in the party. Soon after taking over, she tried to clarify the party's stand on all key issues, and made several politically correct statements such as offering an apology over the 1984 anti-Sikh riots and demolition of Babri Masjid. 'Just about a month before he was assassinated, my husband had said to me that if ever an attempt was made to touch the masjid he would stand in front of it, and they would have to kill him first,' she said.

She also expressed her anguish over Operation Blue Star in 1984 that saw large-scale destruction of the Golden Temple, the Sikhs' holiest shrine. In her apology for the anti-Sikh riots of 1984 that followed Indira's assassination by two of her Sikh bodyguards, she said, 'I feel that this kind of an incident should not have happened, and my husband Rajiv Gandhi felt the same.'[6]

She said she decided to join the Congress because she wanted to serve the poor—'Mujhe koi rajnaitik post nahi chahiye. Main is liye aayi hoon ki aapki taklif meri taklif hain' (I do not aspire to any position. I have joined politics to share people's problems). The AICC chief said the Congress alone knew how to govern, 'We have the experience to run a government . . . The politics of division is destroying what was carefully nurtured over the years by our great leaders.'

On numerous occasions, Sonia declared her love for India, that it was inseparable from her life as she became a bride here—'Yeh mere suhaag ka desh hai aur meri akhri saans tak rahega. Meri mang ka sindoor is zamin mein mila hai. (This is the country where I got married. Until my last breath, this will remain my country.)'[7]

There were occasions that showed that Sonia may be a politician, but not always a calculating one. She stumped Mamata Banerjee soon after the Trinamul Congress chief was sworn in as Cabinet minister on 14 October 1999 by asking her to return to the Congress.

In what was obviously a spur-of-the-moment move, Banerjee strode straight towards Sonia, seated in the front row in the forecourt of Rashtrapati Bhavan, after being sworn in. The two ladies hugged warmly, as startled politicians watched. And then Sonia did her own spontaneous bit. 'Congratulations,' she said, 'But will you come back?'[8]

Both realized that the invitation was only a gesture, an impulse of the moment, but there were tears in Banerjee's eyes nevertheless. There were tears in her eyes even on the drive back home, Trinamul leaders said. 'For a while I could not understand whether she is with the BJP or the Congress,' one of her associates said.[9]

They maintained, though, that there was no question of even thinking about returning to the Congress. Sonia too was not expecting her to respond. If her advisers are to be believed, she uttered the words without expecting anything in return. 'This was one of the things which cannot be explained in words. It was as if she could not help saying that,' a party leader who witnessed the encounter said.

Banerjee repaid Sonia's gesture by blocking a piece of legislation that was aimed at barring persons of foreign origins from holding high office. When the proposal was made in one of the first Cabinet meetings convened by Vajpayee, Banerjee led the charge saying that such a gesture would not go down well with a great many. Ram Vilas Paswan and some others backed her. Vajpayee then intervened and the move was shelved.

The personal bond between Banerjee and Sonia came in handy when the Trinamul chief left the NDA to join hands with the Congress in the West Bengal assembly polls in 2001. However, the bond could not withstand the stigma of defeat and the intrigues of Somen Mitra, Pranab Mukherjee and A.B.A. Ghani Khan Chowdhury. Banerjee abruptly snapped ties with the Congress and returned to the NDA. The AICC chief made no bid to keep the alliance going. However, she did convey to her the regret over the defeat of the alliance. Banerjee too called up Sonia regretting the parting, but she emphasized that she would continue to value her.

In her chequered political career, Sonia has shown that she is a great learner. She may not have been outstanding in academics, but she has a good grasp of major issues confronting the nation. She does not believe in purging and summary removals. When Arjun Singh and others had raised the banner of revolt, Sonia did not join them, though she had sympathy with their cause. She did not want to head a faction of the Congress. She was even reluctant to throw out Pawar, Sangma and Tariq Anwar though she had reason to feel betrayed. Pranab Mukherjee, Arjun Singh and others convinced her that party workers would not settle for anything less than the trio's removal. As of now, she is willing to take them back provided they give up the issue of her foreign origins.

Is Sonia serious about taking a shy at the top job? Will she propose someone else's name in case she is not acceptable?

Some consider her as saintly, a benevolent sort of person who would give up power to go higher in the public esteem. They say Indians hero-worship a person who shuns power. Some political editors had gone to the extent of claiming that Sonia wanted Dr Manmohan Singh to be the Prime Minister when the Vajpayee government fell in April 1999. Nothing could be farther from the truth. Sharad Pawar, who was leader of the Opposition, had collected letters of support and each letter had specifically mentioned Sonia's name. Rashtrapati Bhavan sources too confirmed that when Sonia met President Narayanan as the Congress Parliamentary Party leader, she made no mention of Dr Singh or anyone else. It is also a fact that Sonia's mother and sisters had all come to Delhi in April 1999 ostensibly to witness Sonia's swearing in that never took place.

Sonia does not disclose her intentions, but those who are in the know assert that she alone would be a claimant for the top job. After all, the crowds that come for her public meetings accept her. They say a lot of hard work goes into being Congress president. It is not easy for a chronic asthma patient to tour 140-odd dusty places in sixty days to campaign for the party and work sixteen hours a day round the year.

A lot would also depend upon the numbers game in future

elections. If the Congress gets more than 200-250 parliamentary seats in the next round of general elections, Sonia would face least resistance. However, if the Congress tally stops around the 200 mark, the third front leaders like Mulayam Singh Yadav will have a say in forcing her to opt for a coalition in which she would have a clear disadvantage to head the government. If the Congress further slips and gets under 200, the party chief may face greater leadership challenge. In such a scenario, leaders like P.V. Narasimha Rao, if free from legal tangles, would become active on grounds of a proven track record.

More significantly, the composition of the Congress is such that the winner takes it all. The party has a tradition that there can be just one power centre. Till Nehru was alive, he was everything and the organization had to bow before him. During the Narasimha Rao regime too it became clear that he alone was in command. It is a different matter that the party paid a political price, but Rao had little difficulty in completing the full term as Prime Minister.

In 2004, Sonia will be held accountable if the party fails to cross the 200 Lok Sabha seats mark. To win a clear mandate demands 272 seats, but Sonia would not face much of problem as the Left would back her to bring her closer to South Block. However, if the party fails to get near the 200 mark, there would be a different set of permutations and combinations that may force Sonia to stay out.

For many Congress leaders, there is a Priyanka angle in Sonia becoming the Prime Minister. She must provide continuity for Priyanka to shape up as a politician.

In the past few years Sonia has matured as a parliamentarian, and during her visit to the US the international community accepted her as leader of the Opposition. Sources close to her said in a Cabinet form of government with Dr Manmohan Singh, Arjun Singh, Natwar Singh, Digvijay Singh, Ajit Jogi, Mani Shankar Aiyar and other younger MPs, Sonia would be able to run the government satisfactorily as long as she remained sincere to her causes.

Congressmen also realize that the task of crowning Sonia would not be easy. But they do not fear much protest. In their assessment, by the time that happens, Sonia's main adversary, the BJP, would be far too discredited to raise the bogey of foreign origins. Moreover, Sonia is no alien before the masses as she has already gained acceptability as a politician. What needs to be proved to the great Indian middle class is administrative skill.

NOTES

Chapter One: A Tragedy in Sriperumbudur

1. Sonia Gandhi, *Rajiv* (New Delhi: Penguin Books India, 1992), 15.
2. Suman Dubey, *Hindustan Times* (23 May 1991).
3. As told to the author by M. Afzal.
4. Gandhi, *Rajiv*, 9.

Chapter Two: The Search for a Successor

1. As stated by a senior Congress leader.
2. Author's conversations and interviews with leaders present outside 10 Janpath on that day.
3. Congress party records. The annual general secretary's report.
4. This input was given to the author by more than one leader who was present in the meeting.
5. This input was given to the author by more than one leader who was present in the meeting.
6. Based on inputs from senior party leaders.
7. Sonia's statement was reported in the media and read out at the CWC meeting.
8. *Hindustan Times, Telegraph, National Herald* (24 May 1991).
9. *Hindustan Times, Telegraph, National Herald* (24 May 1991).
10. *Hindustan Times* (25 May 1991).
11. As narrated by Pawar in a meeting with the press at his residence in March 1999.

12. Input from a chief minister of a Congress-ruled state.
13. In conversation with the author.
14. Stated by those present on the occasion.
15. *Hindustan Times* (25-26 May 1991).
16. As told to the author.
17. *Hindustan Times* (26 May 1991).
18. Narrated by close associates of Pawar.
19. As told to the author later on.
20. Dhawan's interview to news agencies in July 1991.
21. *India Today* (31 August 1991).

Chapter Three: A Long Journey from Orbassano

1. Tim McGirk, 'That Gandhi Magic,' *Time Asia* (2 March 1998).
2. Vaiju Naravane, 'In Maino Country…,' *Frontline* (25 April-8 May 1998).
3. Mohammad Yunus, *Persons, Passions, Politics* (New Delhi: Vikas, 1980), 30.
4. Jaipal Reddy, Congress's chief spokesman.
5. In telephonic conversation with the author.
6. Authenticated by Peter Bingley of the Cambridge Advisory Service via email to the author.
7. Gandhi, *Rajiv*, 1.
8. Gandhi, *Rajiv*, 1.
9. Gandhi, *Rajiv*, 2.
10. Rupa Chatterjee, *Sonia Gandhi: The Lady in Shadow* (New Delhi: Butala Publications, 1998), 17.
11. Eric Silver et al., 'Political Pilot Who Learned a Bit Too Fast: Obituary of Rajiv Gandhi,' *Guardian* (UK) (22 May 1991), and Suzanne Goldenberg, 'Gandhi assassination' *Guardian* (UK) (22 May 1991).
12. Gandhi, *Rajiv*, 3.
13. As told to the author by Mohammad Yunus and Mohsina Kidwai.
14. Nicholas Nugent, *Rajiv Gandhi: Son of a Dynasty* (London: BBC Books, 1990), 44-45.

Chapter Four: A Tale of Two Bahus

1. Yunus, *Persons*, 45.
2. B.K. Nehru, *Nice Guys Finish Second* (New Delhi: Penguin Books India, 1997), 579. Also cited in Chatterjee, *Sonia*, 37.

3. Khushwant Singh, *Truth, Love and a Little Malice: An Autobiography* (New Delhi: Penguin Books India, 2002), 287.
4. Narrated by Biju Patnaik to the author in 1993.
5. A. Surya Prakash quoting the Gupta Commission report in the *Pioneer* (10 May 1999) in Dina Nath Mishra, ed., *Sonia 'The Unknown'* (New Delhi: India First Foundation, 1991), 145.
6. Minhaz Merchant, *Rajiv Gandhi: The End of a Dream* (New Delhi: Penguin Books India, 1991), 73.
7. As told to the author.
8. Vrinda Gopinath, op-ed interview of Maneka Gandhi, *Indian Express* (New Delhi) (12 November 2001).
9. Pupul Jayakar, *Indira Gandhi* (New Delhi: Penguin Books India, 1992), 435. See also Khushwant Singh, 'Of Love and Loathing,' *India Today* (31 October 1995).
10. Gandhi, *Rajiv*, 6.
11. Gandhi, *Rajiv*, 7.
12. Based upon off the record conservation with those who were in the know and closely followed the events then.
13. *Indian Express* (12 November 2001).
14. Doordarshan interview (11 September 1999). This interview was the basis of an article by UNI called '"Sonia Is Unfit to Become PM" Says Sis-in-law Maneka' and published on Rediff.com (11 September 1999). See also 'Sonia, Rajiv Deserted Indira in '77: Maneka,' *Times of India* (New Delhi) (19 February 1999).

Chapter Five: The Prime Minister's Wife

1. Pushpa Bharti, 'Sonia Gandhi,' *Dharmayug* (15 June 1985). Also in Chatterjee, *Sonia*, 80.
2. As narrated by close family friends.
3. Pawar made these observations while speaking to a group of journalists, including the author, in February 1999 in Baramati, Maharashtra.
4. *Indian Express* (12 November 2001).
5. As told to the author.
6. Gandhi, *Rajiv*, 13.
7. As told to the author.
8. The incident was related to the author by Chandrakar.

Chapter Six: A Tug of War

1. Inputs from senior Congress party leaders.
2. Sonia's letter to Prime Minister P.V. Narasimha Rao in 1991.
3. Widely reported in media. Also confirmed by sources close to Narasimha Rao and members of the Congress Working Committee.
4. As told to the author by two RGF trustees.
5. As witnessed by the author.
6. The sequence of events was narrated by Karunarakan and others.
7. As told to the author.
8. Based on the author's interaction with Jogi and Digvijay Singh.
9. Ritu Sarin, *Asia Week* (22 September 1995).
10. *Asian Age* (26 August 1995).
11. As told to the author.

Chapter Seven: Educating Sonia

1. Gopal Sarvepalli, *Jawaharlal Nehru: A Biography* (New Delhi: Oxford University Press, 1975), 643-45.
2. Nicholas Nugent, *Rajiv Gandhi: Son of a Dynasty* (London: BBC Books, 1990), 40, and Silver, 'Political Pilot.'
3. Gandhi, *Rajiv*, 12.
4. J.B. Patnaik's interview with Nirmal Pathak in *Dainik Jagran* (10 February 1999).
5. Told to a group of journalists including the author in Baramati in February 1999.
6. Close Pawar associates had confirmed that a survey was conducted.
7. Bhavdeep Kang, 'Educating Sonia,' *Outlook* (6 July 1998).
8. Told to Pushpa Bharti, 'Sonia Gandhi,' *Dharmayug* (15 June 1985). Also in Gandhi, *Rajiv*, 3.
9. Also admitted by several Congress party MPs.
10. Speaking to the author soon after the debate (29 October 1999).
11. Mishra, *Sonia 'The Unknown'*, 6-7.

Chapter Eight: Sonia Takes Over the Congress

1. These observations were made in the author's presence.
2. These remarks were made by Kesri days before his death when he called the author for a chat.
3. Vaddakan later rose to become secretary of the AICC's media department.

4. Inputs given by persons extremely close to Sonia.
5. Sonia's speeches at Bangalore on 12 and 21 January 1998 in Jodhpur, Rajasthan.
6. Narrated by a person who was on the flight.
7. CWC resolution adopted on 5 March 1998.
8. Kesri made these observations in the presence of the author.

Chapter Nine: The Favoured Few

1. The observation was arrived at by numerous informal interactions with these leaders.
2. As told to the author.
3. Gadgil was the Congress's longest serving party spokesman.
4. Gadgil made the observation to the author on several occasions.
5. As told to the author by Gadgil.

Chapter Ten: Sonia's Faith

1. The incident was narrated by a Karnataka Congress MP.
2. Subbi Rami Reddy is currently the AICC secretary in charge of media.
3. Gadgil made these views public through articles and press statements.
4. As told to the author.
5. Sonia made these remarks on 12 January 1999 at the Ramakrishna Mission in New Delhi.
6. Sangma made these observations speaking to a senior journalist.
7. Deliberations at the CWC meeting on 14 January 1999.
8. Mishra, *Sonia 'The Unknown'*, 16.
9. As told to the author.

Chapter Eleven: The New Generation

1. *Hindustan Times* (12 January 1998) and *Telegraph* (12 January 1998).
2. *Telegraph* (12 January 1998).
3. Karnataka Congress unit leaders.
4. Nugent, *Rajiv Gandhi*, 5, and inputs from family sources.
5. Bhavna Vij, *Indian Express* (9 March 1998).
6. Gandhi, *Rajiv*, 1.
7. As told to the author.
8. *Times of India* (4 January 2002).
9. *Outlook* (15 January 2002).

10. Addressing the press at Mount Abu in November 2002.
11. The author was on board the plane with Sonia and Priyanka when she made the remark.
12. As told to the author.
13. Gandhi, *Rajiv*, 8.
14. *Sportsworld*, 13-19 September 1989.
15. *Sportsworld* 13-19 September 1989.
16. *Sportsworld* 13-19 September 1989.
17. *Sportsworld* 13-19 September 1989.
18. *Indian Express* (24 June 2000).
19. *Probe* (1988) quoted in Chatterjee, *Sonia*, 174.
20. S. Gurumurthy, *Indian Express* (Chennai) (17 May 1999).

Chapter Twelve: The Rebels

1. Sonia made the remark in the presence of Ahmad Patel, Ambika Soni, Ghulam Nabi Azad and others.
2. Gadgil narrated the incident to the author and dubbed Pawar as 'unreliable'.
3. Account based on inputs from sources in 10 Janpath.
4. Ashok Gehlot, Sheila Dikshit and all other chief ministers of the Congress made similar remarks.
5. Pawar's press statement.
6. Sonia's speech at the AICC session at the Talkatora Stadium on 24 May 1999.
7. Sonia's speech at the AICC session at the Talkatora Stadium on 24 May 1999.
8. Sonia's speech at the AICC session at the Talkatora Stadium on 24 May 1999.

Chapter Thirteen: The Controversies

1. *Telegraph* (15 March 1998).
2. *India Today* (15 December 1998).
3. Based upon inputs from well-placed sources in the BJP.
4. Ram Jethmalani, *Statesman* (16 May 1999).
5. B. Raman in the *Statesman*, 1999 quoted in Mishra, *Sonia 'The Unknown'*, 63.
6. S. Gurumurthy in Mishra, *Sonia 'The Unknown'*, 126.
7. From the author's meeting with Sonia.

8. These formulations are based on inputs from CBI sources.
9. Jayakar, *Indira*, 321.
10. Gupta panel report quoted in *Sonia 'The Unknown'*, 145.
11. Vir Sanghvi quoted on Rediff.com (23 September 1999).
12. Mahendra Ved, *Times of India* (3 February 1998).
13. Sonia Gandhi's press conference.
14. Quattrocchi quoted by UNI on 22 December 1999.
15. Jayakar quoted in Mishra, *Sonia 'The Unknown'*, 45.
16. An off-the-record statement made by a senior minister.
17. As posted on <http://www.indiannationalcongress.com>.

Chapter Fourteen: Sonia the Leader

1. Jairam Ramesh quoted in the *Times of India* (17 November 2002).
2. Told to the author by senior Congress leaders from Bengal.
3. Azad made the remark in the CWC meeting held in November 2002.
4. Natwar made the remark in the CWC meeting.
5. Highly placed sources close to Sonia and Mufti gave these inputs to the author.
6. Jaipal and Somath went public with their views criticizing Vajpayee.
7. Arun Jaitley in the *Times of India* (17 November 2002).
8. As told to the author.
9. While interacting with media, Prasada later made fun of that MP without naming him.
10. As told to the author by Prasada.
11. Sonia's presidential address at Bangalore on 17 March 2001.
12. Kamal Nath's note to the Congress chief submitted on 16 December after the party's defeat in assembly polls.
13. A senior party leader and CWC member made the remark to the author.
14. Kanti Bajpai in the *Times of India* (17 November 2002).
15. Mahesh Rangarajan in the *Times of India* (17 November 2002).

Chapter Fifteen: Looking to the Future

1. The Panchmarhi brainstorming session of the Congress was held in September 1998 to fine-tune the party's programmes and policies.
2. Sanjeev Sinha died in an air crash when he was accompanying Madhavrao Scindia on 30 September 2001.
3. Uma Bharti made the remark in an informal chat with the author

during the 1999 general elections.

4. Based on Election Commission data.
5. Digvijay Singh, however, believes that Sonia's own instincts were against backing Yadav in Bihar in 2000.
6. Sonia made the remark during her visit to the Golden Temple.
7. From the AICC session at the Talkatora Stadium on 24 May 1999.
8. The remark was made in the presence of the author and several other correspondents on 14 October 1999.
9. As told to the author.

REFERENCES

Books

Alexander, P.C. *My Years with Indira Gandhi*. New Delhi: Vision Books, 1991.

Ali, Tariq. *The Nehrus and the Gandhis: An Indian Dynasty*. London: Picador, 1991.

Brass, Paul. *The Politics of India since Independence*. Cambridge: Cambridge University Press, 1994.

Bright, J.S. *Indira Gandhi*. New Delhi: New Light Publishers, 1984.

Chatterjee, Rupa. *Sonia Gandhi: The Lady in Shadow*. New Delhi: Butala Publications, 1998.

Dhar, P.N. *Indira Gandhi: The Emergency and the Indian Democracy*. New Delhi: Oxford University Press, 2000.

Frank, Katherine. *Indira: The Life of Indira Nehru Gandhi*. London: HarperCollins, 2001

Gandhi, Indira. *My Truth (as Told to Emmanuel Pouchpadass)*. New Delhi: Vision Books, 1981.

Gandhi, Sonia. *Rajiv*. New Delhi: Penguin Books India, 1992.

Gandhi, Sonia. (ed.) *Freedom's Daughter. Letters between Indira Gandhi and Jawaharlal Nehru 1922-39*. London: Hodder, 1989.

Gandhi, Sonia. (ed.) *Two Alone, Two Together: Letters between Indira Gandhi and Jawaharlal Nehru 1940-64*. London: Hodder, 1992.

Gill, S.S. *The Dynasty. A Political Biography of the Premier Ruling Family of Modern India*. New Delhi: HarperCollins India, 1996.

Gupta, Bhabani Sen. *Rajiv Gandhi: A Political Study*. New Delhi: Konark, 1989.

Gupte, Pranay. *India: The Challenge of Change*. New York: Mandarin, 1989.

Hasan, Zoya, 'The Prime Minister and the Left.' In *Nehru to the Nineties*.

Edited by Manor James. Albany, N.Y.: State University of New York Press, 1993.

Gandhi, Indira (in conversation with Pupul Jayakar). *What I Am*. New Delhi: Indira Gandhi Memorial Trust, 1986.

Jayakar, Pupul. *Indira Gandhi*. New Delhi: Penguin Books India, 1992.

Malhotra, Inder. *Indira Gandhi: A Personal and Political Biography*. London: Hodder and Stoughton, 1989.

Manor, James. 'Innovative Leadership in Modern India: M.K. Gandhi, Nehru and Indira Gandhi.' In *Innovative Leaders in International Politics*, Edited by Gabriel Sheffer. Albany, N.Y.: State University of New York Press, 1993.

Merchant, Minhaz. *Rajiv Gandhi. The End of a Dream*. New Delhi: Penguin Books India, 1991.

Mishra, Dina Nath (ed.), *Sonia 'The Unknown'*. New Delhi: India First Foundation, 1991.

Nehru, B.K. *Nice Guys Finish Second*. New Delhi: Penguin Books India, 1997.

Nehru, Jawaharlal. *Letters from a Father to His Daughter*. Allahabad: Kitabistan, 1938.

Nugent, Nicholas. *Rajiv Gandhi: Son of a Dynasty*. London: BBC Books, 1990.

Paul, Swraj. *Indira Gandhi*. London: Robert Royce, 1985.

Rao, P.V. Narasimha. *Insider*. New Delhi: Penguin Books India, 1998.

Sahgal, Nayantara and E.N. Mangat Rai. *Relationships: Extracts from a Correspondence*. New Delhi: Kali for Women, 1994.

Sarvepalli, Gopal. *Jawaharlal Nehru: A Biography*. New Delhi: Oxford University Press, 1975.

Shourie, Arun. *The Assassination and After*. New Delhi: Roli Books, 1985.

Singh, Khushwant. *Truth, Love and a Little Malice: An Autobiography*. New Delhi: Penguin Books India, 2002.

Singh, K. Natwar. *Count Your Blessings*. New Delhi: Har-Anand Publications, 1993.

Thakur, Janardhan, *All the Prime Minister's Men*. New Delhi: Vikas, 1977.

Tully, Mark and Zareer Masani. *From Raj to Rajiv: Forty Years of Indian Independence*. London: BBC Books, 1988.

Vasudev, Uma. *Indira Gandhi: Revolution and Restraint.* New Delhi: Vikas, 1973.

Wolpert, Stanley. *A New History of India.* New York: Oxford University Press, 1989.

Yunus, Mohammad. *Persons, Passions, Politics.* New Delhi: Vikas, 1980.

Articles

Bharti, Pushpa. 'Sonia Gandhi.' *Dharmayug,* 15 June 1985.

Chowdury, Neerja. 'Power Play: Sonia Set for a Poll Vault.' *Indian Express* (New Delhi), 18 March 2002.

Dua, H.K. 'It Is Sonia Gandhi Versus India.' *Pioneer* (New Delhi), 1 June 1999.

Elliott, John. 'In Asia, the Dynasties Still Rule.' *New Statesman* (UK), 8 November 1999.

Goldenberg, Suzanne. 'Gandhi Assassination.' *Guardian* (UK), 22 May 1992.

Harding, Luke. 'Gandhi Family Fortunes, Despite the Numerous Failings of India's Coalition Government, the Likelihood of the Opposition's Sonia Gandhi Becoming Prime Minister Remains Small.' *Guardian* (UK), 20 August 2001.

Kang, Bhavdeep. 'Educating Sonia.' *Outlook,* 6 July 1998.

Jain, Sandhya. 'Double Speak, Dubious Intentions.' *Pioneer* (New Delhi), 2 February 1999.

McGirk, Tim. 'That Gandhi Magic.' *Time Asia,* 2 March 1998.

Mitra, S.K. 'India, Dynastic Rule or the Democratization of Power?' *Third World Quarterly* 10 (January 1988).

Naravane, Vaiju. 'In Maino Country....' *Frontline,* 25 April–8 May 1998.

n.a. 'Readying for Race Course Road.' *Times of India* (New Delhi), 17 November 2002.

Philipose, Pamela. 'Centrestage, Interview of the Week. Khushwant Singh "Mrs Gandhi-Maneka Spats Will Do Well on TV. A Political "Tu Tu, Main, Main"!' *Sunday,* 23 September 2001.

Prakash, A. Surya. 'What A.C. Gupta Commission Had Said about Sonia's First Scandal: Gupta Commission Report.' *Pioneer* (New Delhi), 10 May 1999.

Sanghvi, Vir. 'Looking Back at the Bofors Scandal.' <http://www.rediff.com>, 23 September 1999.

Sarin, Ritu. 'Breaking the Silence: Sonia Gandhi Grows More Vocal, But Is the Dynastic Head Ready to Enter Politics?' *Asia Week*, 15 September 1995.

―――. 'Sonia's Silence and the Importance of Being Vincent George.' *Asia Week*, 29 November 1997.

―――. 'Sonia—No Longer the Saviour, Dissent against Her Leadership Is Growing.' *Asia Week*, 12 May 2000.

Shenoy, T.V.R. 'Surely There's Life Beyond Bofors—Sonia's Somnambulism.' *Indian Express* (New Delhi), 4 January 2000.

Shourie, Arun. 'Indira Gandhi as Commerce.' *Indian Express* (New Delhi), 15 March 1982.

Silver, Eric et al. 'Political Pilot Who Learned a Bit Too Fast: Obituary of Rajiv Gandhi.' *Guardian* (UK), 22 May 1991.

Ved, Mahendra. *Times of India* (New Delhi), 3 February 1998.

INDEX

MONTANA

Norma Tirrell

Photography by John Reddy

First published in Great Britain in 1992

© 1991 Compass American Guides, Inc.
Maps © 1991 Compass American Guides, Inc.

Distribution in the UK, Ireland, Europe and certain Commonwealth countries by Hodder & Stoughton, Mill Road, Dunton Green, Sevenoaks, Kent, TN13 2YA

Editors: Barry Parr, Don Pitcher
Series Editor: Kit Duane
Designer: David Hurst
Map Design: Bob Race

ACKNOWLEDGEMENTS

THANKS ARE DUE FIRST TO STAN MEYER, for his vote of confidence, and to Barry Parr, for his encouragement and unyielding demands as an editor and writing coach. Grateful recognition goes to my technical advisers: historians David Walter and Vivian Paladin; geologist Ray Breuniger; wildlife and conservation pro Jim Posewitz; census and economic research specialists Patrica Roberts and Jan Clack; arts advocates David Nelson, Jo-Anne Mussulman, and Julia Smith; and photo archivists Becca Kohl and Lory Morrow. Thanks are also due my informal council of advisers: backroads buffs Rick Rogne, Ken Walchek, Doug Monger, and Tom Palmer; community insiders Sally Mullen, Mick Mills, Becky Tirrell, Shirley Zupan, Dale Herbert, Patty Rambo Short, and Deirdre Boggs; bed and breakfast sleuth Paula Deigert; and restaurant consultants Ila Jesme, Janet Lowe, Barb Skelton, Wdythe McCleary, Pep Jewell, Mary Tietjen, Dore Schwinden, and Ann German. I am grateful, as always, to Sherryl Vaughn for her generous proofreading assistance. And I salute John Reddy for images that speak louder than words.

The Publishers wish to thank the following institutions and individuals for the use of their illustrations: Montana Historical Society, Helena, pp. 9, 31, 32, 34, 37, 63, 70, 81, 85, 93, 95, 101, 153, 163, 171, 192, 202, 221; Bancroft Library, University of California at Berkeley, pp. 30, 126; C.M. Russell Museum, Great Falls, pp. 121–123, 129, 243; Independence National Historic Park, Philadelphia, p. 42; Travel Montana, pp. 109, 246; Douglas O'Looney, pp. 38, 71, 72, 111, 215; Don Pitcher, p. 254; and Harry S. Robins, p. 51.

The quote on pages 148–149 by Richard Ford from *Rock Springs*, copyright 1987 is reprinted by permission of Atlantic Monthly Press.

British Library Cataloguing in Publication ███████████████
Produced by Twin Age ███████████████
Printed in Hong Kong ███████████████

*For Bennett, with whom I share Montana's mountains and headwaters,
and for Janet, with whom I walked its deepest valley.*

CONTENTS

Maps

Literary Quotes

Cycles of life and seasonal change are evident across Montana's uncluttered landscape.

AUTHOR'S PREFACE

LIKE MOST GUIDEBOOKS, THIS ONE IS A PERSONAL REFLECTION of its author. If I dwell on rivers and mountains, it is because that is where I spend much of my time. What will it be this weekend, Ten Lakes or the Missouri River? Bighorn Canyon or the Big Hole River? Cross-country skiing in Glacier or Yellowstone? These are the hard, year-round choices a Montanan faces. All national treasures, they are but a handful of gold nuggets in Montana's outdoor recreation bonanza.

If history keeps bobbing up, it is because the past is never out of reach in a state so young you can still sit at the knees of wranglers, homesteaders, miners, and tribal elders who keep it alive. Visit old Jake Hoover's sod-roof cabin in the Judith River country, and you'll see where cowboy artist Charlie Russell spent his early years and derived the inspiration to create his inimitable Western landscapes. Or take a walking tour of uptown Butte to sense the magnitude of the rivalry that existed between William Clark and Marcus Daly in their quest for dominance of the copper industry and the statehouse. Clark may have built the most ostentatious mansion, but it wasn't long before Daly blocked his view with a massive apartment house next door.

No longer boss of Montana's economy and politics, copper remains the symbol of a colonial state, historically driven by outside interests. After more than 150 years of long-distance promises about beaver pelts, gold, copper, silver, oil, coal, cattle, wheat, and timber, the nation's fourth-largest state still can't muster sufficient economic vitality to support more than one-third of one percent of the U.S. population—800,000 souls in all, scattered across nearly 150,000 square miles (388,500 sq. km).

But it is the resilience and diversity of its meager population that give Montana its fresh face and big heart. Smoke rising from Crow Indian sweat lodges beside Interstate 90 and cornucopian displays of fresh produce at Montana's Hutterite colonies hint at the cultural mix. Full-tilt Western blowouts, like the Miles City Bucking Horse Sale and Lewistown's Cowboy Poetry Gathering, are brassy statements about Montana's overriding cowboy culture and its attendant mythology.

In one of his essays, Wallace Stegner speaks of the importance of "placeness" in an increasingly "placeless" society. "If you don't know where you are," he says, "you don't know who you are." Montanans may be uncertain of their future, but they have never entertained doubts about their sense of place. It means more to them than money in the bank.

Through my own subjective mix of places, people, and events, I have tried to familiarize you with this addictive place. Mine is the view of a native who loves her state, and a journalist with no formal training in history, economics, or any of the isms or ologies that would lend this text the weight of authority. With any luck, it will send you searching for many of the titles that distinguish Montana nationally as a literary heavyweight. Good reading and happy travels.

Homesteaders were told of the mild winters, prodigious crop yields, and unlimited opportunity that awaited them in Montana; what many found was isolation, dust, drought, and drudgery. (Montana Historical Society)

(following pages) A perfect rainbow crowns Walton Mountain in Glacier National Park.

INTRODUCTION

■ LAND AND SPACE, MOUNTAINS AND SKY

DRIVING ACROSS EASTERN MONTANA—from, say, Sidney to Lewistown—can be an uneasy, or an exhilarating, experience. Uneasy if you find comfort in crowds; exhilarating if space is what you seek. The trip will take the better part of a day, and still you will be only halfway across the state. You will travel through all or part of five counties (roughly the equivalent of driving from Maine to New York) with a total population of fewer than 30,000. Of those counties, Garfield has 1,600 residents scattered over an area about the same size as Connecticut, with its 3.3 million people.

If you are open to a new perception of beauty, the lunar landscapes of eastern Montana can be endlessly absorbing. This is the Earth itself speaking, but if you have been conditioned to the babel of humanity, you may not hear it. So pack along a cassette tape of *High Plains Music* by Montana native, Phil Aaberg. His high-spirited and haunting piano celebrates the landscape and beckons you to the uninterrupted stretch of highway ahead. Soon, you will realize that you are surrounded not by emptiness, but by *space*. In Montana, there is a difference.

Eastern Montana space is filled with the subtlest forms of beauty. Shifting light and shadow play on coulees, badlands, and breaks. Western meadowlarks remind you with one astonishing trill that it's good to be alive. Neutral earth tones of ocher and sage magnify a 180-degree backdrop of sky that broods and shimmers in primary colors.

Driving south from Lewistown, the space becomes more immediate, more dramatic. It is defined by solitary mountain ranges that appear as islands in an ocean of grass—the Big Snowies, the Little Belts, the Castles, and the Crazies. Keeping to themselves in the distance, these isolated ranges are your signal that the landscape is about to change dramatically.

■ FROM PLAINS TO MOUNTAINS

Turning west at Big Timber, you might as well be in a different state. In fact, you have reached Montana's mid-point. Yet to come are the mountains that gave

Montana its name. First, the Absarokas and the Bridgers, then the Madison Range, the Tobacco Roots, the Pioneers, the Sapphires, and on and on, range after range, until they meld into one hazy ridge floating on the horizon. These views need no introduction; you've seen them on movie screens and travel posters. This is the Montana that outsiders know about: the mountains and trout streams, guest ranches and ski resorts, national parks and wilderness areas. You may have missed where the Dakota plains ended and the plains of eastern Montana began, but the imprint of the Northern Rockies will stay with you forever.

Scooped out of each range of mountains is a glaciated valley fed by rivers and streams that begin as snowfall on peaks that range from 7,000 to 12,000 feet (2,000 to 3,600 m) above sea level. But for an occasional town or small city, these timbered valleys and granite ranges are the domain of wildlife—abundant populations of elk, deer, moose, mountain goats, bighorn sheep, waterfowl, upland birds, and trout. The roster includes endangered and threatened species like the bald eagle, gray wolf, and grizzly bear. A popular Montana guest ranch offers this comparison to illustrate the company Montanans keep and the space they enjoy:

PER SQUARE MILE IN MONTANA

1.4 elk or antelope

3.3 deer

896 catchable-size trout

6 people

The conventional view of a remote, sparsely populated state like Montana is that there is nothing going on out here. Just land and space. In his *Montana: High, Wide, and Handsome,* Joseph Kinsey Howard wrote: "Montana is a remote hinterland about as well known to the average eastern seaboard citizen as East or West Africa. But it is this space that defines Montana and shapes the outlook of its residents." The newsman and historian also said of this place:

> This sums up what I want in life—room to swing my arms and to swing my mind. Where is there more opportunity than in Montana for creation of these broad margins, physical and intellectual? Where is there more opportunity to enjoy the elemental values of living, bright sun and clean air and space? We have room. We can be neighbors without getting in each other's hair. We can be individuals.

The fact that there is still a place like Montana, where humanity does not dominate the landscape, is immensely important in a world that is overrun with people and their impact. Space and an unspoiled landscape are increasingly hard to come by, and herein lies Montana's appeal.

■ LIFESTYLE

Montanans treasure their space and the lifestyle it allows. Residents of even the largest cities can be skiing, hiking, fishing, or hunting in less than an hour. The Rattlesnake Wilderness is only a mile from the city limits of Missoula, western Montana's largest city. The people of Kalispell regard Glacier National Park as their own backyard. Bozeman skiers can choose between two of Montana's premier downhill areas—Bridger Bowl is 15 miles (24 km) north, Big Sky 30 miles (48 km) south. And one of Montana's finest floating and fishing rivers, the Missouri, is a half-hour drive from Bozeman, Helena, and Great Falls.

Isolation, a harsh climate, and a fickle, resource-based economy over which they have little control are the trade-offs Montanans are willing to make for this lifestyle. Global markets control the commodities that come from Montana: grain, livestock, minerals, energy fuels, and timber. Because of Montana's isolation from the nation's commercial centers, most of these are shipped out of the state as raw materials. It is cheaper to refine them near the markets where they will be used. The result back home is what one newspaperman has described as a "niche-poor" economy that cannot provide enough good-paying jobs to keep people, especially young people, in the state.

Montana's history has been marked by uneven growth and decline, a pattern that repeated itself as recently as the last decade. Following nearly three decades of prosperity starting in the 1950s, Montana's population reached a peak of 824,000 in 1985. By 1990, it had slipped to just under 800,000. Per capita income dropped from 12 percent above the national average in the 1950s to 20 percent below in 1987. In 1983 the state's largest employer, the Anaconda Company, abandoned its mining and smelting operations in Butte, Anaconda, and Great Falls. By the end of the eighties, Montanans were also adjusting to upheavals in the state's oil and gas, transportation, and timber industries. The clincher was a persistent drought that collapsed the agriculture industry in much of eastern Montana, and kindled

When the weather behaves, Flathead Lake cherries are one of Montana's most eagerly awaited crops.

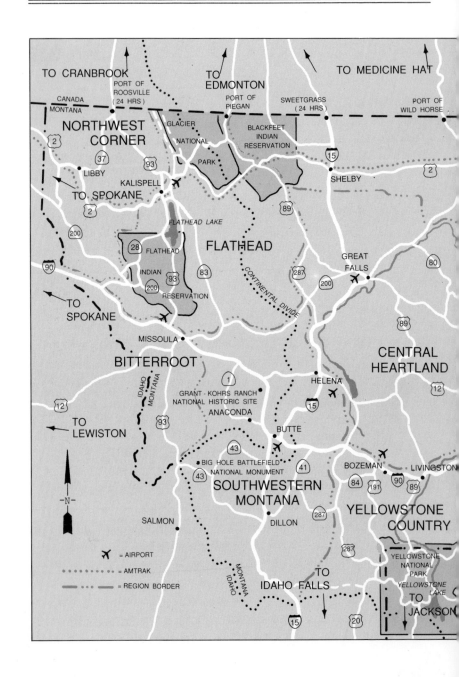

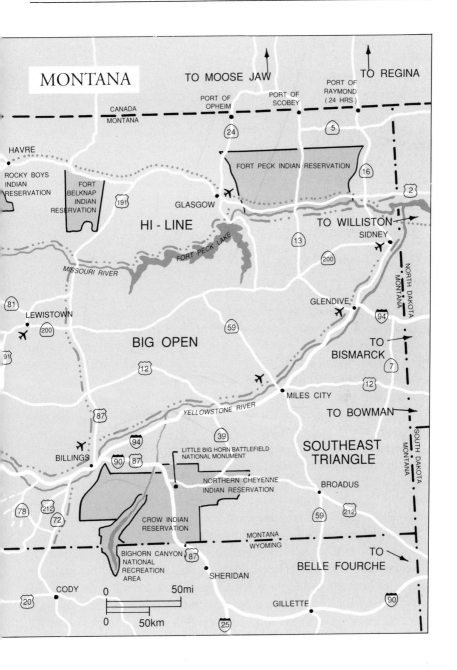

massive forest fires in the west. In just one decade, Montana's economy shrunk by nine percent.

The outlook for the nineties is brighter if only because most Montanans believe it can't get worse. But *Newsweek* presented a different forecast for the upper Great Plains and northern Rocky Mountain region, including Montana, in a 1989 article entitled "America's Outback." Describing the area as a "lost frontier" prone to chronic recession and decline, the magazine pronounced it, for all intents and purposes, dead. Montanans had mixed reactions to the article, rejecting the death sentence but warming up to a new nickname. America's Outback. They liked it. In two words, it sized up what they love about their state.

No one ever said it was easy to live in Montana. But for the few who can afford it, it is the *only* place to live.

■ A Land at Odds with Itself

From the high plains of eastern Montana to the Rocky Mountain west, Montana has never made much sense as one state. Physically, economically, politically, and socially, it has always been at odds with itself. Back in 1880, when Montana was still a territory, the vast majority of its residents lived in the west, as a majority do today. According to the historian K. Ross Toole, no one gave much thought to the plains at that time. In his 1959 history of the state, *Montana: An Uncommon Land,* he theorized that in 1889, when it came time to draw state boundaries, the plains were "simply marked off and drawn in."

The result is a sprawling state that is pulled in opposite directions. Endowed with adequate rainfall, minerals, timber, rivers, and abundant wildlife, the mountains and valleys of western Montana support a diversified economy of farming and ranching, mining, logging, tourism, and recreation. Most of Montana's population live in these stream-fed western valleys. (Even so, the region's largest city, Missoula, has a population of just under 43,000.)

While western Montana is considered an extension of the Pacific Northwest, it is hard to tell where eastern Montana ends and the Dakotas begin. Eastern Montana is the heart and soul of the northern Great Plains, and it has nothing to do with western Montana. Residents of Montana's extreme eastern corners travel regularly to nearby Williston, North Dakota, and Belle Fourche, South Dakota, for

The Rocky Mountain Front is where the mountains meet the plains, and where the views and the weather are always dramatic.

shopping and entertainment, and are oriented toward the Dakotas' media and public affairs. To compound this east-west schism, Montanans living along the sparsely populated northern tier are as much at home in the western Canadian cities of Regina, Moose Jaw, and Lethbridge as they are in Glasgow, Havre, and Great Falls.

WESTERN MONTANA

Topography and climate are the obvious factors that divide Montana. While the very name, Montana, is derived from the Spanish word for mountain, in fact, it applies to only a third of the state. In the mountainous west, more than two dozen distinct ranges comprise Montana's share of the Rocky Mountains. Elevations swing from 3,500 feet (1,050 m) on valley floors to the peaks of the Beartooth Plateau near Yellowstone National Park that rise above 12,000 feet (3,650 m). Many of these ranges are high enough to make their own weather, inducing precipitation that supports dense coniferous forests of fir, pine, cedar, spruce, and larch. While snow often piles up hundreds of inches, measurable precipitation ranges from 14 to 23 inches (36 to 58 cm).

The valleys that divide western Montana's mountain ranges vary from narrow, steep-sided slots to broad floors up to 50 miles (80 km) wide. Many of the state's most unforgettable mountain valleys—the Big Hole, Bitterroot, Yellowstone, Gallatin, and Madison—are named after the rivers that drain them. Beginning their journeys as nameless streams and freshets at 10,000 feet (3,050 m) and higher, these legendary rivers support agriculture, tourism, and life itself in a dry western state.

Western Montana is the land that comes to mind when most people think of the state. Powder-white peaks, alpine meadows, trout streams, and small, friendly towns. It's an addictive landscape for both residents and visitors, but not for those who thrive on the infinite sky and open spaces of eastern Montana.

EASTERN MONTANA

Unlike spectacular western landscapes, the plains of eastern Montana are regarded by many as monotonous. In truth, however, they are full of topographical surprises, like badlands and breaks, sandstone outcrops, glacial lakes, coulees, ice caves, and even an occasional pine forest and cluster of hills or low-lying mountains. Unlike western Montana, where weather arrives on westerly air flows from the Pacific

Ocean, eastern Montana is raked by arctic air from the north. January temperatures seldom exceed 10° F (-12° C) in northeastern Montana, and snow rarely stays because steady winds whisk it away. In summer, these plains bake in the sun; temperatures in the 90s F (30s C) are not uncommon. Officially classified as semiarid, the plains of eastern Montana receive meager amounts of moisture, with normal precipitation levels ranging from 12 to 16 inches (30 to 40 cm). Drought is a fact of life here.

Other than occasional scrub-pine forests and cottonwood-lined river bottoms, the plains consist largely of short grasses that bend to prevailing west winds and starve the landscape of eye-catching color. These protein-rich grasses support a proud livestock industry, a legacy of the great trail drives that moved cattle and cowboys from Texas to Montana beginning in the 1860s. Much has changed since the days of the open range. Blizzards and barbed wire have reduced herds significantly, but cattle still outnumber people three to one in Montana. Underlain by immense coal beds and a portion of the massive Williston Oil Basin, the eastern Montana plains also conceal vast reserves of energy fuels.

Eastern Montana is hard country. Its sharp edges are branded on the weather-creased faces of its residents. It is also austerely beautiful country. If you seek a vision of what the West was like before filmmakers and fashion designers got hold of it, a trip to the high plains of eastern Montana will satisfy your soul.

THE LAND BETWEEN

No one can point to a line where eastern Montana becomes western Montana. Some say it's as far west as the Rocky Mountain Front, where the mountains literally meet the plains; some say it's as far east as the lower Musselshell River, beyond which both population and topographical relief are in short supply. Between these extremes lies Montana's middle ground—a vast area of isolated mountain ranges, buttes and plains, great rivers and small streams, a grain-rich farm belt, and Montana's two largest cities—Billings and Great Falls.

Residents of this mid-section enjoy the best of both Montanas. The mountains are never out of view; instead of dominating the landscape, however, they lend it depth and perspective. The contrast between mountains and plains is nowhere more striking than it is along the Rocky Mountain Front, seen from the stretch of highway between Augusta and Browning. To the west is a solid wall of peaks and domes, a view that changes seasonally, daily, even hourly, as clouds and storms collide above and around them. To the east is an unrelenting stretch of plains, broken only by the geometry of crop rotation and an occasional shadowy butte suspended on the horizon.

The Rocky Mountain Front is responsible for a unique weather pattern that can take the edge off winter in central Montana. Known among Indians as "snow eaters," warm winter winds called Chinooks sweep down the eastern slopes of the Rockies, raising temperatures and melting snow along the way. Montana's Chinook winds have been known to lift January temperatures as much as 47° F (26° C) in seven minutes. A meteorologist in Havre onces witnessed something even more startling: a rise of 26° F (15° C) in 45 seconds. Strongest at the base of the Rockies, Chinooks run out of steam as they scoot across the plains, but their moderating effects are felt as far east as the Upper Yellowstone Valley near Billings.

In addition to year-round recreation, the mountains of central Montana provide relief from the weather extremes that beset the plains. In summer, they offer cool refuge from the simmering lowlands; in winter, they block frigid weather systems and, in some cases, produce their own.

Besides their physical differences, east and west differ in the character and outlook of their residents, and the source of their affection for Montana. In the east, that affection begins and ends with the sky and stretches to the horizon in every direction. Although the mountains of western Montana are responsible for the state's name, eastern Montana can rightfully claim Montana's most popular nickname, "Big Sky Country." To an eastern Montanan, mountains are a clutter on the landscape, a barrier that wrecks the view and shackles the spirit. But to a western Montanan, they are food for the soul, and the trade-off that makes Montana's lackluster economy worthwhile. For it is in these mountains—along their hiking trails and trout streams, in their roadless backcountry, and on their skytop peaks—that western Montanans find the compensation that matters most to them.

While Montana's diverse landscape is inherently divisive, the land in all its contours and moods is the glue that binds Montanans together. Whether they are digging out from under six feet (two m) of snow in Red Lodge or facing their fourth heart-breaking year of drought in Wolf Point, Montanans share a camaraderie that comes from a love of the land and a willingness to take it on nature's terms.

The Pryor Mountains are a remote, highland junction of desert and ice west of Bighorn Canyon on Montana's southern border.

H I S T O R Y

■ GEOLOGY AND PREHISTORY

SOME OF MONTANA'S MOST SCENIC FEATURES and historic treasures were born in violent natural acts that place the exploits of humanity in the realm of light comedy. Fire and ice, wind and water, massive glaciers, rivers of molten lava, shallow seas, swamps, and deserts: these are the ancient forces that sculpted the mountains, scoured the plains, chiseled river canyons, scooped out great basins, and nurtured a prehistoric kingdom of dinosaurs.

While the so-called "basement" rocks that underlie the northern Rockies can be traced back 2.5 to 3 billion years, the Rockies themselves did not begin forming until some 100 million years ago. Before that, Montana was a flat plain, flooded periodically by shallow seas. The action that created the dramatic landscape we know today began when giant masses of molten rock deep within the Earth began rising to the surface. Pushing and heaving, they broke the surface to create some of the peaks that distinguish the Western mountain ranges. The action was compounded by tectonic pressure that pushed, folded, and thrust soft, upper sedimentary rocks eastward. Further tension stretched the Earth's crust east and west, allowing north-south blocks to tilt upward. The result was a massive jumble of mountains ranges, whose peaks and valleys have been further defined by rivers and glaciers over millions of years. As the mountains grew from the plain, surrounding seas drained away. Plants that had accumulated in swamps along the edge of an inland sea were added to the layers of marine sediment formed by periodic flooding. Millions of years of pressure cooked and compacted this material into thick beds of sediment containing the petroleum, gas, and coal that now lie beneath the plains of central and eastern Montana.

After the Rockies were formed, some of the peaks were buried under thick caps of ice during several ice ages. This was an era of colder climates and massive snowfall, when more snow fell during the winter than melted in summer. Gradually, these snow accumulations turned to glaciers—rivers of solid ice that flowed and slid down mountains, gouging valleys and carving the details of today's landscape. Vestiges of these ice ages are most visible in northwestern Montana's **Glacier National Park,** which gets its name not from the glistening white snow patches that cling to its mountains today, but from the ancient ice sheets that molded this magnificent park. Glacier's photogenic vistas, its sculptured peaks, chiseled valleys, dazzling lakes, waterfalls, and cascades are all testimony to the last great glaciers that melted about 10,000 years ago.

Fire and ice were the artists in **Yellowstone National Park.** Floods created by melting snow and glaciers etched the majestic Grand Canyon of the Yellowstone, and superheated water just below the crust continues to erupt from complex underground plumbing as spouting geysers, bubbling mud caldrons, hot springs, and steaming fumaroles. Yellowstone was created by a series of volcanic eruptions, the most recent of which began more than a million years ago and culminated in a blast 600,000 years ago that has no peer in recorded history. The explosion spewed tons of gases and hot ash across North America, with fragments landing more than a thousand miles away. Estimates rank this cataclysmic blowout anywhere from 1,000 to 10,000 times greater than the Mount St. Helens blast of 1980. Intense geothermal forces are still at work beneath the Earth's shallow surface in Yellowstone Park, making it the biggest and busiest hot spot on the globe.

■ THE AGE OF DINOSAURS

For 140 million years—more than twice as long as mammals have dominated the Earth—dinosaurs ruled the world. No one knows for sure why they vanished so abruptly, but research in Montana is shifting attention to how these prehistoric creatures lived. Recent fossil discoveries by Montana paleontologist Jack Horner have forced scientists to rethink old theories about dinosaurs, long perceived as solitary, cold-blooded beasts that relied more on their brawn than their brains for survival. Horner, who presides over the paleontology wing of Montana's Museum of the Rockies, made one of his field's most important discoveries in 1978. Following a tip from an amateur paleontologist, he unearthed a nest of dinosaur eggs and hatchlings on the eastern slope of the Rocky Mountains near Choteau. Later digs revealed more nests and a huge bone bed that lend credence to an emerging theory that dinosaurs were warm-blooded creatures that behaved more like birds than reptiles, traveled in herds, and cared for their young.

It is no mere coincidence that Montana is the epicenter of some of the most significant research taking place in the field of paleontology. Its prehistory makes it a perfect laboratory. As the Rockies were forming and dinosaurs were dying, sediment sloughed off the rising slopes and formed a layer over their remains. Then came the glaciers, scouring the plains and removing the layers of sedimentation that had buried the dinosaurs. Today, fossils are found on or near the surface of a land that has been largely undisturbed by industrial or residential development.

A must-see attraction for dinosaur lovers of all ages is the **Museum of the Rockies**, located on the campus of Montana State University in Bozeman. In addition to lifelike displays, exhibits, and a fossil preparation room where visitors can watch scientists at work, the museum sponsors summer field trips that enable visitors to participate in dinosaur digs with knowledgeable "bone hunters." Field training in fossil location and identification is also available at the **Old Trail Museum** in Choteau, near the site where dinosaur nests were first discovered. Visitors to southeastern Montana will be surprised by the **Carter County Museum** in the tiny town of Ekalaka. Developed by local amateur paleontologists, the museum houses an impressive collection of bones and fossils, including the 35-foot-long

A robotic Triceratops family greets visitors at the Museum of the Rockies in Bozeman.

(11-m) skeleton of a duck-billed dinosaur named *Anatosaurus.* Long recognized as an important paleontological site, this area has also turned up some of the oldest evidence of humanity in North America.

■ THE HUMAN RECORD

THE FIRST MONTANANS

Montana's human record is but a millisecond on the geologic timetable. It is believed that Asiatic peoples first entered North America between 10,000 and 30,000 years ago during a period of glaciation when sea levels dropped enough to form a land bridge across the Bering Strait. These Asian migrants traveled south from Alaska along the eastern slope of the Rockies on what has become known as the "Great North Trail." Some wandered all the way to South America.

Those who remained in the north left evidence indicating they hunted big game animals, including the now extinct mammoth. Following a major climatic change that turned the Great Plains into a desert, both the hunters and the hunted disappeared. Beginning about 5,000 to 4,000 B.C., a different crowd moved north from the desert southwest. More foragers than hunters, these migrants occupied the western valleys. About 2,000 years later, the last wave of prehistoric migrants—the so-called "late hunters"—entered Montana from the south and west. Historians believe they were the direct ancestors of today's Indian tribes. Evidence of their culture lingers in the teepee rings and buffalo jumps that still exist on the plains of central and eastern Montana.

Plains Indians as we know them today did not arrive in Montana until after 1620. Flathead Indians, the only Montana tribe living west of the Continental Divide, came about a century earlier. In a period of little more than 250 years, several tribes flourished on the plains and in the western valleys before they were displaced by non-native expansionism. By the early 1880s, hide hunters had shot the buffalo to virtual extinction, and similarly rubbed out the lifestyle and culture of the Indians who relied on it for their food, shelter, clothing, and tools. In their *Montana: A History of Two Centuries,* historians Michael Malone and Richard Roeder describe Montana's native peoples as a "highly diversified group, combining plateau-mountain peoples from the west, Great Basin Indians from the south, hardy plainsmen from the north and east." They sum up the brief rise and fall of recent Indian culture in Montana this way:

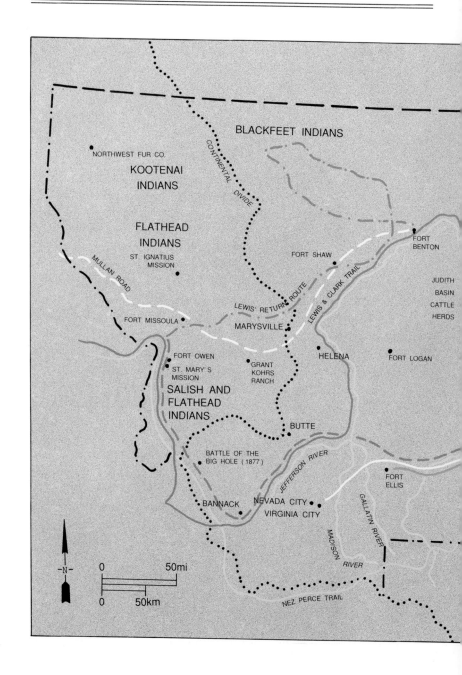

BLACKFEET INDIANS

NORTHWEST FUR CO.

KOOTENAI
INDIANS

CONTINENTAL DIVIDE

FLATHEAD
INDIANS

ST. IGNATIUS
MISSION

FORT SHAW

FORT
BENTON

MULLAN ROAD

JUDITH
BASIN
CATTLE
HERDS

LEWIS' RETURN ROUTE

LEWIS & CLARK TRAIL

FORT MISSOULA

MARYSVILLE

FORT OWEN

HELENA

FORT LOGAN

ST. MARY'S
MISSION

GRANT
KOHRS
RANCH

SALISH AND
FLATHEAD
INDIANS

BUTTE

BATTLE OF THE
BIG HOLE (1877)

JEFFERSON RIVER

FORT
ELLIS

GALLATIN RIVER

BANNACK

NEVADA CITY

VIRGINIA CITY

MADISON

RIVER

-N-

0   50mi

0   50km

NEZ PERCE TRAIL

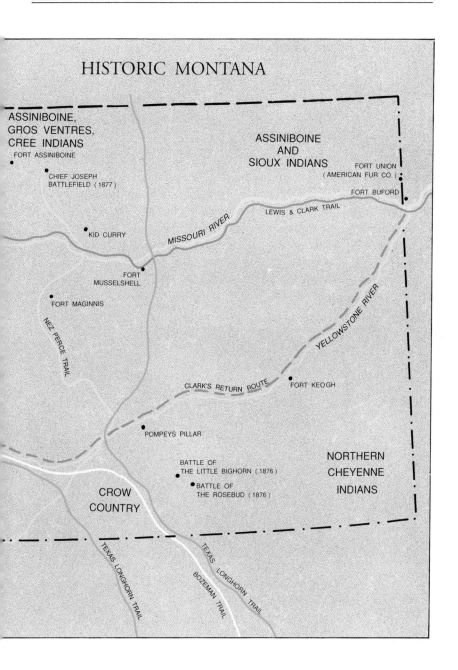

HISTORIC MONTANA

ASSINIBOINE,
GROS VENTRES,
CREE INDIANS
FORT ASSINIBOINE

CHIEF JOSEPH
BATTLEFIELD (1877)

ASSINIBOINE
AND
SIOUX INDIANS

FORT UNION
(AMERICAN FUR CO.)

FORT BUFORD

LEWIS & CLARK TRAIL

MISSOURI RIVER

KID CURRY

FORT
MUSSELSHELL

FORT MAGINNIS

NEZ PERCE TRAIL

YELLOWSTONE RIVER

CLARK'S RETURN ROUTE

FORT KEOGH

POMPEYS PILLAR

BATTLE OF
THE LITTLE BIGHORN (1876)

BATTLE OF
THE ROSEBUD (1876)

NORTHERN
CHEYENNE
INDIANS

CROW
COUNTRY

TEXAS LONGHORN TRAIL

TEXAS LONGHORN TRAIL

BOZEMAN TRAIL

Prior to 1800, Montana was the eye of a cultural hurricane, where Indians migrating from all directions, bringing horses and guns with them, met to create new and unusual societies. These Indians would share a common fate in the years following 1800, as Americans and Canadians drove them from their lands, reduced them by war, disease, and alcohol, and shattered their native cultures.

By the 1800s, international interest in the North American fur trade was threatening a cultural showdown between natives and newcomers. But no single event hastened the inevitable clash as did the first U.S. government contact with the Indians—the Lewis and Clark Expedition of 1804–06. Among the goals of the expedition was an inventory of the West's fur-trade potential. Shortly after Meriwether Lewis reported that "that portion of the continent watered by the Missouri and all its branches . . . is richer in beaver and otter than any country on earth," trappers and traders arrived in great numbers, and the West, as the Indians knew it, was changed forever.

Lewis and Clark hold a council with some of the Indians they met on their transcontinental trek. (Bancroft Library, University of California at Berkeley)

ANGLO SETTLERS

As a state, Montana is just a kid. Only 100 years old, it is a state where you can learn history at the knee of an elder who has lived it. Among Montana's native peoples, the "Old Ones" sustain a rich oral tradition with songs and stories about the buffalo and coyote, the seasons, "Sun Chief," and the "Above Ones." Homesteaders recount the isolation, dust, drought, and drudgery that awaited them in Montana after they swallowed the railroads' claims of mild winters, prodigious crop yields, and unlimited opportunity. Old-timers in the stockgrowers industry heard first-hand accounts of the brutal winter of 1886–87 which, together with overgrazing and barbed wire, brought an end to Montana's legendary open-range era. Retired miners can pinpoint the hour of the Smith Mine disaster in Bearcreek, when 74 coal miners were killed in an under-

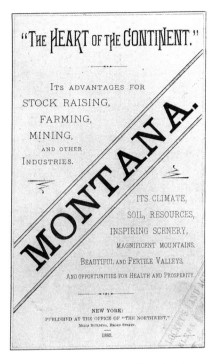

Early homestead hype promised health and prosperity to all who ventured west. (Montana Historical Society)

ground explosion, or the night radical labor leader Frank Little was hanged in Butte after delivering a fiery speech against U.S. involvement in World War I. All significant in the development of the West, these legends and events are still within reach in Montana, where history is a hands-on affair.

True to its genre, the romance of the West is a highly idealized account of great deeds and adventures, conquest, and fortune. Indeed, great fortunes were made in Montana, but always at the expense of the state and its residents. The fresh face of Montana that greets visitors today belies a past of abuse and exploitation. Since 1805, when Lewis and Clark unlocked the West for the fur traders, prospectors, miners, loggers, stockmen, and sodbusters who followed, Montana's history has been that of an isolated colony held captive by outside interests. Armed with capital to develop the riches of this sprawling land, they trapped its beaver, slaughtered its buffalo, plowed its virgin grasslands, fenced its plains, logged its timber, mined its precious metals, and removed tons of earth to expose its thick seams of coal.

Nowhere is the legacy of Montana's extractive economy more apparent than in Butte, where the environmental wreckage that began a century ago still blights the landscape. In its heyday, Butte was known as "the richest hill on Earth." The hill that produced more than $2 billion worth of gold, silver, copper, and zinc is now a crater. Underground mines were gradually replaced by a huge open-pit mine that opened in 1955. Until it was closed in 1983, the Berkeley Pit ate away at the city like a beast that feeds on its own flesh. Once the nation's largest producer of copper and silver, Butte now has the distinction of being one of the nation's largest Superfund sites, targeted by the federal government in 1983 as part of a massive effort to rid the nation of hazardous wastes.

Once the "richest hill on Earth," the copper-mining town of Butte is still known for its scarred landscape and spirited people. (Montana Historical Society)

AN ERA OF EXPLOITATION

The colossal fortunes created by Butte's concentrated deposits of metal ores never remained in Butte long enough to mitigate the damage created by their extraction. Instead, they wound up in the hands of three principal entrepreneurs, who came to be known as Montana's "copper kings," and the Wall Street investors who backed them in their mining ventures. Montanans had an opportunity to re-examine this chapter in their state's history of exploitation in 1989, the year they celebrated their statehood centennial. Residents got a glimpse of the fabulous wealth one of those copper kings amassed when the Corcoran Gallery of Art in Washington, D.C., agreed to lend a portion of its priceless William A. Clark art collection to Montana for temporary display at the Yellowstone Art Center in Billings. Clark assembled his collection of European paintings, Renaissance ceramics, sculpture, and antiquities after building a mining fortune in Butte and buying a seat in the United States Senate. Driven by political and financial ambitions, Clark had barely won election to the Senate in 1899 before he was derailed by rival copper king Marcus Daly, who engineered a Senate investigation of alleged campaign fraud and bribery. Earlier, the two went head to head and pocketbook to pocketbook over Clark's campaign to become a territorial delegate to Congress and his successful drive to make Helena the permanent state capital. Following the Daly-inspired investigation into Montana politics, Clark was found guilty of bribery and promptly unseated. Clark then formed an alliance with Butte's third rising star, Augustus Heinze, who built his mining empire by bribing the courts to settle property ownership disputes in his favor. Together, Clark and Heinze set out to discredit Daly and elect a pro-Clark legislature, which they did. Because United States senators were still elected by state legislatures at that time, Clark soon regained the Senate seat he had so long desired.

Following a single, undistinguished term in the Senate, Clark took his Montana-made fortune to New York City, where he built an elegant mansion on Fifth Avenue and filled it with one of America's major turn-of-the-century art collections, consisting of approximately 800 works of original art. Thought to be one of the world's eight richest men at the time, Clark is said to have left an estate valued at $150 million upon his death in 1925. Heinze reaped $10 million from the sale of his Butte mining interests in 1906. He, too, was drawn to New York. But unlike Clark, who built his fortune over a lifetime of studied and shrewd investments, Heinze engaged in some madcap ventures on Wall Street and lost his millions almost as soon as he arrived. Daly, who died in 1900, divided his assets between the town of Anaconda, where he built a huge smelter to process his ore, and southwestern Montana's scenic Bitterroot Valley, where he built a 42-room mansion and pursued his passion for breeding and racing fine horses on a baronial country estate.

The ultimate victor of the so-called "war of the copper kings" was Marcus Daly's original mining company, the Anaconda Copper Mining Company, which gradually absorbed the interests of all three men. At one time controlled by Standard Oil and William Rockefeller, Anaconda's Montana empire held mines, smelters, lumber and railroad operations, coal fields, and most of the state's major daily newspapers in the snakelike grip for which the company was named. The loser was Montana, which was dominated for years by one corporation.

Surely the most colorful story of conquest and development of Montana's vast resources, the story of the copper kings is not unique in Montana history. The importation of capital, exploitation of resources, and exportation of profits has been a recurring pattern since the fur-trade era, when beaver pelts left Montana by the boatload. Later in the century, Montana's "free grass" and "free water" gave rise to

a cattle boom that was financed largely by British capitalists and East Coast investors, the same crowd that developed the mining frontier and stretched railroad tracks across the continent.

In his *Montana: An Uncommon Land*, historian K. Ross Toole captured Montana's historic dilemma: "Distance meant cost, cost meant capital, capital meant absentee ownership, absentee ownership meant absentee control, and absentee control meant operation in the essential interest of outsiders with local interests a very secondary consideration. And so it was with beaver, beef, sheep, silver, copper, oil, and, to a lesser extent, even with lumber and wheat."

Marcus Daly, founder of Anaconda and one of Butte's "copper kings."
(Montana Historical Society)

SAVING THE LAND

Beginning in the 1970s, during an unusual period of prosperity, urbanization, and political activism, Montanans began to write a new chapter of history by fighting back to save the land they loved. Fueled by a global energy crisis, large, out-of-state coal companies were sending their lease hounds into the cattle country of southeastern Montana to secure mineral rights to the low-sulfur coal that lay in thick seams beneath prairie grasslands. In 1971 the federal government released a study calling for construction of 42 new coal-fired generating plants in the northern Plains states, half of them targeted for Montana. In addition to threatening eastern Montana's agricultural values and diverting enormous quantities of precious water from the Yellowstone River, the power plants would have obscured Montana's open spaces with a network of high-voltage transmission lines designed to carry electricity from the mines to urban markets.

Determined not to repeat their history, Montanans pulled together to keep their state from becoming what some described as a "national sacrifice area." In the end, the energy crisis dissipated and the North Central Power Study was shelved. Millions of tons of coal were stripped from the plains of southeastern Montana, however, creating a boom that gave rise to a burst of landmark environmental legislation. Some of the nation's most stringent conservation laws can be traced two decades back to Montana's legislative halls and courtrooms.

Inevitably, the prosperity of the seventies gave way to a recession in the eighties, liberals lost ground to conservatives, and jobs became the paramount issue of the day. Daily newspaper headlines focus attention on disputes between Montana's conservation community and the state's industrial giants over forest and mining practices, wilderness classification, cleanup of hazardous wastes, subdivision development, air pollution, oil drilling along the Rocky Mountain Front, grizzly bears, bald eagles, gray wolves, and a seemingly endless array of issues that won't go away.

Montanans are torn. While they wring their hands about the emigration of their youth who cannot find good-paying jobs at home, they are reluctant to let go of the reasons why they live here. Face it. Montana simply wouldn't be Montana without its bright skies, open spaces, great trout streams, and abundant wildlife.

MONTANA'S ETHNIC ROOTS

The contrary values of independence and neighborliness define the character of a Montanan. This dual personality can be traced more than a century back to the explorers, fur traders, prospectors, miners, laborers, stockmen, and homesteaders who abandoned all that was familiar to them for the promise of freedom and independence in the American West. They came, one by one and family by family, from the East and Midwest, and from ancestral neighborhoods—the Piedmont region of northern Italy, the Volga River valley of Russia, the Pyrenees, Croatia, Scandinavia, and other European enclaves. Together with relatives and friends, they brought Old World place names that still remain in the neighborhoods and towns they built. Finn Town, Caledonia, Scotch Coulee, Dublin Gulch, Belgrade, Glasgow, Frenchtown, and Amsterdam, to name just a few in Montana.

While the state's European ethnic heritage has been diluted over four and five generations as it has elsewhere in America, remnant populations of these clannish settlements still exist in the once-booming mining and smelter towns of Butte, Anaconda, Red Lodge, East Helena, and Black Eagle. The colorful mining city of Butte, which erupted in the 1880s as the greatest mining camp in the West, has the most visible ethnic mix. St. Patrick's Day is the biggest day of the year here, drawing thousands of Butte Irish and would-be Irish from throughout the state and across the nation. But Serbian Christmas and Chinese New Year are also observed in Butte, where as many as 60 different nationalities once lived and worked together.

Scandinavian immigrants left their imprint on farming communities and lumber towns, and Scottish names are still prevalent in ranching communities, like Miles City. Germans were the largest, single ethnic group to settle in Montana. They came as homesteaders and their descendants still farm near small communities throughout northern and eastern Montana. To the south, the Yellowstone River Valley attracted Russian Germans who became successful sugar beet producers.

NATIVE PEOPLES

Preceding all of these immigrant groups and later yielding to their new society were the Indians of the plains and plateau. Unlike the immigrants who settled in one place, the ancestors of Montana's present-day Indian tribes roamed the plains as hunters, relying on vast herds of bison that once ranged throughout the American West. Like the European immigrants, they left an imprint on the land in the colorful place names that honor their chiefs and perpetuate their language: Chinook, Ekalaka, Charlo, Kalispell, and Yaak.

OWNING THE EARTH

*T*he earth was created by the assistance of the sun, and it should be left as it was . . . The country was made without lines of demarcation, and it is no man's business to divide it . . . I see the whites all over the country gaining wealth, and see their desire to give us lands which are worthless . . . The earth and myself are of one mind. The measure of the land and the measure of our bodies are the same. Say to us if you can say it, that you were sent by the Creative Power to talk to us. Perhaps you think the Creator sent you here to dispose of us as you see fit. If I thought you were sent by the Creator I might be induced to think you had a right to dispose of me. Do not misunderstand me, but understand me fully with reference to my affection for the land. I never said the land was mine to do with it as I chose. The one who has the right to dispose of it is the one who has created it. I claim a right to live on my land, and accord you the privilege to live on yours.

—Chief Joseph, 1832-1904

Chief Joseph of the Nez Perce Indians. (Haynes Foundation Collection, Montana Historical Society)

Moving into Montana from the north and east were the powerful Blackfeet Indians, whose fierce war parties dominated north-central Montana and whose influence reached as far south as present-day Yellowstone National Park. Montana's largest Indian tribe, they now live on the Blackfeet Indian Reservation at the eastern edge of Glacier National Park. To the east of the Blackfeet were the Atsinas, who came to be known as the Gros Ventres, or "Big Bellies." Once allies of the Blackfeet, the Gros Ventres later aligned themselves with the Assiniboine and now live with them on the Fort Belknap Indian Reservation between the Milk River and the Little Rocky Mountains in north-central Montana. Another band of Assiniboine Indians aligned themselves with the Yanktonai Sioux; the two tribes now live together on northeastern Montana's Fort Peck Indian Reservation.

Moving into the Yellowstone River valley from the east were the Crows, enemies of the Blackfeet. Once ranging over a broad area that stretched from the upper Yellowstone River into the Big Horn and Wind River mountains of Wyoming, they now live on the Crow Indian Reservation, covering most of Big Horn County in south-central Montana. Between the Crow reservation and the Tongue River to the east is the Northern Cheyenne Indian Reservation. The Northern Cheyenne arrived in Montana later than most other Plains Indians but were here in time to join forces with the Sioux to defeat Gen. George Armstrong Custer in 1876 at the Battle of the Little Bighorn. The last Plains Indians to arrive were the Chippewas and Crees of Algonquin heritage, and the Metis or "mixed Bloods" which represent a racial mixture of Cree, Assiniboine, Chippewa, and French. Rocky Boy's Indian Reservation lies northwest of the Bear Paw Mountains in north-central Montana.

To the west of the Continental Divide were the tribes of the Columbia Plateau, which clustered in villages and relied on plants and fish. Plateau Indians living in Montana, most notably the Salish and Kootenai, combined the two lifestyles, crossing the mountains to hunt buffalo in the summer and returning to their villages in the winter. Today, the Salish and Kootenai live together on Montana's westernmost Flathead Indian Reservation. Once dominant, these native peoples now comprise only six per cent of the population. They live on seven semi-sovereign reservations. Although they coalesce on some issues, they are, in essence, seven separate nations living within the borders of Montana.

Indian teepees still cut a distinctive profile against the sky, especially at powwow time.
(photo by Douglas O'Looney)

MONTANANS TODAY

With nearly 800,000 residents, Montana has been likened to a mid-size American city, each town representing a different neighborhood with a distinct personality. Helena is the government town, Miles City the cowboy town, Billings the business town, and Missoula the university town. Each of these larger cities appears in bold type on the map of Montana and is, in itself, a bold expression of what Montana is about. But for a deeper understanding of what it is like to live in a rural Western state, look to the smaller towns, like Libby, Browning, Wolf Point, and Roundup.

Small-town America is in decline nationally, and so it is in Montana. But don't be fooled by sleepy-looking towns like Malta and Big Timber, and so many others with populations of less than 2,500. Compared with America's urban centers and mid-size cities, these small communities look like the end of the line. What do they do here, you will wonder. Not to worry. Between kids, sports, church, and local government, most residents are busy every night of the week. There are 4-H programs, basketball practices, choir rehearsals, and fund-raisers for the volunteer fire department, the senior citizens' center, and the family whose budget has been ravaged by a medical crisis. Somehow, though, there always seems to be half an hour to catch up with friends over coffee, or half a day to help a neighboring farm family with harvest.

Because Montana is so sparsely settled, neighbors are valued. Without asking, neighbors rely on one another to watch their homes while they are away or fill in when help is needed at critical times of the year, like calving and branding. Here is how one rancher describes relations in the low-lying Bull Mountains of south-central Montana: "We've worked together so long, we know what needs to be done without being told. If something happens to one of our families, our neighbors know our business better than we do and the work just goes on." This is what community is all about, and it is engendered by Montana's rural demography. Montanans rely on the entire state to provide the network of friends and business contacts most Americans find in the cities where they live and work.

The difference between commuting across the state in Montana and across town in one of America's major metro areas is that in Montana, there is nothing between Point A and Point B. Nothing manmade, that is, except an occasional gas station or roadside saloon. Montanans become intimately familiar with the look of the land as they drive to Helena to testify at legislative hearings, Miles City to place a bid at a livestock auction, or Great Falls to do some shopping. And they are all too familiar with ground blizzards, black ice, and snow-packed mountain passes. As soon as they learn to drive a car or handle a rifle, Montanans learn self-sufficiency. Neighbors are to be trusted, but it is this ability to take care of one's self that defines the Montana spirit.

THE LEWIS AND CLARK EXPEDITION

Twentieth-century moon walks aside, the Lewis and Clark Expedition remains America's greatest adventure. This was its first transcontinental trek, and much of it took place across what is now Montana. The nation's third president, Thomas Jefferson, saw westward expansion as the key not only to inland commerce but also to control of a growing trade with China via the Pacific. With a single real estate deal, Jefferson doubled the size of the United States when he bought Louisiana Territory from France in 1803 for a sum of $16 million. The Louisiana Purchase reached from the Gulf of Mexico to the Canadian border through what is now the nation's midsection; its width stretched from the Mississippi to the Rockies.

To explore this vast and uncharted land, Jefferson appointed a secret "Corps of Discovery" headed by his private secretary—Meriwether Lewis—along with William Clark, younger brother of Gen. George Rogers Clark. On May 14, 1804, their party of 45 soldiers, guides, interpreters, and others set out from St. Louis, poling up the Missouri by flatboat and keelboat. They spent that winter in a North Dakota Mandan village, and continued upriver in canoes and keelboats the following spring.

The expedition crossed into what is now Montana on April 27, 1805, and followed the Missouri to its Montana headwaters, and to what Lewis described as the "snowy barrier" of the Continental Divide. Here, Shoshone Indians provided guides and horses to cross the Rockies. The party then followed the Clearwater, Snake, and Columbia rivers down the western slopes, reaching the Pacific Ocean that fall. They built a fort near the mouth of the Columbia River for winter quarters, and re-crossed the mountains the following summer.

On the return trip east, Lewis and Clark split the expedition into two parties near what is now Lolo, Montana. Lewis and his detachment went northeast to explore the Blackfoot, Sun, and Marias rivers; Clark and his group headed southeast to explore the Yellowstone River. Six weeks later, they reached their rendezvous, near the mouth of the Yellowstone River, within nine days of one another. In the words of Robert Fletcher, popularizer of Montana history: "Considering distance and unexplored terrain, they were tolerably punctual."

On September 23, 1806, the expedition finally arrived back in St. Louis, long after everyone but President Jefferson had given them up for dead. The trip proved a vital step in bringing the Northwest under the U.S. flag, and in revealing the great wealth of this land to those back east. In just over 28 months, the expedition had traveled more than 8,000 miles (12,800 km) by foot, horseback, and boat. Well over a quarter of that distance encompassed what is now Montana.

William Clark

RETRACING LEWIS AND CLARK'S FOOTSTEPS

Travelers in Montana can visit several spots along the Lewis and Clark National Historic Trail, some developed, some not. Developed sites accessible by car are: **Missouri Headwaters State Park** near Three Forks, where the expedition traced the "heretofore conceived boundless Missouri" to its birthplace at the confluence of the Jefferson, Gallatin, and Madison rivers; **Giant Springs State Park** in Great Falls, where Clark discovered a huge "fountain or spring" during a formidable, 18-mile (29-km) portage around a series of waterfalls (now altered by dams and development); and the **Lolo Pass Visitor Center** on US 12 at the Montana-Idaho border, which explains the significance of both the Lewis and Clark Expedition and the Nez Perce Indians in this part of the state. A national Lewis and Clark Historic Center, emphasizing the expedition's encounters with the Indian culture, is scheduled to open in 1993 at Giant Springs State Park.

Meriwether Lewis

Portraits courtesy of Independence National Historic Park, Philadelphia

BOAT TOURS

One of the most enjoyable ways to retrace Lewis and Clark's journey is by boat. Commercial boat tours operate on the Missouri at the **Gates of the Mountains,** off Interstate 15 north of Helena where the river flows through a narrow canyon flanked by what Lewis described as "the most remarkable clifts that we have yet seen," and also at the White Cliffs area of the **Upper Missouri National Wild and Scenic River** below Fort Benton. A canoe rental and shuttle service on the river near Loma offers floaters the option of exploring the river on their own.

MAPS

Several maps provide detailed information on the paths of Lewis and Clark. These include: **"Lewis and Clark Trail,"** a National Park Service map available from Travel Montana, tel. (800) 541-1447; **"Lewis and Clark in the Rocky Mountains,"** a map of the expedition's route through western Montana, available from the U.S. Forest Service, Box 7669, Missoula, MT 59807; tel. 329-3511; **"The Explorers at the Portage,"** a map of the expedition's portage route around the Great Falls of the Missouri, available from the Great Falls Chamber of Commerce, Box 2127, Great Falls, MT 59403, tel. 761-4434; and **"Floater's Guide to the Upper Missouri National Wild and Scenic River,"** available from the Bureau of Land Management, Airport Rd., Lewistown, MT 59457, tel. 538-7461.

Frontier still life, displayed at Fort Benton's Museum of the Upper Missouri

THE GREAT OUTDOORS

IF HOME IS WHERE THE HEART IS, THEN THE SOUL OF A MONTANAN resides in the great outdoors. Here, it is still possible to retreat to the woods or the plains and never see another person.

Not all states were created equal—within Montana, there are two national parks and a national recreation area, 10 national forests, 15 wilderness areas, eight national wildlife refuges, 370 miles (590 km) of national wild and scenic river, and several national scenic trails, including the Continental Divide Trail. Complementing these federal holdings are 60 state parks, seven state forests, and roughly 600 miles (1,000 km) of prized, blue-ribbon trout streams.

These natural areas are the result of visionary Montanans who fought to preserve their state's rivers, forests, and open spaces. A vigilant conservation community continues this tradition by keeping watch on many fronts, ranging from forest practices and mined land reclamation to streambed protection and cleanup of toxic wastes. Priceless resources like the free-flowing Yellowstone River and the trout-rich Madison, the northern Yellowstone elk herd, and the lower 48's largest populations of grizzly bears and bighorn sheep are the reward for these efforts.

In Montana, hunting and fishing are inalienable, if not divine, rights. Montanans worship at holy places like the Big Hole River, Freezeout Lake, and the C. M. Russell Game Range. They celebrate holy days like the salmon fly hatch and the opening day of antelope season. Beyond the need to feed their souls and fill their freezers, Montanans are just plain in love with wildlife. Fishing and hunting news is reported regularly in most newspapers, and a wolf sighting or the results of a new grizzly bear study merit front-page coverage. A reporter for Kalispell's *Daily Inter Lake,* published next door to Glacier National Park and the Bob Marshall Wilderness, once told a fellow journalist, "Every time a grizzly farts, we are expected to be there."

The harmony and perfect grace of trumpeter swans in flight, the soulful song of coyotes calling, or the tonic sleep that follows a day outdoors will verify the ancient doctrine that the best things in life are free. If you have forgotten that lesson and allowed your priorities to shift in accordance with the demands of careers, possessions, and other false idols, Montana outdoors is a good place to get a fix on the planet and your place in it.

■ WILDLIFE WATCHING

The best places to observe wildlife native to the northern Rockies are the parks, refuges, and wilderness areas established for their protection. On Montana's northern border, **Glacier National Park** hosts a diversity of wildlife, ranging from a five-ounce mammal called a pika to the lower 48's largest carnivore, the grizzly bear. Glacier is probably best known for the bighorn sheep and mountain goats that grace its rocky outcrops and mountaintop perches, far removed from predators. Bands of bighorns are readily seen in the Many Glacier and Haystack Butte areas. **Wildhorse Island State Park**, surrounded by Flathead Lake, is another good place to view bighorn sheep. Bighorns have flourished on this 2,165-acre island since they were transplanted here in 1940. Other wildlife include deer, coyotes, waterfowl, raptors, and songbirds. Access is by boat.

South of Flathead Lake is the **National Bison Range**, where 400 to 500 buffalo share 19,000 acres of grassland with deer, elk, bighorn sheep, and pronghorn antelope. Set amidst stunning views of the Flathead Valley and the Mission Mountains, this refuge preserves a vestige of the estimated 13 million buffalo that once roamed Montana's plains. Established in 1909, it is one of America's oldest wildlife preserves. During the summer, visitors can explore the range by car on a self-guided tour, and in spring, they are likely to see newborn calves. The most dramatic time comes with the annual buffalo roundup of early October when visitors are treated to the drama of rumbling hooves and flying dust as cowboy rangers thin the herd.

Charles M. Russell National Wildlife Refuge on the grasslands of northeastern Montana, where buffalo once roamed, is a sprawling, million-acre refuge that protects elk, bighorn sheep, deer, pronghorns, waterfowl, and upland game. It surrounds enormous Fort Peck Lake on the Missouri River, home to trout, sauger, bass, catfish, perch, pike, and paddlefish. Together with the UL Bend Wilderness, this is the only area in Montana where elk still occupy their native prairie year-round.

Pryor Mountains Wild Horse Range near Bighorn Canyon in south-central Montana forms a unique refuge. The nation's first wild horse range, this highland desert supports about 130 free-roaming mustangs, some of which may have descended from Spanish explorers' stock. This is rugged country with year-round opportunities for hiking, birding, and fossil hunting.

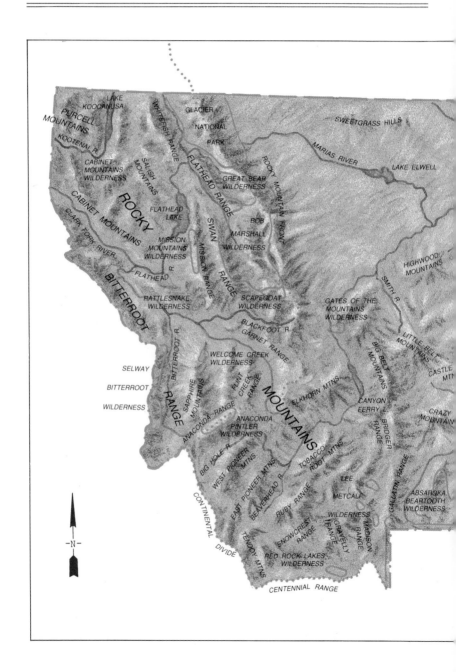

NATURAL FEATURES

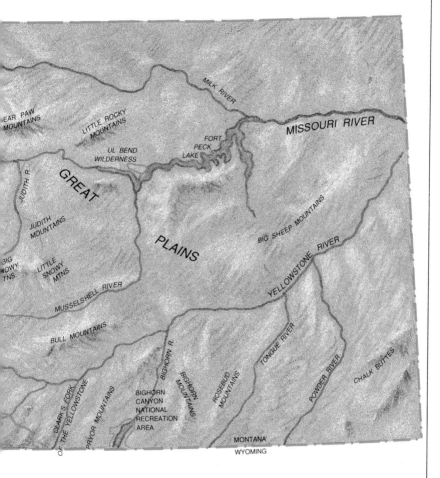

MILK RIVER

BEAR PAW MOUNTAINS

LITTLE ROCKY MOUNTAINS

MISSOURI RIVER

UL BEND WILDERNESS

FORT PECK LAKE

JUDITH R.

GREAT

JUDITH MOUNTAINS

BIG SHEEP MOUNTAINS

PLAINS

YELLOWSTONE RIVER

BIG SNOWY MTNS

LITTLE SNOWY MTNS

MUSSELSHELL RIVER

BULL MOUNTAINS

BIGHORN R.

TONGUE RIVER

POWDER RIVER

CHALK BUTTES

CLARK'S FORK OF THE YELLOWSTONE

PRYOR MOUNTAINS

BIGHORN CANYON NATIONAL RECREATION AREA

BIGHORN MOUNTAINS

ROSEBUD MOUNTAINS

MONTANA
WYOMING

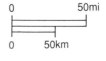

0   50mi

0   50km

Although primarily within Wyoming, **Yellowstone National Park** is a major drawing card for Montana visitors. Elk and bison regularly graze alongside highways, causing traffic to back up while otherwise responsible motorists simply abandon their vehicles for a better view. September is an especially good time to visit the park, when bull elk are challenging one another for possession of harems numbering as high as 30 cows each. There are usually one or two harems lolling around National Park Service headquarters at Mammoth under the jealous gaze of the bulls.

■ BIRDWATCHING

Among Montana's best birding opportunities are the refuges at Freezeout, Medicine, and Red Rock lakes. During peak migration periods, up to a million waterfowl can be observed at **Freezeout Lake,** a state-managed refuge about 40 miles (64 km) northwest of Great Falls in north-central Montana. Snow geese and tundra swans arrive by the thousands. Other resident and migratory birds include Canada geese, mallards, teal, pintails, eagles, hawks, owls, sandhill cranes, egrets, and ibis.

Spring and fall migrations bring up to 250,000 waterfowl to the **Medicine Lake National Wildlife Refuge** between Culbertson and Plentywood in Montana's extreme northeast corner. Especially important for white pelicans and occasional whooping cranes, this refuge also attracts great blue herons, cormorants, gulls, and most species of North American ducks. It encompasses Montana's smallest designated wilderness, also named Medicine Lake, which supports a small parcel of mixed-grass prairie and a large population of white-tailed deer.

Red Rock Lakes National Wildlife Refuge in southwestern Montana provides one of North America's most important nesting sites for the majestic trumpeter swan. This largest of all North American waterfowl has made a comeback here, in Montana's remote Centennial Valley. When the refuge was established in 1935, there were fewer than 100 known swans in the entire country, two-thirds of them living in this valley. Today, about 500 nesting swans in the Greater Yellowstone area are joined by another 1,000 wintertime migrants from Canada and Alaska. The refuge's lakes, marshes, and creeks also sustain 23 different kinds of waterfowl. Other residents and visitors include sandhill cranes, sage grouse, hawks, falcons, moose, elk, deer, and pronghorns.

(top) Bald eagles hold fall conventions on selected Montana rivers, where they feast on spawning salmon. (bottom) Swaison's hawk is commonly seen in summer at Red Rock Lakes National Wildlife Refuge in the remote Centennial Valley. Best known for its nesting population of trumpeter swans, the refuge supports more than 200 species of birds.

■ GRIZZLY COUNTRY

Of all the animals that grace the northern Rockies and Great Plains, the one that keeps Montana truly wild is the grizzly bear. Indeed, many biologists regard the presence of the grizzly as an indicator of the quality of wilderness: where there are grizzlies, there is wilderness; where there are none, there is no wilderness. Ever since Lewis and Clark crossed what is now Montana in 1805–06, trouble has been brewing between people and bears. Grizzlies once numbered as high as 50,000, with a range extending east to the Mississippi River. Unfortunately, rapid Anglo expansion decimated grizzly numbers and pushed them into remote Western wilderness areas where today they are federally protected under the Endangered Species Act. Gradual recovery of bear populations, especially in Montana, has stirred debate over whether the grizzly should be "delisted" as a threatened species.

Of the thousand or so grizzlies that remain in the American West, most survive in two major ecosystems: the Northern Continental Divide Ecosystem, which includes Glacier National Park and the Bob Marshall Wilderness; and the Greater Yellowstone Ecosystem which, in Montana, includes the Absaroka-Beartooth and Lee Metcalf wilderness areas and surrounding forests.

Chances of seeing a grizzly in the wild are slim. Bears do not seek human encounters. Indeed, grizzlies are so elusive that frequent visitors to bear country say they would regard it as a privilege to see one. With growing numbers of hikers visiting these wild places, however, there are bound to be conflicts. Between 1950 and 1980, visitors to Glacier Park—regarded as one of the nation's premier hiking destinations—tripled from 500,000 to 1.5 million a year. It was during that period that Glacier witnessed its first fatal mauling. Bear attacks are not always fatal to people; more often the bear is the loser. If a bear becomes conditioned to human food or cannot be successfully relocated from popular trails and campgrounds, park officials may have no choice but to destroy it. Between 1967 and 1989, eight people were killed by grizzlies in Glacier National Park. During the same period, 19 grizzlies were killed for management reasons.

If hikers are not aware of the dangers of hiking and camping in grizzly country when they arrive in Glacier or Yellowstone, they will be by the time they reach the trailhead. In an effort to keep bears and people apart, the National Park Service publishes and distributes all manner of pamphlets, leaflets, fliers, and "bear alerts," warning visitors about the hazards of entering grizzly country. Some may think the park service is resorting to scare tactics, but maulings in both parks have forced park officials to become aggressive managers of human traffic inside park boundaries.

Visitors are urged to take these precautions when hiking or camping in bear country:

- Hike in groups and make noise.
- Keep your food preparation area away from your sleeping area.
- Store food in closed containers and hang all food well away from campsites, and at least 12 feet (4 m) above the ground.
- If you encounter a bear, stay calm and give it wide berth, especially if it is a sow with cubs or a bear defending a carcass; slowly detour or quickly look for a tree to climb.
- If a bear charges, drop a pack or jacket to distract it, climb a tree, or as a last resort assume a "cannonball" position to protect your head and stomach while playing dead; never try to outrun a grizzly.

Of all the animals that dwell in Montana's spacious backcountry and federally protected wilderness areas, the one that keeps Montana truly wild is the grizzly bear. (illustration by Harry S. Robins)

Most maulings occur when people take chances with bears, by hiking alone, moving in too close to a bear, or camping away from designated camping areas. A little common sense goes a long way in bear country. So does a sense of perspective. Far more people have been killed by drownings, falls, and car accidents in Glacier and Yellowstone than by bears. Don't let the remote prospect of a bear encounter spoil your trip. For all who love the outdoors, this is a land of unspeakable beauty, where grizzlies remain a symbol of wildness.

At 10,000 feet (3,048 m) above sea level, the rugged Centennial Mountains capture winter's snowfall to replenish the lakes and marshes of southwestern Montana's Red Rock Lakes National Wildlife Refuge.

TROUBLE ON THE RANGE

Montanans are happy to share their space with the kinds of animals most people see only in zoos. Most will never meet a grizzly bear or a mountain lion in the wild, but knowing they could is a source of pride. They may well be in love with the idea of wildlife, but their love is not unconditional. Livestock producers, in particular, live in perpetual tension with wildlife. While ranchers are accustomed to sharing their haystacks and grain fields with deer and antelope, they draw the line on predators that threaten their cash crop of newborn lambs and calves.

Recently, grizzly bears have begun wandering out of the mountains and onto the plains near Choteau, Dupuyer, and other ranching communities along the Rocky Mountain Front. Actual depradation along the Front has been limited to a few sheep and commercial beehives, but fear of depradation has marshalled the livestock industry against the grizzly. Troublesome bears are usually trapped and transplanted to remote mountain areas. If they stay in the mountains, chances are good that they will survive their brief encounter with humanity. But if they are tempted back to the plains by the prospect of vegetation or the scent of a fresh carcass, they may wind up as good bears, which in the minds of most ranchers, are dead bears.

Chances of seeing a grizzly in the wild are slim. With growing numbers of visitors to Montana's backcountry, however, human-bear encounters are on the rise. The inevitable loser is the bear.

RUDYARD KIPLING GOES FISHING

*F*rom Livingstone the National Park train follows the Yellowstone River through the gate of the mountains and over arid volcanic country. A stranger in the cars saw me look at the ideal trout-stream below the windows and murmured softly: "Lie off at Yankee Jim's if you want good fishing." They halted the train at the head of a narrow valley, and I leaped literally into the arms' of Yankee Jim, sole owner of a log hut, an indefinite amount of hay-ground, and constructor of twenty-seven miles of wagon-road over which he held toll right. There was the hut—the river fifty yards away, and the polished line of metals that disappeared round a bluff. That was all. The railway added the finishing touch to the already complete loneliness of the place. Yankee Jim was a picturesque old man with a talent for yarns that Ananias might have envied. It seemed to me, presumptuous in my ignorance, that I might hold my own with the old-timer if I judiciously painted up a few lies gathered in the course of my wanderings. Yankee Jim saw everyone of my tales and fifty better on the spot. He dealt in bears and Indians—never less than twenty of each; had known the Yellowstone country for years, and bore upon his body marks of Indian arrows; and his eyes had seen a squaw of the Crow Indians burned alive at the stake. He said she screamed considerable. In one point did he speak the truth—as regarded the merits of that particular reach of the Yellowstone. He said it was alive with trout. It was. I fished it from noon till twilight, and the fish bit at the brown hook as though never a fat trout-fly had fallen on water. From pebbly reaches, quivering in the heat-haze where the foot caught on stumps cut four-square by the chisel-tooth of the beaver; past the fringe of the water-willow crowded with the breeding trout-fly and alive with toads and water-snakes; over the drifted timber to the grateful shadow of big trees that darkened the holes where the fattest fish lay, I worked for seven hours. The mountain flanks on either side of the valley gave back the heat as the desert gives it, and the dry sand by the railway track, where I found a rattlesnake, was hot-iron to the touch. But the trout did not care for the heat. They breasted the boiling river for my fly and they got it. I simply dare not give my bag. At the fortieth trout I gave up counting, and I had reached the fortieth in less than two hours. They were small fish,—not one over two pounds,—but they fought like small tigers, and I lost three flies before I could understand their methods of escape. Ye gods! That was fishing, though it peeled the skin from my nose in strips.

—Rudyard Kipling, *Sea to Sea: Letters of Travel,* 1899

■ TROUT FISHING

What's so special about the fishing in Montana? All of the Rocky Mountain states are headwaters states, and all are endowed with icy, clear-running mountain streams—the kind that grow up to be legendary trout rivers. So why is it that only Montana ranks consistently with the upper Great Lakes states in terms of nonresident fishing license sales? And why is it that most trout fishermen, given a choice, would rather fish the Madison, the Gallatin, or the Yellowstone than other rivers in the continental U.S.?

The answer lies in the cooperation of visionary sportsmen's and conservation groups, and an aggressive state fish and game agency that gets high marks among its peers for fisheries management. While other states still stock their streams and rivers with hatchery-reared trout, Montana manages its thousands of miles of streams and rivers for *wild* trout. And that means taking care of the land and water that support trout.

The importance of habitat was recognized by state lawmakers in 1963 with passage of the nation's first stream preservation law. What followed over the next 20 years was a series of laws designed to protect water quality, instream flows, streambank cover, and streambed integrity. These laws provide a solid framework for the conservation of Montana's streams and rivers. Together with aggressive regulations and a growing catch-and-release ethic, they have enhanced a sport fishery of national, if not international, significance.

The rivers of southwestern Montana are the heavyweights in a statewide lineup of champions. Premier trout streams include the upper Missouri and its headwaters: the Madison, Jefferson, Gallatin, Beaverhead, and Big Hole, and the waters in and around Yellowstone National Park, including the Yellowstone itself, the Firehole, Gibbon, Lamar, Gardner, and Lewis rivers, plus Slough Creek and, just over the Idaho border, the Henry's Fork of the Snake. To the northwest are the Clark Fork and Bitterroot; to the east is the Bighorn. And in between are the countless smaller streams that feed these rivers and reward the anglers who seek them out with the promise of a day well spent.

Writer Norman Maclean in his wonderful book, *A River Runs Through It,* talks of growing up in a Montana fishing family:

In our family, there was no clear line between religion and fly fishing. We lived at the junction of great trout rivers in western Montana, and our father was a Presbyterian minister and a fly fisherman who tied his own flies and taught others. He told us about Christ's disciples being fishermen, and we were left to assume, as my brother and I did, that all first-class fishermen on the Sea of Galilee were fly fishermen and that John, the favorite, was a dry-fly fisherman.

Fishing is an important part of the Montana lifestyle, and it can't be learned too early.

Montana is a headwaters state. Countless rivers are born in the snowmelt that cascades down Montana's mountain ranges.

THE RODEO CIRCUIT

The Western sport of rodeo grew out of cowboys' passion for their occupation. When they weren't movin', sortin', and brandin' cows, or breakin', buyin', and sellin' horses, cowboys were testing their day-to-day skills against one another to see who was the best calf roper or bronc rider. Before long, these barnyard contests were attracting kids and neighbors, and a professional sport was born. Cowboys began traveling from rodeo to rodeo, and the good ones won enough prize money to finance next year's circuit. Few actually make a living as rodeo cowboys, but most come away with something; if not a cash prize or a new belt buckle, often a busted jaw and a crooked grin. Some have even died doing what they loved best. But all have been lassoed by a sport that requires skill, courage, a good deal of luck, and a love of livestock. From Thompson Falls in timber country to Brockway on the plains, cities and towns across Montana celebrate their Western heritage with a weekend of rodeo, usually in summer. Popular rodeos on the Montana circuit are listed under "Top Events" in "PRACTICAL INFORMATION."

Most rodeo events fall into two categories: riding and roping. Riding events include saddle bronc riding, bareback bronc riding, and bull riding, while roping events include steer wrestling and calf roping. Women's barrel racing, along with various other sports, complete the roundup. In most events, luck has a lot to do with who wins. Much of the scoring is based on the difficulty of the ride (the toughest broncs or bulls are favorites because they mean higher scores), and times for ropers are dependent upon the speed and behavior of the calf or steer they are trying to tackle.

STEER WRESTLING

Steer wrestling, or bulldogging, involves leaping from a quarter horse onto the back of a 700-pound Mexican steer running at 25 miles an hour, grabbing his horns and wrestling him to the ground. If you think that sounds easy, try it some time! The sport originated in 1903 when Bill Pickett, a black Texas cowboy (many early cowboys were black), jumped on the back of an ornery steer, grabbed its horns, bent over its head and bit the steer's lower lip like an attacking bulldog. Soon he was repeating the stunt for the 101 Ranch Wild West Show. Others copied this feat, and though the lip-biting part has long since disappeared, the name bulldogging has stuck.

Steer wrestling today involves two men: a dogger and a hazer. When the steer hurtles into the arena, the two spur their horses in quick pursuit, with the hazer trying to force the steer to run straight ahead while the dogger gets into position to leap onto the steer's horns, wrestling him to the ground with his feet and head facing the same direction. Since they are competing with other doggers on time, every second counts. Good doggers can get a steer down in less than seven seconds.

CALF ROPING

Calf roping originated in the Old West when ropers would pull down a calf and quickly tie it up for branding. Today, this is the most competitive of all rodeo events, and there is often big money for the winners. Calf ropers chase a 200- to 350-pound (91- to 159-kg) calf on their expertly trained horses, roping it and then quickly throwing it on its side. After a quick wrap of the piggin' string around three ankles, followed by a half hitch knot, the calf is allowed to try to break free. If it can't within six seconds, the time stands and an untie man rides in to free the calf.

SADDLE BRONC RIDING

The oldest of all rodeo sports, saddle bronc riding originated from cowboys' attempts to train wild horses. Broncs are saddled up in the chutes (fenced-in enclosures along the edge of the arena) and riders climb on, grabbing a thick hemp rope in one hand and sinking their boots into the stirrups. When the gate opens, the bronc goes wild, trying to throw the rider off. The smooth back and forth motion of a good saddle bronc rider makes it appear that he is atop a rocking chair. Rides only last eight seconds; when the horn sounds, a pickup man rides alongside the bronc and the rider slides onto the other horse.

BAREBACK BRONC RIDING

Bareback riding is similar to saddle bronc riding, but the cowboy rides with only a minimum of equipment—no stirrups and no reins. A small leather rigging held on by a leather strap around the horse is topped with a suitcase-like handle. A second wool-lined strap goes around the flank of the horse to act as an irritant so that they buck more. The cowboy holds on with one hand and bounces back and forth in a rocking motion, an effort akin to trying to juggle bowling pins while surfing a big wave. Eight seconds later it's over and a pickup man comes in to rescue the rider (if he hasn't been thrown to the ground).

BULL RIDING AND RODEO CLOWNS

Bull riding is in a class of danger all its own. Unlike broncs who just want that man off their back, bulls want to get even. When a bull rider is thrown off (and this is most of the time, even with the best riders), the bull immediately goes on the attack, trying to gore or trample him. Many bull riders are seriously injured and some die when hit by this 2,000 pounds (909 kg) of brute force. There are no saddles in bull riding, just a piece of thick rope wrapped around the bull's chest with the free end wrapped tightly around the bull rider's hand. A cowbell hangs at the bottom of this contraption to annoy the bull even more. When the chute opens, all hell breaks loose as the bull does everything it possibly can to throw his rider off—spinning, kicking, jumping, and running against the fence.

If the rider hangs on for the required eight seconds (style isn't very important), the next battle begins, getting out of the way of one very angry bull. Here the rodeo clown comes in. Dressed in baggy pants and bright red and white shirts, clowns look like human Raggedy Andy dolls. In reality they are moving targets. Clowns use every trick in the book—climbing into padded barrels that the bulls butt against, weaving across the arena, mocking the bulls with matador capes, and simply running for their lives to reach the fence ahead of the bull. Frequently, two clowns work in tandem to create confusion, one acting as the barrel man, and the other as a roving target. Rodeo clowns also play another role, that of entertainer between events. Their stock of supplies includes rubber chickens, trick mules, a series of pantomimed jokes with the announcers, and anything else that might keep folks from getting restless.

BARREL RACING

One of the only female-dominated events, barrel racing is found at nearly every rodeo, and consists of a triangular course of three barrels arranged a hundred feet apart. The event requires riding a fast horse in a set pattern around these barrels, trying not to knock any over.

—Don Pitcher

Grant-Kohrs Ranch National Historic Site at Deer Lodge preserves the legacy of one of the frontier's largest and most prosperous cattle empires.

THE HI-LINE
MONTANA'S NORTHERN TIER

THE SO-CALLED "HI-LINE" IS MONTANA'S NORTHERN TIER, an immense land of cattle and grain, wildlife, waterfowl, and open space. The region's few people meet for coffee in small towns and cities along U.S. Route 2—also known as the Hi-Line—which links the high plains of eastern Montana with the Rockies to the west. Sparsely populated as it is, the sociology of northern Montana is as diverse as any you will find in the state. Scattered across this broad landscape are the descendants of immigrant farmers, ranchers, and railroad workers, the members of six Indian tribes living on four reservations, and the German-speaking residents of nearly two dozen Hutterite colonies. Adding to the mix is a regular flow of traffic to and from the Canadian provinces of Alberta and Saskatchewan, Montana's closest neighbors to the north.

■ A RESILIENT PEOPLE

The communities that dot the Hi-Line bespeak the resilience of their founders and residents. Appealing as it is, no one ever said it was easy to live in Montana, and life on the Hi-Line can be especially challenging. In addition to extremes in weather that scour the plains with arctic winds in winter and scorch them in summer, the Hi-Line has ridden out all manner of ups and downs, including the collapse both of the open range cattle industry and the homestead movement, the changing fortunes of the Great Northern Railway, cyclical drought, dust, and grasshoppers, boom and bust in the northern oil fields, and the vagaries of federal farm legislation and global grain markets. Ever since the massive farm foreclosures of the twenties, when half the state's farmers lost their land and Montana lost 60,000 residents, population along the Hi-Line has declined, due primarily to a steady out-migration from the eastern counties.

Yet, it is in the face of hardship and decline that the character of the Hi-Line reveals itself. Because people are so scarce, people matter. Neighbors are valued, and visitors frequently make the pages of the weekly newspaper. The bygone traits of compassion, good will, and humor are still palpable in communities like Malta and Glasgow. As one Hi-Liner put it: "You have to value people as the main thing when you live up here." In addition to the county fairs, church suppers, rodeos, and bull sales that bring area residents together, school sports draw passionate crowds from one end of the Hi-Line to another. It is not unusual for a Hi-Liner to drive 300 miles (480 km) from, say, Cut Bank to Wolf Point, in the dead of winter, to see a closely contested high school basketball game.

Many of the settlements along U.S. Route 2 got their start as railroad towns in 1887. Later, the Great Northern Railway Company continued west through Shelby and Cut Bank, crossed the Continental Divide at Marias Pass on Glacier National Park's southern border, and reached Seattle in 1893. Linked to the Great Lakes and the Pacific Coast by rail, these brand new towns became important storage and shipping centers for grain and livestock. **Havre** and **Shelby** are still important railroad towns along the track, now owned by the Burlington Northern Railroad. Since the discovery of oil and gas fields in north-central Montana in the 1920s and '30s, energy fuels have also been important, if fickle, partners in the local economies of Shelby and **Cut Bank**. Farther east, Fort Peck Dam and now-defunct Glasgow Air Force Base both significantly added to—then just as significantly subtracted from—the

Much of the Hi-Line was settled in the late 1880s, when Jim Hill's Great Northern Railway laid tracks across the northern Great Plains to link the Great Lakes with the Pacific Coast. (Montana Historical Society)

population of **Glasgow**. Smaller towns almost wholly dependent on farming and ranching are Malta, Harlem, Chinook, Chester, and, in the northeast corner, Scobey and Plentywood.

The Canadian border is less than an hour's drive north of U.S. Route 2 in most places. Ever since the 1920s, when bootleggers wore ruts into these and other "whiskey roads" hauling cargoes of smuggled booze into the states in defiance of Prohibition, there has been a steady flow of traffic between Canada and Montana. More than a dozen border stations are spaced along the 570-mile (910-km) international border Montana shares with Canada. The busiest border crossing between Seattle and Minneapolis is at Sweetgrass, north of Shelby on Interstate 15, which funnels traffic into the United States from the Alaska and MacKenzie highways and the province of Alberta.

■ DRIVING THROUGH

U.S. Route 2 is a relentless double lane of "oil"—in the local vernacular—that follows the Missouri and the Milk rivers from the North Dakota state line to Havre, then highballs west through Shelby and Cut Bank to Glacier National

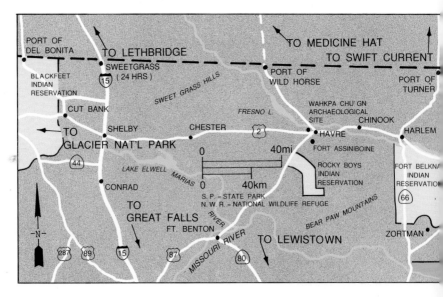

Park. The accommodations and cafés are few and far between in this remote country, but most of the small towns have all-American food and homey motels. See "PRACTICAL INFORMATION" for specifics.

Just when you think the plains will never end, the Sweet Grass Hills, the Bear Paw Mountains, and the Little Rockies appear like ghosts on the horizon. AMTRAK'S *Empire Builder*—named after nineteenth-century railroad magnate James J. Hill, whose Great Northern Railway stretched from Minneapolis to Seattle—follows a similar route across northern Montana.

Earlier visitors did it the hard way, pushing upstream against the **Missouri River,** original highway of the West. Upon first entering what is now Montana at the confluence of the Missouri and Yellowstone rivers, Meriwether Lewis noted in his journal that "we can scarcely cast our eyes in any direction without perceiving deer Elk Buffaloe or Antelopes." The date was April 29, 1805. By the end of the century, the buffalo had been shot to near extinction by hide hunters and the elk had been forced to higher ground. But the vast plains, rivers, and reservoirs of northern Montana are still home to a great variety of wildlife. Ducks and geese eclipse the moon during spring and fall migrations.

Motorists commonly spot big game and birds from the road throughout Montana, but several refuges and reservoirs along the Hi-Line assure more intimate

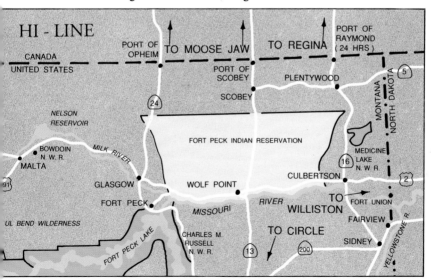

views. One of North America's largest nesting colonies of white pelicans returns to **Medicine Lake National Wildlife Refuge** each spring, along with about 100,000 ducks and geese. Get here via a paved-then-gravel road that turns east from scenic Montana State Highway 16, halfway between Culbertson and Plentywood. Medicine Lake also provides sanctuary for the threatened piping plover and an occasional endangered whooping crane. This isolated refuge in Montana's extreme northeast corner encompasses Montana's smallest classified wilderness, also called Medicine Lake, which preserves the lake's islands and waters, a small parcel of mixed-grass prairie, and a prehistoric teepee ring.

Another bird sanctuary, **Bowdoin National Wildlife Refuge,** lies about a half-day's drive west on U.S. Route 2. Spring is a busy time at Bowdoin. Starting in late March, bald eagles arrive to feast on winter-kill fish. Male sharp-tailed grouse bow and strut, coo and cackle, as they compete for mates on traditional dancing grounds in April and May. The best months to view waterfowl are May and June, as migration winds down and nesting begins. More than 200 species of birds in all, in addition to deer and antelope, make Bowdoin a favorite spot for wildlife watchers. **Nelson Reservoir,** just across the highway, is best known for its walleye, northern pike, and perch fishing, but birders visit, too, for views of its abundant waterfowl and shorebirds. Fresno Lake, Lake Elwell, and Lake Frances are also popular oases along U.S. Route 2 for fishing and hunting, wildlife viewing, and water sports.

Among the wildlife they sighted, Lewis and Clark made numerous diary entries about the "uncommonly large" and "excessively tormenting" mosquitoes they endured as they made their way up the Missouri and past its tributaries, including the Milk. Like so many other aspects of the Lewis and Clark Trail in Montana, this one has not changed. Mosquitoes are still a summertime nuisance in the Milk River valley, especially around Malta and Saco in a wet year.

■ THE FUR TRADE

Of all the wildlife reported by Lewis and Clark along the Missouri, none had more immediate impact on Montana's history than the beaver. The West presented a brand new frontier for the expanding fur trade, and eastern and European entrepreneurs lost no time in exploiting it. In 1828, John Jacob Astor's powerful American Fur Company established what was to become the preeminent fur-trading post on the Missouri River. From its strategic location at the mouth of the Yellowstone River, Fort Union dominated the northern plains and Rocky Mountain fur trade from the 1830s to the Civil War. A colorful cast of characters enlivened this lonely outpost—eastern capitalists and Plains Indians, boorish mountain men, Jesuit missionaries, artists, scientists, and European royalty anxious to glimpse America's exotic new frontier. Untold thousands of beaver pelts were floated downriver from Fort Union to St. Louis. The demand for beaver fur declined when men switched from fur to silk hats.

Fort Union Trading Post, on the Montana-North Dakota border just south of U.S. Route 2, has been preserved by the National Park Service as a historic site. Here, in this unlikely location, visitors can explore the fort's Bourgoise House, once the setting of elegant dinners for distinguished guests like the German explorer Prince Maximilian, naturalist John James Audubon, and artists Karl Bodmer and George Catlin. Newly restored to its nineteenth-century glory, Fort Union reflects one of the most colorful eras of the nation's westward expansion.

A lively chapter in Western history, this era brought death and disease to the native culture. Once nomadic, self-sufficient buffalo hunters, many Plains Indians grew dependent on the whiskey and guns they received in exchange for furs. Trappers and traders also brought smallpox, a disease that proved fatal to Indians who had no immunity. The Mandan tribe of North Dakota was almost entirely wiped out by the smallpox virus, and throughout Montana, thousands more Plains Indians died. The *coup de grâce* was the wholesale extermination of buffalo, in the mid-1870s, when buffalo hides replaced beaver pelts as the West's most profitable commodity. By 1883, the buffalo was gone and so was the Plains Indian culture it supported. Unable to provide for themselves and defend their way of life, the tribes were vulnerable to the federal government, which confined them to reservations. Even these limited reservations diminished as settlers demanded more land for farming, ranching, mining, and railroads.

■ INDIAN RESERVATIONS

The present boundaries of the Fort Peck, Fort Belknap, and Blackfeet reservations were established by the Sweetgrass Hills Treaty of 1888. The federal government created the Hi-Line's fourth reservation—Rocky Boy's—in 1916. Like Indian

A Grassy Clean Wind

*A*cross its empty miles pours the pushing and shouldering wind, a thing you tighten into as a trout tightens into fast water. It is a grassy, clean, exciting wind, with the smell of distance in it, and in its search for whatever it is looking for it turns over every wheat blade and head, every pale primrose, even the ground-hugging grass. It blows yellow-headed blackbirds and hawks and prairie sparrows around the air and ruffles the short tails of meadowlarks on fence posts. In collaboration with the light, it makes lovely and changeful what might otherwise be characterless.

It is a long way from characterless; "overpowering" would be a better word. For over the segmented circle of earth is domed the biggest sky anywhere, which on days like this sheds down on range and wheat and summer fallow a light to set a painter wild, a light pure, glareless, and transparent. The horizon a dozen miles away is as clean a line as the nearest fence. There is no haze, neither the woolly gray of humid countries nor the blue atmosphere of the mountain West. Across the immense sky move navies of cumuli, fair-weather clouds, their bottoms as even as if they had scraped themselves flat against the flat earth.

The drama of this landscape is in the sky, pouring with light and always moving. The earth is passive. And yet the beauty I am struck by, both as present fact and as revived memory, is a fusion: this sky would not be so spectacular without this earth to change and glow and darken under it. And whatever the sky may do, however the earth is shaken or darkened, the Euclidean perfection abides. The very scale, the hugeness of simple forms, emphasizes stability. It is not hills and mountains which we shall call eternal. Nature abhors an elevation as much as it abhors a vacuum; a hill is no sooner elevated than the forces of erosion begin tearing it down. These prairies are quiescent, close to static; looked at for any length of time, they begin to impose their awful perfection on the observer's mind. Eternity is a peneplain.

—Wallace Stegner, *Wolf Willow,* 1962

Northern Montana is an immense land of cattle and grain, space and sky.

reservations throughout America, these four offer a bleak insight into the conquest of one culture by another. Unemployment runs as high as 80 percent on some, and all have been ravaged by poverty and alcoholism. Cultural leaders trace a loss of pride and purpose to federal policies at the beginning of this century that outlawed traditional ceremonies like the Sun Dance and prohibited Indians from speaking their native tongues. On reservations across Montana, these people are now working with missionary zeal to heal the wounds of cultural deprivation by rescuing the language, songs, stories, and spiritual traditions of their ancestors.

Visitors can witness this cultural revival at any of the Indian powwows, where traditional dancing, drumming, singing, and games blend spirit and spectacle, reverence and revelry. The **Museum of the Plains Indian** in Browning uses Blackfeet Indian tribal artifacts and other exhibits to explain the culture and history of the tribes that inhabited northern Montana.

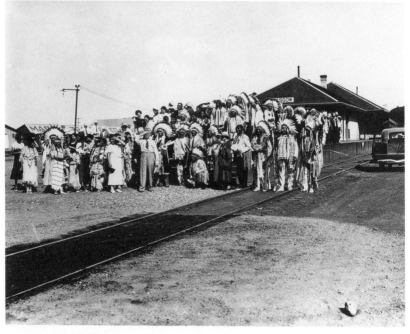

Assiniboine Indians at Glasgow awaiting the arrival of President Franklin Roosevelt in 1934 to launch construction of Fort Peck Dam. (Montana Historical Society)

CHIEF JOSEPH AND THE NEZ PERCE

One of the last major battles of the United States' campaign to win control of the plains took place about 16 miles (26 km) south of the Hi-Line town of **Chinook**. In 1877, the federal government tried to force the Nez Perce Indians of Oregon's Wallowa Valley onto an Idaho reservation so that white ranchers could have their lands. The Nez Perce stubbornly refused. A few drunk young men killed four whites, and subsequent raids led to the deaths of at least 14 more. The U.S. Army retaliated, but was turned back by the Indians.

Rather than face government reinforcements and certain defeat, more than a thousand Nez Perce began an 1,800-mile (2,900-km) flight in a desperate bid to reach safety in Canada. A series of running battles followed as the Indians used their geographic knowledge and battle skills to confound the inept Army. Finally, just 45 miles (70 km) from the international border with Canada, the Army of Gen. Nelson A. Miles caught up with the Nez Perce. After the fierce, four-day Battle of the Bears Paw, Chief Joseph is remembered for closing one of the great speeches in the history of the West with these words: "Hear me, my chiefs, I am tired; my heart is sick and sad. From where the sun now stands, I will fight no more forever." The Nez Perce were forced to surrender, though 300 made good their escape to Canada. Despite promises that they would be allowed to return home, the Nez Perce were hustled onto a reservation in Oklahoma, while whites remained on their ancestral lands farther west. Chief Joseph died in 1904, reportedly of a broken heart.

Now managed as a state park, **Chief Joseph Battlefield** has been proposed as part of a new Nez Perce National Historic Park.

(following pages) Costumes are elaborate and spirits are high as native dancers from throughout the country compete at Crow Fair. (photos by Douglas O'Looney)

■ ISLAND MOUNTAIN RANGES

Whether traveling north-south or east-west through Montana's northern tier, you will be struck by the sheer size of the landscape. With the exception of three small but surprising mountain ranges, there is nothing to interrupt the view for miles in every direction. Mere suggestions of the mountain landscape that lies to the west, the Little Rockies, Bear Paw Mountains, and Sweet Grass Hills add welcome dimension to the linear geometry of the plains. Buckhorn Cabins (see "Accommodations" in "PRACTICAL INFORMATION") in Zortman provide a pleasant stopping place at the base of the Little Rockies.

The **Little Rocky Mountains** are nearly as rich in Old West romance as they are in precious metals. Surrounded by a sea of grass and the rugged breaks of the Missouri River, these mountains provided refuge for outlaws, whiskey traders, and assorted scamps and scoundrels with names like Kid Curry, Butch Cassidy, Pike Landusky, Jew Jake, and the Sundance Kid. Tales of their Christmas shoot-outs, train robberies, and other carryings-on are as colorful as the gold that glittered in the gulches. Gold was first discovered here in 1884, and by World War II, the Little Rockies are said to have yielded $25 million in gold. Mining resumed in 1979 when the Pegasus Gold Co. developed a huge open-pit gold mine above the historic mining camp of Zortman. Today the mine produces 70,000 to 100,000 ounces of gold annually, and about three times as much silver.

Zortman and Landusky once fell within the borders of the adjoining Fort Belknap Indian Reservation. After the discovery of gold, however, agents of the federal government persuaded the Assiniboine and Gros Ventre Indians to give up this mineral-rich chunk of land for a mere $350,000. This land grab shows up clearly on the map as a big bite taken from the reservation's southern border.

Similarly, the Blackfeet Indians lost a precious piece of their traditional homeland in the **Sweet Grass Hills,** north of Chester, after gold was discovered there in 1885. The gold in these hills never amounted to a major strike. Nonetheless, this area, long regarded by the Blackfeet as a sacred site, is still held privately by non-Indians.

Chief Joseph Battlefield lies south of Chinook along Montana State Highway 240. The battlefield is well marked but otherwise undeveloped, allowing visitors to use their imagination in re-creating the last battle of the Nez Perce Indian War (15 miles, 25 km). The **Bear Paw Mountains** rise invitingly behind Havre—the Hi-Line's largest city—and Rocky Boy's Indian Reservation—Montana's smallest

Indian reservation. Said to resemble a giant paw print from a distance, the grassy buttes and rounded peaks of the Bear Paws offer cool refuge from summer's sunscorched plains. Hill County maintains a 10,000-acre public park along Beaver Creek leading into the Bear Paws, south of Havre. Billed as the largest county park in the nation, **Beaver Creek Park** offers ready access to fishing, camping, swimming, and wildlife watching for local sportsmen and outdoor lovers.

Like a portent in a well-crafted novel, these isolated mountain ranges foreshadow the drama that lies ahead when the plains run headlong into the towering wall of the Rockies.

THE HUTTERITES

Montana's cloistered Hutterites are conspicuous to the outside world by the homespun skirts, scarves, and black, Western-cut suits they wear when they come to town. These German-speaking exiles are masters of the soil and devout servants of God.

The plains of Montana, the Dakotas, and Canada provided the isolation and productive land that the Hutterite Brethren sought when they fled from intolerance and religious persecution in Russia after 1870. Firm in their insistence on adult baptism, communal living, and their refusal to bear arms or participate in prevailing social and economic institutions, these Anabaptists had already been driven from Austria, Moravia, and several eastern European countries. Between 1874 and 1877, the Hutterites established a beachhead in South Dakota, where they prospered until the patriotic fervor of World War I forced them north to Canada to avoid military conscription in the United States. Government-imposed limitations on land ownership in Canada pushed some of them back over the border after the war, and in 1937, the Hutterites established their first colony in Montana near Lewistown. About 40 colonies, each with a population of 60 to 100, now dot the plains of central and north-central Montana, where a live-and-let-live attitude has allowed the Hutterite people to flourish.

Self-sufficient and isolated by choice, Hutterites do not mix with secular society. This is not to say they are secretive or standoffish. Always willing to help non-Hutterite farmers and ranchers with repairs and chores, they are good neighbors. They visit nearby towns as necessary to pick up supplies, vote in elections, or deliver fresh produce to grocery stores.

At home and in their colonies, Hutterites speak German as a first language. English is used at school and in dealings with the outside world. Hutterite men work the land and raise the livestock; women perform all household duties. Children attend school until age 16, the minimum required by the state; then, they go to work for the colony. Hutterite women marry outside their own colony and take up residence in their husband's colony. When a colony outgrows the basic farm-ranch operation, it splits in two, with half the population moving to a new site. At the heart of every colony is a philosophy of communal sharing and caring. All members work for the colony and the colony takes care of them from cradle to grave.

Visitors can get a glimpse of colony life during late summer and fall when Hutterites harvest truckloads of fresh vegetables from their large gardens. Many colonies display signs near their entrances announcing fresh tomatoes, corn, beans, potatoes, and squash. And for many Montana families, Christmas would not be Christmas without a fat, grain-fed Hutterite goose.

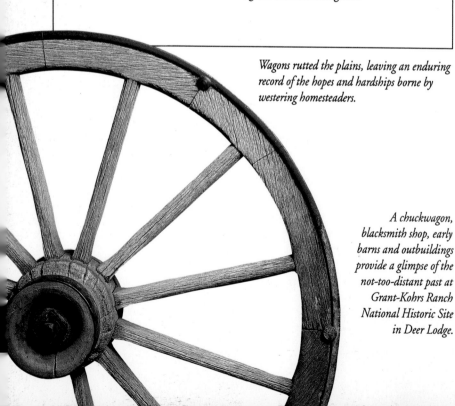

Wagons rutted the plains, leaving an enduring record of the hopes and hardships borne by westering homesteaders.

A chuckwagon, blacksmith shop, early barns and outbuildings provide a glimpse of the not-too-distant past at Grant-Kohrs Ranch National Historic Site in Deer Lodge.

THE BIG OPEN
EAST-CENTRAL MONTANA

I glance higher for some hint of the weather, and the square of air
broadens and broadens to become the blue expanse over the Montana
rangeland, so vast and vaulting that it rears, from the foundation-line of
the plains horizon, to form the walls and roof of all life's experience that
my younger self could imagine, a single great house of Sky.
—Ivan Doig, *This House of Sky: Landscapes of a Western Mind,* 1978

THE MID-SECTION OF EASTERN MONTANA—the lonely expanse of plains wedged
between the Yellowstone River on the south and the Missouri on the north—has
inspired many epithets over the years. Insiders have long known it as the "Big Dry
Country" and "Next Year Country." Lately, journalists and academicians have
brought their enlarged world-view to this forgotten place with such exotic names
as American Outback, American Serengeti, and Buffalo Commons. But frontier
photographer L. A. Huffman gets the credit for giving it the name that stuck—the
Big Open.

The Big Open is exotic. Even Montanans feel like foreigners here. Barely rele-
vant to western Montana, let alone mainstreet America, it is the fulfillment of our
folklore about the West. Undoubtedly the state's most unadulterated travel destination, the Big Open has no resorts, no gourmet restaurants, no shopping centers.
About the closest thing to a privately developed tourist attraction is a handful of
working cattle ranches that take in guests. (See "Accommodations" in "PRACTICAL
INFORMATION" for specifics.) Its two largest cities are **Jordan** (pop. 494), once described by a New York radio station as "the lonesomest town in the world," and
Circle (pop. 805), which made the news a couple of winters back when Montana
State Highway 13 north of town was clogged with tumbleweeds after a November
blow. The state highway department responded, as it does to most winter emer-
gencies, by dispatching snowplows to the site.

With roughly 4,000 people scattered over 12,000 square miles, (31,080 sq. km)
the Big Open encompasses just under 10 percent of Montana's land base, while ac-
counting for only one-half of one percent of its population. People have been quitting the Big Open ever since the homestead experiment, which failed miserably in
a land that gets 12 to 13 inches (30 to 33 cm) of moisture in a good year.

■ THE OPEN RANGE

Ironically, this was a land of opportunity in the glory days of the open range cattle boom. In a New Deal-era guidebook to Montana, the Federal Writers' Project reported that "a man who could ride a horse and do his share of corral work was always sure of a job here." This was a land of big cow outfits like the Texas-based XIT, which employed more than 200 cowboys to ride herd on 15,000 head, and the CK, part of a four-state, million-acre cattle empire owned by Conrad Kohrs. This was also the land that invented the rugged individualist, a way of life that survives, even though today's stockgrowers are tethered to the land, the next weather report, cattle futures, global markets, and international trade policies over which they have no control.

Overgrazing, compounded by the brutal winter of 1886–87 and the arrival of plows and barbed wire, brought an end to the days of the open range. The end of an era, perhaps, but by no means the end of an industry. Numbering more than 300,000 head, cattle and sheep still outnumber people nearly a hundred to one in the Big Open.

On land that requires 30 to 40 acres to support a cow and a calf, it takes a big spread and a friendly banker to build a ranch "that a cow can pay for," as the folks out here would say. This is the kind of ratio that inspires Rutgers University professors Frank and Deborah Popper to carry on their campaign to rid this and other semi-arid Western lands of cattle and give them back to grass and buffalo, creating a "Buffalo Commons." Describing the Homestead Act of 1862 as "the largest, longest-running agricultural and environmental mistake in United States history," they propose that the government buy back the land, tear down the fences, replant the shortgrass, and restock the plains with buffalo. The result would be the world's largest national park, an idea whose time has decidedly not arrived in the Big Open.

■ THE PEOPLE

Those who live outside the Big Open have long questioned the rationale of those inside. But for the few who remain and the occasional outsiders who yearn for the open road, there's no place like it. Let's start with those few souls who live here. Most live on a piece of land that has been under the stewardship of one family for three, four, perhaps five generations. It is all they know, but it is more than that. It

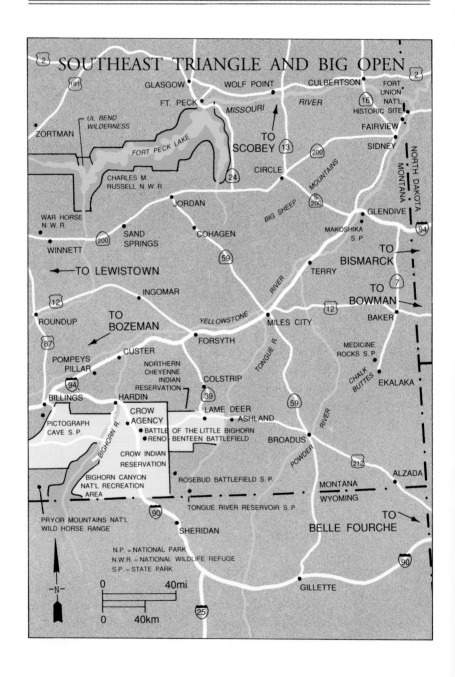

SOUTHEAST TRIANGLE AND BIG OPEN

has to do with ties that bind generation to generation, neighbor to neighbor, rancher to earth, earth to sky. In a land of infinite space, relations out here are skintight. Next door may mean 20 miles (32 km) away, but due to everlastingly busy telephone lines, neighbors know more about one another's lives here than they do in Billings or Great Falls.

In this land of isolation, people hang together. In a land of harsh winters and cyclical droughts, they sell off their herds or commute to temporary, hard-to-find jobs in Miles City or Glendive. They do what they have to do to make it through this season because things will be better next year. And, in a land of treeless plains bleached by sun, scoured by wind, and engulfed by sky, residents find unsurpassed beauty. This is the land of the long look, the unobstructed view, and they wouldn't trade it for a dozen Glacier Parks.

The inscrutable beauty of the Big Open either eludes visitors altogether or draws them back again and again. As a circuit-riding doctor from Billings describes it, "I used to think you had to have trees where you live. But pretty soon, you start seeing sunrises, sunsets, and incredible skyscapes."

Frontier photographer L.A. Huffman came west with the Army in 1878, and captured an era. His photo of a homesteader breaking the prairie is entitled "The Honyocker." (Montana Historical Society)

(top) A hopeful graingrower checks his barley crop before harvest.
(bottom) Rhythm and texture play their parts in the business of farming.

(top) Not everyone rides a horse in Montana, but they're not hard to come by.
(bottom) Grain bins form the skyline of many small farming communities.

It takes a good, long while to traverse the Big Open. Rolling ahead for as far as the eye can see, Montana State Highway 200 was made for those who travel for the sheer love of driving. Figure five hours of driving from Sidney to Lewistown, and that's with no stops. It will take at least that long to disengage from the world as you know it and adopt a new outlook. The view from the Big Open begins and ends with the sky. It has little to do with humanity, and yet it raises fundamental questions about existence. How do they make it out here, you will wonder. Wits, humor, tolerance, and style are some of the required traits, and they are visible in the weathered faces and egalitarian dress of the locals. They are audible in the no-frills dialect of the plains. When novelist Jim Harrison visited the Big Open, he had his notebook out when a cowboy blew into town and hollered that he had just "outdrove a storm down the creekbed." No need to waste time on words when there is work to be done. A soda at the general store in Sand Springs, a rib steak at the QD Cafe in Jordan, or a bowl of pinto beans at the Jersey Lilly in Ingomar (to the south, on U.S. Route 12) are all good excuses to stop, listen up, and get acquainted.

For a more formal introduction to the development of this country, plan to spend some time at the **McCone County Museum** in Circle. It took a 6,400-square-foot building to house the artifacts and memorabilia that have been assembled by this preservation-minded community. Besides comprehensive displays of the area's homestead and cattle range eras, the museum has impressive collections of firearms, Indian artifacts, arrowheads, and fossils.

■ DINOSAUR COUNTRY

Although much of Montana east of the Rockies is dinosaur country, one of the richest areas lies north of Jordan. Paleontologists and trained excavation crews comb these plains each summer for the fossilized remains of the plant and animal life that thrived here 65 million years ago, when the area was covered by swamps and shallow seas. The latest major find, discovered a couple of years ago by two amateur fossil hunters, appears to be the most complete skeleton ever found of *Tyrannosaurus rex,* largest of the predatory dinosaurs. Standing more than 18 feet (5 m) tall and weighing about seven tons, T-rex is thought to have been the most ferocious of all dinosaurs. Its six-inch-long (15-cm) serrated teeth prompted Montana paleontologist Jack Horner to describe this prehistoric giant as having had "a

Fort Peck Dam, near its completion in 1938. (Montana Historical Society)

mouth full of steak knives." Of the seven other partial T-rex skeletons that have been unearthed, five were taken from this general area of Montana. The latest skeleton has been added to the already impressive paleontology collection at the **Museum of the Rockies** in Bozeman.

More fossils from the bone beds of the Big Open can be seen at the **Fort Peck Museum,** on the northeast end of Fort Peck Lake. Salvaged from what is now the bottom of Fort Peck Lake during the construction of Fort Peck Dam, they are but a remnant of the rich prehistory of the area.

■ DAMMING THE MISSOURI

Once free-flowing and spirited, the Missouri River has been tamed dramatically since the days when explorers and mountain men muscled their way upriver to unlock the West. Several dams now control the upper river's once-treacherous current, generating electrical power and providing irrigation and recreation in the upstream states and flood control and navigation downriver. The Missouri's largest dam in Montana is at Fort Peck. Indeed, **Fort Peck Dam** is one of the world's largest earth-fill dams, and the single greatest manmade alteration to Montana's landscape.

Public policy experts now debate the wisdom of this and other dams on the Missouri, but back in the "dirty thirties," the only resistance to Fort Peck Dam came from the handful of ranchers whose lands were inundated by its floodwaters. Montana was in the grip of drought, dust, and the Great Depression. Families across the nation were desperate for work. President Franklin Roosevelt responded with the New Deal, and one of the largest New Deal projects in the country was Fort Peck Dam. When Glasgow mayor Leo Colemen learned of plans to build a dam 250 feet (76 m) high and 21,000 feet (6,400 m) across, he responded with an incredulous: "Hell, a dam like that might cost a million dollars." In fact, Fort Peck Dam cost $156 million.

Workers flocked to the site and boomtowns sprang from the plains of northeast Montana. Clusters of tents, tarpaper shacks, dance halls, and flop houses, these now-forgotten towns carried names like New Deal, Square Deal, and Wheeler. At the height of construction in 1936, nearly 11,000 workers were employed on the project. Despite the dust, danger, and drudgery, these were happy times in Montana. Paychecks came regularly and booze flowed again following the repeal of Prohibition.

Fort Peck Dam remains a monument to this troubled and triumphant era in U.S. history. Travelers today are more likely to visit Fort Peck for its recreational opportunities than its historic value, but in 1936, journalists sensed a big story here. Pulitzer Prize-winning reporter Ernie Pyle visited Fort Peck that year and described the town of Wheeler as "the wildest wild-west town in North America." Also that year, *Life* magazine was born, and Fort Peck Dam appeared on its first cover. Be sure to visit the museum located in the powerhouse at the dam, just south of U.S. Route 2 between Wolf Point and Glasgow. Besides telling the human story behind this massive public works project, the **Fort Peck Museum** has an impressive collection of fossils found during construction of the dam. The government-built town of Fort Peck is smaller and much more sedate today than it was during its dam-building days, but it offers one of Montana's finest summer playhouses, the **Fort Peck Theatre**, which features lively musicals and drama every weekend during the summer.

■ FORT PECK LAKE

Stretching 134 miles (214 km) across the northern rim of the Big Open, Fort Peck Lake covers portions of six counties and draws half-a-million visitors each year to its 1,520-mile (2,430-km) shoreline, campgrounds, and recreation areas. In recent years, however, drawdowns by the Army Corps of Engineers to satisfy demands by downstream users have dropped water levels and raised heck with the lake's recreation industry. Montana and the Dakotas have taken the federal agency to court in an effort to preserve water levels in the so-called Upper Basin states.

Between the lake and the surrounding Charles M. Russell National Wildlife Refuge, visitors can choose from boating, fishing, hiking, horseback riding, wildlife watching, and hunting. Until recently, many of the roads into the area have been impassable in wet weather because eastern Montana's clay soil turns to a greasy gumbo that grabs tires and won't let go. Today many roads have been graveled for all-weather travel, but it is always a good idea to check weather and road conditions before leaving pavement in the Big Open. Two fine drives are the gravel roads leading from Winnett (Crooked Creek Road), and Jordan (Hell Creek Road) to Fort Peck Lake—not many people, but plenty of wildlife, along with impressive badlands topography.

Every year in July, amateur and professional anglers from throughout the nation converge on Fort Peck Lake to compete in the annual Governor's Cup Walleye Tournament. While walleye is Fort Peck's best known game fish, it is by no means the only fish in this inland sea. Other popular game fish are sauger, northern pike, smallmouth bass, channel catfish, lake trout, perch, and chinook salmon. Montana's largest fish, the paddlefish, is also found in these waters, but prefers the river to the lake for its spring spawning run.

Lunkers like this chunky rainbow trout are plentiful in Montana, especially in stocked lakes and reservoirs. But a growing number of river and stream fishermen prefer to release their catch for future enjoyment.

■ CHARLES M. RUSSELL WILDLIFE REFUGE

C. M. Russell Wildlife Refuge was named for cowboy artist **Charlie Russell,** whose oil paintings and watercolors portrayed the austere beauty of the Missouri River's bluffs and coulees, badlands, breaks, and buttes. Isolated by the harsh climate, forbidding terrain, and sheer space of the Big Open, this million-acre range provides sanctuary for at least 200 species of birds, 45 different mammals, and a wide variety of reptiles and fish. Bighorn sheep have replaced the now extinct Audubon sheep that once grazed this prairie wilderness. Mule deer are the refuge's most abundant big game animals and elk are its most surprising. Together with the UL Bend, a 20,800-acre peninsula of federally protected wilderness within the refuge, this is the only place in Montana where elk still occupy their native prairie year-round. Prairie dog towns make this a good spot for burrowing owls that nest in the rodents' holes, and plovers thrive on the shortgrass and sagebrush.

The prospect of seeing strutting grouse or eavesdropping on a spring convention of Canada geese make the refuge well worth visiting, but the undefiled footprint of history makes the C. M. Russell Refuge a national treasure. Dinosaur bones, buffalo kill sites, and teepee rings mark the nothingness of the prairie like random tombstones, while abandoned homesteaders' shacks and wagon-wheel ruts reveal more recent hardships. Paleontologists and archaeologists from museums and universities throughout the country visit the refuge and surrounding area each summer in search of clues to the past.

This isolated landscape is not easily reached, but is well worth the effort. Wildlife watchers should approach the refuge from U.S. Route 191, north of Lewistown and south of Malta. A 20-mile (32-km), self-guiding auto tour starting near the west end of the refuge, off U.S. Route 191, follows an all-weather road into the bottomland of the Missouri River as it makes its way east to Fort Peck Lake. Other roads are passable only in dry weather. Morning and evening are the best times of day, when animals are moving around; spring and fall are the best seasons.

The U.S. Fish & Wildlife Service manages three outlying refuges southwest of the Russell Refuge as breeding sites and migratory rest stops for a variety of birds. Pelicans, cormorants, great blue herons, gulls, eagles, owls, and grouse are commonly seen at the **War Horse, Hailstone,** and **Lake Mason** refuges. The sage and shortgrass prairie surrounding these small lakes provides habitat for game animals, too. Located on backroads and lacking developed recreation facilities, these outposts see few visitors.

The Big Open is for nesting grebes and dancing grouse. It is for bobcats and bighorn sheep that are seldom seen in the rugged prairie wilderness of the Missouri breaks. It is for grass that needs little moisture and people who need few conveniences. The Big Open is for beasts and birds whose very existence depends on open, unpeopled places. It is for a very few people whose spirit requires the same.

THE BUFFALO DRIVE

*O*n the north we passed a precipice about one hundred and twenty feet high, under which lay scattered the fragments of at least one hundred carcases of buffaloes, although the water which had washed away the lower part of the hill must have carried off many of the dead. These buffaloes had been chased down the precipice in a way very common on the Missouri, and by which vast herds are destroyed in a moment. The mode of hunting is to select one of the most active and fleet young men, who is disguised by a buffalo skin round his body; the skin of the head with the ears and horns fastened on his own head in such a way as to deceive the buffalo: thus dressed, he fixed himself at a convenient distance between a herd of buffalo and any of the river precipices, which sometimes extend for some miles. His companions in the meantime get in the rear and side of the herd, and at a given signal show themselves, and advance towards the buffalo: they instantly take the alarm, and finding the hunters beside them, they run towards the disguised Indian or decoy, who leads them on at full speed towards the river, when suddenly securing himself in some crevice of the cliff which he had previously fixed on, the herd is left on the brink of the precipice: it is then in vain for the foremost to retreat or even to stop; they are pressed on by the hindmost rank, who, seeing no danger but from the hunters, goad on those before them till the whole are precipitated and the shore is strewed with their dead bodies. Sometimes in this perilous seduction the Indian is himself either trodden underfoot by the rapid movements of the buffalo, or missing his footing in the cliff is urged down the precipice by the falling herd. The Indians then select as much meat as they wish, and the rest is abandoned to the wolves, and creates a most dreadful stench. The wolves who had been feasting on these carcases were very fat, and so gentle that one of them was killed with a spontoon.

—Meriwether Lewis, journal entry from Arrow Creek
along the upper Missouri River on May 30, 1805

SOUTHEAST TRIANGLE

IF THE MISSOURI RIVER IS A WINDOW ON MONTANA'S PAST, then the Yellowstone embodies its future. The longest free-flowing river in the lower 48 states, the Yellowstone is a river's river, valued for what it is, not what it could become with a little intervention from, say, the Army Corps of Engineers. From its headwaters in the mountains of Wyoming's northwest corner to its confluence with the Missouri 670 miles (1,070 km) downriver, the **Yellowstone River** is unshackled by dams. As it makes its way along a gradual northeasterly course, the river forms the hypotenuse of Montana's southeast triangle.

Born in snowmelt at 12,000 feet (3,657 m), the Yellowstone cascades down mountains, catches its breath on the Yellowstone Plateau, then gouges out canyons, carves mountain valleys, races traffic along Interstate 94, and hurries past Montana's largest, most industrialized city before it settles down to the broad and braided, cottonwood-lined prairie river that dumps four trillion gallons of water into the Missouri each year. Along the way, it flowers the plains, irrigates croplands and hay pastures, supplies municipal water needs, powers industry, builds side channels, islands, and bottomlands for wildlife, sustains abundant fish populations, and provides unrivaled recreation for floaters, anglers, hunters, rockhounds, and all who find renewal in the presence of a great spirit.

■ WATER WARS

In the early 1970s, the Yellowstone was a river under siege. Proposals to dam the river had been debated off and on for 40 years, but the real threat came after the Arab oil embargo, when the federal government, together with the mining and utility industries, began eyeing the potential of eastern Montana coal fields for powering huge electrical plants. The power plants would require unprecedented diversions of water for cooling, and the logical source was the Yellowstone and its tributaries. When it was discovered that up to 80 percent of the river's total flow might be drained off in dry years, even the most ardent boosters of economic development began to question the wisdom of selling off their river as a solution to the energy problem.

Rising like tabletops out of the plains, the Chalk Buttes, near Ekalaka, are part of the southeastern Montana mosaic.

After three years of intensive research and public debate, the Montana Board of Natural Resources and Conservation set aside 5.5 million acre-feet of water in the Yellowstone and its tributaries for fish, wildlife, recreation, and protection of water quality. Water for the sake of water. It was unheard of in the West, where once-great rivers like the Colorado and the Columbia have been dammed nearly to death. Even in Montana, with 10 dams on its main stem, the Missouri ain't what she used to be.

The board's action reversed more than Montana's traditional, consumptive approach to water use. It challenged a century of resource exploitation by outside interests and said, in effect, "This is our river and we will determine its fate." With millions of tons of coal still lying in shallow underground seams nearby, the Yellowstone's future is by no means secure. But the precedent set by state policy makers in 1978, backed by public support, and bolstered by a solid framework of water protection laws assures that anyone who tries to tame the Yellowstone will have to put up quite a fight to do it.

■ THE LAND

Like the Big Open, southeastern Montana is dramatically big country. It is a land of canyons and badlands, fossils and agates, timbered hills, treeless plains, and rivers that sustain life in a near-desert climate. Southeastern Montana is good grass country, and therefore, cattle and cowboy country. It is Indian country, more specifically, Crow and Northern Cheyenne country. It is the site of last century's most celebrated clash between native and non-native cultures and this century's most heated resource debate between ranchers and coal developers. It includes Montana's largest city—Billings—along with a cowtown straight out of *Lonesome Dove*, a string of river settlements that owe their existence to the Yellowstone and the Northern Pacific Railroad, and a smattering of one-horse towns in the middle of nowhere.

Montana's southeast corner developed in much the same way as the rest of the plains. Before the end of the eighteenth century, explorers and fur traders had discovered the Missouri's great southern tributary, which carried a French name—"la Roche Jaune," or Yellow Rock. Crow Indians knew it as the Elk River, but the French name stuck when Captain William Clark Anglicized it. In July 1806, after

Powder River roundup, framed by Army post photographer L.A. Huffman.
(Montana Historical Society)

Lewis and Clark had divided their forces to further explore Montana on their return trip to St. Louis, Clark reached the Yellowstone near present-day Livingston and drifted all the way downriver to the Missouri where he and Meriwether Lewis were reunited. The only physical evidence of Clark's Yellowstone River trip is the frontier graffiti he left on a rock outcropping about 30 miles (48 km) east of Billings. He carved his signature in what he described as a "remarkable rock" and named it Pompy's Tower in honor of Sacagawea's son, whom he had nicknamed "Pomp." The federal Bureau of Land Management is negotiating with a private owner to purchase the landmark, now known as **Pompey's Pillar**, and plans to manage it as a national historic site.

■ CATTLE COUNTRY

Later in the century, while prospectors were rushing to the gold camps of western Montana, Texas cowboys began trailing hundreds of thousands of longhorn cattle north to the rich grasslands that had once supported great buffalo herds. Growing demand for beef, not only in the Eastern cities but in Western mining camps, at military forts, and on railroad construction sites, provided the market. The northern territory's vast open range provided free grass and water. The sheep industry was not far behind, but the "woolies" never matched the numbers of Montana's open range cattle. Montana's top sheep-producing county is Carter County, in the extreme southeast corner, where the woolies outnumber people about fifty to one.

■ MILES CITY

Trappings of the stockmen's trade are readily apparent in any eastern Montana town. But the heart and soul of the livestock industry, particularly the cattle industry, resides in **Miles City**, midway between Billings and Sidney, where the Tongue River joins the Yellowstone. Long recognized as the "cow capital" of Montana, Miles City pulls on its Justin "Ropers" and Tony Lamas every morning, tunes into KATL for rock or KIK for country-western, and caps the work day with beers and bourbon ditches at the Bison Bar, the Range Riders, and a half-dozen other main-street saloons. In May, the city celebrates its cowboy culture with a three-day rodeo that fills the town with thousands of spectators and participants ranging from local ranch hands to U.S. senators. The **Miles City Bucking Horse Sale** is the season opener, and it is no ordinary rodeo. Unlike other rodeos on the summer circuit, where cowboys and girls shine in skilled events like bareback riding, calf roping, steer wrestling, and barrel racing, the Bucking Horse Sale is exactly what it says it is: a showdown between the wildest, orneriest, most ill-behaved horses, and cowboys who are compulsive enough to climb aboard because "it's there." The guys who stay on top of the meanest horses longest get the prizes, and the horses that give the wildest rides sell for top dollar to rodeo stock contractors who come from throughout the United States and Canada. At the end of each day, participants and spectators mingle in downtown saloons, where videotapes of the day's buckouts are shown on big-screen TV, and the latest fashions run to canvas dusters and teal chaps.

If you can't make the Bucking Horse Sale, there are plenty of places to soak up cowboy lore year-round in Miles City. Downtown, the scent of leather wafts from the door of the **Miles City Saddlery**, drawing you inside the way a sidewalk bakery does. Tourists delight in the racks of Western clothing, and the hats and boots stacked floor to ceiling on the main level, while working cowboys head downstairs for overalls, long underwear, bits and spurs, shoeing hammers, hoof knives and rasps, nippers, and ferrier aprons—the essential gear of their trade. A couple of blocks up the street is the exquisitely restored **Montana Bar**, built in 1902 "for those early cattlemen who stayed in Montana and parlayed a bull and a handful of heifers into herds that, when trailed, were about half the size of Connecticut."

On the western outskirts of town, the cowboys and pioneers who settled these parts are memorialized at the **Range Riders Museum**, a sprawling complex that

END OF THE FRONTIER

*K*ind fate had it I should be Post Photographer with the Army during the Indian campaigns close following the annihilation of Custer's command. This Yellowstone-Big Horn country was then unpenned of wire, and unspoiled by railway, dam or ditch. Eastman had not yet made the Kodak, but thanks be, there was the old wet plate, the collodion bottle and bath. I made photographs. With crude home-made cameras, from saddle and in log shack, I saved something.

Round about us the army of buffalo hunters—red men and white—were waging the final war of extermination upon the last great herds of American bison seen upon this continent. Then came the cattleman, the "trail boss" with his army of cowboys, and the great cattle roundups. Then the army of railroad builders. That—the railway—was the fatal coming. One looked about and said, "This is the last West." It was not so. There *was* no more West after that. It was a dream and a forgetting, a chapter forever closed.

—L. A. Huffman quoted in Mark H. Brown and W. R. Felton,
Before Barbed Wire, 1956

Cheyenne Indians being interviewed about the Battle of the Little Bighorn by journalist Olin D. Wheeler. (Montana Historical Society)

exhibits relics of the range and homestead eras, period clothing, Indian artifacts, a 400-piece gun collection, and replicas of early buildings and street scenes. The museum occupies the site of a military cantonment established in 1876 by the city's namesake, Col. Nelson A. Miles, who gets most of the credit for removing the Indian "menace" from the plains after Lt. Col. George Armstrong Custer's humiliating defeat at the Battle of the Little Bighorn. The cantonment was abandoned in 1877 when Fort Keogh was built two miles to the west. Once Montana's largest army post, Fort Keogh now serves all of eastern Montana as a USDA Livestock and Range Research Station, specializing in range improvement and the science of cattle breeding.

Lonesome Dove fans will remember Miles City as the place where their favorite cowboy, Gus McCrae, bit the dust after he and Captain Call trailed their herd of stolen cattle from the Mexico border to the grass bonanza of Montana Territory. Much has changed in Montana since those glory days, but much remains the same. Though the range is now fenced, ranches are still measured in miles, and many are still in the hands of the families that first staked them out.

While southeastern Montana is largely cattle country, the rich bottomlands along the Yellowstone River invited homesteaders to try their luck at farming. Completion of the Northern Pacific Railroad in 1883 brought another wave of settlers into the area. Russian Germans saw the climate and soil of the Yellowstone River Valley as prime sugar beet country, and to this day, sugar beet farms stretch all the way from Laurel to Sidney, making Montana one of the nation's top beet-producing states. Other irrigated crops include corn, alfalfa, oats, wheat, and barley.

■ BILLINGS

The farm and livestock industry is the first order of business for most of the cities and towns of southeastern Montana, but energy production has also played a prominent role in this part of the state. The 1951 discovery of the Williston Basin—a huge oil field that underlies eastern Montana, western North Dakota, and southern Saskatchewan—brought prosperity to small communities like Glendive and Sidney, Baker and Wibaux. The biggest winner was Billings, which emerged as headquarters for the state's promising new petroleum industry. Its claim to the title of energy capital was secured by the energy scare of the seventies, which brought major-league mining and four new coal-fired generating plants to the coal fields of nearby Rosebud County. By the mid-1980s, world oil prices had collapsed. As Montana's largest and most diversified city, Billings withstood the decline, but not without substantial losses of businesses, jobs, and people.

Located midway between Minneapolis and Seattle, Denver and Calgary, **Billings** remains a major trade and distribution hub, headquarters for the region's farm and ranch economy, medical center for all of eastern Montana and northern Wyoming, business and convention center, cultural oasis, and a gateway to Yellowstone Park and the Custer Battlefield. With its handsome, new performing arts center, two college campuses, sprawling shopping malls, high-rise hotels, and buttoned-down, pin-striped business community, Billings puts on big-city airs. But behind the neon lights and theater marquees, the symphony balls and country club shindigs, Billings is a stockmen's town at heart. From the annual stockgrowers' and woolgrowers' conventions to the Northern International Livestock Exposition and Cowboy Christmas Reunion, Billings is where cowboys go when they get all slicked up for business or a night on the town. If ever there were doubt about the city's allegiance to the cattle industry, it vanished in the dust of 10,000 hooves in September 1989. Billings residents lined city streets to cheer the riders and wranglers of the "Great Montana Centennial Cattle Drive" on the last leg of their six-day, 60-mile (100-km) celebration of the way things were, here on the range, before plows turned the grass upside down and fences got in the way.

A heroic-size bronze sculpture of a cattle drover commemorates the "Drive of '89" and welcomes travelers to the **Billings Visitor Center** on South 27th Street, just off Interstate 90. This is a worthwhile stop for first-time visitors to the greater Billings area, which numbers about 100,000 residents concentrated primarily between the prominent rimrock terrace of the city's north face and the Yellowstone River on the south. In addition to its many shops, restaurants, motels and hotels, hospitals and clinics, Billings has several cultural and historic attractions. From the Royal New Zealand Ballet to the "Cowboy Review," the curtain rises one night out of three at the **Alberta Bair Theater,** Billings' brand new, $5.2-million performing arts center. The nearby **Yellowstone Art Center,** housed in the original county jail, has the best contemporary art collection in Montana. Not to be outdone by the arts community, a dedicated bunch of Billings boosters opened **ZooMontana,** a 70-acre wildlife park and botanical garden, in 1991. The **Western Heritage Center** ·

draws residents and visitors to its changing exhibits about the Yellowstone River Valley and the West. The **Moss Mansion** perpetuates the elegance of one of the city's early bankers, while **Pictograph Cave State Park** preserves the drawings of a prehistoric culture.

■ CROW AND CHEYENNE

Like the plains north of the Missouri River and the mountain valleys to the west, the "ground-of-many-gifts" south of the Yellowstone was Indian country long before it was exploited by fur traders and trampled by trail drives. Crow Indians once ranged across a gigantic sweep of mountains and plains from the upper Yellowstone River near what is now Yellowstone National Park, across southern Montana and into Wyoming's Wind River country and Bighorn Basin. A series of treaties with

Billings is a business town, and its Moss Mansion is a monument to one of the city's early banker-developers, Preston B. Moss.

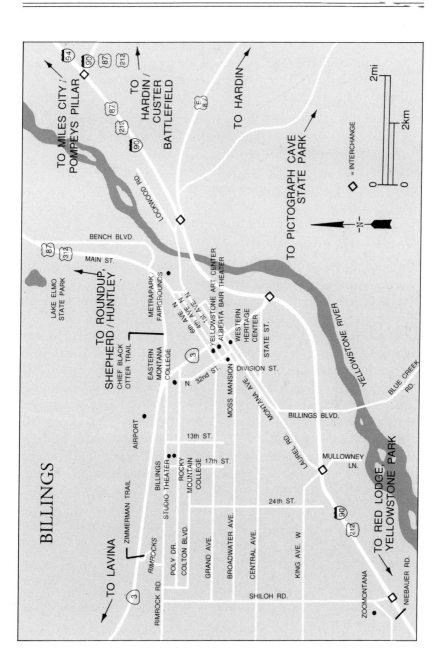

BILLINGS

the U.S. government confined them to their current two-million-acre reservation encompassing most of Big Horn County between Hardin and the Wyoming state line. Their immediate neighbors to the east, on a much smaller reservation, are their historic enemies, the Northern Cheyenne. Unlike other tribes that now inhabit Montana, the Crow developed friendly relations with the federal government before and during the Indian war years. They saw the government as a potential ally in their attempt to protect their land from encroachment by Northern Cheyenne and Sioux, many of whom had left their reservation in the Black Hills of South Dakota when it was overrun by gold prospectors.

■ CUSTER BATTLEFIELD

The **Custer Battlefield National Monument** and **Rosebud Battlefield State Park** immortalize an explosive moment and a dramatic era in Western history. The U.S. campaign to rid the plains of Indians and to open the West to development began right after the Civil War and was achieved by 1890. In just 25 years, one culture crushed another, and life would never be the same for a people whose borders were once defined by natural barriers like mountains and rivers, and whose sustenance was assured by now-extinct buffalo herds.

Scholars and Custer buffs throughout the world visit the Custer Battlefield each year in search of clues to explain the mystery of the Seventh Cavalry's misguided strategy. Casual visitors come by the thousands to walk the grounds of a battle so deeply entrenched in the lore of the American West. Some say ghosts still haunt the site, troubled visions of the violence that detonated these plains more than a century ago. A mass grave atop "Last Stand Hill" makes it a likely spot for disembodied visitors. Ironically, Custer Battlefield is also a place where all of the monuments are to the losers. Working to reverse nearly 120 years of history slanted toward Custer and his cavalry, Indian activists are promoting placement of a monument at the battlefield to the Sioux and Cheyenne victors, as well as a change of name from Custer to Little Bighorn National Battlefield.

Visitors to the Custer Battlefield are in good position to explore the culture and history of the neighboring Crow and Northern Cheyenne tribes. **Chief Plenty Coups State Park,** at Pryor, preserves the home and burial site of Plenty Coups, last chief of the Crows. The Indian leader, whose name translated means "Many

THE BATTLE OF LITTLE BIGHORN

Few events seem so fixed in the American psyche as the 1876 massacre of Gen. George Armstrong Custer and his men at Little Bighorn. The battle seems to reverberate through the years with echoes of that entire tumultuous era when whites and Indians fought over the West. Born to a middle-class Michigan family in 1839, George Custer began his military career as a rather undistinguished student at West Point. After graduating just as the Civil War was beginning, Custer proved himself an able and daring soldier, and moved quickly up the ranks, becoming a major general of the Michigan volunteers. After the war, he gained attention for his exploits in the West, and his autobiographical *My Life on the Plains* attracted national attention. There was even talk of future presidential ambitions for this rapidly rising star whose flowing yellow hair became a trademark.

Sitting Bull, Sioux chief
(Montana Historical Society)

Lt. Col. George Armstrong Custer
(Montana Historical Society)

GOLD IN THE HILLS

The events leading up to the climactic confrontation at Little Bighorn were familiar ones, centering around the discovery of a glittering yellow rock, gold. It was the same substance that had earlier stimulated the heady rush of miners and profiteers of all stripes to California, Colorado, and western Montana. This time it was to the Black Hills of Dakota Territory.

The Black Hills had long been fought over by various Indian tribes, but the ·1868 Fort Laramie Treaty promised the land to the Sioux, for "as long as the grass shall grow and the buffalo shall roam." According to the treaty, "no persons except those designated herein . . . shall ever be permitted to pass over, settle upon, or reside in the territory described in this article." As with previous treaties, however, this one proved difficult to enforce, particularly when reports kept emerging of rogue miners emerging with gold dust. To check out these rumors, Gen. Custer was sent to head a massive expedition of 1,000 men into the Black Hills in 1874. His geologists/miners did indeed find gold, an event quickly trumpeted by newspapers across the nation. Unfortunately, the 1868 treaty stood in the way of thousands of whites anxious to get rich on the latest mother lode.

Although the government officially disapproved of whites invading the Black Hills, little was done to halt their advance. Gen. William T. Sherman commented, "I understand that the President and the Interior Dept will wink at it." Even if they *had* wanted to do something, it is unlikely that the Army could have stopped the hordes of miners clamoring to get into the Black Hills. When the government attempted to buy the land for $6 million, the Sioux responded by demanding $600 million along with a guarantee of food and clothes for the next seven generations. The U.S. then took the next predictable step: they decided to simply take the Black Hills by force.

THE BUILDUP

By the fall of 1875, Sioux on the reservations faced starvation due to negligence by the U.S. government and the corruption of its Indian agents. Many of the Sioux headed west to Montana, joining the Cheyenne on hunting grounds along the Little Bighorn River. The government issued an order that all Indians who did not reach the reservations by January 31, 1876, would be considered hostiles and subject to whatever action the U.S. Army might take. The Sioux and Cheyenne either ignored the order or were too far away to be aware that it even existed. In either case, the Army was sent out to bring them in.

All of the monuments at Custer Battlefield are to the losers. Indian activists are working toward placement of a monument to the Sioux and Cheyenne victors.

The Army converged on the Sioux and Cheyenne from three directions under the overall command of Gen. Alfred H. Terry. General George Crook headed north from Fort Fetterman in Wyoming, while Gen. John Gibbon moved in from western Montana. The third column rode west from Fort Abraham Lincoln in Dakota Territory, headed by Gen. Terry, and including Gen. Custer's Seventh Cavalry.

Gen. Crook's column, reinforced by Shoshone and Crow warriors and scouts, met a force of more than a thousand Indians in the Rosebud Valley (south of the present-day Northern Cheyenne Reservation) on June 17, 1876. The Battle of the Rosebud was more or less a draw, but Crook was forced to retreat back to the south. Meanwhile, Gen. Gibbon was moving toward the Bighorn from the west, joining up with Gen. Terry on June 21. Custer and his men were directed to follow an Indian trail from the south into the Little Bighorn Valley while the force of Terry and Gibbon pressed down from the north.

The Sioux and Cheyenne were well aware that an attack was imminent. Not only had scouts warned of the advancing columns, but so had visions. Chief Sitting Bull had taken part in a Sun Dance along Rosebud Creek in which 100 pieces of flesh were cut from his arms as a blood sacrifice. Afterwards, he dreamed of a great victory over the bluecoats, a victory that was drawn out on the sand. Custer's scouts found the sand pictograph and understood its meaning. It was a warning that went unheeded by the blue coats.

THE BATTLE

On the morning of June 25, Custer's scouts had located the combined Sioux and Cheyenne village along the Little Bighorn River. His 600 men prepared to attack, unaware that at least 10,000 Indians and up to 4,000 warriors were waiting for him. To surround the village, Custer split his regiment into three battalions, putting one under the command of Maj. Marcus Reno and another under Capt. Frederick Benteen. Custer himself led the remaining 225 men.

When Reno attacked, his men were forced back by a fierce Indian counterattack, and were quickly joined by Benteen's force on the high riverside bluffs. Everyone knew that something must be terribly wrong with Custer and his men, for they heard gunfire and saw the smoke from a battle to the north. A messenger from Custer brought a note saying "Come on, big village, be quick, bring packs," but Reno and Benteen's men found themselves pinned down. Here they held out until the following evening when the Indians who had encircled them finally withdrew.

(Although an official military inquiry cleared Reno and Benteen, many historians place the blame for Custer's destruction on their shoulders for not moving up to help.)

Meanwhile, Custer had met up with the full force of several thousand battle-hardened Sioux and Cheyenne warriors. None of his command survived the Battle of the Little Bighorn to explain what had happened. Sioux and Cheyenne accounts varied, but seemed to point to complete chaos among the cavalry, with many apparently going insane in the battle and committing suicide. It appeared a fate better than being tortured to death. Among the 225 who died were Custer himself, along with two brothers, his brother-in-law, and a nephew. Probably fewer than 50 Indians were killed.

THE AFTERMATH

After the battle, Indian women moved onto the site, stripping off the soldiers' clothes and joining in a macabre mutilation of the bodies. Gen. Custer (whose hair was cut short at the time) was one of the few whose heads remained unscalped. His body was relatively untouched; some say because it was protected by two women who knew that Custer had taken a Cheyenne girl as a wife. It is also said that the two women punctured Custer's eardrums with a sewing awl so that he would be able to hear better in the next life. He had certainly not heard the warnings in this one. Two days later, the Army finally stumbled upon the gruesome carnage at Little Bighorn, the place that the Sioux called Greasy Grass.

A magnificent triumph for Sitting Bull, Crazy Horse, Gall, and other Indian leaders, victory was short-lived for the Sioux and Cheyenne. Back East, word of the massacre came as tragic news to a spirited nation in the midst of its first centennial celebration, evoking an immediate national outcry for revenge. The War Department dispatched a third of the U.S. Army to Montana Territory to put an end to the Indian resistance. Many Sioux and Cheyenne fled to temporary safety in Canada, but with the buffalo gone and their ancestral lands seized by American interests, there could be no return to the old days. Custer's Last Stand was in many respects the last stand of the Plains Indians as well. Within a few years, the last of a proud people straggled into the reservations, desperate for food. The death knell came in 1890 when medicine man Sitting Bull was shot by Indian policemen in a botched arrest.

—Don Pitcher

Achievements," is remembered for trying to save the Crows' beloved homeland by getting along with the white man. A museum at the site houses a cultural center for Crow tribal history.

Ashland's **Plains Indian Museum,** on the adjacent Northern Cheyenne Reservation, uses artifacts, clothing and beadwork, even a sweat lodge, to explain the culture of the tribes that inhabited this area. To this day, a careful observer driving through a reservation can detect random plumes of smoke that indicate Indians are heating rocks in outdoor lodges for a therapeutic or ceremonial sweat bath. The adjacent **Little Coyote Gallery** features hand-crafted headdresses, beaded moccasins, jewelry, leatherwork, and paintings. The reservation lies west of the rolling, pine-studded hills of Ashland Forest and north of Tongue River Breaks, an austere, wind-scrubbed landscape of red shale and juniper canyons near Montana's southern border. A gravel road parallels the river through Tongue River Canyon, providing fine views of the coulees and breaks. **Tongue River Reservoir State Park** offers good fishing for walleye, crappie, and bass. Four species of fish from the reservoir hold the state records for size.

The city of **Hardin,** on the northern edge of the Crow reservation, has an excellent visitor center to orient travelers to the area's past and present. A complex of restored buildings and rotating exhibits, the **Big Horn County Historical Museum and Visitor Center** portrays local history from the settler's point of view. With its outdoor park, well-stocked bookstore, and gift shop, it makes a pleasant stop.

■ BIGHORN CANYON

Less than an hour's drive south is **Bighorn Canyon National Recreation Area,** a scenic gorge sunk between the Pryor and Bighorn mountains on Montana's southern border. Canyon walls tower above 71-mile-long (114-km) Bighorn Lake, created by Yellowtail Dam near the park's northern entrance. Water sports and walleye fishing are the main attractions here, but the area also draws hikers, birders, and wildlife watchers. Endangered bald eagles, peregrine falcons, and even an occasional whooping crane round out the Bighorn Canyon bird list to 260 species. Backcountry camping, scenic drives, canyon overlooks, historic homesteads and ranches, and one of Montana's least-visited mountain ranges await visitors to the west side of the canyon. Boat tours of Bighorn Canyon are available from the Wyoming side of the canyon; see "Tours" in "PRACTICAL INFORMATION" for specifics.

Bighorn Canyon National Recreation Area, from the Devil Canyon overlook.

The **Pryor Mountains** are a remote, highland junction of desert and ice on the west side of Bighorn Canyon. Low-lying limestone peaks and plateaus are rutted with deep canyons and dotted with ice caves so numerous that visitors can still find some that have never been explored. The best known is **Big Ice Cave**, which tunnels into a hillside blanketed with wildflowers during the summer. But the Pryors' biggest attraction is its wild horse range, the nation's first. Established in 1968, this outback preserve is home to about 130 mustangs managed by the Bureau of Land Management. Descended from both Spanish stock and horses of local ranchers, they have reverted to truly wild animals in the sequestered meadows and box canyons of this 44,000-acre refuge. Visitors frequently see the horses from the Trans-Park Highway (Montana State Highway 37), on the west side of Bighorn Canyon.

Bighorn River below Yellowtail Dam on the east side of the canyon is a nationally renowned trout stream, supporting as many as 10,000 trout per mile, mostly good-sized browns. These may sound like great odds, but statistics are not synonymous with success. Fishing for wild trout in mountain rivers and streams is not as easy as it may appear. Beginners' luck aside, landing trout is directly proportional to knowledge of the water. And here on the Bighorn, there are plenty of fishing guides who know every inch of the river. If you are new to this or any river in Montana, it's a good idea to hire a guide the first day out. Drill your guide for information, then head out on your own the next day. One day's guide service on a new river is a good investment in any fishing vacation. (See "Useful Addresses" in "PRACTICAL INFORMATION" for the Montana Outfitters and Guides Association address.)

■ FISHING AND FLOATING THE YELLOWSTONE

Native cutthroat and other trout give the upper Yellowstone River its national reputation among anglers. Somewhere between Columbus and Laurel, however, the Yellowstone and its tributaries give up their cold-water traits and take on a prairie personality. The climate becomes warmer and so does the water. The river supports 45 species in all, including sauger, walleye, bass, pike, burbot, sturgeon, and channel catfish.

The lower Yellowstone's most exotic fish is also its oldest and largest. More than 65 million years old, the bottom-dwelling **paddlefish** has a distinctive, spatula-like snout and a hulking frame of cartilage and meat covered with a tough, leathery skin. The Yellowstone and the Missouri rivers support one of the world's few remaining reproducing populations of paddlefish. In May and June, the fish make spawning runs up the two rivers from Lake Sakakawea in North Dakota, signaling the start of one of Montana's most athletic sporting events. Anglers crowd the Yellowstone's banks at Intake Diversion Dam, between Glendive and Sidney. Because paddlefish are plankton eaters that filter microscopic organisms through their gills, they are never caught the conventional way, but by snagging. So, with a little blind luck, fishermen may snag one of these 25- to 50-pound (11- to 23-kg) beasts. The prize, besides a memorable catch and photo opportunity, is a freezer full of boneless, white, lobster-like steaks. Hoping to cash in on a resource that lies literally under its nose, the city of Glendive has even begun marketing paddlefish caviar.

■ AGATES

Other treasures from the lower Yellowstone include colorful moss agates, jasper, and petrified wood. Formed some 50 million years ago, agates are a form of quartz that contains dendritic, or branchlike, patterns in the shape of trees, flowers, and other "pictures." They range in color from yellow and orange to brown and black, making distinctive jewelry when cut and polished.

Not much for looks, the ancient paddlefish provides great sport for fishermen along the lower Yellowstone and Missouri rivers.
(Travel Montana)

Agates can be found all the way from Custer, where the Bighorn joins the Yellowstone, to Sidney, near the North Dakota state line. The best times to look are in early spring, when ice breaks up and scours the riverbed, and after June, when spring runoff has exposed new stones. Raw agates are not easily spotted by amateur rockhounds, but there are plenty of rock shops along the lower river, where tips and guidance are freely given. One of Montana's finest agate collections is displayed in Glendive's Best Western Holiday Lodge, where guided float trips can be arranged for agate hunters.

Whether searching for agates, fish, white-tailed deer, a family of Canada geese, or simply peace of mind, drifting down the Yellowstone is a lovely introduction to southeastern Montana. Unlike the upper river—where trout fishing and white water draw thousands of recreationists each year—the lower river is relatively unknown, a forgotten place where you can float for two or three days without seeing another person.

■ EASTERN BORDERLANDS

Land lovers will enjoy a similar, off-the-beaten-path experience most anywhere in southeastern Montana, but two of the more accessible sites are Makoshika and Medicine Rocks state parks. **Makoshika** is a badlands park, just outside of Glendive, that has been shaped over the past 70 million years by wind and water. Derived from a Sioux Indian word meaning "bad or stinking earth," Makoshika preserves 8,800 acres of sculpted sandstone and shale dotted with pine, juniper, and a frenzy of wildflowers. Fossilized remains of primitive plants and dinosaurs open windows to the prehistory of this area, once a vast swamp covered by giant ferns and inhabited by reptiles. During the summer, visiting paleontologists conduct "dig-a-dinosaur" tours to teach amateurs how to identify fossils without disturbing them. The **Frontier Gateway Museum** in Glendive has a fine collection of fossils from the area. The park's most popular current inhabitants are the turkey vultures that return each spring from the Southwest. Area residents mark the event, usually around mid-April, with "Buzzard Day," an excuse to get together at the park for games and activities. The park has a visitor center, campground, picnic tables, scenic drives, nature trails, and archery and shooting ranges.

Medicine Rocks is another badlands park, south of Makoshika in Montana's isolated southeast corner. As its name implies, this was a place of big medicine, where

Indian tribes came to seek strength and guidance from the spirits that dwelled here. The Sioux name for medicine rock, *Inyan-oka-la-ka,* means "Rock with a hole in it." In fact, these rocks look more like Swiss cheese than sandstone. The steady wind that sweeps the plains appears to be the master craftsman at Medicine Rocks, sculpting the soft sandstone deposits over millions of years into sand castles, knobs, pillars, and buttes. An early visitor to this quiet corner of Montana, Theodore Roosevelt, was captivated by the sight of "as singular a bit of country as I have ever seen." He described the formations as "caves, columns, battlements, spires, and flying buttresses . . . mingled in the strangest confusion." Once the domain of giant herds of buffalo, this area still hosts mule deer, pronghorn, coyote, fox, and raptors of all kinds. Relatively

Makoshika is a badlands park near Glendive; its Sioux Indian name means "bad or stinking earth." (photo by Douglas O'Looney)

undeveloped, Medicine Rocks State Park provides camping, picnic tables, toilets, drinking water, and a loop road with scenic turn-outs.

■ EKALAKA

A trip to this out-of-the-way corner of the world would be incomplete without a visit to Ekalaka, said to be founded by a bartender who was out here hunting buffalo when his horses balked and his wagon bogged down. "Hell," he said, "any place in Montana is a good place to build a saloon." Whereupon he dropped his load and built the Old Stand Bar, which still serves as the social center of this small but spirited outpost. While Carter County was named after the bartender, Ekalaka, its county seat, derived its curious name from a Sioux Indian girl said to be the niece of Sitting Bull. A town of only 400, Ekalaka has one of the most significant local museums in Montana. The **Carter County Museum** is nothing short of a prehistory bonanza. In addition to the 35-foot-long (11-m) skeleton of a duck-billed dinosaur, assembled bone-by-bone from fossilized remains found nearby, the museum houses the thousand-pound skull (455-kg) of a *Triceratops,* the remains of a giant marine lizard, a bonehead dinosaur, and artifacts from a much more recent find—an 11,000-year-old archaeological site where ancient peoples killed and butchered buffalo. All of the museum's treasures were found in Carter County.

South of Ekalaka are the **Chalk Buttes, Ekalaka Hills,** and **Long Pines,** three distinct scenic areas managed as units of the Custer National Forest. A number of enjoyable scenic gravel roads cut through this remote country, offering the chance to savor an austerely beautiful landscape. One of the nicest, Powderville Road, crosses the plains to tiny Powderville and then on to Chalk Buttes. Together with the Pryor Mountains, the Ashland Forest, Makoshika and Medicine Rocks, the diverse public lands of southeastern Montana have little in common except their isolation and the region's ubiquitous cattle crop. Canyons and mesas, badlands and breaks, limestone cliffs, terraces, pine forests, meadows, and grasslands are all part of the southeastern mosaic. Not long ago, many of these lands were regarded as sacred places where Indians gathered to seek visions and spiritual renewal. Largely overlooked by visitors who seek the grander scale of Glacier and Yellowstone, they remain an appealing destination for modern vision seekers.

(top) The post office, general store, and gas staion are the social center of tiny Volborg in southeastern Montana. (bottom) A well-placed sign beats a highway map when you leave the pavement in eastern Montana.

CENTRAL HEARTLAND

CENTRAL MONTANA IS A LAND OF TRANSITIONS. Moving east to west, from Roundup to the Rocky Mountain Front, it rises gradually from semi-arid plains and low-lying hills to fertile valleys, benches and buttes, forested mountains and isolated peaks. Along the way, grass and sage give way to cultivated fields of wheat and barley as the rainfall increases. Baseball caps outnumber cowboy hats and the people who wear them use tractors, not horses, to get the work done. If Montana has a heartland, this is it.

The tallest structures on the skyline are grain elevators, and one of the most pleasing sights in all of Montana is the inland ocean of plump, golden grain that ripples across the plains of central and northern Montana in late summer. Central Montana shares the grain-rich **Golden Triangle** with the Hi-Line. Find Great Falls, Havre, and Cut Bank on a map, and you will have traced the triangle's outline, but you will never see it named. It exists in the minds of Montanans, a perceptual region made real by the cash receipts of its annual output of grain. In a state that consistently ranks among the nation's top five wheat and barley producers, this area produces fully 50 percent of the statewide total. Indeed, it is one of the nation's breadbaskets.

Headquarters for the region's agriculture industry are Great Falls, which services the Golden Triangle, and Lewistown, a smaller city that pinpoints the state's geographic center. Dozens of small farming communities dot the heartland, remnants and survivors of Montana's homestead experiment.

Lewistown got an earlier start as a trading post on the Carroll Trail between Helena and the mouth of the Musselshell. It has served as a regional trade center ever since. With a population of about 6,000, Lewistown has the heart of a small town and a head for exploiting its assets. Its central location, together with a busy main street, the preservation of historic buildings erected by Croatian stone masons-turned-homesteaders, and plenty of outdoor recreation opportunities all contribute to Lewistown's appeal. Set against a backdrop of three mountain ranges—the Snowies, the Judiths, and the Moccasins—it is one of Montana's most attractive small towns.

■ GREAT FALLS

Great Falls, a city of about 55,000, straddles the Missouri River where a series of waterfalls once roared, giving the state's second-largest city its name. It was at this point on the river that Lewis and Clark encountered one of the most formidable challenges of their entire expedition. Meriwether Lewis described the falls as a "sublimely grand specticle" when he first saw them in June 1805, but the enchantment wore off quickly. He and co-captain William Clark were stalled at this site for nearly a month while they portaged 18 miles (29 km) around the falls before continuing upriver. Later harnessed by dams for their hydroelectric power potential, the falls also gave the city its most enduring nickname, the "Electric City." Scenic overlooks at some of the dams give visitors a chance to stretch their imaginations as they envision an earlier obstacle course of freeflowing falls and cascades.

By Montana standards, Great Falls is a large city with a diversified economy. Yet, it is in their past that civic leaders see the city's future. Through their efforts, a national Lewis and Clark Historic Center is scheduled to open in 1993 at **Giant Springs State Park,** on the Missouri River east of town. The center will emphasize the native cultures Lewis and Clark encountered on their route, and will include a dugout canoe demonstration area and an encampment along the river, in addition to a visitor center.

The city of Great Falls has assembled one of the world's largest collections of Charles M. Russell original art and memorabilia, on display at the **C. M. Russell Museum.** Great Falls is the logical spot for this national treasure because this is where the cowboy artist spent his most productive years as a painter, sculptor, and master storyteller of the romantic West. The city also celebrates Russell's life and legacy every year by throwing a colossal birthday party for him in March. Artists, art lovers, and collectors of Western art from throughout the world come to Great Falls to immerse themselves in four days of seminars, exhibits, and auctions at the **C. M. Russell Auction of Original Western Art.** Over 20 years old, the event has raised more than $1 million for the Russell Museum, which includes several galleries, Russell's turn-of-the-century home, and his original log cabin studio. Covering 46,000 square feet, the museum features the work of Russell and his contemporaries, and houses 7,500 works in its permanent collection. Not to be missed!

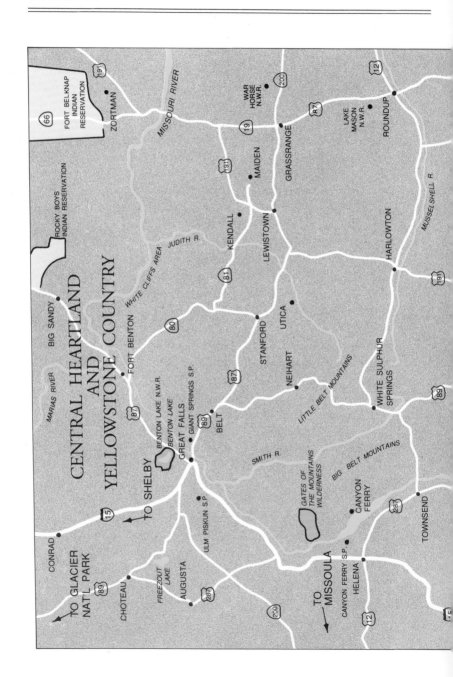

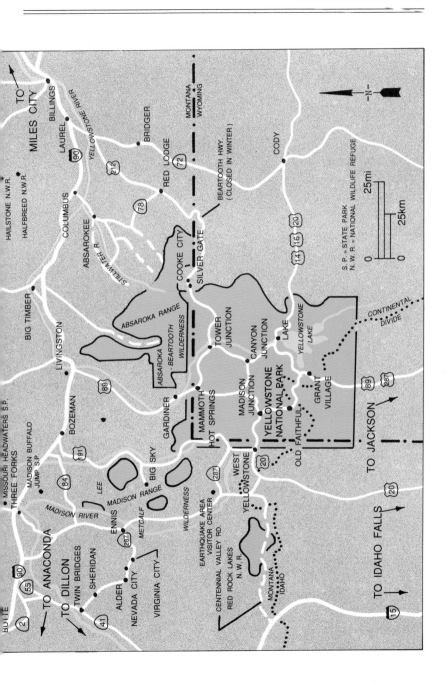

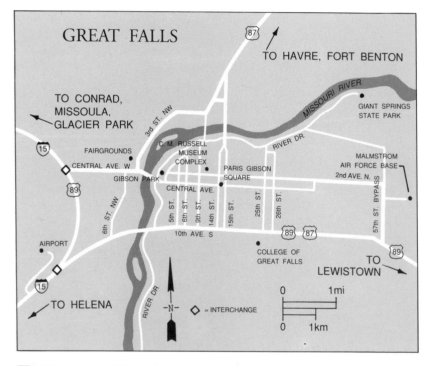

■ NUCLEAR HEARTLAND

If Russell condemned his nation's early incursions, he undoubtedly would have had some salty comments about today's military presence in Great Falls and the surrounding plains and grainfields of central Montana. Beneath this quiet, life-sustaining landscape lie 200 long-range nuclear missiles, each equipped with one to three warheads capable of producing a nuclear firestorm up to 100 times greater than the blast that incinerated Hiroshima in 1945. Installed in the early 1960s at the height of the Cold War, they comprise a portion of the 1,000 Minuteman missiles (some now being replaced by MX) seeded in the plains of seven Western and Midwestern states. Aimed at the Soviet Union, they are similarly targeted by that nation's ground-based, nuclear missiles. Residents and visitors rarely comprehend the fact that they are traversing Ground Zero when driving through central Montana because the missiles are housed—out of sight, out of mind—in underground silos. Covered by concrete slabs and surrounded by tall, chain-link fencing, they resemble

C. M. RUSSELL, COWBOY ARTIST

Cowboy artist Charles Marion Russell was born in 1864 to a wealthy St. Louis family, but spent his childhood in rebellion against the strictures of society. In desperation, Charlie's father sent the lad to Montana at age 16 to give him a dose of reality. His family expected to see a chastened young man return to their doorstep, but instead, Charlie fell in love with the wide open spaces of the West. His first Montana job—as a sheepherder along the Judith River—proved a disaster when Charlie lost the entire flock of sheep. Shortly thereafter, mountain man Jake Hoover found the shivering kid hunkered beside a flickering fire. Under Jake's tutelage, Charlie learned to survive on the open range. The small, sod-covered cabin he shared with Jake still stands along the South Fork of the Judith, an unmarked but unmistakable shrine to the romance and freedom he sought out West.

Eventually, Charlie landed a job as night wrangler for a cattle outfit. The job provided a perfect outlet for his pent-up creative energy; it meant his days were free to paint, draw, or make models from clay or wax. Russell continued to wrangle cattle for more than a decade, gaining first-hand knowledge of the cowboy life that became a central feature of his art work. Our most enduring reminder of the disastrous winter of 1886–87 is a small watercolor of a starving steer painted by Russell, who titled it "Waiting for a Chinook." Stalked by coyotes, the dying animal portrayed the end of an era.

Russell was a humorous, lighthearted man given to good times with good friends. Those who knew him were delighted by his marvelous, long-winded tales of the Old West. But Russell was saddened by the changes and injustices he saw during the rapid development of the West. A cowboy at heart, he had no affection for the homestead movement, which turned the plains "grass side down." Writing to a friend in 1913, he said, "The boosters say it's a better country than it ever was but it looks like hell to me. I liked it better when it belonged to God. It was shure his country when we knew it."

Russell spent a winter with the Blood Indians, a branch of the Blackfeet, and learned to speak Piegan. Using sign language, he could communicate with any of the Plains Indian tribes, and lamented the demise of their culture and the government's policy of displacing the West's native inhabitants. "Those Indians have been living in heaven for a thousand years," he once told a friend, "and we took it away from 'em for forty dollars a month." Russell was one of several prominent Montanans who lobbied for creation of the Rocky Boy's Reservation in 1916 for landless members of the Chippewa and Cree tribes.

Russell documented the West he loved in more than 4,500 oil paintings, watercolors, sculptures, and illustrated letters. In later years, he gained an international following for his self-taught artwork, commanding up to $20,000 for a single painting. Despite national acclaim, he continued to live in Great Falls, working in an artifact-filled log cabin studio next to his home. Russell died in 1926, but left behind his passionate legacy of paintings documenting the American West, many of which are on display in the outstanding C. M. Russell Museum in Great Falls.

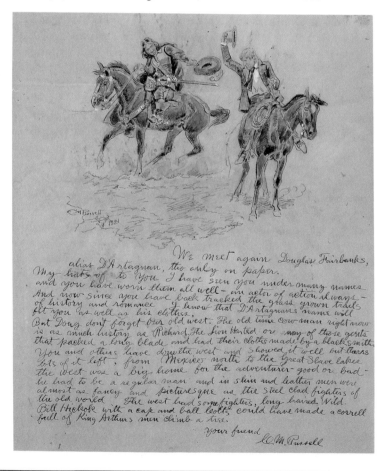

One of Charlie Russell's illustrated letters, this one to Douglas Fairbanks, Jr.

(top) "The Jerkline," oil painting by C.M. Russell. (C.M. Russell Museum)
(bottom) "He Aimed and the Snake was Shattered," pen and ink drawing by C.M. Russell.
(C.M. Russell Museum)

"Flying Lead and Splinters," ink wash by C.M. Russell. (C.M. Russell Museum)

Russell was a humorous, light-hearted man but he was saddened by the changes and injustices he saw during the rapid development of the West. (C.M. Russell Museum)

small electrical power substations. But there is no denying the fact that these are weapons of annihilation, controlled around the clock by personnel of the 341st Strategic Missile Wing based in Great Falls. A major influence on the Great Falls economy, Malmstrom Air Force Base operates an aerial refueling mission as well as the missile program.

■ FORT BENTON

An earlier military installation, **Fort Benton** is now a peaceful community loaded with history and small-town charm. Lewis and Clark camped at this site, less than an hour downriver from Great Falls, in June of 1805. Because of the trouble they and other early travelers encountered with waterfalls upriver, Fort Benton became the head of commercial navigation on the great river route of the West. Fort Benton came to be known as the "birthplace of Montana" after the first steamboat from St. Louis arrived in 1859. Within a year, it was also a terminus on the Mullan Road, which linked the Missouri to the Columbia River and the Pacific Northwest. Other wagon roads soon radiated from this river port like spokes from a hub, and by the mid-1860s, thousands of miners were passing through town en route to the gold camps of southwestern Montana. It is said that two-and-a-half tons of gold dust were shipped downriver from Fort Benton in 1866, and that between 1872 and 1882, 445,000 buffalo robes made the same trip. By the same token, tons of supplies and equipment destined for Montana's gold camps were freighted

Logo on a steam-powered tractor at Mehmke's Antique Farm Machinery Museum, near Great Falls.

OPEN HOUSE ON THE PRAIRIE

*T*he Air Force personnel who look after the missiles in Montana are stationed at Malmstrom Air Force Base, just outside of Great Falls. The public information officers there answer questions by mail about the Minuteman system with a vague line drawing of a missile in a silo. To callers who wish to chat about the missile installations, they reply in the most general terms. Then, in the summer, the base holds an open house for anybody who wants to come, and officers and enlisted men show their visitors around and tell them just about anything they want to know. This event, called Big Sky Days, is usually on a weekend in July. One year, along with about twenty-nine thousand other people, I went. At the gate, an Air Force guy in a short-sleeve blue uniform shirt was directing traffic. Nearby he had parked a Chevy Blazer with the doors open, so he could listen to the radio. "Standing in the Light," by Fleetwood Mac, was playing. Malmstrom is mostly runway. The thousands of cars parked together took up only a little piece of it. In the distance, heat shimmers rose where it seemed to disappear around the curve of the earth.

Big Sky Days was the kind of summer event where people in shorts walk around dazed and asquint. Long lines waited to go up into the camouflage-painted B-52. In a big hangar, Air Force wives and local groups ran booths selling "Rambo Hotdogs" and "Commie Busters" T-shirts. At one booth, kids could get their faces painted camouflage. By the end of the day, about half the kids had. An M-60 tank in the middle of the hangar drew kids by the hundreds. It was like the most popular rock at monkey island. Members of Air Force security in mesh flak jackets and black berets, with automatic rifles across their backs, helped kids climb on and off. By the hangar doors, pilots in flight suits walked up to each other and put their heads together. Then, after a moment, they threw back their heads and laughed big openmouth pilot laughs.

—Ian Frazier, *Great Plains*, 1989

upriver and dumped on the landing at Fort Benton, then hauled overland by ox and mule teams.

Fort Benton today is a mature, law-abiding town of about 1,600, its ambience a far cry from the lynchings and gunfights that marked its renegade youth. Paved, tree-lined streets have replaced mud- and manure-caked wagon roads. Sleek canoes and motor boats glide where sternwheel steamers once chugged into port. Neat rows of wood-frame residential housing now stand where Indian trading houses, a brewery, an adobe fort, and at least a dozen saloons once sprawled along the river. Fort Benton's preservation-minded residents have rescued their past and now share it with visitors at their riverfront park, historic landmark district, Lewis and Clark Memorial, and museums focusing on agriculture and the upper Missouri River.

■ EXPLORING THE MISSOURI RIVER

Just as it did more than a century ago, Fort Benton still serves as an important starting point for river travel. Not only can you enjoy scenic boat tours right from town, but more adventurous explorers can float the **Upper Missouri National Wild and Scenic River,** which stretches 150 miles (240 km) downriver from Fort Benton

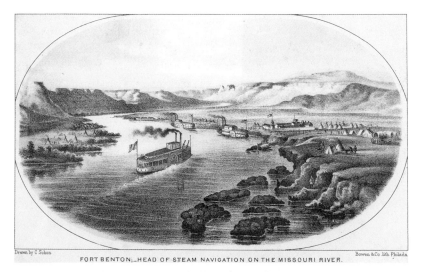

Drawn by C Schon.   Bowen &Co .lith Philada.

FORT BENTON;_HEAD OF STEAM NAVIGATION ON THE MISSOURI RIVER.

By the mid-1860s, thousands of miners were traveling by riverboat from St. Louis to Fort Benton en route to the gold camps of southwestern Montana. (Bancroft Library, University of California at Berkeley)

to Fort Peck Lake. The Bureau of Land Management maintains a visitor center in Fort Benton to orient floaters to the only major portion of the 2,300-mile-long (3,700-km) Missouri that has been preserved in its natural, freeflowing state.

As it courses through a lunar landscape of eroding breaks and badlands, sagebrush and sandstone formations, this turbid stretch of river moves relentlessly forward, yet reaches back in time. What it does not offer in white-knuckle rapids and icy, fresh water, the Missouri more than compensates with historic drama and its own isolated beauty.

Once the domain of Blackfeet, Assiniboine, and Cree Indians, the Missouri was a moving stage on which many of the major players in Montana history made their first appearance. Lewis and Clark marveled at the "seens of visionary inchantment" they viewed in the scenic White Cliffs area. Prince Maximilian, Albert Bierstadt, Karl Bodmer, and other European explorers and artists weren't far behind. Anxious for a look at the New World's exotic frontier, they sought a romantic view of the American West and recorded it in priceless illustrations and paintings of the landscape, wildlife, and native cultures they encountered as they made their way upriver. Indians and fur traders swapped beaver pelts for beads and whiskey at riverside trading posts. Near the end of their ill-fated, three-month march to Canada, Chief Joseph and his band of Nez Perce crossed this stretch of river en route to the destination they never reached. Steamboats puffed upriver, supplying a steady market for fuel supplied by "woodhawks" along the river. Cattlemen turned their herds out to graze the river's rough edges, a formidable landscape that came in handy for cattle rustlers and outlaws. Homesteaders found this country too harsh to cultivate but not before they built the weathered shacks that remain as evidence of their optimism.

For all the action this river has seen, it is hauntingly quiet now, the perfect tonic for anyone wishing to escape the babel of humanity. But for an occasional chorus of Canada geese or the distant song of coyotes calling, the isolated breaks of the Missouri are silent and refreshingly lonesome. Despite the disappearance of some of its earlier residents, like the grizzly bear, wolf, and buffalo, the Missouri still provides refuge for a diverse bunch of mammals, birds, amphibians, reptiles, and fish.

Rattlesnakes are among the strangers you might encounter here, so be prepared to rely on yourself because you are miles—on river and bad roads—from medical help. Essential gear, besides food and camping equipment, includes hiking boots, rain jackets, plenty of fresh water, and all manner of sunscreens: lotion, long

(following pages) "Indian Village" C.M. Russell Museum

sleeves, wide brims, and sunglasses. A canoe trip on the Missouri can last from a day to a week, the longer the better. Popular launching spots, besides Fort Benton, are Coal Banks Landing and Judith Landing. Lewis and Clark Cruises (see "Tours" in "PRACTICAL INFORMATION" for specifics) provides boat tours down the Missouri from Fort Benton.

While the river below Fort Benton is a national treasure, preserved for its historic and scenic values, the Missouri above Great Falls is prized as one of Montana's great trout streams. Fed by mountain headwaters and regulated by four dams, the upper river supports sizeable populations of catchable rainbows and browns. No slouch as a scenic river, this stretch is also popular with rafters and canoeists as it makes its way through canyons, past mountains, and onto open plains. Diverse habitats, ranging from bottomlands and backwater sloughs to dense forests and short-grass prairies, provide sanctuary for a variety of wildlife, including waterfowl, raptors, and upland game, deer, elk, smaller mammals, and furbearers.

■ CENTRAL MONTANA MOUNTAINS

To the east are the plains, rivers, and isolated mountain ranges of central Montana. Not as famous as southwestern Montana's Madison and Gallatin, the streams that meander through central Montana are uncrowded and fun to fish. Not as post-card-perfect as the high-rise peaks to the northwest, the mountains are smaller, more manageable, and easily reached.

Two of the most uncommonly beautiful river valleys in all of Montana carry the deceptively ordinary names of the Smith and the Judith. Both rivers rise in the mountains of central Montana and find their separate ways to the Missouri. Born in the Castle Mountains east of White Sulphur Springs, the **Smith River** winds beneath imposing limestone walls and through remote, largely private sheep and cattle ranching country between the Little Belt and Big Belt mountain ranges. Because of its isolation and limited public access, the Smith is a floater's river. Overcrowding has become a problem in recent years, necessitating the state fish and wildlife agency to regulate the number of people on the river.

In contrast, the **Judith River,** farther east, is surrounded by national forest lands and not so stand-offish. Accessible by improved gravel roads, this is a valley for leisurely driving, biking, hiking, or horseback riding. Not as big a river as the

Smith, the Judith and its mountain-fed tributaries support smallish trout. What they lack in sporting appeal, however, is compensated by the surrounding beauty of lush meadows and limestone canyons.

Up the road, the tiny outpost of Utica carries a sizeable reputation as one of the liveliest towns of the open-cattle-range era, when cowboys from throughout the grass-rich Judith Basin came to town to spend their week's earnings on Saturday night. This area has also enjoyed on-again-off-again eminence as one of the world's few producers of gem-quality sapphires. Valued worldwide for their clarity and deep blue color, sapphires have been mined from Yogo Gulch, in the Little Belt Mountains southwest of Utica, since 1896. Over the years, this lode has produced $10 million worth of gemstones. Synthetic sapphires have crowded the market and devalued the real thing, but rich veins of sapphire-bearing clay still exist in the gulch, making it a popular spot for rockhounds.

Some of the serious money in central Montana's development came from gold and silver. While the gold rush of the 1860s and the silver strikes of the eighties were concentrated in the highly mineralized mountains of southwestern Montana, the boarded skeletons of saloons and assay offices in the Castle, Judith, and Little Belt mountains confirm a fever of epidemic proportions. Fortunes were fabulous but fleeting in the mining camps of Castle, Maiden, Kendall, and Hughesville. Delayed rail service and distant smelting facilities, combined with a panic on the silver market, caused the more isolated camps of central Montana to collapse nearly as quickly as they sprang to life.

A few homes and outbuildings are all that remain of the silver mining center of Castle, once a 14-saloon town in the Castle Mountains southeast of White Sulphur Springs. In the Judith Mountains, northeast of Lewistown, there is even less evidence of Maiden, where an estimated $18 million in gold was produced before a fire leveled the town in 1905. Another mining camp in the Judiths was overestimated in nearly every respect, including its name. Mining operations never amounted to much in Gilt Edge, but legend has it that Calamity Jane was a frequent guest of its jailhouse. Nearby Kendall, in the low-lying Moccasin Mountains north of Lewistown, was a more serious venture. At the turn of the century, it boasted a two-story hotel, opera house, two churches, a mercantile, four stagecoach lines, and several saloons. Kendall became a ghost in 1912, when a branch line of the Milwaukee Road (a partly electrified railroad that spanned central Montana) sidestepped it to establish the town of Hilger nearby. Many of Kendall's buildings collapsed and others were moved to area ranches. In the Little Belts, several small camps rose briefly to prominence, including Hughesville, Barker, Lehigh, Monarch, and Neihart. Once the trade center of this mining district, **Neihart** remains a small but active jumping off place for year-round recreation in the surrounding mountains.

An icicle-lined cave with a frozen waterfall is one of the attractions that draws explorers on hot summer days to the **Big Snowy Mountains,** less than an hour's drive from Lewistown. Lake fishing, hiking trails, more caves and waterfalls, fossils, camping, picnic grounds, and stunning, 360-degree views lure visitors. **Big Spring Creek,** which offers some of Montana's finest trout fishing and best drinking water, originates in these mountains. About seven miles (11 km) south of Lewistown, where the creek emerges from one of the largest freshwater springs in the United States, visitors to the Big Springs Trout Hatchery can see where many of Montana's famed trout get their start. Unlike the wild, self-propagating trout that dwell in Montana's rivers, these hatchery trout will be planted in freshwater lakes and reservoirs. Annual output of up to three million trout and kokanee salmon accounts for a sizeable proportion of the state's total production.

To the south are the **Crazy Mountains,** supposedly named after a westering woman who became deranged and wandered the area alone after everyone else in her family was killed during a Blackfeet Indian raid. Today these mountains are known simply as the Crazies. This small but magnificent range is a favorite of hikers, horsemen, and hunters. Soaring peaks, alpine lakes, cascading streams, and sweeping views make the Crazies one of Montana's most spectacular alpine areas. To the Crow Indians these were sacred peaks, a place to summon spirits. Later travelers sought landmarks to measure their progress, and few were more dramatic than the Crazy Mountains, rising 7,000 feet (2,130 m) above the plains, 11,000 feet (3,360 m) above sea level.

■ ROCKY MOUNTAIN FRONT

Along the western edge of the heartland, travelers find another clearly defined transition point. Here, the plains pour out of the mountains, rolling east of U.S. Route 89/87 as far as the eye can see. The vertical wall of the Rocky Mountains rises abruptly to the west. This is the Rocky Mountain Front, a visual feast cooked

Castle is one of dozens of ghost towns that haunt the mountains and hillsides of central and western Montana.

up about a hundred million years ago in a superheated, over-pressurized, underground kitchen. Today's apparent calm belies the intense forces still at work beneath this transition zone. Earthquakes rumble frequently through western Montana, indicating that these mountains are still on the move.

Rocked by human conflict, the visible landscape is equally dynamic. What appears to be a land of quiet beauty has become a battle zone, where developers and conservationists, ranchers and wildlife advocates square off almost daily over the issues of oil and gas exploration, logging, wilderness protection, and grizzly bear habitat. Oil and gas deposits are believed to lie beneath the overthrust belt that was created when huge slabs of rock formations slid over one another. While conservationists, including Blackfeet Indian traditionalists, fight to preserve these pristine lands, the oil industry wants to explore their potential for commercial drilling.

One of the Front's most controversial residents, the grizzly bear, has stirred debate over another complex issue that raises a fundamental question: Whose land is this, anyway: the wildlife populations that were here first, or the human community that came later? The grizzly's leading defender, the late A. B. Guthrie, Jr., was a celebrated resident of the Front until his death in 1991. Pulitzer Prize-winning author of *The Way West, The Big Sky,* and several other novels about the early development of the West, Guthrie described the grizzly as "a living, snorting incarnation of the wilderness and grandeur of America." His allegiance to the bear was a sore point with his rancher-neighbors, most of whom run their cattle and sheep on the fringe of prime grizzly habitat.

Recognizing the importance of the Rocky Mountain Front to this and other wildlife and plants, The Nature Conservancy has preserved 18,000 acres of prairies, wetlands, foothills, and forests along the east slope of the Rockies, a lowland extension of the adjacent Bob Marshall Wilderness. The Conservancy's **Pine Butte Swamp** is the grizzly's last prairie stronghold, a place where the threatened beast and other wildlife can migrate freely between mountains and plains. Here, the bears come each spring to feed and raise their young in a lush lowland while snow still covers the high country. This merger of diverse habitats is home to more some of Montana's rarest native plants and animals, plus a rich prehistory that includes the nesting sites of dinosaurs, a buffalo jump, and a portion of the Great North Trail, used by Asiatic peoples migrating across the land bridge to North America more than 10,000 years ago. Visitors to Pine Butte Swamp, less than 30 miles (48 km) west of Choteau, can explore the preserve on their own or participate in week-long natural history tours and workshops that feature the area's plants, animals, geology, and paleontology. (See "Guest Ranches" in "PRACTICAL INFORMATION" for lodging at Pine Butte.)

From cattle and sheep to wheat and barley, plains to alpine peaks, the Central Heartland embodies the physical diversity of Montana. An agricultural giant, it is but a pinpoint on America's demographic map. The heartland was built on the backs of farmers and small-town folks who still celebrate the rural lifestyle at county fairs, church suppers, and community dance halls. But their way of life is threatened, their future as uncertain as the grizzly's. As more and more Americans desert the farm, central Montana supports fewer and fewer residents. Yet, it remains the kind of place most people would love to call home.

(following pages) Rising 7,000 feet (2,130 m) above the plains of central Montana, the Crazy Mountains were a landmark for early travelers, and a sacred place for Crow Indians.

YELLOWSTONE COUNTRY

IF YELLOWSTONE PARK WERE SIMPLY A PIECE OF REAL ESTATE defined by the legal boundaries that established it as the world's first national park in 1872, Montana would hardly be justified in claiming it as a major attraction. Barely overlapping Montana's southern border, the park's 2.2-million-acre expanse lies almost entirely in Wyoming's northwest corner. But Yellowstone is more than the largish square it occupies on both states' highway maps. It is the centerpiece of one of the nation's most intact ecosystems, the so-called **Greater Yellowstone Ecosystem,** which shapes the landscape and penetrates the mindset of three states—Wyoming, as well as Montana and Idaho. An immense wilderness plateau, it straddles the Continental Divide radiating an aura of elemental power.

Rising in the mountains of Yellowstone's backcountry, icy creeks gather size and strength as they surge north, providing Montana with some of the world's finest trout streams. Elk, grizzly bears, buffalo, geese, swans, and other Yellowstone residents migrate freely in and out of the park, making Montana a second home. It is conceivable that even the park's thermal waterworks gurgle north through underground plumbing to create the random hot springs that dot southwestern Montana. Indeed, the forests and wildernesses, pristine waters, wildlife refuges, and roadless areas that surround the park, together with the park itself, constitute some 14 million acres of wild country within the Northern Rockies. Montana's claim on Yellowstone Country extends north from the park roughly to Bozeman, Livingston, and Big Timber on Interstate 90. To the west, it stretches to the Madison River and beyond to the Gravelly Range and the Tobacco Root Mountains; to the east, it reaches to Red Lodge, at the base of the 12,000-foot-high (3,650-m) Beartooth Plateau.

Given the nature of the landscape, Yellowstone Country is as close to heaven as most outdoor lovers will get in this life. Sacred sites range from the Grand Canyon of the Yellowstone to 12,799-foot-high (3,901-m) Granite Peak (Montana's apex), from the trout-rich Madison River to feather-friendly Red Rock Lakes, a wildlife sanctuary for the trumpeter swan. Most residents devote their leisure time to fishing and hunting, hiking, biking, climbing, camping, horseback riding, and in winter, skiing and snowmobiling. Even driving is a pleasure when the road follows a sparkling river and promises glimpses of golden eagles, elk, and bighorn sheep along the way.

Four scenic highways—the Beartooth, along with the Paradise, Gallatin, and Madison valley routes—provide access from south-central Montana into Wyoming's Yellowstone National Park. All four are destinations in their own right. Three flank great rivers, and one, the Beartooth Highway, has been stealing hearts and testing flatlanders' acrophobia since its completion in 1936.

■ BEARTOOTH HIGHWAY

The **Beartooth Highway** (U.S. Route 212) is an engineering triumph. Ascending the glacier-carved walls of Rock Creek Canyon south of Red Lodge, it teeters up switchbacks and hairpin curves with names like "Mae West" and "Frozen Man," delivering travelers from one heart-in-the-throat view to the next until it levels off at about 11,000 feet (3,350 m) on the Beartooth Plateau. Snow-white peaks and plateaus, alpine lakes, elk, moose, lupine, buttercups, and daisies are all part of the view from the top of the world. First-time visitors are literally breathless by the time they reach the rarefied air on top. After catching their breath and stabilizing their knees, most put the Beartooth Highway near the top of their most-loved-trips list. CBS news correspondent Charles Kuralt once described it as "the most beautiful roadway in America."

The highway is generally open from late May to mid-October, but snow can come at any time to this high country. While marmots celebrate summer by sunning themselves on newly exposed rockslides, visitors play in snowfields by the side of the road, and Olympic-class skiers descend snow-encrusted headwalls as part of their training at the Red Lodge International Ski Race Camp. Give yourself at least three hours to drive the 68-mile-long (109-km) Beartooth Highway between Red Lodge and Yellowstone's northeast entrance. This is a drive to be relished, not rushed.

Born as a coal-mining camp, **Red Lodge** grew on the backs and brawn of European immigrants. Today, this spirited mountain village relies on agriculture, recreation, and tourism for its economic well-being, but it has never lost sight of its proletarian roots. Ethnic distinctions have been diluted here as elsewhere in Montana, but neighborhoods still wear names like Finn Town, Little Italy, and "Hi Bug"—a schoolyard tag invented by kids to describe where the English-speaking upper class lived. Every August, the international stew that simmered here is served up at Red Lodge's nine-day-long Festival of Nations.

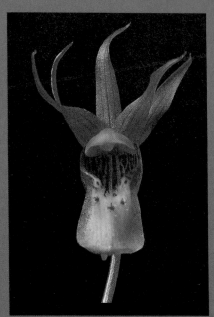

Sitting at the base of the skyscraper Beartooth Range, Red Lodge can count on a good six to seven months of snow, making it one of the state's top ski and winter sports areas. A dumping of six feet (two meters) of snow in April is not uncommon. While the rest of Montana is rejoicing in green grass and crocus, hardcore skiers are stretching the season at **Red Lodge Mountain,** one of the Northern Rockies' premier spring skiing areas. (See "WINTER RECREATION" for specifics.) When the snow finally retreats, Red Lodge embraces summer the way someone with a terminal illness clings to each day of life. This is a season of celebrations, ranging from the **Peaks to Prairie Relay** and the uphill-all-the-way **Beartooth Run** to the **Red Lodge Music Festival, Home of Champions Rodeo,** and the **Festival of Nations.**

◼ ABSAROKA-BEARTOOTH WILDERNESS

The Absaroka-Beartooth Wilderness is to hikers what Yellowstone National Park is to motorists. Just as adjoining Yellowstone Park was envisioned more than a

Rough Lake is one of nearly 1,000 lakes that dot the alpine plateaus of the Absaroka-Beartooth Wilderness in south-central Montana.

Wildflowers embroider the plains and the mountains in a patchwork of color. Pictured here (clockwise from top left) are false lupine, fairy slipper, blue bonnet, and shooting stars.

century ago as a national pleasuring ground for the masses, the Absaroka-Beartooth Wilderness is the legacy of visionary conservationists who recognized the value of keeping this heavenly plateau forever wild. Remote and rugged, this alpine wilderness encompasses the lower 48's largest single expanse of land above 10,000 feet (3,050 m). Indeed, 28 peaks, all within the Beartooth Range, rise to 12,000 feet (3,660 m) or higher. At their base, mammoth boulders and icy lakes are strewn across the landscape like giant fistfuls of confetti. The less rugged, more rounded mountains of the Absaroka Range form the western half of a backcountry playground that covers nearly a million acres within two national forests in south-central Montana.

Snow can come at any time to this high country, making it one of Montana's least hospitable destinations. Yet, backpackers arrive like pilgrims at this high ground, making it one of the most heavily used wildernesses in America. About 700 miles (1,120 km) of trails take visitors seemingly to the top of the world. Many of the lakes are stocked with trout, mostly cutthroat and brookies, but also prized golden trout and arctic grayling. Rocky cliffs and remote river drainages shelter some of the Northern Rockies' most distinguished residents, including bighorn sheep, mountain goats, elk, bear, and moose. Prolific wildflowers defy one of Montana's harshest climates with audacious blossoms of phlox, orchids, and lilies during a spring season that lasts all summer.

July and August are the most reliable months for dry weather, but a trip into the Absaroka-Beartooth Wilderness is never to be entered into lightly. The Beartooths stir up their own weather, and violent storms frequently pound the plateau as if Zeus himself were hurling thunderbolts from Granite Peak. This is not to say that wilderness visitors invariably encounter snow, sleet, hail, rain, wind, or hypothermia in the wilderness. But they had better be prepared for all of the above, as well as the blinding purity of sunlight at more than two miles (three km) above sea level.

■ PARADISE VALLEY

For some travelers, particularly those from the East and Midwest, the Beartooth Highway is too much, too soon. A devious service station owner in Billings used to delight in directing Yellowstone Park-bound tourists up the Beartooth, insisting it was the only way to get to the park from Billings. Most went on their way and were never heard from again, but a few made a point of returning to Billings to blister their informant for sending them on a journey that unnerved them from the moment they rounded their first switchback. Especially when they realized there was an alternate route to the park, another 100 miles (160 km) west of the Beartooth turnoff.

For those who prefer their mountains from a distance, U.S. Route 89 through Paradise Valley delivers stunning alpine scenery. The road itself follows a well-mannered riverside route between Livingston and the north entrance to Yellowstone National Park at Gardiner. To the east lies the imposing face of the Absarokas; to the west, the foothills of the Gallatins. Gouging out the broad valley between these two ranges is the **Yellowstone River,** one of Montana's finest fishing and floating rivers.

Encircled by mountains, Paradise Valley has a way of lifting your eyes upward, which seems a good enough explanation for the origin of its name. Horace Albright, once superintendent of Yellowstone Park and later the head of the National Park Service, said of the valley, "If that area were in any other state, it would have been a national park." Area ranchers would never put up with such a foolish notion, but even the most vocal opponents of land-use planning now wish the valley had been protected from free market economics in 1981 when the late publisher Malcolm Forbes sold his 12,000-acre ranch along the north edge of Yellowstone Park to the Church Universal and Triumphant (CUT). A highly controversial cult-like church that claims a worldwide membership of anywhere between 30,000 and 150,000, CUT transferred its headquarters from southern California to Park County, Montana, when it bought the ranch, and has been enlarging the property and altering the landscape ever since. Housing developments, mobile home parks, farming and ranching operations, even a massive, underground complex of fallout shelters occupy 30,000 church-owned acres at the south end of the valley, with additional holdings in Livingston and nearby Gallatin and Yellowstone counties.

Whether due to its scenic appeal, its isolation, or more likely, its fly-fishing, the valley has attracted another unusual crowd in recent years, this one from the celebrated world of arts, letters, and motion pictures. Over the years, fame's exiles, including writers Tom McGuane, William Hjortsberg, Tim Cahill, and Richard Brautigan, artist Russell Chatham, movie director Sam Peckinpaugh, and actors Peter Fonda, Margot Kidder, Warren Oates, and Jeff Bridges have all sought refuge in the Paradise Valley. They come and go, but some, like Chatham

and Cahill, have stayed, and others, like McGuane, have abandoned Paradise Valley for even more remote properties.

About an hour north of Yellowstone Park, the small city of **Livingston** was once a principal operations center for the Northern Pacific Railroad. With hundreds of workers employed by the NP's extensive machine shops, Livingston's dependence on the railroad made it vulnerable to every national recession that came along. In the early 1980s, the railroad, then under the ownership of Burlington Northern, consolidated its operations and laid off well over half the workers at the Livingston shops. But the real blow came in 1986, when BN abandoned the shops altogether. A new business, Montana Rail Link, bought BN's southern Montana line. Another new company, Livingston Rebuild Center, refurbished the BN facilities and now employs up to 150 mechanics, machinists, and painters to rebuild locomotives, railcars, and other heavy equipment from throughout the United States and Canada. Once boss of the Livingston economy, the rail industry now shares the reins with recreation and tourism.

The ornate Livingston passenger depot, built at the turn of the century, proclaimed the Northern Pacific's prominence as the "Yellowstone Park Line" and Livingston as the "Original Entrance to Yellowstone Park." Now a museum and exhibition hall, the **Depot Center** anchors Livingston's downtown historic district, characterized by the elaborate brickwork and cornices on turn-of-the-century commercial and residential buildings that once housed the town's founders, its blue-collar workers, and a busy red-light district.

Across from the depot, on West Park Street, is another Livingston landmark, **Dan Bailey's Fly Shop.** A must-see attraction for fly-fishermen, the shop was opened in 1938 by one of the sport's founding fathers, Dan Bailey. Bailey's sells everything from $400 graphite fly rods to 75-cent scraps of dyed rabbit fur, and does a sizable mail-order business. This is one of the world's largest wholesalers of fishing tackle. Bailey's employs about two dozen fly tiers on a piecework basis to produce more than half a million trout flies a year. Thousands of anglers and amateur tiers visit the shop to watch as these professionals turn out royal wulffs, blue-winged olives, and other intricate patterns with remarkable speed and precision. Livingston's scenic location and its prominence as a fly-fishing destination has inspired an abundance of fine landscape, wildlife, and Western art. This community of 6,700 supports half a dozen art galleries plus small, specialized collections within fly-fishing shops.

The Gallatin Gateway Inn, south of Bozeman, was built in 1927 as a hotel and railway depot for visitors en route to Yellowstone Park.

■ GALLATIN CANYON

The Yellowstone River is but one of dozens of renowned rivers in south-central and southwestern Montana that draw anglers from around the world. Another is the Gallatin, which flows right off the cover of *Field & Stream*. Born in the northwest corner of Yellowstone Park, the Gallatin dodges boulders and scours tree-lined banks as it rushes down mountains and through canyons to meet the Missouri at Three Forks. Along the way, it furnishes habitat for fish and wildlife, rapids for rafters, riffles and pools for anglers, and refuge for campers, picnickers, and foot danglers. From Bozeman to Yellowstone Park, it shares the Gallatin Canyon with U.S. Route 191, a narrow, twisting highway that ushers motorists to the splendid Spanish Peaks area of the Lee Metcalf Wilderness, Cottonwood Canyon, Hyalite Canyon, and the Palisades Falls National Recreation Trail. Dozens of campgrounds and picnic areas and hundreds of miles of trails cater to outdoor enthusiasts. Accommodations along the route include Montana's most complete, all-season, destination resort at **Big Sky**, plus cabins, guest ranches, fishing and hunting lodges, and even an elegantly restored railroad hotel (see "Accommodations" in "PRACTICAL INFORMATION" for specifics). In winter, there are enough slopes, lifts, trails, lodges, and restaurants along this route to keep downhill and cross-country skiers and snowmobilers happy for a week, if not the entire season.

■ BOZEMAN

Gallatin Canyon is peopled at each end by two contrasting communities, both wholly devoted to outdoor recreation. At the north end, Bozeman has enough other interests to stand on its own as a regional trade center and the home of **Montana State University.** But underlying this academic and cultural façade is a sports-crazy town that lives for the ski season and longs for opening day on nearby trout streams. A city of under 25,000, Bozeman is jammed with mountain bikes, kayaks, ski racks, and car-top carriers, and has more than its share of sporting goods shops, guides and outfitters, outdoor writers and photographers, subscribers of *Outside Magazine,* and devotees of Patagonia equipment and clothing. With its proximity to Yellowstone National Park, Bridger Bowl and Big Sky ski areas, hiking, climbing, and fishing, it is no mere coincidence that Patagonia has relocated its mail-order division to Bozeman.

Influenced, perhaps, by its magnificent setting, Bozeman cares about its appearance and presents an appealing face to visitors. Bookstores, art galleries, a bakery, coffee house, and half a dozen memorable restaurants are reason enough to spend a day in downtown Bozeman, which has withstood the threat of outlying shopping malls better than most Montana cities. And visitors return every year for festive events like the **Taste of Bozeman,** when Main Street is closed to traffic so that all those good restaurants can serve up their specialties to hundreds of guests outdoors, banquet-style.

Bozeman's top attraction is the newly expanded **Museum of the Rockies,** the town's 1989 centennial gift to Montana. Famous in paleontological circles as the home of dinosaur guru Jack Horner, the museum greets visitors with life-like, robotic re-creations of a *Triceratops* family, roaring and rooting around an interior fern garden. Although Horner's presence casts an aura of paleontological primacy over the institution, the Museum of the Rockies is more than a testing ground for new thinking on a growing collection of timeworn bones. With the ambitious goal of explaining the Northern Rocky Mountain region over the past 80 million

The annual Bobcat-Grizzly football game between Montana State University and the University of Montana dates back to 1897.

years, the museum gives nearly equal time and space to prehistoric peoples, the birth of the Rockies, the impact of man on the region, and Plains Indian art, history, and culture. It also attempts to teach us about our place in the universe with its digital Taylor Planetarium, the only one of its kind in the Northern Rockies that is open to the public.

A LOVE STORY

I was at the Top Hat having a drink with Little Troy Burnham, talking about the deer season, when a woman who had been sitting at the front of the bar got up and came over to us. I had seen this woman other times in other bars in town. She would be there in the afternoons around three, and then sometimes late at night when I would be cruising back. She danced with some men from the air base, and sat drinking and talking late. I suppose she left with someone finally. She wasn't a bad looking woman at all. Blond, with wide, dark eyes set out, wide hips, and dark eyebrows. She could've been thirty-four years old, although she could've been forty-four or twenty-four, because she was drinking steady, and steady drink can do both to you, especially to women. But I had thought the first time I saw her: Here's one on the way down. A miner's wife drifted up from Butte, or a rancher's daughter just run off suddenly, which can happen. Or worse. And I hadn't been tempted. Trouble comes cheap and leaves expensive is a way of thinking about that.

"Do you suppose you could give me a light," the woman said to us. She was standing at our table. Nola was her name. Nola Foster. I had heard that around. She wasn't drunk. It was four o'clock in the afternoon, and no one was there but Troy Burnham and me.

"If you'll tell me a love story, I'll do anything in the world for you," Troy said. It was what he always said to women. He'd do anything in the world for something. Troy sits in a wheelchair due to a smoke jumper's injury, and can't do very much. We had been friends since high school and before. He was always short, and I was tall. But Troy had been an excellent wrestler and won awards in Montana, and I had done little of that, some boxing once was all. We had been living in the same apartments on Ryman Street, though Troy lived there permanently and drove a Checker cab to earn a living, and I was hoping to pass on to something better. "I *would* like a little love story," Troy said, and called for whatever Nola Foster was drinking.

"Nola, Troy. Troy, Nola," I said, and lit her cigarette.

"Have we met?" Nola said, taking a seat and glancing at me.

"At the East Gate. Some time ago," I said.

"That's a very nice bar," she said in a cool way. "But I hear it's changed hands."

"I'm glad to make your acquaintance," Troy said, grinning and adjusting his glasses. "Now let's hear that love story." He pulled up close to the table so that his head and his big shoulders were above the tabletop. Troy's injury had caused him not to have any hips left. There is something there, but not hips. He needs bars and a special seat in his cab. He is both frail and strong at once, though in most ways he gets on like everybody else.

"I *was* in love," Nola said quietly as the bartender set her drink down and she took a sip. "And now I'm not."

"That's a short love story," I said.

—Richard Ford, *Rock Springs*, 1987

■ WEST YELLOWSTONE

Ninety miles (144 km) south of Bozeman, **West Yellowstone** *is* a city of visitors. Well over one million people enter the park each year through this small town of 900 year-round residents, making it the busiest of the park's five gateways. In July and August, at the height of the season, "West" looks like a tourist trap, but give it a chance and it will grow on you, especially if you came to fish. Listen to the conversation as you stroll down Madison or Firehole or Gibbon avenues, and you will know why the streets are named after some of the world's best-known trout streams, all located within 30 minutes of town. West Yellowstone is to serious anglers what Carnegie Hall and the Metropolitan Opera are to music lovers. Headquarters for the International Federation of Fly Fishers, it has top billing on every angler's dream list of places to go and things to do.

Not far from town, dead trees poke through the surface of **Quake Lake,** an eerie reminder of the mega-jolt that toppled half a mountain into the Madison River canyon on the night of August 17, 1959. The landslide dammed a river, created a lake, and buried 28 campers in an unmarked grave. About 250 vacationers were trapped overnight in the canyon when whole sections of U.S. Route 287 cracked like eggshells and dropped into existing Hebgen Lake. Registering 7.1 on the Richter scale, the earthquake was one of the strongest in U.S. history and

YELLOWSTONE NATIONAL PARK

Wyoming's Yellowstone National Park is the magnet that pulls most visitors into south-central Montana, where three of the park's five entrances are located. America's largest national park outside of Alaska, Yellowstone has been drawing curiosity seekers from throughout the world ever since mountain man John Colter reported tales of hissing geysers, burbling mud pots, and pools of boiling paint to an unbelieving public in 1810. For many years, this mysterious place was known simply as "Colter's Hell." In his journal of American travel notes, Rudyard Kipling described it as "a howling wilderness of three thousand square miles, full of all imaginable freaks of a fiery nature."

Several short, self-guiding trails introduce visitors to headline attractions, like the Grand Canyon of the Yellowstone and Upper Geyser Basin, which encompasses the world's greatest cluster of geysers, including Old Faithful. A longer but lovely introductory trail is the three-mile (five-km) climb to the top of Mount Washburn, between Tower and Canyon. From the summit, visitors enjoy panoramic views of Yellowstone Canyon, Hayden Valley, Yellowstone Lake, and on clear days, the Tetons, Absarokas, and Gallatins. Hikers can also view the mosaic burn pattern created by the historic fires of 1988. More than a third of the park's 2.2-million-acre landscape was altered by the fires, with more than 790,000 acres of forest blackened to one degree or another. But meadows and forest understory have bounded back, creating prodigious wildflower displays and increased forage and habitat for wildlife.

For those who want to know more about fire ecology, bears, geysers, or the many other features that make Yellowstone one of America's greatest outdoor classrooms, the **Yellowstone Institute** offers more than 80 field courses each year (see "Useful Addresses" in "PRACTICAL INFORMATION"). The Institute is housed at the historic Buffalo Ranch in the Lamar Valley, near the park's northeast gate.

AVOIDING THE CROWDS
Close to three million people now visit the park each year. During the peak months of summer, traffic crawls along the park's Grand Loop Road and grinds to a standstill every time a bison or bull elk is sighted within camera range. There are a couple of ways to beat the crowds, however. One is to visit the park during the off-season. In September, hormone-crazed bull elk entertain visitors with their

Midway Geyser Basin's Grand Prismatic Spring is one of more than 10,000 thermal features in Yellowstone National Park.

macho antics at the outset of breeding season. In spring, at the other end of the cycle, a drive through Yellowstone is like visiting a wildlife nursery. Satisfied bison and elk moms suckle their wobbly calves in roadside meadows, while Canada geese drill downy, yellow goslings on paddle and splash missions in a watery wilderness.

A welcome hush settles over Yellowstone as it fills up with snow in winter. If the park's spouting geysers and fumaroles seem eerie in summer, they are unearthly in winter. Frosty bison move in and out of view as clouds of mist and steam roll through, transforming the powerful beasts into shaggy ghosts. Snow whites-out the roads and confines travel to skis, snowshoes, snowmobiles, and guided snowcoach tours.

Yellowstone watchers fear the winter season may be too popular for the good of the wildlife that top the list of reasons why people visit. They warn that the park's bison and elk don't need the added impact of snarling snowmobile engines and backcountry interlopers on top of the rigors of winter. It's hard not to love this park to death, even in the off-season when visitation is markedly down.

INTO THE BACKCOUNTRY

The best way to avoid peak-season congestion is to abandon your car for day hikes or extended hiking and horseback trips through Yellowstone's spacious backcountry. The park has more than a thousand miles of backcountry trails to acquaint visitors with its many moods and curiosities. The privileged few who use them are gifted with sights never seen from a Winnebago: the secret eruptions of the remote Shoshone Geyser Basin, the terraced waterfalls and wilderness jacuzzis of the "Cascade Corner," the chance view of a golden-tipped grizzly sow steering her cubs across Hayden Valley, the unexpected burps and splats of unnamed mud pots.

Yellowstone's backcountry is bear country. There are an estimated 700 bears in and around the park, including about 200 grizzlies. While few people actually see *Ursus horribilis*, the great bear ranges throughout the park. Hikers should generally avoid traveling alone, and should always check trail conditions and bear sightings before heading out. Given the National Park Service's aggressive efforts to reduce bear-human conflicts, it is difficult to avoid these precautions. Brochures, leaflets, and fliers litter the park.

Preaching at Pulpit Terrace in the Mammoth Hot Springs area of Yellowstone Park.
(Montana Historical Society)

shook an eight-state region. People across Montana were startled from their sleep, but the heaviest damage was at this site, where the U.S. Forest Service maintains a memorial visitor center and vista point.

The vast majority of tourists visit the West Yellowstone area during the summer, but fall and winter are becoming increasingly popular. With the growing popularity of snowmobiling and cross-country skiing, Yellowstone Park and the town of West Yellowstone have become one of the Northern Rockies' hottest winter destinations. Billing itself as "the snowmobile capital of the world," West Yellowstone goes all out for power sledders, who use the town as a base camp to explore not only Yellowstone Park but hundreds of miles of trails on national forest lands outside the park. There's plenty of room for cross-country skiers, who also flock to West Yellowstone and the park. An excellent public trail system, right in town, provides early winter training for the U.S. Nordic and Biathlon teams.

■ MADISON RIVER VALLEY

Flanked on the east by the soaring peaks of the Madison Range, this drive offers skyward views of Montana's second-highest mountain range and the broad, alluvial plains that fan out from its base to create one of the state's most handsome valleys. Heavy timbers frame entrances to ranches that lie at the end of long, gravel roads. The names etched into these gates—Bar Seven, Longhorn, Jumping Horse—are clues to one of the major occupations that drive the economy of the valley. But the real evidence is a landscape dotted with cattle and sheep as far as the eye can see. Year after year, Madison County ranks among Montana's top cattle- and sheep-producing counties. And year after year, the **Madison River** draws more nonresident anglers to its banks than any other trout stream in Montana. Originating in Yellowstone Park, the river follows U.S. Route 287 for about 60 miles (100 km) from West Yellowstone to Ennis, then leaves the highway before joining the Gallatin and Jefferson rivers at Three Forks to form the Missouri.

Ranching and fishing converge in the small community of **Ennis,** where well-heeled anglers meet high-heeled cowboys over beers in watering holes like the Longbranch and Silver Dollar. Over the years, fly shops and art galleries have replaced farm and ranch supply stores, but the atmosphere in Ennis remains distinctly Western. At no time is the valley's love affair with livestock more apparent than during rodeo weekend, when the population of Ennis swells to accommodate contestants and spectators at one of Montana's most popular Fourth of July rodeos. An attractive purse, a sure crowd, and a wild horse race make Ennis one of the top rodeos for professional cowboys and cowgirls working the summer circuit, as well as for local ranch hands. When the dust has settled and the professionals have moved on to the next arena, spectators turn their attention to the many nearby attractions that make Ennis such a popular base camp for summer visitors.

■ HISTORICAL DETOURS

Two of Montana's liveliest ghost towns, Virginia City and Nevada City, lie just 15 miles (24 km) west of Ennis, on Montana State Highway 287. An 1863 gold strike brought thousands of prospectors to the area and secured Virginia City's place in history as Montana's second territorial capital. (See "Ghost Towns" in "SOUTHWEST MONTANA" for more about this area.)

Most Montana communities support a historic home or museum like the
Headwaters Heritage Museum in Three Forks.

Three state parks north of Ennis reach back even further in history. Just outside the aptly named community of Three Forks, three of southwestern Montana's great rivers—the Jefferson, the Madison, and the Gallatin—join to form the Missouri River. The site was an important crossroads for several Indian tribes. The Lewis and Clark expedition also camped here in July 1805, nearly 2,500 miles (4,000 km) above their starting point near St. Louis, where the Missouri feeds into the Mississippi. In his journal, Meriwether Lewis said he and his co-captain, William Clark, agreed to name the forks after President Thomas Jefferson, "the author of our enterprize," Secretary of the Treasury Albert Gallatin, and Secretary of State James Madison. They proceeded westward along the Jefferson, certain, as were most early explorers, that the Missouri headwaters would take them to the Pacific Ocean. The history of the area is preserved in a beautiful setting at **Missouri Headwaters State Park,** a popular spot for camping, picnicking, hiking, fishing, and floating.

For 2,000 years before the arrival of guns and horses, Indians killed the buffalo they needed for food, clothing, shelter, and tools by stampeding them en masse over cliffs. Not far from the Missouri Headwaters, **Madison Buffalo Jump State Park** preserves one of these early killing grounds. Layers of bones and remnants of primitive tools mark these slaughtering sites, where Indian parties often spent several days gutting carcasses, removing hides, and drying meat.

Montana's first and best-known state park preserves one of the largest limestone caverns in the Northwest, less than 20 miles (32 km) west of Three Forks on Montana State Highway 2. **Lewis and Clark Caverns** began forming more than 300 million years ago. Sediments at the bottom of a shallow inland sea hardened into limestone and were eventually exposed to air as the sea drained away and the nearby Tobacco Root Mountains were uplifted. As groundwater penetrated and dissolved fractured limestone, a network of channels began forming. Today, these channels and caves are punctuated by stalactites, stalagmites, columns, and crystals. Visitors can explore the caves on guided tours during the summer. The park also has a visitor center, café and gift shop, campground, picnic area, and nature trail.

■ ROADS LESS TRAVELED

For those who seek a more intimate, less developed view of this landscape, several rugged roads wind tentatively through the wild country that borders Yellowstone

Park. Starting as ordinary, two-lane highways, they taper off first to gravel, then dirt. Some wind up at trailheads that designate foot and horse traffic only. These memorable trips make few demands in proportion to the pleasures they yield. A flexible itinerary and a tolerance for bumpy, dusty roads are a small price to pay for a chance view of a golden eagle feeding by the side of the road or mountain goats perched on rocky outcrops overhead. For extended visits, most travelers are self-sustained. There are some private cabins and guest ranches, however, in addition to a number of public campgrounds.

The remote **Centennial Valley**, just west of the park, is an essential trip for photographers, birders, and wildlife watchers. The valley is bordered on the south by a wall of mountains that approach the 10,000-foot (3,050-m) level. The rugged Centennials catch heavy snows that replenish the lakes and marshes of 42,000-acre **Red Rock Lakes National Wildlife Refuge,** which provides sanctuary for the trumpeter swan. This vast wetland sustains a multitude of other birds and animals. Because of its location halfway between West Yellowstone and Monida on a dirt and gravel road, passage is slow and subject to weather conditions. The best time to visit is between May and September when the road is generally dry. Recently designated a national scenic backroad by the BLM, the Centennial Valley Road has its own built-in speed bumps to ensure that motorists take it slow.

North of the park, **Columbus** is the starting point for a cluster of secondary routes into the Beartooth Range along the Stillwater and Rosebud drainages. Though long dependent on farming and ranching, this Yellowstone River community is enjoying an economic revival tied to mining and manufacturing. The Stillwater Mining Company, located at the edge of the Absaroka-Beartooth Wilderness near Nye, is the nation's only producer of platinum-palladium metals, used widely in industry and technology. Columbus is also the home of Montana Silversmiths, the world's largest manufacturer of Western-style silver products, including belt buckles, jewelry, and saddle and bridle trim.

The last outpost of any size before heading into the mountains is **Absarokee**, 15 miles (24 km) south of Columbus on Montana State Highway 78. The small town bears an Indian name that originally was used to identify the Crow tribe. Once part of the Crows' vast homeland, Absarokee was on the Crow Reservation until the reservation was reduced to its current size and location near Hardin. The historic **Bozeman Trail** also crossed through this southern portion of Stillwater County. In 1862, founder John Bozeman envisioned the route as a shortcut from

eastern Wyoming, through Indian territory, and on to the gold fields of Virginia City. Despite its ease of travel and abundance of water, grass, and game, the trail was abandoned in 1868 due to persistent attacks by the Sioux. Today, travelers can retrace a portion of the trail on short wagon-train vacations (see "Tours" in "PRAC-TICAL INFORMATION"). Visitors can enjoy another Western tradition, still very much alive in Montana, at either of two lively rodeos held in Absarokee each summer. In early June, the Northern Rodeo Association kicks off its season here, and in July, seasoned contestants from throughout the area entertain a spirited crowd at the **Old Timers' Rodeo.**

Absarokee is the jumping-off point for deeper exploration of Beartooth country on different routes, each constituting a variation on the theme of grandeur. Follow East Rosebud Creek 14 miles (23 km) to the tiny settlement of Roscoe, then another 12 miles (19 km) on gravel to East Rosebud Lake, which marks the beginning of one of the Beartooth's most spectacular canyons. A short hike up East Rosebud Creek reveals a Yosemite landscape with an El Capitan-like upthrust at nearly every bend in the trail. An extended hike or horseback ride on the same trail takes conditioned explorers over the top of the boulder-strewn, lake-studded Beartooth Plateau before dropping down to Cooke City, at the northeast corner of Yellowstone National Park.

A 20-mile (32-km) road follows West Rosebud Creek from tiny Fishtail to a hydroelectric plant below Mystic Lake. Early in the century, the Montana Power Company chose the site to build its 300-foot-long (90-m) concrete dam and power plant in these highest of all Montana mountains because of its vertical drop and massive snowfall. Considered an engineering feat at the time of its construction, such a proposal today would generate far more controversy than electricity. Hikers and horsemen en route to the Absaroka-Beartooth Wilderness begin their journey with a three-mile (five-km) ramble up to Mystic Lake, itself a popular fishing spot.

A 40-mile (64-km) journey along the Stillwater River packs plenty of scenic views, camping, and stream fishing in the heart of Beartooth country. The route also leads to the the nation's richest deposits of platinum, palladium, and related metals, and the Stillwater Mining Company's highly automated mining operation near Nye.

Beartooth country is a skyscraper wilderness of granite peaks, boulder-strewn plateaus, and alpine lakes.

■ BOULDER RIVER

The 1964 Wilderness Act, passed to preserve the pristine qualities of certain natural areas forever, defines wilderness as "an area where the earth and its community of life are untrammeled by man, where man himself is a visitor who does not remain." The act prohibits motorized travel within wilderness boundaries, but people who shun hiking and horseback riding can still surround themselves with wilderness on the **Boulder River Road.**

Reaching some 50 miles (80 km) south of Big Timber to the abandoned mining town of Independence, this partially paved road fingers its way into the Absaroka-Beartooth Wilderness along a non-wilderness corridor. As a result, travelers are enveloped on three sides by "capital W" wilderness for about a third of the distance. For the entire distance, they are encircled by sublime views of rivers and peaks, canyons and gorges, and meadows and hay fields where sheep mingle with elk and deer. Eagles and hawks soar overhead, while rainbow trout flash in rivers and streams below.

"They don't make land like that anymore," said NBC newsman Tom Brokaw in an interview after purchasing a ranch on the nearby West Fork of the Boulder. "Montana is special in the world. I come over a rise there and I feel like I'm in Tibet." Other celebrities attracted to the exotic frontier of the Boulder Valley include Brooke Shields, Michael Keaton, novelist Tom McGuane, and Robert Haas, chairman of Levi Strauss & Co. They come for the unspoiled beauty and the unhurried lifestyle. Here, they come and go without a fuss, even in nearby **Big Timber,** a small Western town of about 1,600 where the real stars are the cowboy poets who convene at the high school gymnasium every August to croon their lonely ballads and recite their latest rhymes of the range. Heaping servings of Western lore and a good time to boot make the two-day **Montana Cowboy Poetry Gathering** a gut-buster for anyone with a hankering for a taste of the West.

The cosmopolitan views of visiting anglers and hikers, combined with those of the valley's new luminaries, are tempered by the rock-hard, conservative politics of Sweet Grass County and the mores and folkways of ranchers who have raised sheep and run cows here for over a century. The sociology of Big Timber is nearly as engaging as the landscape that surrounds it.

Horse and wagon trips add history and adventure to a Montana vacation.

SOUTHWEST MONTANA

FEWER THAN 60 YEARS AFTER LEWIS AND CLARK ENTERED the unmapped wilderness of what is now Montana, miners and merchants were beating a path across the mountains and deserts of California, Colorado, and Idaho to reach its southwestern gold fields. News of gold strikes on Grasshopper Creek in 1862 and Alder Gulch the following year traveled fast. By the mid-1860s, Montana had nearly 30,000 permanent, non-Indian settlers, where five years earlier there had been none. Another strike in 1864, this one on Last Chance Gulch, established Helena as the "Queen City of the Rockies" and southwest Montana as the progenitor of the state's most enduring nickname, the Treasure State.

In the 1860s at the height of the gold rush in Montana, the strikes were so rich it was said that a prospector could shake a dollar's worth of dust from an uprooted sagebrush. In five years, the digs at Alder Gulch (now Virginia City) produced $30–$40 million worth of gold; Last Chance Gulch produced an estimated $19 million in just four years. By 1866, Montana was second only to California as a gold producer. But the gold played out, and so did silver. Then in 1882, the fortuitous discovery of a thick vein of copper beneath the undistinguished gold camp of Butte ushered in the greatest era of all in Montana mining history and immortalized Butte as "the richest hill on earth."

Right behind the miners came the stockmen who supplied Montana's mining camps with fresh meat. The valleys were as rich in grass as the mountains were in precious metals. While the plains of eastern Montana fattened hundreds of thousands of cattle for the export market during the state's great open range cattle era of the 1870s and '80s, Montana's early mining camps provided a ready market for pioneer stockmen. Those who mastered the basics of building a herd and selling in the Deer Lodge and Beaverhead valleys emerged as leaders of Montana's developing livestock industry.

Computerized livestock breeding programs and technology-driven mining operations are still the bones and sinew of this corner of the state. But its spirit resides in the weathered ghost towns, Victorian mansions, and carriage houses that bespeak the bonanza years of Montana's colorful mining frontier. Much of Montana's political and economic history was written in this part of the state, and it is easily revisited in galleries, museums, mansions, and miners' union halls. Where

COPPER MONEY

*W*hen the late Senator Robert LaFollette listed [William A.] Clark as one of one hundred men who owned America, and cited fourteen great corporations in his hands to prove it, he neglected to recite a more revealing fact. Differing from the other ninety-nine "owners of America," Clark stood alone, unique, in the fact that of all the great enterprises with which he was connected, not one share of stock nor bond issue by any one of them was either listed or quoted or could be bought on any stock exchange in the United States.

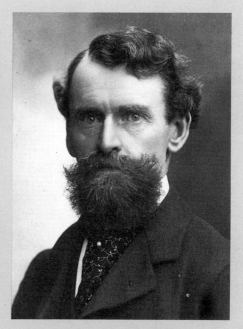

William A. Clark, "copper king."
(Montana Historical Society)

WILLIAM ANDREWS CLARK
PIONEER PROSPECTOR AND MINER
MERCHANT BANKER RAILROAD BUILDER
BENEFACTOR OF CHILDREN AND PHILANTHROPIST
THIS MEMORIAL IS ERECTED BY
THE SOCIETY OF MONTANA AND OTHER FRIENDS
AS A TRIBUTE TO HIS GREAT ACHIEVEMENTS
AND TO PERPETUATE HIS MEMORY

Inscription from bas-relief in capitol rotunda in Helena

—C. B. Glasscock,
The War of the Copper Kings: Builders of Butte and Wolves of Wall Street, 1935

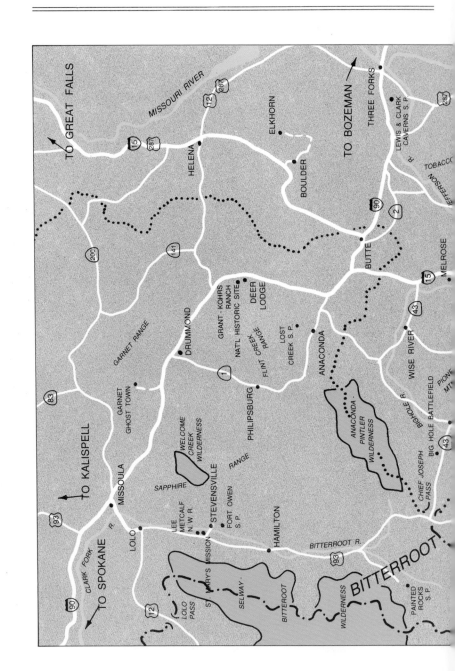

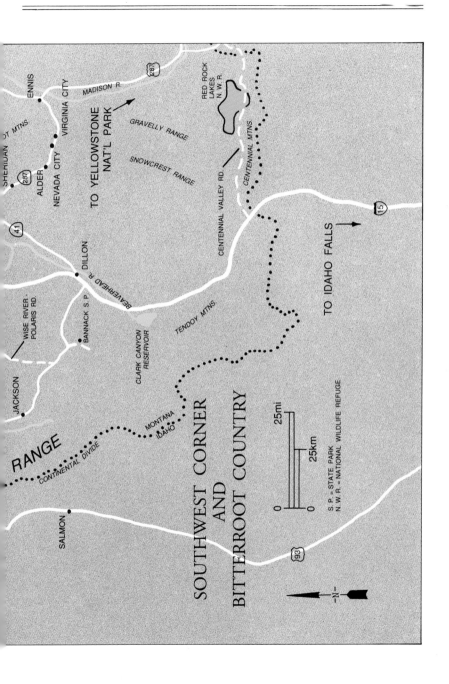

SOUTHWEST CORNER
AND
BITTERROOT COUNTRY

S.P. = STATE PARK
N.W.R. = NATIONAL WILDLIFE REFUGE

TO YELLOWSTONE NAT'L PARK

TO IDAHO FALLS

RED ROCK LAKES N.W.R.

GRAVELLY RANGE

SNOWCREST RANGE

CENTENNIAL MTNS.

CENTENNIAL VALLEY RD.

TENDOY MTNS.

CLARK CANYON RESERVOIR

BANNACK S.P.

BEAVERHEAD R.

DILLON

WISE RIVER-POLARIS RD.

JACKSON

SALMON

RANGE

CONTINENTAL DIVIDE

MONTANA
IDAHO

SHERIDAN

MADISON R.

ENNIS

VIRGINIA CITY

NEVADA CITY

ALDER

287

287

41

15

93

25mi

25km

0

0

prospectors once mined these hills and panned these streams for the sparkling "color" that meant instant prosperity, visitors today mine the area not just for its history but also for its natural beauty and recreational opportunities—its trout streams and forested mountains. Georgetown Lake, the Anaconda-Pintler Wilderness, the Big Hole River, and Gates of the Mountains are just some of the getaways that make this part of the state so attractive to sightseers and sportsmen.

Most of the region's small cities grew from primitive mining camps after the discovery of gold placers and silver lodes, as well as rich deposits of copper, lead, and zinc. The two largest are Helena and Butte.

■ HELENA

Helena's early fortunes were made of gold. The city's main street is still named **Last Chance Gulch,** a permanent memorial to four discouraged prospectors who declared this unlikely spot to be their "last chance" after following strike after played-out strike around the West. It turned out to be their best chance when, in 1864, they discovered the first of several gold deposits that catapulted Helena into second place, right behind Alder Gulch, as Montana's leading gold producer. Within 10 years, tents and crude log cabins had given way to mansions, mercantiles, and hundreds of small businesses. By 1888, an estimated 50 millionaires lived here, making it the richest city per capita in the United States. Strategically located on early travel routes and at the center of Montana's mining district, Helena's survival was assured. In 1875, it became Montana's third territorial capital (after Bannack and Virginia City, the sites of Montana's first two major gold strikes). Then, in 1894, it became the permanent state capital in a runoff election against Anaconda, after a $3 million campaign financed by rival copper barons Marcus Daly and William A. Clark.

Much of Helena's early history has been preserved in its architecture, both downtown and in adjacent residential neighborhoods. The extravagant jumble of Baroque, Gothic, Italianate, and Romanesque designs reflects the exuberance of Helena's Victorian period. Arched windows, ornate pillars and masonry patterns, sculpted metal, carved faces, flowers, and lion heads are all visible on the massive stone buildings that anchor Helena's historic Last Chance Gulch. While fires, earthquakes, demolition, and decay have leveled many of Helena's historic

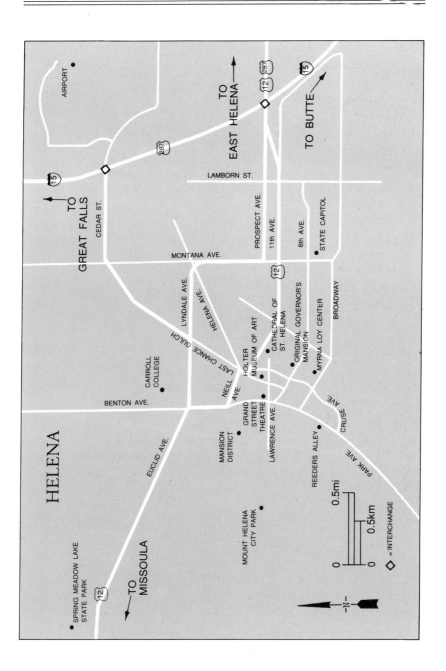

buildings, nearly a hundred still stand as reminders of the city's golden era. The growth of Helena can be traced from the gulch eastward as downtown fixtures like the original Governor's Mansion and the territorial and original State Capitol (now the Lewis and Clark County Courthouse) were abandoned for more modern buildings on the east side of town.

The century-old mansions of Helena's venerable west-side neighborhoods flaunt an opulent mix of styles and designs that combine parquet floors, Tiffany windows, tile fireplaces, handcrafted woodwork of oak and cherry, gracious, high-ceilinged rooms, spacious front porches, gazebos, and carriage houses. The **original Governor's Mansion,** (304 North Ewing), built as a private residence in 1888 by entrepreneur William Chessman, is open to the public for tours. The nearby Sanders mansion, built by politician and vigilante Wilbur Fisk Sanders in 1875, is now a gracious bed and breakfast inn. (See "Accommodations" in "PRACTICAL INFORMATION" for specifics.)

Towering above all these secular monuments to the earthly treasures of an earlier period is the magnificent **Cathedral of St. Helena.** Modeled after the Votive Cathedral of the Sacred Heart in Vienna, it boasts stained-glass windows from

The State Capitol in Helena is crowned with a copper dome.

The cathedral of St. Helena lends European dignity to the capital's skyline.

Bavaria, a white marble altar from Italy, and twin spires crowned with gilded crosses that face east and west to catch the first and last light of day. Rising 230 feet (70 m) above the tree-lined streets of Helena—as if to compete with the surrounding peaks of the Rocky Mountains—the cathedral lends European dignity to the city's skyline.

History and the arts are a source of pride to Helena residents. Many are involved in efforts to restore downtown buildings and neighborhood mansions, one of which even transformed their abandoned, turn-of-the-century jail into the **Myrna Loy Center,** a performing arts and film center. Helena is home to the **Archie Bray Foundation,** an internationally recognized center for the ceramic arts; the **Holter Museum of Art** and its annual **Rendezvous of Western Art;** and **Grandstreet Theatre,** a lively school and stage for the dramatic arts. The **Montana Historical Society,** 225 North Roberts, houses two museums—the Montana Homeland Historical Museum and the smaller F. Jay Haynes Museum, which depicts frontier photography. Also here are two art galleries, one of which features the works of C. M. Russell, along with a fine archives and historical library.

While the city's early growth was financed by gold dust and nuggets, Helena now owes its existence to the less tangible but self-perpetuating occupation of politics. Much of the business of state government is conducted beneath the dome of the **State Capitol,** but state offices are located in buildings throughout town. Crowned in copper, the capitol serves as a reminder that while gold shines brighter, the reddish-brown ore coming out of Butte, beginning in the 1880s, was the dominant star in Montana's mining and political history.

■ BUTTE

The discovery of rich copper ores in Butte coincided with the introduction of the electric light bulb and telephone on the world market, and the rest, as they say, is history. Large mining interests turned to Butte, and between 1882 and 1890, copper production increased from nine million to 130 million pounds; Butte's population tripled. The population peaked right around World War I with an estimated 20,000 miners and 100,000 residents, making it one of the West's largest inland cities. Once Montana's largest city, Butte now ranks fourth, with about 33,000 residents.

This mile-high mining town is known affectionately as "Butte, America," because the valley in which it lies was lost in a frontier twilight zone between the Louisiana Purchase and Oregon Territory, and never legally procured as part of either chunk of real estate. A true melting pot, it drew thousands of foreign-born immigrants in search of a living wage. They clustered together in ethnic neighborhoods that still bear the names of Corktown, Dublin Gulch, Finntown, Chinatown, and Little Italy. Some of these enclaves were literally devoured by the huge open-pit mine that began replacing underground mining operations in 1955, but Butte, more than any other city or town in Montana, has retained its ethnic character. While the Irish dominate Butte in body and spirit, there are still distinct pockets of Finns, Slavs, and Italians, and remnant populations of many other nationalities.

Whether due to its ethnic roots, its labor heritage, or both, Butte is a rough town with a tender heart. Surrounded by gallow frames, mine spoils, ore dumps, and mine shafts, and perched on the edge of the defunct, mile-wide Berkeley Pit, Butte stands uncontested as Montana's most unattractive city. It has been described in the national press as "the ugliest city in America." Behind its bleak, pock-marked face, however, shine the smiling eyes and indomitable spirit of its

The Wah Chong Tai Co. thrived in Butte's turn-of-the-century melting pot. (Montana Historical Society)

Improved technology and market conditions for precious metals have created a resurgence in mining. This open-pit gold mine (top) is south of Helena. These gold bricks (above) are not as pure as they look; they will be further processed outside the state. (opposite) Molten gold.

residents. People are the power behind Butte and they have been ever since they muscled the ore and fought the labor wars that made Butte the most militant union town in the nation.

Butte was all business when it went to work, but when the shift changed, Butte knew how to have fun. Hundreds of saloons and gambling parlors stayed open around the clock to serve three shifts of miners. This was a town that never shut down and never gave up. Market fluctuations, changes in mining technology, overseas production, and depletion of high-grade ores all inflicted near-fatal blows to the economy of Butte over the years. What everyone but Butte interpreted as the final blow came in 1983, when the Atlantic Richfield Company (ARCO) announced the suspension of all mining operations in Butte. Mining in Butte will never be what it was during the nation's industrial era, but small-scale copper mining has made a comeback, and Butte has diversified its economy with a sound mix of businesses built on mining, energy and environmental research, along with public utilities, education, and medical services.

For most of its existence, Butte was a company town, held captive by global markets and corporate policies beyond its control. Forced to take control of its destiny when it was abandoned by ARCO, Butte now stands as a role model for other Montana towns singing the American heartland blues. While Butte had the vision to contemplate life after copper, it never lost sight of its rich ethnic-labor heritage and mining history. The entire city is a living museum, with real-life exhibits in the card room of the M&M bar and café, the tightly packed miners' shanties that cling to steep hillsides, uptown mansions that memorialize the copper kings, Irish wakes that celebrate the lives of the departed, Christmas Eve at the Serbian Church, St. Urho's Day at the Helsinki Bar, and St. Patrick's Day in every bar and on every sidewalk.

Visitors can familiarize themselves with Butte's mining heritage on walking tours of uptown Butte, driving tours of underground mine sites, guided trolley tours of the city, and at the **World Museum of Mining,** the **Mineral Museum** on the campus of **Montana Tech,** the **Copper King Mansion,** the **Arts Chateau,** and the visitor center at the **Berkeley Pit,** for many years the nation's largest truck-operated open-pit copper mine. The **Butte Chamber of Commerce** at 2950 Harrison Ave. has info on all these options. Two other attractions stand as monuments to the characteristic determination of "Buttians" to beat the odds: a 90-foot (27-m), 51-ton lighted statue of **Our Lady of the Rockies** that overlooks Butte from atop the Continental Divide; and the multi-million-dollar U.S. **High Altitude Sports Center,** which grew out of Butte's speedskating tradition and serves as a training facility and competition skating rink for Olympic-class athletes.

On first impression, Butte offers little more than a tarnished landscape and the services that are bound to appear at the junction of two interstate highways. But venture past the convenience stores and fast-food joints clustered at the exit ramps and poke around uptown Butte. Drop into **Gamer's Confectionery,** where customers operate the cash register and make their own change, or any of the neighborhood bars. A warm reception is guaranteed, and it won't be long before "yous guys" see the heart of gold that beats behind the homely facade of the city built on copper.

■ ANACONDA

About 25 miles (40 km) west of Butte is another small city that owes its existence to copper. Indeed, **Anaconda** would be known today as "Copperopolis" if its founder, Marcus Daly, had had his way. Hand-picked by Daly as the site of a giant reduction works to process the ores coming from his Anaconda mine in Butte, Anaconda became a classic company town whose fortunes were tied directly to those of Daly's mining operations. When the mines were producing, life was good in Anaconda, and Marcus Daly was its patron saint. Besides providing good jobs for hundreds of smelter workers, he endowed his beloved Anaconda with a trolley line, an amusement park, a magnificent hotel, and a racetrack. (Only the amusement park is still in operation.) At one time, the 585-foot-high (180-m) smelter stack was the tallest in North America; the plant had the world's largest smelting capacity. By the end of World War II, the Anaconda Copper Mining Company (ACM), which had absorbed the interests of Daly and the other early copper barons of Butte, had also acquired copper mines in Chile and Mexico, becoming the world's largest producer of copper.

ACM lost its monolithic stature in the worldwide copper industry in 1970, when a Marxist government rose to power in Chile and nationalized all of that nation's copper mines. Trouble in Latin America coincided with the domestic challenge of meeting new air pollution standards, and the company began divesting itself of its Montana properties, one by one. In 1977, ACM merged with the

Atlantic Richfield Company, and in 1980, the company suspended its smelting operations in Anaconda and Great Falls indefinitely. For the first time in its existence, the company town of Anaconda was without a company.

While still unsure of its future, Anaconda has a firm grip on the significance of its role in Montana history. It is said that seven truckloads of printed material from the Anaconda Reduction Works are preserved by the local historical society, along with maps, photographs, and memorabilia of Anaconda's early ethnic groups and social organizations. For those who prefer their history condensed, try a historic walking tour (see the chamber of commerce), or head to the museum and art gallery. Anaconda's elaborate **Washoe Theater** is an art deco classic, and its **Hearst Free Library,** donated to the city by newspaper eminence Phoebe Hearst (whose husband helped finance Daly's mining ventures), is yet another reminder of the outside money that influenced the development of southwestern Montana. **Washoe Park,** a gift of Daly to the city, is still Anaconda's favorite playground with its ball fields, flower gardens, picnic areas, swimming pool, and state fish hatchery.

Anaconda's Washoe Theatre is an art deco classic.

Nearby **Lost Creek State Park** is one of the best-kept secrets in the state parks system. Spectacular limestone cliffs and granite formations, waterfalls, mountain goats, and bighorn sheep make this a worthwhile sidetrip for anyone visiting Anaconda.

■ STOCKGROWERS' TOWNS

Southwestern Montana has two other mid-sized communities, both firmly rooted in the livestock industry. Deer Lodge, 25 miles (40 km) north of Anaconda, and Dillon, about 80 miles (130 km) south, lie along major rivers flowing through broad mountain valleys. Just as the mountains around Butte and Helena yielded rich deposits of copper and gold, these valleys provided the grass and water that launched Montana's cattle industry.

Canadian trapper and mountain man Johnny Grant was the first to make a go of ranching in the Deer Lodge Valley, and he is sometimes acknowledged as the founder of the industry in Montana. By 1863, only 10 years after acquiring a few rundown cows, he was running 4,000 head and nearly as many horses on his Deer Lodge property and supplying most of the beef for the mining camps of Bannack and Virginia City. Grant sold his spread in 1866 to a German immigrant, Conrad Kohrs, who built it into one of the most prosperous cattle ranches in the West. As headquarters for an empire that covered more than a million acres of grazing land in the western United States and Canada, Kohrs' operation was one of few that survived the brutal winter of 1886-87.

Today, the **Grant-Kohrs Ranch** is preserved on the outskirts of **Deer Lodge** as a National Historic Site. Visitors can poke around in the early barns and outbuildings, or tour the original ranch house, once regarded the finest in the Territory. Cattle still graze here and draft horses are still used to work the land, making this the next best thing to a working ranch for visitors who desire to know more about ranching without getting their cowboy boots dirty. Plan to stay awhile in Deer Lodge, especially if you enjoy history, because the **Old Montana Prison,** the **Montana Law Enforcement Museum,** the **Towe Ford Museum,** and the **Powell County Museum** are all located in the same block downtown.

For a larger view of the livestock industry, you can't do better than a drive through the scenic **Big Hole Basin** in the heart of the region. Watered by the

This antique Ford (top) is one of 90 on display at the Towe Ford Museum in Deer Lodge. (bottom) The Tow collection covers the period from 1903 to the 1960s, and includes Henry Ford's personal Lincoln camper.

meandering Big Hole River, the hay grows wild in this high mountain valley, contributing heavily to Beaverhead County's standing as the top cattle and hay producer in the state. Mountain valleys were "holes" to the early trappers and mountain men, and this was one of the biggest in the area, so the name stuck. Known today as the "valley of 10,000 haystacks," the Big Hole looks like an agrarian landscape from the past, with haystacks piled high as houses throughout the valley's 50-mile (80-km) length and 15-mile (24-km) width. Cutting a cleaner profile than the haystacks are the 30-foot-high (nine-meter) beaverslides that are used to stack the hay. The derrick-like, wooden structures were devised by two Big Hole ranchers in 1907.

The trade center for Big Hole and Beaverhead valley ranchers is **Dillon,** which got its start as a railroad town on the route to mineral-rich Butte. The stately homes of early merchants and stockmen still preside over Dillon's older, tree-lined neighborhoods. Once Montana's largest wool shipping point, Dillon is better known today as the home of **Western Montana College,** which specializes in improving rural education and serves as a branch campus of the University of Montana. Dillon is also a base camp for recreation in the surrounding Beaverhead National Forest, the nearby Beaverhead and Big Hole rivers, Clark Canyon

Taking a break during one of several wagon train rides that rolled across Montana in 1989, the statehood centennial.

Reservoir, and the Wise River-Polaris scenic byway. Dillon's **Labor Day Rodeo,** locally billed as "Montana's Biggest Weekend," ranks among the state's best rodeos with its dances, rodeo performances, a wild horse race, parade, and barbecue.

■ GHOST TOWNS

For every gold camp that survived, there are dozens that went bust when the diggin's played out. The century-old drama of prospectors, road agents, vigilantes, harlots, and abandoned wives and children is etched in the weathered frames of cabins, saloons, hotels, and assay offices that once lined the folds and gulches of these mountain valleys. A few ghost towns, especially Bannack and Virginia City, have been preserved, their stories intact. Most, however, are blown-down, rusted-out relics whose stories can only be imagined by the visitors who seek them out.

For beginning students of ghost town lore, **Bannack** is an illustrated primer on Montana's gold mining history. The site of Montana's first major gold rush, Bannack erupted when hundreds of prospectors flocked to a strike on nearby Grasshopper Creek in 1862. Within a year, the population had swollen to 3,000, and in 1864 Bannack became Montana's first Territorial capital. Eventually the gold played out and so did Bannack, but not before a sizable community had been established. Gunfights and hangings once shattered the silence of this remote valley, while more peaceable citizens crowded the saloons, dance halls, miner's court, church, and school. Today, Bannack is a quiet park, managed by the state for its historic value. A walking tour and visitor center familiarize visitors with the social and structural fabric of this 1860s' gold rush town. In late July, Bannack celebrates its history with a weekend of frontier crafts and food, music, buggy rides, gold panning, a black powder rifle shoot, and frontier church service. **Bannack Days** is the biggest weekend of the year in this otherwise lonely outpost. The park is located west of Dillon, off Montana State Highway 278.

Visitors can still stroll the boardwalks of one of the West's richest and most colorful mining districts, about 60 miles (100 km) east of Dillon, on Montana State Highway 287. **Virginia City** and **Nevada City** lie within a mile of one another along Alder Gulch. News of an 1863 gold strike here spread like knapweed, and within a year several thousand prospectors had crowded into makeshift camps along the gulch. The most enduring of these overnight mining camps was Virginia

MINERS AND MAYHEM

*O*f the settlements in Alder Gulch, Virginia City was the principal, though Nevada, two miles below, at one time was of nearly equal size and population. A stranger from the Eastern States entering the gulch for the first time, two or three months after its discovery, would be inspired by the scene and its associations with reflections of the most strange and novel character. This human hive, numbering at least ten thousand people, was the product of ninety days. Into it were crowded all the elements of a rough and active civilization. Thousands of cabins and tents and brush wakiups, thrown together in the roughest form, and scattered at random along the banks, and in the nooks of the hills, were seen on every hand. Every foot of the gulch, under the active manipulations of the miners, was undergoing displacement, and it was already disfigured by huge heaps of gravel, which had been passed through the sluices, and rifled of their glittering contents. In the gulch itself all was activity. Some were removing the superincumbent earth to reach the pay-dirt, others who had accomplished that were gathering up the clay and gravel upon the surface of the bed-rock, while by others still it was thrown into the sluice boxes. This exhibition of mining industry was twelve miles long. Gold was abundant, and every possible devise was employed by the gamblers, the treaders, the vile men and women that had come with the miners to the locality, to obtain it. Nearly every third cabin in the towns was a saloon where vile whiskey was peddled out for fifty cents a drink in gold dust. Many of these places were filled with gambling tables and gamblers, and the miner who was bold enough to enter one of them with his day's earnings in his pocket seldom left until thoroughly fleeced. Hurdy-gurdy dance-houses were numerous, and there were plenty of camp beauties to patronize them. There too, the successful miner, lured by siren smiles, after an evening spent in dancing and carousing at his expense, steeped with liquor, would empty his purse into the lap of his charmer for an hour of license in her arms. Not a day or night passed which did not yield its full fruition of fights, quarrels, wounds, or murders. The crack of the revolver was often heard above the merry notes of the violin. Street fights were frequent, and as no one knew when or where they would occur, every one was on his guard against a random shot. Sunday was always a gala day. The miners then left their work and gathered about the public places in the towns. The stores were all open, the auctioneers specially eloquent on every corner in praise of their wares. Thousands of people crowded the thoroughfares, ready to rush in any direction of promised excitement. Horse-racing was among the most favored amusements. Prize rings were formed, and brawny men engaged at fisticuffs until their sight was lost and their bodies pommelled to a jelly, while hundreds of on-lookers cheered the victor. Hacks rattled to and fro between the several towns, freighted with drunken and rowdy humanity of both sexes. Citizens of acknowledged respectability often walked, more often perhaps rode side by side on horseback, with noted courtesans in open day through the crowded streets, and seemingly suffered no harm in reputation. Pistols flashed, bowie-knives flourished, and braggart oaths filled the air, as often as men's passions triumphed over their reason. This was indeed the reign of unbridled license, and men who at first regarded it with disgust and terror, by constant exposure soon learned to become part of it, and forget that they had ever been aught else. All classes of society were represented at this general exhibition. Judges, lawyers, doctors, even clergymen could not claim exemption. Culture and religion afforded feeble protection, where allurement and indulgence ruled the hour.

—Nathaniel Pitt Langford,
Vigilante Days and Ways,
1890

Road agent's grave at Boot Hill cemetery in Virginia City.

This weathered façade (top) is one of several restored buildings from Montana's gold rush days at Virginia City. (above) Mining memorabilia on display at the World Museum of Mining in Butte.

City, which mushroomed into a commercial hub of 10,000 and served as Montana's second Territorial capital from 1865 to 1875. In one year, $10 million in gold nuggets was panned from the streams that feed into the gulch, and since the initial strike, an estimated $70 million has been taken from the area. Thanks to the painstaking restoration efforts of a Montana ranch family headed by the late Charles and Sue Bovey, visitors can drop coins into a nickelodeon, photograph a two-story outhouse, and browse through shops, buildings, merchandise, and memorabilia that are true to the era. One of Montana's foremost summer theater troupes, the **Virginia City Players**, performs nineteenth century melodrama every night during the summer at the Virginia City Opera House.

Less developed but equally diverting are the 1870s' gold camp of **Garnet**, north of Drummond; the 1880s' silver boomtown of **Granite**, near Philipsburg; the 1870s mining camp of **Elkhorn**, near Boulder, which produced both gold and silver; and **Marysville**, north of Helena, home of the fabulous Drumlummon mine, which yielded $16 million in gold and silver. Dozens of other ghost towns haunt the mountains of southwestern Montana. The **Ghost Town Hall of Fame**, at Fairmont Hot Springs east of Anaconda, displays photos and narrative descriptions of many of them. You can buy comprehensive guides to Montana's ghost towns at many bookstores around the state.

■ OUTDOOR RECREATION

The abiding treasures of this region are not the gold placers, silver lodes, and copper veins whose value is determined by a fickle metals' market. In an increasingly crowded and polluted world, this mining district's trump card may well be its rivers and lakes, its vast, untrammeled wilderness and roadless areas, its unpeopled space, and natural beauty. Small cities and towns that once drew prospectors and immigrant laborers now attract retirees, sportsmen, and refugees from urban America.

The centerpiece of the region's natural attractions is a superlative trout fishery nurtured by the headwaters of the Missouri River. Ever since August 22, 1805, when Meriwether Lewis noted in his journal that his party had landed "528 good fish, most of them large trout," the **Beaverhead River** has become famous for its "porkchops," chunky browns and rainbows that tip the scales at four-plus pounds (two kg) each. Indeed, the upper Beaverhead produces more trophy-size trout per mile than any other stream in the state.

More accessible and easier to fish, the **Big Hole** draws more anglers each year than the Beaverhead. Many come in June to fish the Big Hole's famed salmonfly hatch, which triggers Montana's most celebrated trout feeding binge. Others come for the opportunity to catch rare, river-dwelling arctic grayling, thought to be extinct everywhere in the lower 48 states except for the upper Big Hole drainage. Rising as a trickle in the Beaverhead Mountains, the Big Hole flows through wild hay meadows, skirts the north end of the Pioneer Mountains in a grand, graceful arc, and plunges through a canyon before merging with the Beaverhead at Twin Bridges to become the Jefferson River.

Beyond the veinous network of rivers and streams that surge through its valleys, the region is studded with lakes and reservoirs. One of the most scenic is **Georgetown Lake,** actually a reservoir built in 1901 by the Anaconda Company to ensure a lasting water supply for its smelting operation in nearby Anaconda. Shimmering beneath the 10,000-foot-high (3,050-m) peaks of the Anaconda Range, Georgetown Lake is one of Montana's most popular boating and fishing spots, with reliable yields of rainbow trout and kokanee salmon. To the south, near Dillon, **Clark Canyon Reservoir** is an excellent rainbow trout fishery with plenty of camping and boat-launching facilities. To the north, near Helena, three dams on the Missouri have created a chain of recreation opportunities on Canyon Ferry, Hauser, and Holter lakes. Stretching 25 miles (40 km) from the valley east of Helena to Townsend, **Canyon Ferry Lake** draws people from throughout the state to fish its stocked waters, sail and surf its wind-chopped surface, and play on its sandy beaches.

The river below Canyon Ferry Dam has become an important fall feeding ground for bald eagles. Here, just 20 minutes away from the state capital, hundreds of eagles gather around Thanksgiving to feast on spawning kokanee. Hundreds of wildlife watchers also gather to view the magnificent birds with seven-foot (two-meter) wingspans as they cruise the thermals above the same river where, in 1805, Meriwether Lewis noted that "the Bald Eagle are more abundant than I ever observed them in any Part of the country." Lewis and Clark left their imprint just a few miles downriver where the Missouri flows through a narrow passage flanked by what Lewis described as "the most remarkable clifts that we have yet seen." Because these cliffs first appeared as if they would block the expedition's passage, then seemed to open as the explorers got closer, Lewis named this scenic gorge the Gates of the Rocky Mountains. Visitors today can see the same illusion on commercial boat tours departing from the **Gates of the Mountains** boat landing on Holter Lake.

Nearby **Gates of the Mountains Wilderness** is one of Montana's smallest and least visited wilderness areas. Most people are content to view a fraction of the wilderness from the tour boats that glide past it (see "Tours" in "PRACTICAL INFORMATION"). For those willing to don hiking boots and a backpack, the "Gates" offer a truly primitive experience within the same distinctive limestone formations and cliffs that can be seen from the river. Canyons, coulees, and gorges invite deeper exploration. A popular hunting area, they provide a home to sizable populations of elk, bighorn sheep, mountain goats, and mule deer. The adjacent **Beartooth Game Management Area** furnishes winter range for the area's large elk herd. Another small, easily accessible recreation area is the **Humbug Spires Primitive Area,** south of Butte. Erratic limestone rock formations, located just off Interstate 15, draw hikers, rock climbers, and geologic sightseers.

Southwestern Montana's foremost wilderness area is the lofty Anaconda-Pintler, straddling the Continental Divide southwest of Butte and Anaconda. Much larger than the Gates of the Mountains or the Humbug Spires, the **Anaconda-Pintler Wilderness** receives surprisingly moderate use. This is high country characterized by alpine meadows, lakes, windswept ridges, and several peaks above 10,000 feet (3,050 m). Nearly all of the land is above 7,000 feet (2,134 m), meaning that snow can come at any time and remains on the ground for more than half the year. There are nearly 300 miles (480 km) of trails in this wilderness, including 45 miles (72 km) of the Continental Divide National Scenic Trail. The Anaconda-Pintler encompasses several lakes and streams, including headwaters of nationally renowned **Rock Creek,** an exceptional trout stream that flows north approximately 70 miles (110 km) to its confluence with the Clark Fork, en route to the Pacific Ocean. Many of the lakes and streams in the wilderness area hold cutthroat and rainbow trout, while mountain goats, elk, moose, deer, bear, and mountain lion occupy the higher ground.

■ SCENIC BYWAYS

People need not climb these mountains nor fish these rivers to catch their spirit. Just being in their presence, surrounded by their majesty and grace, is enough for most visitors to the Northern Rockies. Two scenic roads penetrate the region, providing lavish views as well as access to hiking trails and trout streams, campgrounds, ghost towns, and other historic sites. Montana State Highway 1, known as the **Pintler Scenic Route,** is an inviting alternative to Interstate 90 between Missoula and Butte. For 60 miles (100 km), it parallels sparkling streams, climbs mountain passes, skirts the shores of Georgetown Lake, and visits the towns of Anaconda and Philipsburg, all beneath the towering backdrop of the Anaconda Range. When combined with Interstate 90, it forms a loop that takes in the community of Deer Lodge.

For a closer look at this Northern Rockies landscape, the **Wise River-Polaris National Forest Scenic Byway** bisects a half-million acres of peaks, lakes, and headwaters in the Pioneer Mountains. For half its 30-mile (48-km) length, this mostly unpaved road follows the Wise River, then crosses a divide and emerges from the Beaverhead National Forest near Dillon. Along the way, it delivers motorists to a variety of scenic, historic, and cultural gems, including the ghost town of **Coolidge,** which served as a base camp in the 1920s for miners working the nearby Elkhorn silver mine; 1930s-era campgrounds constructed by the Civilian Conservation Corps; prehistoric Indian sites; and a New Ager's mecca called **Crystal Park,** where small quartz crystals and amethysts are commonly found. Campgrounds, hiking trails, trout streams, and abundant wildlife can stretch what appears on the map to be a short jaunt into an extended tour.

Nez Perce Indians captured the Army's howitzer on this ridge overlooking the Big Hole Battlefield during the 1877 Battle of the Big Hole.

Upon reaching Montana State Highway 278 at the south end of the Wise River-Polaris Road, Bannack State Park and Clark Canyon Reservoir are but a few miles to the south. **Big Hole Battlefield National Monument,** site of an 1877 battle between the U.S. Army and Chief Joseph's Nez Perce Indians, lies to the northwest. This was one of four major battles along the Nez Perce's flight to Canada. (See "Hi-Line: Montana's Northern Tier," for more on this trek.) While the Nez Perce escaped the army here and technically won the Battle of the Big Hole, their numbers and morale were seriously diminished. A visitor center at the Big Hole Battlefield, 12 miles (19 km) west of Wisdom on Highway 43, explains the significance of the Nez Perce Indian War. Walking trails take visitors to the camp site where soldiers surprised the sleeping Nez Perce, a wooded area where Col. John Gibbon and members of the Seventh Infantry were besieged by warriors for 36 hours, and the ridge where Indians captured the army's howitzer and a pack mule carrying 2,000 rounds of rifle ammunition.

■ PROSPECTING FOR SAPPHIRES

While the early visitors to this part of the state were fortune seekers lured by talk of fabulous gold strikes, many of today's visitors are rockhounds, drawn to one of the few places where modern prospectors can dig for sapphires. These brilliant gemstones are found in a rainbow of colors. The most common is green-blue, while blue is the best known and ruby one of the most highly prized. At commercial sapphire mines, visitors can screen "paydirt" from buckets or purchase bags of gravel to sift at home. Some of the mines also have custom gem-cutting shops on site. Most sapphire hunters spend a day or two at the mines for the fun of it, gathering gemstones that range from one-half to 10 carats. But it's easy to get hooked on these treasure hunts, knowing that sapphires as large as 150 carats have been found, then sold for thousands of dollars. Three of these mines line the Missouri River northeast of Helena—the **Spokane Bar, Cleatus** and **El Dorado** mines. Another large deposit lies along Rock Creek, southwest of Philipsburg. Once mined commercially by the St. Louis-based American Gem Mining Syndicate, today's **Gem Mountain Sapphire Mine** is open to rockhounds and recreational prospectors.

BITTERROOT COUNTRY

*W*herever mountains are, there exist people to whom mountains are where life should be lived. To millions more they are a fascination, an exhilaration, a challenge, a solace; but when a man tries to state why, he finds himself using the impotent abstractions. Like magnificence. Like solitude. Like self-humility. Like freedom and beauty. Or he goes the other way and speaks of fresh air and fishing, of bighorn and bear. None of these suffices, and together they don't explain. Maybe we can't improve on the simple statement that mountains are mountains.

—A. B. Guthrie, Jr., *Big Sky, Fair Land,* 1988

THE BITTERROOT VALLEY TAKES ITS NAME FROM THE RIVER that flows its entire length, the mountain range that forms its dominant western wall, and the diminutive flower that grows wild among its forests of ponderosa pine. This distinctive valley, which resembles a snout on the face of western Montana, appears isolated from the rest of the state but is central to its history.

As early as 1500, Flathead Indians are said to have lived here, having drifted east with other Salish-speaking tribes from the Columbia River country of the Pacific Northwest. They moved freely across the Continental Divide to hunt buffalo until around 1700, when the arrival of Shoshone and Blackfeet Indians east of the divide forced them back to the western valleys. By the time Lewis and Clark came upon them in 1805, they had established the Bitterroot Valley as their central homeland.

In the 1830s, curious about reports of "Black Robes" who could speak to the Great Spirit, the Flatheads sent delegates east to St. Louis to request that a Catholic mission be established in their valley. In September 1841, the Jesuits founded **St. Mary's Mission,** the first church in the Northwest, in what is now the community of **Stevensville.** By Christmas of that year, more than 700 Indians had been baptized. But the original church did not last beyond its first decade. It faced a number of problems, including scarce funds, continual threats from hostile Blackfeet Indians, and growing disenchantment among the Flatheads. In 1850, the mission closed and the property was sold to Major John Owen, who transformed it into a lively trading post he named **Fort Owen.**

Never a military base, Fort Owen flourished as the commercial hub of Bitterroot Valley. Owen himself had resigned his position as a licensed trader with the U.S. Army to go independent. At Fort Owen, he built on the grain and livestock operations begun by the Jesuits of St. Mary's and soon became a major supplier to nearby gold camps. Fort Owen was also a popular gathering spot for adventurers, trappers, new settlers, and several Indian tribes. Here, travelers were welcome, parties and feasts were frequent, and Indians and whites were friends. Married to a Shoshone, Owen was sympathetic to the growing problems of the natives and became the agent of the Flathead Nation, a position he later resigned out of disgust with the federal Indian Bureau's indifference and neglect. Fort Owen served as Flathead Agency Headquarters until 1860, when the headquarters was moved to its existing location in the Jocko River Valley, north of Missoula. A remnant of this once humming "bastion of civilization" in the remote wilderness of the Northwest has been preserved in Stevensville as **Fort Owen State Park.** Set on the banks of the Bitterroot River, surrounded by the lush pasturelands that supported Fort Owen's livestock, the dimly lighted East Barracks is about all that remains of the enterprise.

Less than half a mile (one km) away is the mission, reconstructed in 1866 by an Italian Jesuit, Father Anthony Ravalli. St. Mary's remained an Indian mission until 1891, when the last band of Flatheads in the Bitterroot were forced to move north. A prominent Stevensville landmark, it memorializes not only the long-standing friendship between the Flathead Indians and the Catholic church, but also the importance of this valley to the peopling of Montana. In terms of permanent settlement, the Bitterroot Valley is where it all began.

■ THE VALLEY TODAY

To reach both St. Mary's and Fort Owen, travelers must leave U.S. Route 93 and cross the Bitterroot River to reach the East Side Highway (State Highway 203/ 269). This secondary route stretches about 30 miles (50 km) through the valley's interior, between Florence and Hamilton, and provides a leisurely alternative to its major north-south artery. With views of the low-lying Sapphire Mountains to the east and the canyons and peaks of the Bitterroot Range to the west, visitors will understand the magnetic pull this valley has had on visitors ever since the Flathead

St. Mary's Mission was established by Jesuit priests in 1841 at the request of Flathead Indians; they'd heard about "Black Robes" who could speak to the Great Spirit. The present church was built in 1866.

Indians were first attracted by its mild climate. Stretching nearly 100 miles (160 km) south of Missoula to the Idaho border, the valley lies in the protective rain shadow of the Bitterroot Mountains, whose 8,000- to 10,000-foot (2,440- to 3,050-m) summits wring eastbound moisture from the Pacific out of the air before it reaches the valley. Logging and livestock are the traditional pillars of the Bitterroot economy, with a growing number of cottage and service industries that reflect the valley's appeal as a retirement community and refuge for urban emigrés. From gardening and beekeeping to horse breeding and log home construction, anything goes in this valley of scattered housing and small ranches.

"Outsiders" have been discovering the Bitterroot ever since mining industrialist Marcus Daly traveled through the valley in 1864 searching for a mining friend, George Hearst, who was feared lost in Canada. Later in his career he remembered the valley's natural beauty and climate, not to mention its thick stands of timber, which he needed for his mine tunnels and smelter works in Butte and Anaconda. In 1888–89, he and his agents began acquiring land for timber as well as for Daly's personal use. He built a 28,000-acre estate on the outskirts of Hamilton that became his summer residence and stock farm. He called it "Riverside," and added a covered and heated horse track for his beloved race horses. After the copper king's death, the **Daly Mansion** was remodeled extensively by his wife, and is now open

Early logging was done with horses. (Montana Historical Society)

to the public during the summer. A beautiful, tree-lined driveway leads to the three-story, 42-room Georgian Revival residence with its 24 bedrooms and 15 bathrooms.

The legacy of Daly's logging and milling operations may well be the log home manufacturing industry that now dominates the valley's economy. Nearly two dozen log home companies are headquartered here. The assembly yards where logs are peeled and notched, then shipped as kit log homes to buyers throughout the world, can be seen just off U.S. Route 93 throughout the valley.

■ HAMILTON

Another major employer in the valley is the medical research industry, which grew from turn-of-the-century efforts to conquer the deadly Rocky Mountain spotted fever, carried by the wood ticks so prevalent in the foothills of the Bitterroots and other Western mountains. Dr. Howard T. Ricketts, one of many fine scientists drawn to the valley to take up the challenge, discovered the link between infected

The logging and sawmill industry today is highly mechanized. (Montana Historical Society)

ticks and spotted fever in 1906. He is remembered by the name "rickettsia," given to the tiny organisms responsible for typhus, spotted fever, and related illnesses. Later scientists developed a successful vaccine against spotted fever, which is still produced at **Hamilton's Rocky Mountain Laboratories,** built in 1928 by the U.S. Public Health Service and now an arm of the National Institutes of Health. In addition to producing the vaccine, which is shipped all over the world, the laboratories conduct basic and applied research in immunologic, allergic, and infectious diseases. A private, spin-off business, Ribi ImmunoChem Research, Inc., markets veterinary pharmaceuticals and conducts cancer research. Begun by a former member of the Rocky Mountain Laboratories staff, the Hamilton company is one of 14 Montana businesses traded publicly on the stock market.

The small but diverse community of Hamilton is a crossroads of scientific and technical workers, U.S. Forest Service personnel, and the valley's more traditional loggers and ranchers. As county seat of Ravalli County, it is also the government and commercial center for the valley's 25,000 residents. It has a substantial retirement population consisting largely of former visitors who were permanently attracted by the area's climate, rural lifestyle, and outdoor recreation. Prized assets are the Bitterroot River, which flows right through town, and Blodgett Canyon, a magnificent gorge through the Bitterroot Range just 20 minutes away.

Another nearby natural treasure is the **Lee Metcalf National Wildlife Refuge,** outside of Stevensville. Named after the late U.S. Senator Lee Metcalf, a native son and conservation giant, the refuge is an island of serenity in the midst of the rambling development of the Bitterroot Valley. It protects 2,800 acres of marshes, meadows, river bottoms, and uplands that sustain more than 200 different kinds of birds, notably blue herons, osprey, and a multitude of ducks, swans, and geese. White-tailed deer are also abundant. A county road accessible from the East Side Highway bisects the lower half of the refuge, and a seasonal hiking trail with observation blinds is open mid-July to mid-September.

■ THE MOUNTAINS

The enduring appeal of the Bitterroot lies in the dramatic skyline etched by Trapper Peak, El Capitan, and the other summits and spires that run the entire length of the Bitterroot Range. The crest of this glacially sculpted range forms the jagged border separating Montana from Idaho. The two states share not only one of the most rugged massifs in the Northern Rockies but also one of the largest federally protected wilderness areas in the lower 48. The 1.3-million-acre **Selway-Bitterroot Wilderness** straddles the border, providing refuge for abundant elk and other wildlife. At first the sheer granite faces of these mountains appear cold and forbidding, but it won't be long before you feel the pull of their valleys and saddles, canyons and crests. Distinctive, U-shaped chasms cut east-west across the range, opening cool, pine-covered avenues of exploration along trout streams fed by icy lakes in the wilderness interior. Several secondary roads lead from U.S. Route 93 to trailheads at the mouths of these canyons.

When the Bitterroots are continually stealing the show, it is easy to overlook the valley's eastern rim, formed by the gentler ridges and folds of the Sapphire Mountains. Easy to reach and well worth the effort, the Sapphires' high meadows and basins shelter elk, moose, bears, mountain lion, bighorn sheep, and mountain goats, as well as a number of smaller mammals and birds. A good trail system awaits hikers, but most visitors prefer driving the Skalkaho Pass Road, which climbs the east face of the range on Montana State Highway 38, west of Hamilton, crosses Skalkaho Pass at 7,260 feet (2,210 m), then drops into Rock Creek Valley and Georgetown Lake near Anaconda. This popular back road for summer loiterers is closed in winter.

At the north end of the Bitterroot Valley, U.S. Route 12 takes motorists over the historic Lolo Trail into Idaho. This was a busy route, used by the Flathead and Nez Perce, and later by non-Indian explorers beginning with Lewis and Clark in 1805. After following the Bitterroot River in September of that year, their expedition camped at a place they named Travellers Rest, near the junction of U.S. Routes 93 and 12 at Lolo. Shortly, they reached Lolo Pass on what is now the Montana-Idaho border, and began the most difficult leg of their westward journey. Hampered by deep snow, bad weather, and a scarcity of wild game, their progress was slow but they managed to reach the Pacific by November. The following July, on their return trip east, they camped again at Travellers Rest, and it was here that they split the outfit into two groups for further exploration of the Yellowstone, Marias, and Missouri rivers. Well over a quarter of the expedition's entire 8,000-mile (12,800-km) journey was spent here in Montana. The U.S. Forest Service

(following pages) Lolo Peak, south of Missoula, is one of many distinctive landmarks along the Bitterroot Range.

maintains a visitor center at Lolo Pass that explains the significance of the Lolo Trail in the opening of the West. The history of the area was also illustrated by early Montana painter Edgar S. Paxson in several of the murals that adorn the walls of the Missoula County Courthouse in the valley's gateway city.

■ MISSOULA

Presiding over the north end of the valley is Montana's cultural superstar and third-largest city. Best known as home to the **University of Montana**, Missoula is a yeasty brew of students and independent small businesspeople, professors, truckers, foresters, artists, and writers. The common denominator of this often factious community is a lifestyle revered by all. "One of the most sophisticated small cities in America" . . . "One of the top 10 universities for education and recreation" . . . "One of the top 10 bicycling cities in the United States": these are some of the badges of distinction Missoula wears, awarded over the years by national magazines and rating guides. At the head of five scenic valleys and the junction of three great rivers, Missoula has no shortage of recreational opportunities. Here is a city of 43,000 residents with more than 140 restaurants, all within minutes of a wilderness trailhead. Here is western Montana's commercial, industrial, educational, and transportation hub, with a trout stream flowing through the center of town.

Loggers, foresters, railroaders, and merchants may have put this town on the map, but it is Missoula's writers, artists, and dramatists who keep it there. Past literary lights include critic Leslie Fiedler, the late poet Richard Hugo, and Western novelist Dorothy Johnson. Still shining brightly are novelists James Welch and James Crumley, essayist and novelist William Kittredge, writer and filmmaker Annick Smith, nonfiction writer Bryan Di Salvatore, and poet Patricia Goedicke. Many are the products of the university's 70-year-old creative writing program, which awards MFA degrees to a select group of graduate students from throughout the nation.

Readings and writing seminars are regular fare in and around Missoula. So are the live performances and exhibits of dozens of performing artists, musicians, dancers, painters, sculptors, potters, and crafters. Missoula is the home of the **Montana Repertory Theatre**—a first-rate regional touring company; the **Missoula**

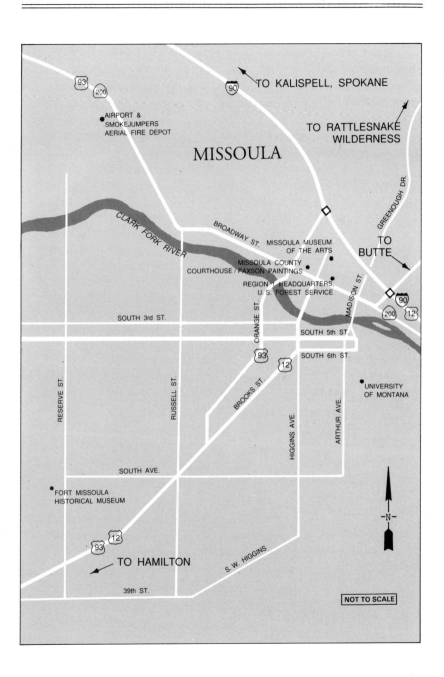

Children's Theatre—largest touring children's theater in America; the **String Orchestra of the Rockies**; the **Garden City Ballet Company**; and a number of other university and community-based music and drama groups. Each spring, the world's top wildlife films are screened and judged at the week-long **International Wildlife Film Festival.**

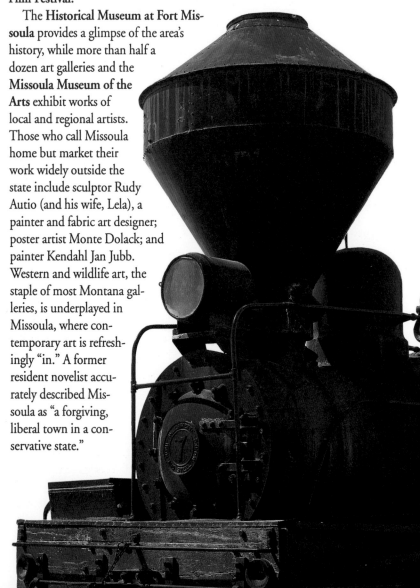

The **Historical Museum at Fort Missoula** provides a glimpse of the area's history, while more than half a dozen art galleries and the **Missoula Museum of the Arts** exhibit works of local and regional artists. Those who call Missoula home but market their work widely outside the state include sculptor Rudy Autio (and his wife, Lela), a painter and fabric art designer; poster artist Monte Dolack; and painter Kendahl Jan Jubb. Western and wildlife art, the staple of most Montana galleries, is underplayed in Missoula, where contemporary art is refreshingly "in." A former resident novelist accurately described Missoula as "a forgiving, liberal town in a conservative state."

'Dirty Murphy' plays events in several of Montana's cities.

Missoula is also a town—perhaps the only one in Montana—where day in and day out the mike is on and the curtain is up. There is always something happening on the cultural front. Which is not to say that a new stage production or   concert would preempt a fall hunting trip, or sell out as quickly as a Lady Griz basketball game or the annual Bobcat-Grizzly football game (one of the nation's oldest inter-collegiate rivalries, reenacted alternately on the UM campus in Missoula and the MSU campus in Bozeman). Even though many eastern Montanans discount it as "that liberal college town" on the state's western fringe, Missoula is still in Montana. And Montana priorities are firmly in place here.

■ MISSOULA OUTDOORS

The **Rocky Mountain Elk Foundation,** one of the nation's fastest-growing wildlife conservation organizations, is based in Missoula, as is **Bikecentennial,** America's bike-touring headquarters. Cartop carriers are always in place, ready to receive the bikes, skis, kayaks, and rafts that are the essential gear of a Missoulian. Surrounded

A steam railroad engine is one of many artifacts and displays at Fort Missoula's historical museum.

JEANNETTE RANKIN: ACTIVIST FOR PEACE

As the home of Montana's leading liberal arts university, Missoula attracts and nurtures political activists. But the city's most famous pacifist pre-dates the university, and even statehood. Born in 1880 on a ranch outside of Missoula, Jeannette Rankin became the first woman elected to the U.S. House of Representatives and the only member of Congress to vote against U.S. entry into both world wars. A progressive Republican, Rankin came to the peace movement through her involvement in the campaign for woman suffrage. As she worked on a variety of issues to benefit women and children, she became convinced that the quest for peace also belonged in the suffrage movement.

Rankin launched her political career in 1911, when she urged the Montana Legislature to grant women the right to vote. In 1916, she won her first campaign for Congress on a platform calling for woman suffrage, protective legislation for children, prohibition, and peace. After casting her first antiwar vote in April, 1917—five days after being introduced in Congress as its first female member—

Jeannette Rankin speaking in Washington, D.C., before proceeding to the Capitol to be installed as the first woman member of Congress, 1917. (Montana Historical Society)

she said, "I have always felt that there was more significance in the fact that the first woman who was ever asked what she thought about war said NO and I believe that the first vote I had was the most significant vote and a most significant act on the part of women, because women are going to have to stop war."

On that vote, she had the support of 56 other members of Congress. Twenty-four years later, after her re-election to Congress, Rankin stood alone in her opposition to war. On December 8, 1941, the day after Pearl Harbor, she cast the lone vote against U.S. entry into World War II. Asked to justify her unpopular position, she replied, "A just nation never votes unanimously for war." It was her political undoing. Defeated in her 1942 reelection bid, Rankin carried on her crusade through public appearances and antiwar statements. In 1968, the Vietnam War coalesced a group of women who marched on Washington under the banner of the Jeannette Rankin Brigade. In 1972, a year before her death, Ralph Nader noted, "If aging is the erosion of one's ideals, then Jeannette Rankin is young forever."

Statues of Montana's most outspoken feminist and pacifist stand today in both the U.S. Capitol and the State Capitol in Helena. Her ideals still inspire activists at Missoula's Jeannette Rankin Peace Resource Center.

by national forests, mountains, and rivers, locals either inherit or quickly acquire a love of woods and water. Those who lack the time or ability to hike, hunt, bike, fish, or float can enjoy Missoula's addictive environment at one of Montana's most attractive urban parks, which stretches along the Clark Fork River as it passes through downtown Missoula on its way to the Pacific Ocean. Almost as convenient as the park is the **Rattlesnake National Recreation Area and Wilderness,** a 61,000-acre preserve of hiking trails, rocky peaks, and lake-filled basins that lies literally in Missoula's backyard, just a mile north of town.

As Northern Region headquarters for the U.S. Forest Service, Missoula has always been tied to the wood-products industry and the forestry profession. One of the university's strongest programs is its forestry school, which supplies the agency with many of its professionals. Missoula is also the home of the **Smokejumper Training Center and Aerial Fire Depot,** the oldest and largest of its kind in the nation. Stationed west of town near the airport, this is one of the U.S. Forest Service's nerve centers during the summer firefighting season, generally July through mid-September. Visitors can tour the center during the summer and view the action as retardant-filled planes squat for refueling and smokejumpers fuss with their parachutes and wait for the call that will signal their next mission. Photographs, murals, and videos further illustrate the highly technical business of fighting fires from the sky, and the unusual history of firefighting.

■ THE UNIVERSITY INFLUENCE

With an enrollment of about 10,000, the university is Montana's leading liberal arts school. In addition to its College of Arts and Sciences, it maintains seven professional schools of business, education, fine arts, forestry, journalism, law, and pharmacy and allied health sciences. The university also conducts significant research at the UM Biological Station on Flathead Lake, the Lubrecht Experimental Forest, and the Bureau of Business and Economic Research.

Besides the cultural, sports, and entertainment benefits supplied by the university, UM delivers a built-in clientele to the city's constellation of bookstores, music stores, art galleries, restaurants, and food markets. Downtown Missoula has risen to the challenge of shopping malls, franchises, and fast-food restaurants by creating an appealing commercial district, complete with its inviting riverfront park and a farmers market that confirms its standing as Montana's "Garden City." Downtown Missoula is a place where people still practice the leisurely art of browsing as they drift from coffeeshop to bookstore to bakery, gathering up fresh herbs and spices, croissants, and imported cheeses along the way. Except for a few days in winter, when warm air aloft creates a temperature inversion and traps smog and wood smoke in the valley, Missoula's urban environment is as inviting as its natural setting.

In 1987, the Confederated Salish and Kootenai Tribes of the Flathead Indian Reservation staged a vigil on the University of Montana campus against erosion of treaty rights.

THE FLATHEAD
WESTERN WILDERNESS

IF MONTANA HAS A DESTINATION RESORT AREA, THIS IS IT. Bordered by wilderness, encircled by mountains, watered generously by lakes and rivers, and soothed by a Pacific Northwest climate, the Flathead Valley makes its living hosting visitors. Art galleries, championship golf courses, resorts, sailing, skiing, and whitewater rafting are the industry of the Flathead. The raw materials are Flathead Lake and a stockpile of nationally protected recreational resources: Glacier National Park; the adjacent Bob Marshall Wilderness; the National Bison Range; Jewel Basin Hiking Area; Mission Mountains Wilderness, and Flathead National Wild and Scenic River. Add The Big Mountain ski resort and a chain of lakes called the Seeley Swan, and you have a year-round playground of immense proportions.

Summer is the high season here. Visitors cluster on beaches and mingle at resorts, marinas, and yacht clubs. They clog the parking lots and gift shops at Glacier Park. Local businesses cater to a growing nonresident market with fine wines and the cuisine of schooled chefs. But come September, after the crowds have subsided, residents take back their beloved Flathead and preoccupy themselves with the same concerns of other Montanans: squeezing in as many fishing trips as possible before hunting season begins and making ends meet in an area that supports few large employers. Outside of the tourism and forest industries, an aluminum plant at Columbia Falls, and public-sector employment, residents find work on family farms and ranches or in their own creative genius.

The rural lifestyle and natural beauty of the Flathead Valley have drawn a disproportionately large number of Western and contemporary painters, sculptors, ceramicists, and craftworkers to the area. Their work can be seen in studios and galleries and at art fairs throughout the valley, particularly in the Bigfork and Kalispell areas.

What little land is not textured by mountains and managed by the federal government as national forest is cultivated in crops peculiar to the climate and soil of the Flathead Valley, like peppermint, Christmas trees, cherries, and champagne grapes. Assuming it comes at the right time of year, the generous moisture that falls west of the Continental Divide also produces profitable yields of barley, wheat, oats, hay, and seed potatoes.

◼ FLATHEAD LAKE

The heart of Flathead Valley lies in a shimmering expanse of water that cultivates both an economy and a lifestyle that are unique in Montana. Stretching nearly 30 miles (48 km) from Bigfork and Somers on the north to Polson on the south, Flathead Lake is the West's largest natural, freshwater lake. Its commanding presence governs not only the climate of this northern valley but also the disposition of all who dwell here. Until recently, Flathead Lake was perhaps most famous for its cherry orchards. The moderating influence of the lake creates a micro-climate conducive to the commercial production of some of the nation's plumpest, sweetest cherries.

Until 1989, mile upon mile of orchards formed a fragrant boulevard of blossoms along the lake's east shore each spring, followed by summer's festive harvest. But that year, orchardists around the lake were reminded that they are no different from other farmers and ranchers in Montana who have learned they cannot trust the weather. On February 1, a brutal, once-in-50-years cold snap sent temperatures plummeting 53 degrees (11°C) in 24 hours, flash-freezing trees and destroying the valley's cherry industry. Some growers have replanted their orchards, but it will be several years before they are producing at pre-1989 levels. Other growers are experimenting with apples, pears, peaches, and apricots. But the crop that is getting the most attention is the vineyard on the west shore of the lake near Dayton.

A recent addition to the producers whose exotic crops distinguish the Flathead Valley from the grain and livestock mainstays of central and eastern Montana, **Mission Mountain Winery** grows pinot noir grapes that are bottled as a pale, ruby champagne. The pinots thrive on the Flathead's long, hot days and cool nights, but to survive in Montana, their vines must be buried in soil over the winter. Mission Mountain also bottles a white riesling, chardonnay, muscat canelli, and Johannisberg riesling, using grapes that are grown in the Yakima Valley of Washington. The tasting room south of Dayton off U.S. Route 93, is open daily from early May to late October.

Flathead Lake supports Montana's largest sailing community, as well as sizeable fleets of motor craft and charter fishing boats. The lake is a favorite among fishermen who enjoy the needle-in-the-haystack approach to fishing,—that is, searching out large trout in deep lakes. Flathead is unrivaled in Montana as a prime fishery

for trophy Mackinaw, or lake trout. Because of the lake's size and depth, fishing on Flathead takes on the appearance of an ocean expedition. Serious anglers arm themselves with steel line and saltwater rods, and probe this inland sea at depths of 130 feet (40 m) from large boats fitted for downriggers. For visitors who would like to try their luck at catching a 20-pound (nine-kg) Mac, there are several guides on the lake, plus boat rentals, tackle shops, and marinas in lakeshore communities.

Visitors who don't need to fish to enjoy a beautiful lake can choose from several boat tours (see "Tours" in "PRACTICAL INFORMATION"). In addition to several private campgrounds and resorts, there are six state parks with camping facilities and boat launches around the lake. A seventh state park, **Wildhorse Island**, sprawls across the southwest arm of Flathead Lake. Accessible only by boat, the island shelters about a hundred bighorn sheep, along with a variety of other mammals and birds. Positioned within the boundaries of the Flathead Indian Reservation, the island was once used by Salish and Kootenai Indians as a hiding place for their horses when they were threatened by Blackfeet horse-raiding parties. Horses that were never retrieved gave the island its name.

■ KALISPELL

With roughly 12,000 residents, the city of Kalispell is as urban as it gets in this valley. Founded in 1891 along the main line of the Great Northern Railway, Kalispell has served northwestern Montana as a transport and trade center ever since. Its patriarch, Charles Conrad, was a pioneer entrepreneur who arrived in Montana on a Missouri River steamboat after losing his Virginia plantation during the Civil War. He rebuilt his fortune in the freighting business at Fort Benton, then moved to the Flathead Valley. In forming the Kalispell Townsite Company, he reserved 72 acres for himself and built a three-story, 23-room, Norman-style mansion, said to be the best example of luxurious, turn-of-the-century architecture in the Pacific Northwest. The mansion (on Woodland Avenue between 3rd and 4th streets) remained in the Conrad family until it was given to the city in 1975, and is open daily, from mid-May to mid-October, for guided tours.

Several other historic homes grace the tree-lined residential neighborhoods of "old" Kalispell. Beyond these dignified roots, Kalispell has branched and sprawled into a typical small city that serves the surrounding valley with a revitalized

The heart of Flathead Valley lies in the shimmering expanse of Flathead Lake, largest natural freshwater lake in the West.

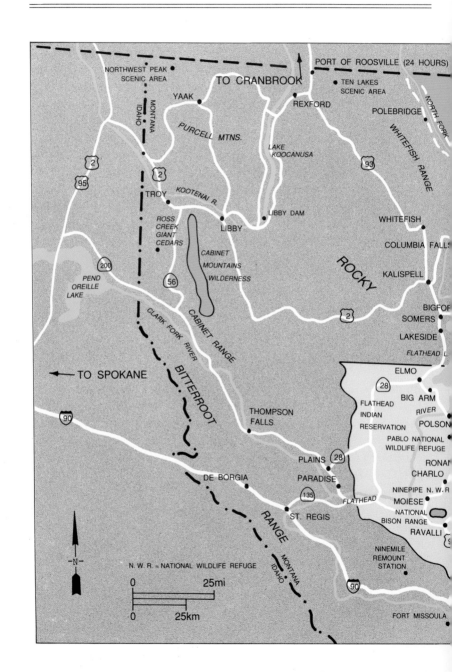

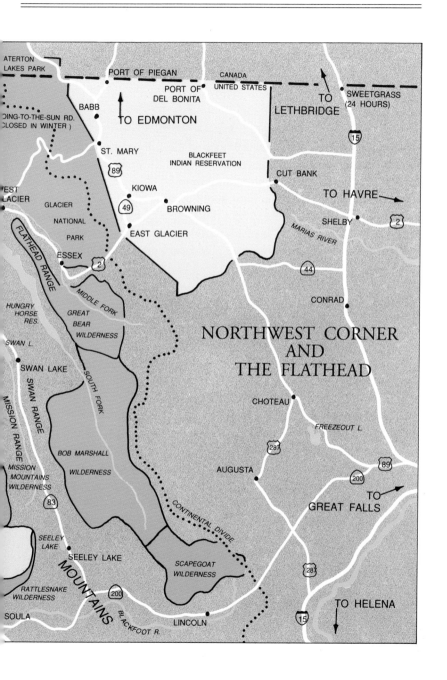

ATERTON
LAKES PARK

PORT OF PIEGAN

PORT OF
DEL BONITA

CANADA
UNITED STATES

TO
LETHBRIDGE

SWEETGRASS
(24 HOURS)

BABB

DING-TO-THE-SUN RD.
CLOSED IN WINTER)

TO EDMONTON

15

ST. MARY

89

BLACKFEET
INDIAN RESERVATION

CUT BANK

TO HAVRE

EST
LACIER

GLACIER

KIOWA

49

BROWNING

SHELBY

2

NATIONAL

MARIAS RIVER

FLATHEAD RANGE

PARK

EAST GLACIER

ESSEX

2

44

HUNGRY
HORSE
RES.

MIDDLE FORK

GREAT
BEAR
WILDERNESS

CONRAD

SWAN L.

SWAN LAKE

SOUTH FORK

NORTHWEST CORNER
AND
THE FLATHEAD

SWAN RANGE

MISSION RANGE

CHOTEAU

FREEZEOUT L.

BOB MARSHALL
WILDERNESS

AUGUSTA

89

MISSION
MOUNTAINS
WILDERNESS

83

CONTINENTAL DIVIDE

200

TO
GREAT FALLS

SEELEY
LAKE

SEELEY LAKE

SCAPEGOAT
WILDERNESS

287

RATTLESNAKE
WILDERNESS

MOUNTAINS

200

SOULA

BLACKFOOT R.

LINCOLN

15

TO HELENA

downtown commercial district, convention facilities, a community college, airport, and numerous restaurants, motels, and art galleries.

■ WHITEFISH

While Kalispell serves the functional needs of the valley, some of the Flathead's smaller communities are better examples of the distinctive lifestyle enjoyed by area residents. To the north is the sports-loving town of Whitefish, which sits on the shore of Whitefish Lake, just minutes from Montana's largest ski resort, **The Big Mountain** (see "WINTER RECREATION" for specifics). In summer, its 4,400 residents celebrate their place on Earth with canoe races, regattas, and Olympic-style summer games; in winter, they host one of Montana's most festive winter carnivals.

■ COLUMBIA FALLS AND POLEBRIDGE

The timber products industry and the Columbia Falls Aluminum Plant are the major employers in nearby Columbia Falls. Nearly as important as the paychecks they provide are the recreational benefits of living within minutes of Glacier Park, the North Fork of the Flathead River, 34-mile-long (55-km) Hungry Horse Reservoir, and the Great Bear and Bob Marshall wilderness areas.

One of the most distinctive communities in this region is Polebridge, halfway up the gravel road that lines the western edge of Glacier Park. Consisting of a historic general store known by its patrons as the Polebridge Merc, along with a hostel, café, saloon, and ranger station, Polebridge is the social center of the scattered North Fork community. Deep in logging country, where roads are outfitted with signs proclaiming "this family is supported by timber dollars," the independent thinkers of Polebridge are among Montana's most outspoken proponents of wilderness protection. Typical of the Polebridge spirit is the sign outside the Northern Lights Café announcing "this business is supported by people from all walks of life." If you need to make a phone call or intercept a message from the outside world while exploring the remote reaches of the North Fork of the Flathead, this is the place to do it. The Merc has the only public telephone in these parts, and it's a busy one.

■ BIGFORK

Less than 60 miles (100 km) south, but light years away, is the picture-perfect village of **Bigfork**, overlooking Flathead Lake from a sheltered bay at the mouth of the Swan River. Influenced by the climate of the Pacific Northwest, winters are long and gray here and elsewhere in the Flathead Valley. But when the sun comes out of hibernation, Bigfork blossoms like the potted geraniums and petunias that line its main street and the sweet peas that grow wild in the draws and gullies at its outskirts.

With a year-round population of less than 1,000, Bigfork swells in summer to accommodate the many visitors who come to enjoy its art galleries, live theater, sidewalk cafés, restaurants, resorts, golf courses, and genteel ambiance. Well known as one of Montana's leading fine arts communities, Bigfork is also a growing center for the performing arts. A new, million-dollar theater houses the town's popular **Bigfork Summer Playhouse** and a fledgling springtime event, the **Gathering at Bigfork,** draws some of the nation's leading playwrights to conduct workshops and readings, and to premier new works. It is no wonder that urban refugees from San Francisco, Los Angeles, and elsewhere have settled in the so-called "village by the bay." Bright red barns stand out against the towering blue mountains of the Swan Range; cows graze on steep hillsides; neat rows of junior Scotch pine stretch for miles at Christmas-tree farms throughout the valley. Bigfork is the good life, Montana-style.

■ POLSON

At the opposite end of Flathead Lake, **Polson** is a community of about 3,000 that reaches back to 1840, making it the first settlement on the lake. It is fitting that the community was named after pioneer rancher David Polson, who was also a fine fiddler. Every summer, in late July, Polson hosts the state's biggest fiddling contest when members of the Montana Oldtime Fiddlers Association come to town. All of Polson is a stage, as contestants—ranging in age from six to 90—tune up at various campsites around town. Formal competition takes place inside the middle-school gymnasium. Other attractions, besides the lake and the water-based lifestyle it supports, are the nearby Flathead River and one of the valley's oldest and loveliest lakeshore golf courses.

■ FLATHEAD INDIAN RESERVATION

Polson is the largest city on the 1.2-million-acre **Flathead Indian Reservation,** which takes in the southern half of Flathead Lake and stretches south nearly to Missoula. This is the only Indian reservation in Montana west of the Continental Divide. Unlike the Plains Indians who inhabit Montana's six other reservations, the Salish and Kootenai tribes of the Flathead Reservation are the descendants of a coastal culture. Together, the tribes are known as the Flathead Indians, a name that carried over to many of the land forms in the area despite its disputed origin. Some say that Lewis and Clark gave the Flatheads their name, but there is no evidence that these Indians ever adopted the practice of flattening their children's heads as some of the coastal tribes farther west are believed to have done. Before the arrival of non-native explorers, the Flathead moved freely throughout the Bitterroot and Flathead valleys, with frequent forays east of the Rockies to hunt buffalo.

Intrigued by early stories of Christianity that drifted West with some visiting Iroquois Indians in the 1830s, the Flatheads sent east for "Black Robes," thus bringing Roman Catholicism to Montana. One of the most historic monuments to the church's early development is the mission at St. Ignatius. Set against the magnificent backdrop of the Mission Range, the **St. Ignatius Mission** was established in 1854 by the Jesuits after they abandoned their original mission in the Bitterroot Valley. The new mission began as a simple wooden chapel, cabin, blacksmith, and carpentry shop. The imposing brick church that stands today was built a century ago and includes a number of spectacular murals depicting biblical history, painted by Brother Joseph Carignano. It is the oldest continuously operating mission in Montana and remains one of the Flathead Valley's most prominent landmarks.

In 1855, the Flatheads signed what came to be known as the Hellgate Treaty, which established the current reservation in the Jocko River Valley, north of Missoula. The treaty also promised a reservation in the Bitterroot Valley, but growing pressure from white settlers forced its residents onto the Jocko reservation in 1891. Loss of aboriginal lands in the Bitterroot Valley did not signal the end of encroachment by the U.S. government. In 1887, Congress passed legislation allowing the federal government to partition tribal holdings into 80- and 160-acre parcels. The effect was to destroy the Indians' communal way of life and force them to become individual farmers. With the natives each allotted their piece of

POWWOWS

Powwow is a time of pageantry and celebration on Montana's seven Indian reservations, and there is nothing quite like it in the state's dominant white culture. For three to five days, tribal members abandon the day-to-day challenge of reservation life and come together for renewal and reunion. They perform traditional ceremonies and compete in dancing and games. They race prized horses and parade in beautifully beaded buckskins and feathered headdresses. They call on spirits, give gifts, and look to tribal elders to keep ancient stories alive. Through it all, they fortify the bonds that tie Indian families and clans so closely together.

Non-Indian visitors are welcome as spectators, but don't expect these events to conform to the schedules and comforts of the American middle class. Leave your own cultural trappings behind and go to powwow with the expectation of enriching your understanding of the West by learning about its native culture. Some of Montana's best-known powwows are included in the list of events in "PRACTICAL INFORMATION."

Powwow is a time of celebration and renewal of spirit for Montana's Indian tribes. (photo by Douglas O'Looney)

land, remaining lands were deemed "surplus," and opened to non-native settlers. In the case of the Flathead Reservation, the Allotment Act was especially damaging to the Indians' land base because of the reservation's agricultural potential. Under the act, just over half of the land was opened to homesteading. As a result, the Flathead Reservation has a much larger non-Indian population than Montana's other reservations; in fact, the Salish and Kootenai Indians who live here are a minority within their own reservation. Of the nearly 20,000 people living on the reservation, fewer than one-fifth are enrolled members of the tribe. Because of the loss of so much of their land to homesteaders, the Salish and Kootenai tribes have been aggressive in controlling ownership of their remaining tribal lands, which include a rich body of timber and agricultural lands. In addition, they receive sizeable rent payments from the Montana Power Company for the operation of Kerr Dam near Polson. Of all seven Montana Indian reservations, the Flathead is wealthiest in terms of natural resources.

Bordered on the east by the imperial Mission Range and watered by Flathead Lake, the Flathead and Jocko rivers, the reservation is also rich in scenic and recreational assets, including the nation's first tribally established and managed wilderness. The **Mission Mountains Tribal Wilderness** is an 89,500-acre tract of airy peaks and alpine lakes that provide Flathead Indians with an important link to their ancestral heritage. It adjoins another 74,000-acre parcel managed by the Flathead National Forest as the **Mission Mountains Wilderness**. While these rugged lands are managed cooperatively, there are differences in management practices. Hunting in the tribal wilderness is reserved for tribal members only, and each summer a 12,000-acre portion of the tribal wilderness near 9,820-foot (3,000-m) McDonald Peak is closed to protect an estimated 25 grizzly bears that come to feed on cyclical swarms of ladybugs and cutworm moths. To help finance management of the wilderness, the tribe sells use permits to non-tribal members for a small fee. Permittees are entitled to hike, fish, and camp on tribal wilderness lands. No special permits are required for these activities on the federally designated wilderness, which lies east of the crest of the Mission Range.

The Flathead Reservation also encompasses an important piece of Western Americana—the National Bison Range—as well the Ninepipe and Pablo national waterfowl refuges. Established in 1908 with the progeny of bison that survived the mass extermination of buffalo from the plains in the previous century, the **National Bison Range** now supports a sizeable herd of 400 to 500 bison on 19,000 acres of natural grassland. Visitors can expect to see bison, as well as pronghorn, elk, deer, and bighorn sheep along an auto tour route that takes in sweeping views of the Mission Range. Newborn bison calves steal the show here in spring; in early October, visitors can witness the drama of an authentic buffalo roundup, when cowboy rangers thin the herd. Range headquarters are at Moiese, west of U.S. Route 93, at the south end of the reservation.

Less dramatic but no less significant is the **Ninepipe National Wildlife Refuge** between St. Ignatius and Ronan. Hundreds of glacial potholes and a large reservoir sustain more than 180 species of birds in this watery environment. Cormorants, herons, gulls, shorebirds, bald eagles, and pheasants round out the roster of birds, primarily waterfowl, that nest and rest here. A few miles north, between Pablo and Polson, the **Pablo National Wildlife Refuge** provides additional wetlands. Spring migration peaks from late March to early May, and fall populations approach 200,000 birds.

■ GLACIER NATIONAL PARK

The entire Glacier Park/Bob Marshall/Seeley Swan wild realm covers about three million, largely unpopulated acres of adjoining public lands, an area roughly the size of Connecticut. The undisputed centerpiece is **Glacier National Park**, which crowns the North American continent with 1,500 square miles (3,885 sq. km) of exquisite ice-carved terrain. Here, serrated ridges and horn-shaped peaks reign over a jumble of turquoise lakes, waterfalls, cascades, river valleys, hanging gardens, and alpine meadows. Born of geologic and glacial violence, this random landscape couldn't be more perfect had it been designed and executed by Michelangelo. Like the ocean, its sheer scope has a way of putting humanity in its place. People are merely visitors here, unable to meet the rigors of a severe northern climate.

Harsh as it is in winter, Glacier Park is on its best behavior during the summer months. Each year, nearly two million pilgrims journey to this place still held sacred by Blackfeet Indians, whose reservation forms the park's eastern border. Travelers come from throughout the world to hike its trails, drive its magnificent **Going-to-the-Sun** highway—the park's magnificent east-west route—or simply to drink in the pristine beauty of one of America's largest intact wild areas. Visitors commonly see mountain goats from roadside turnouts, and need take only a short hike to see bighorn sheep, white-tailed ptarmigan, and many of the other birds and mammals that live here. More than a thousand species of plants, many of them hardy alpine wildflowers, embroider the park in dazzling primary colors and pastels as they follow spring up the mountains all summer long.

With more than 750 miles (1,200 km) of trails in Glacier, there are at least five lifetimes of memorable hikes in this national park. They range from day hikes into hidden lakes and living glaciers to extended treks across snowfields and cloud-covered mountain passes. Two of the most popular trails lead hikers to Sperry and Granite Park chalets, two backcountry lodges that take the worry out of sleeping in bear country (see "Accommodations" in "PRACTICAL INFORMATION"). The landscape of Glacier will leave a lasting imprint on the minds and in the hearts of visitors who absorb its vistas in a way that only hiking allows.

The 52-mile-long (83-km) **Going-to-the-Sun** road quickens the hearts of motorists as it climbs more than 3,000 feet (914 m) from lush, lake-lined valley floors on either side of the park to its windswept summit at Logan Pass on the Continental Divide. Along the way, it sidesteps gushing waterfalls, winds through glaciated

One of Glacier Park's most popular views is St. Mary's Lake and Wild Goose Island.

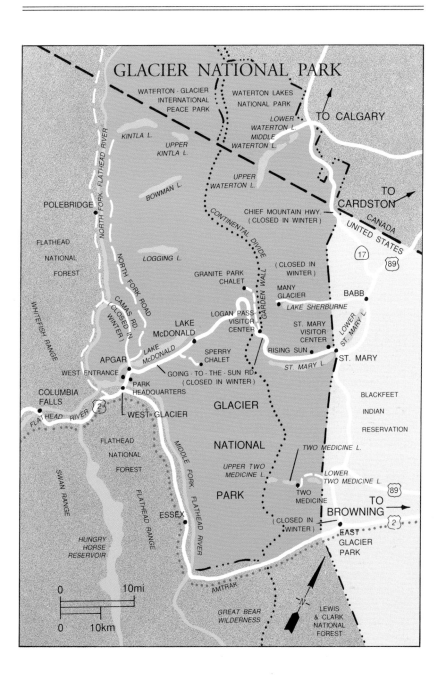

THE CONTINENTAL DIVIDE

Known among the West's native peoples as the "backbone of the world," the Continental Divide runs along the crests of the Rocky Mountains from Canada to Mexico, literally dividing the waters of the North American continent. In Montana, it zigzags across the Rockies, entering the state from the north at Glacier National Park and exiting in Yellowstone National Park on the state's southern border. Waters running west of the Great Divide feed the Columbia River and drain into the Pacific Ocean; waters flowing east fill the Missouri-Mississippi Basin and drain into the Gulf of Mexico. And from one point in Montana—Glacier Park's Triple Divide Peak—water also flows north to Hudson Bay, making Montana the only state that replenishes three oceans.

While the image of the Continental Divide suggests a distinct, knife-like ridge that neatly splits the Atlantic and the Pacific, the topography varies greatly. On prominent peaks and ridges you can actually see the waters of two oceans dividing at your feet, but at other places along the divide it is hard to even pinpoint the ridge as it meanders across broad plateaus. Sometimes obvious, sometimes obscure, the Continental Divide is Montana's single most important topographical feature. More importantly, it is the birthplace of the nation's waterways.

HIKING THE DIVIDE

The **Continental Divide National Scenic Trail** was established by Congress in 1968, making this lofty spine accessible to hikers, horseback riders, and in some cases, motorized travelers. Roughly 800 miles (1,300-km) of the entire 3,100-mile-long (5,000-km) trail lie along or near the ridgetops of Montana's Rocky Mountains. Passing through some of North America's most scenic backcountry, the trail crosses Glacier and Yellowstone national parks, in addition to 10 national forests with designated wilderness areas, including the Bob Marshall, Great Bear, Scapegoat, and Anaconda Pintler. Historic attractions along the trail include several ghost towns and two mountain passes crossed by Lewis and Clark on their 1804–06 search for an inland water route to the Pacific Ocean. In southwestern Montana, the trail passes high above Big Hole National Battlefield, site of the 1877 clash between the U.S. Army and the Nez Perce Indians, and Red Rock Lakes National Wildlife Refuge, a national sanctuary for trumpeter swans.

The trail has yet to be fully constructed and marked in Montana. Temporary routes have been established pending completion of the final route. Anyone considering a Continental Divide trek should contact the U.S. Forest Service before setting out. (See "Useful Addresses" in "PRACTICAL INFORMATION" for Forest Service addresses and phone numbers.)

valleys, and traverses an imposing, knife-like ridge called the Garden Wall before topping out at just over 6,600 feet (2,012 m) above sea level. Begun in 1916 and completed in 1932, the "Sun" road is an engineering masterpiece that deserves the attention of unhurried motorists.

In direct competition with the Canadian Pacific Railway, which was promoting Banff National Park in Alberta, and the Northern Pacific in Yellowstone National Park, the Great Northern Railway marketed Glacier as the "Switzerland of America," and built hotels and chalets to fulfill the slogan's image. The vaulted ceilings, heavy beams, and pillars of Glacier Park Lodge and Many Glacier Hotel evince the exuberance of an earlier era. Other lodges, cabins, and campgrounds are located throughout the park and are generally open from June to Labor Day, with some remaining open until mid- or late-September. There are additional rooms and campgrounds outside the park. See "Accommodations" in "PRACTICAL INFORMATION" for specifics, or contact Glacier National Park for a complete listing of lodging options.

Adjoining Glacier on the north is Canada's **Waterton Lakes National Park.** In 1932, the governments of Canada and the United States established the world's first international park—**Glacier-Waterton International Peace Park**—to commemorate the friendship and good will between the two nations. Smaller than

Many of Glacier's historic chalets no longer exist. However, the park still has two hike-in chalets in addition to its lodges, inns, and campgrounds. (courtesy, Montana Historical Society)

Glacier, Waterton boasts the same magnificent scenery, activities, and services. The primary route between the two parks is Chief Mountain International Highway along the extreme northeast edge of Glacier. Both the Chief Mountain and Going-to-the-Sun highways are closed to winter travel.

■ BOB MARSHALL COUNTRY

Glacier shares its southern border with a kindred spirit named Bob Marshall. This massive wildlife sanctuary and roadless retreat actually consists of three federally designated wilderness areas: the **Great Bear, Bob Marshall,** and **Scapegoat.** The entire 1.5-million-acre expanse is known as Bob Marshall Country in memory of the young forester whose vision of preservation sparked the wilderness movement more than 50 years ago. Known affectionately by its many friends and visitors simply as the Bob, this is one of America's oldest, largest, and best-known preserves, regarded among foresters and conservationists as the "flagship" of the nation's wilderness fleet.

Encompassing entire river drainages and mountain ranges, 2,400 square miles (6,215 sq. km) in all, Bob Marshall Country embodies the spirit of the Wilderness Act of 1964. It is truly a place "where man himself is a visitor who does not remain." Rather, this is the domain of some of North America's largest, most majestic big-game animals. Together with Glacier National Park, the Bob forms a critically important wildlife corridor for the once-dominant, now-threatened grizzly bear. An estimated 250 to 350 of the great bears roam freely throughout this Northern Rockies refuge. Bighorn sheep graze the eastern slopes of the wilderness, while mountain goats take to higher ground, along the mountain crests. Several elk herds, with animals numbering in the thousands, make the Bob a hallowed place for hunters. More than 50 outfitters work the Bob, guiding clients on fall hunts as well as summer horsepack trips.

The Bob appeals equally to land lovers and water bugs. Besides hiking, hunting, and horseback riding, there are rapids to be ridden and pools to be probed for cutthroat trout. The South and Middle forks of the Flathead River penetrate the core of the Bob. Together with the North Fork, which flows along the western edge of Glacier National Park, they form the nation's longest wild and scenic river system. The Middle Fork promises some of the most challenging whitewater in

(previous pages) Looking toward Glacier's snow-capped Mt. Grinnell from Granite Park Chalet.

Montana, with rapids made immortal by names like "Jaws" and "Screamin' Right-Hand Turn." Several rafting companies in the Flathead offer guided trips ranging from half-day whitewater trips and evening dinner floats to extended camp-float, fly-fishing, and combination horsepack/float trips on wilderness rivers.

A trip to the Bob can be a life-changing experience. Because of its sheer size, you can hike or ride horseback for miles and for days, exploring new country each day and living by your wits with a fishing rod, a map, and a compass. At night, you can explore the mysteries of the universe beneath a starry sky and wonder, with friends around a campfire, what it's all about.

■ SEELEY SWAN VALLEY

Lying immediately west of the Bob is an informal wilderness known as the **Seeley Swan Valley.** Flanked by the imposing walls and peaks of the Mission and Swan mountain ranges, this densely forested valley stretches 90 miles (145 km) from Clearwater Junction at the intersection of Montana state highways 200 and 83, into the heart of the Flathead Valley at Bigfork. Montana State Highway 83, the so-called **Seeley Swan Highway,** is a scenic alternative to the Flathead's more heavily traveled U.S. Route 93.

Along the floor of the Seeley Swan, the Clearwater and Swan rivers link a chain of lakes that mirror snow-capped peaks and thick stands of larch, fir, aspen, and birch. When the valley fills up with snow and the lakes glaze over with ice, the boaters, campers, and canoeists of summer give way to ice fishermen, snowmobilers, and cross-country skiers. Year-round, this quiet land of mountains and rivers and forest-clad lakes provides sanctuary for a diversity of wildlife ranging from the elusive loon to the grizzly bear. White-tailed deer are so abundant they pose a hazard to motorists traveling Montana State Highway 83 in early morning and at dusk.

The water corridors around Seeley Lake sustain the largest population of nesting common loons in the Western lower 48 states. Loons and a lot more can be seen on the Clearwater Chain-of-Lakes driving tour, which extends about 18 miles (29 km) from Salmon Lake to Rainy Lake at the south end of Montana State Highway 83. Have the binoculars ready because there are several designated viewing areas just off the highway at Salmon, Seeley, Alva, and Rainy lakes. North of Seeley Lake, the Clearwater Canoe Trail is an easy, four-mile (six-km) float through an outdoor auditorium specializing in loon music.

(following pages) The Flathead River and Swan Range represent some of the finest scenery of northwest Montana.

Outside the small communities of Seeley Lake, Condon, and Swan Lake, the valley consists almost entirely of public land. Campgrounds, motels, and rustic resorts dot the larger lakes of the Seeley Swan. Miles of trails take day hikers to picnics beside waterfalls, and backcountry travelers to remote wilderness destinations in the Missions and the Bob Marshall.

■ JEWEL BASIN

The **Jewel Basin** is just that—a pocket of lakes for hikers only. Visitors limited by time or apprehension about backcountry travel can enjoy a condensed wilderness experience in this special management area of the Flathead National Forest between Kalispell and Hungry Horse Dam. Thirty-five miles (56 km) of trails connect most of the area's 27 alpine lakes, putting them within a two- to three-hour hike of the parking lot. The view from 7,528-foot-high (2,295-m) Mount Aeneus has been described as one of the best 360-degree panoramas in western Montana, with sweeping vistas of Glacier Park, the peaks of the Bob Marshall Wilderness, the Swan and the Mission ranges, as well as the lake-studded interior of the Jewel Basin. Most of the lakes are concentrated on the west side of the basin and hold the promise of pan-size cutthroat and rainbow trout.

Prime time in the Jewel Basin is the same as it is for other mountain treks in Montana—the window of opportunity from July into September, when last winter's snow is gone and next year's has yet to arrive. Visitors are advised that Montana's seasonal window can be slammed shut any month of the year by sudden storms.

NORTHWEST CORNER

IN ALL RESPECTS BUT ONE, NORTHWESTERN MONTANA is the antithesis of the Big Open. Perhaps more than any two regions, they represent the physical diversity of the state. Unlike the thirsty, windswept plains of eastern Montana, the northwest woods fill up with snow each winter, yielding roughly double the moisture of the Big Open. In Montana, the difference between 13 and 26 inches (33 to 66 cm) is the difference between a ranch economy and a timber economy. Here, the trees grow so thick that there isn't space to graze a cow.

Nearly everyone who explored this region, using the 600-mile-long (960-km) **Kootenai River** as a highway, had something to say about the dense forests that grew here and their potential value to an expanding frontier. But it was David Thompson, the first non-native explorer to chart these woods and waters, who nailed down the one feature northwestern Montana shares with the Big Open. In his journals, he noted that the area's isolation left its timber "without the possibility of being brought to market."

Railroads eventually made it possible to market the timber, but the area's population still lives a world apart from "mainland" Montana. Not really on the way to anywhere, the Northwest Corner is in Montana but not of it. Residents are oriented not so much to Kalispell, the hub of the nearby Flathead Valley, but to Spokane, Washington, a good 150 miles (240 km) from Libby, this region's largest community. Like the Big Open, the Northwest Corner remains a remote and undiscovered destination.

But here the similarity ends. To a rancher from the plains, this region's tall, dense forests are cause for anxiety as they close in around him and block his customary 180-degree view of the sky. But to a native of these parts, the deep, dark woods are like a cozy down comforter. To be in their midst is to be snug and secure. These woods are like no other woods in Montana. They are taller, thicker, and far more diversified than the fir and pine forests that grow east of the Rockies. Like the coastal forests to the west, these woods are a fusion of plant species. Cedar, hemlock, pine, fir, larch, and spruce—15 species of conifers in all—grow side by side above a thick understory of shrubs, ferns, berries, and wildflowers.

■ LOGGING

For most of its recorded history, this area has relied on the cyclical fortunes of the timber industry for its economic well-being. Before the turn of the century, settlers were clearing wooded areas and hauling trees to the Kootenai or one of its tributaries, where they awaited massive spring log drives that sent the harvest downriver to mills in Idaho. The arrival of railroads transformed logging from a local practice into an industry, and shortly thereafter the federal government created the National Forest Reserves, forerunner of today's Forest Service, to manage the resource. Besides providing a ready market for railroad ties and bridge timbers, the railroads revitalized local markets by luring more settlers out West, and they opened national markets. They also provided mills with a steady supply of timber, making milling a profitable, year-round enterprise.

Northwest Montana's first sawmill was built in 1889 near Eureka. Since then, millions of logs have been transformed at local mills into billions of board feet of finished lumber, house logs, plywood, pulp, and paper products. Evidence of the logger's trade is everywhere, from the extensive clearcuts and logging roads that scar hillsides to the giant logging trucks that rumble down narrow mountain roads, and the ubiquitous green signs posted outside homes and businesses proclaiming the owner's allegiance to the timber industry.

There is good reason for all those green signs. This industry is in trouble, not just here but in all the timber-producing states. Over-cutting, compounded by a soft market, national concern for endangered species, and protracted debates over wilderness and forest management practices have created a critical shortage of raw timber. In the mills, technology and mechanization have replaced many of the people who once held the good-paying jobs in the community. Today, the mill at Libby employs roughly half the number of workers it did 10 years ago. While a former editor of Libby's *Western News* proclaimed early in the century that "without question, lumbering is Lincoln County's greatest industry and will continue to be so," the future of northwestern Montana's principal industry is very much in question.

■ MINING

More promising are the ore deposits in the Purcell and Cabinet mountain ranges. Ever since gold was discovered along Libby Creek in 1860, miners have been lured

Wild mountain streams and the deep, dark forests of the state's northwest corner are similar to those found in the high country of Idaho and British Columbia.

by the prospect of major deposits in these mountains. Turn-of-the-century mining camps sprang up near Troy, Libby, and the Yaak River Valley to the north. But this is hardrock country, and for many years mining fell off due to the cost of removing precious metals from the ore bodies in this area. New technology has revived the hardrock industry throughout western Montana, however, and the nation's largest silver mine is now operated by the Asarco Corp. near Troy. More than four million ounces of silver are removed annually from this mine alone, and nearby deposits of both silver and copper have attracted investment in additional mining ventures. Known mineral reserves within the Kootenai National Forest are valued at $5 billion.

■ LIBBY

During much of this century, the Lincoln County seat of **Libby** was a company town that owed its existence to a Wisconsin lumberman, Julius Neils, who purchased an existing mill in Libby in 1910 and eventually transformed it into the largest single lumber enterprise in Montana. In addition to the mill, the J. Neils Lumber Company owned timberlands, logging equipment, and railroads. Later purchased by the St. Regis Paper Company and now owned by Champion International, the mill is still a key component of the Libby-area economy, but it is no longer the only show in town. Many now see mining as the industry that will keep Libby employed at the levels it previously enjoyed under Julius Neils' paternal watch.

Nevertheless, this community of 2,500 is proud of its roots and celebrates its lumberjack culture every July during **Logger Days,** the oldest festival of its kind in Montana. Unlike the eastern Montana rodeo circuit that draws working cowboys and cowgirls, whose lean, suntanned bodies are concealed by cowboy hats, boots, and chaps, Libby Logger Days is an exhibition of biceps, beards, and billed caps. Professional loggers compete for prizes, using chainsaws, crosscut saws, and axes.

Nordicfest, celebrating the community's Scandinavian and northern European heritage, draws thousands of visitors to its food booths, juried craft shows, and musical performances in September. Visitors are also attracted at this time of year to the stunning show of fall color that ignites the wooded landscape. Western larch and aspen are the medium by which monochromatic hillsides become an impressionist's canvas of points and strokes applied in every gradation of color between green and gold. More than any other conifer, the western larch, or tamarack, distinguishes these woods from those east of the Rockies because it sheds its lacy web of needles after their seasonal blaze of color has smoldered and died.

■ BULL RIVER VALLEY

Two of the prime spots to view fall colors are the Bull and Yaak river valleys. The Bull River waters a largely unsettled valley south of Troy. Bordered on both sides by the peaks of the Cabinet Mountains, the **Bull River Valley** encompasses public and private forest lands between U.S. Route 2 and Montana State Highway 200. The Bull River Road (Montana State Highway 56) ushers travelers to backcountry lakes and campgrounds, as well as to a noble grove of giant western red cedars and to Montana's westernmost wilderness. Bighorn Lodge near Noxon has a fine country inn and hunting lodge within Bull River Valley (see "Accommodations" in "PRACTICAL INFORMATION").

The **Ross Creek Cedar Grove,** just west of Bull Lake, preserves 100 acres of old-growth cedars that measure up to eight feet (over two meters) wide and 175 feet (53 m) tall. A short, self-guiding nature trail takes visitors through this outdoor cathedral and explains its history and significance.

On the east side of the road lies the 94,000-acre **Cabinet Mountains Wilderness.** This federally protected wilderness extends along the crest of the Cabinet Mountains, whose peaks appear higher than their actual elevation because they rise from the lowest corner of the state. Within viewing distance of 8,712-foot-high (2,655-m) Snowshoe Peak (the Cabinets' highest summit), the Kootenai River leaves Montana at a mere 1,820 feet (555 m) above sea level. The crest of the Cabinets is plenty high to capture eastbound moisture from the Pacific. Snow lies several feet deep in these mountains, providing more than 100 inches (250 cm) of runoff. The result is a tangle of trees, delicate ferns, and berry bushes. A network of trails penetrates this temperate jungle, taking hikers from the edge of the wilderness to its interior alpine lakes and ridgetops. Visitors come primarily for the fishing, berry-picking, and wildlife watching. A remnant population of grizzly bears inhabits the Cabinets, but more abundant are elk, deer, mountain goats, and bighorn sheep. This long, narrow forest preserve can be reached from Libby and U.S. Route 2 on the east side as well as from the Bull River Road on the west.

■ THE YAAK

The **Yaak River Valley,** to the north, is a wilderness without the capital W. If northwest Montana is remote, then this northwesternmost valley, known among Yaakers simply as the Yaak, is the end of the line. A paved road, north of Troy, follows not only the fall colors but the colorful history of the valley nearly to the Canadian border. Abandoned homesteads, mining camps, logging roads, and clearcuts interrupt but never obscure the transcendent beauty of the Yaak River and the surrounding Purcell Mountains. Besides a few stray grizzly bears, caribou, and the usual complement of elk, deer, moose, mountain lions, and black bears, the Yaak is inhabited by loners, loggers, and a handful of urban migrants who believe they have died and gone to heaven. The social and commercial hub of the valley is the town of **Yaak,** which consists of the Dirty Shame Saloon and the Yaak Mercantile, a one-stop, one-room supply depot that stocks gas, propane, and limited groceries, swaps paperbacks, rents pipe dies and cable pulleys, takes phone messages, and dispenses hunting and fishing information.

Loggers, loners, and lions know that Yaak River country is just this side of heaven.

■ LIBBY DAM

From Yaak, motorists can follow Montana State Highway 508 back to Libby, or continue east along a paved forest road to Dodge Summit, then drop down to giant **Lake Koocanusa** at the base of the Purcells. The lake, whose name is an amalgam of Kootenai, Canada, and USA, was created by the impoundment of the Kootenai River, a major tributary of the Columbia River. The massive project, begun in 1966 and completed in 1973, was carried out under the terms of an international treaty signed by the United States and Canada to achieve flood control, navigation, irrigation, and power generation on the river they share. In addition, the construction of **Libby Dam,** just 20 minutes from the town of Libby, created a brand new recreation area. Stretching 90 miles (145 km) north of the dam, Lake Koocanusa crosses the international border about halfway up the lake. Montana's longest and highest bridge spans the lake near Rexford. Numerous campgrounds, boat ramps, and recreation areas surround the reservoir, while a visitor center, observation deck and lounge can be found at the dam.

Like most dams, this one sparked considerable debate over the loss of wildlife habitat, alteration of streamflow, and erosion of the local tax base due to flooding of productive lands. New recreation and wildlife sites have appeased some of the critics, but many residents still mourn the shackling of a great wild river. On the lighter side, the project revealed insight into the Montana mindset the day former President Gerald Ford came to town to dedicate Libby Dam. Local lore has it that the president's bodyguards were alarmed by all the guns they saw, mounted on gunracks in nearly every pickup in town. Instructed to remove all these firearms, the local sheriff is said to have responded with a laugh that said, "You gotta be kidding." Apparently he satisfied visiting law-enforcement personnel with a quick lesson in local culture, explaining that in Montana, hunting is a religion and guns are a birthright.

■ KOOTENAI COUNTRY

When Montanans are not hunting or fishing, they are likely to be scouting their next hunting or fishing trip. In the Northwest Corner, the possibilities are unlimited, not just for sporting expeditions but simply for enjoying the outdoors. Covering 2.25 million acres—an area nearly three times the size of Rhode Island—the

Kootenai National Forest *is* northwestern Montana. In addition to the Kootenai River, Lake Koocanusa, and the Cabinet Mountains Wilderness, the forest encompasses several smaller rivers, more than 100 lakes, and two special management areas in addition to the Ross Creek Cedars.

The **Northwest Peaks Scenic Area** is a rugged 19,000-acre landscape of high peaks and deep valleys that nearly touches both Canada and Idaho. With few trails and unpredictable weather, it appeals to adventurers seeking a primitive experience. **Ten Lakes Scenic Area,** to the east, is for the rest of us. Sculpted by glaciers, this cavernous valley of high lake basins, streams, waterfalls, forests, and wildflowers has

BIG TROUBLE IN A SMALL TOWN

Since our fish were big enough to deserve a few drinks and quite a bit of talk afterwards, we were late in getting back to Helena. On the way, Paul asked, "Why not stay overnight with me and go down to Wolf Creek in the morning?" He added that he himself had "to be out for the evening," but would be back soon after midnight. I learned later it must have been around two o'clock in the morning when I heard the thing that was ringing, and I ascended through river mists and molecules until I awoke catching the telephone. The telephone had a voice in it, which asked, "Are you Paul's brother?" I asked, "What's wrong?" The voice said, "I want you to see him." Thinking we had poor connections, I banged the phone. "Who are you?" I asked. He said, "I am the desk sergeant who wants you to see your brother."

The checkbook was still in my hand when I reached the jail. The desk sergeant frowned and said, "No, you don't have to post bond for him. He covers the police beat and has friends here. All you have to do is look at him and take him home."

Then he added, "But he'll have to come back. A guy is going to sue him. Maybe two guys are."

Not wanting to see him without a notion of what I might see, I kept repeating, "What's wrong?" When the desk sergeant thought it was time, he told me, "He hit a guy and the guy is missing a couple of teeth and is all cut up." I asked, "What's the second guy suing him for?" "For breaking dishes. Also a table," the sergeant said. "The second guy owns the restaurant. The guy who got hit lit on one of the tables."

By now I was ready to see my brother, but it was becoming clear that the sergeant had called me to the station to have a talk. He said, "We're picking him up too much lately. He's drinking too much." I had already heard more than I wanted.

Maybe one of our ultimate troubles was that I never wanted to hear too much about my brother.

The sergeant finished what he had to say by finally telling me what he really wanted to say. "Besides he's behind in the big stud poker game at Hot Springs. It's not healthy to be behind in the big game at Hot Springs."

"You and your brother think you're tough because you're street fighters. At Hot Springs they don't play any child games like fist fighting. At Hot Springs it's the big stud poker game and all that goes with it."

I was confused from trying to rise suddenly from molecules of sleep to an understanding of what I did not want to understand. I said, "Let's begin again. Why is he here and is he hurt?"

The sergeant said, "He's not hurt, just sick. He drinks too much. At Hot Springs, they don't drink too much." I said to the sergeant, "Let's go on. Why is he here?"

According to the sergeant's report to me, Paul and his girl had gone into Weiss's restaurant for a midnight sandwich—a popular place at midnight since it had booths in the rear where you and your girl could sit and draw the curtains. "The girl," the sergeant said, "was that half-breed Indian girl he goes with. You know the one," he added, as if to implicate me.

Paul and his girl were evidently looking for an empty booth when a guy in a booth they had passed stuck his head out of the curtain and yelled, "Wahoo." Paul hit the head, separating the head from two teeth and knocking the body back on the table, which overturned, cutting the guy and his girl with broken dishes. The sergeant said, "The guy said to me, 'Jesus, all I meant is that it's funny to go out with an Indian. It was just a joke.'"

I said to the sergeant, "It's not very funny," and the sergeant said, "No, not very funny, but it's going to cost your brother a lot of money and time to get out of it. What really isn't funny is that he's behind in the game at Hot Springs. Can't you help him straighten out?"

"I don't know what to do," I confessed to the sergeant.

"I know what you mean," the sergeant confessed to me. Desk sergeants at this time were still Irish. "I have a young brother," he said, "who is a wonderful kid, but he's always in trouble. He's what we call 'Black Irish.'"

"What do you do to help him?" I asked. After a long pause, he said, "I take him fishing."

—Norman Maclean, *A River Runs Through It,* 1976

long been considered a candidate for federal wilderness protection. Hiking and horseback trails crisscross its 15,700-acre interior, with public campgrounds at a couple of trailheads. The best approach is from U.S. Route 93, between Fortine and Eureka. Both of these scenic areas are gorgeous and empty.

While nearly all of northwestern Montana is shaded by trees, it is bordered on the north and south by two open, river-fed valleys that support limited agriculture. On the north, the **Tobacco Valley** takes its name from the crop once cultivated here by Kootenai Indians. **Eureka,** its major community, is now more famous for its Christmas trees. To the south, **Thompson Falls** sits on the Clark Fork River and relies on a mix of logging, mining, agriculture, and recreation. The nearby Noxon and Cabinet Gorge reservoirs draw boatloads of skiers, anglers, and other water bums. Both communities enjoy mild climates in an otherwise cool, wet corner of Montana.

STEINBECK'S MONTANA

I am in love with Montana. For other states I have admiration, respect, recognition, even some affection, but with Montana it is love, and it's difficult to analyze love when you're in it. . . . It seems to me that Montana is a great splash of grandeur. The scale is huge but not overpowering. The land is rich with grass and color, and the mountains are the kind I would create if mountains were ever put on my agenda. Montana seems to me to be what a small boy would think Texas is like from hearing Texans. Here for the first time I heard a definite regional accent unaffected by TV-ese, a slow-paced warm speech. It seemed to me that the frantic bustle of America was not in Montana. Its people did not seem afraid of shadows in a John Birch Society sense. The calm of the mountains and the rolling grasslands had got into the inhabitants. It was hunting season when I drove through the state. The men I talked to seemed to me not moved to a riot of seasonal slaughter but simply to be going out to kill edible meat. Again my attitude may be informed by love, but it seemed to me that the towns were places to live in rather than nervous hives. People had time to pause in their occupations to undertake the passing art of neighborliness.

—John Steinbeck, *Travels with Charley: In Search of America,* 1962

T H E   A R T S

MOST VISITORS ARE SURPRISED BY THE VITALITY AND DIVERSITY of the arts in Montana. Those who expect to see quality Western art will not be disappointed. Montana's Western art museums are among the finest. Those who view contemporary art, literature, and the performing arts as strictly East Coast or urban attractions will be astonished. Consider the evidence and a few outside observations:

- Montana has more professional, non-profit art museums per capita than any other state, and its visual artists receive more fellowships per capita than any other state.
- Montana has nine symphony orchestras, plus the New World Symphony of Miami, which has chosen the resort community of Big Sky as its summer residence.
- A 1989 *Los Angeles Times* story named Montana "the literary capital of the country." A year later, *Sunset* magazine singled out Missoula as foundation for the state's literary tradition, and noted that, "One of the area's 174 softball teams, the Montana Review of Books, . . . once even boasted an outfield responsible for 12 published novels."
- The Yellowstone Art Center's annual art auction has been called "the best non-commercial art auction in the United States."

While these declarations come as a surprise to most non-residents, they make perfect sense to Montana artists and art lovers. Because the state's small rural communities are so widely dispersed, each must look to itself for cultural survival. Sheer distance keeps one community from living off another's culture. It is not unusual to find an art center, symphony, and theater group in towns with fewer than 15,000 residents. Other factors are the relatively low cost of living in Montana compared with that of large urban areas, and a natural environment that feeds the soul.

■ WESTERN ART

The **C. M. Russell Museum Complex** in Great Falls boasts the world's most complete collection of Charles M. Russell's original oils, watercolors, bronzes, and illustrated letters in a gallery next door to the cowboy artist's original log-cabin studio.

The museum also exhibits original works by many of Russell's contemporaries. The **Montana Historical Society** in Helena also has an extensive collection of Russell art, as well as a permanent collection of early Western photography by F. Jay Haynes, official turn-of-the-century photographer for the Northern Pacific Railroad and Yellowstone National Park. Large murals depicting the Lewis and Clark expedition and Flathead Indian history, painted by early Western artist Edgar S. Paxson, adorn the foyer of the **Missoula County Courthouse** in Missoula.

The **Museum of the Rockies** in Bozeman has a permanent collection of works by Paxson, Russell, Olaf Seltzer, R. E. DeCamp, and William Standing, and a fine collection of bead and quillwork, clothing, toys, weapons, and ceremonial items used by Plains Indian tribes. The **Museum of the Plains Indian** in Browning also displays a comprehensive collection of Blackfeet Indian artifacts. Original paintings and murals by Charlie Russell and E. S. Paxson appear in the **Montana State Capitol** in Helena. The **Bob Scriver Studio** in Browning features the artist's Western and wildlife sculpture. The **Zemsky-Hines Gallery** in Big Timber presents the work of noted Western artists Jessica Zemsky and Jack Hines, as well as the work

Charlie and Nancy Russell with actor Douglas Fairbanks in Los Angeles. Fairbanks, a great admirer and collector of Russell's work, is dressed for his role as D'Artagnan in the movie "The Three Musketeers."

of other regional artists. Livingston's **Depot Center** shows the works of Charles Russell, Frederic Remington, Edward Borein, Thomas Moran, Karl Bodmer, and others. **Coffrin's Old West Gallery** in Miles City exhibits and sells the prints of L. A. Huffman, who came to Montana Territory as an Army photographer in 1878 and recorded the history of an era dramatized by great buffalo herds, the last of the Indian wars, and the arrival of railroads and ranchers.

■ CONTEMPORARY ART

Although Montana is known for its multitude of Western painters, the state is also blessed with many prominent contemporary artists such as Russell Chatham of Livingston, whose landscapes come alive with the spirit of this spacious land. The **Yellowstone Art Center** in Billings has the most significant contemporary collection in Montana, and its annual art auction is said to be the best of its kind in the nation. The **Montana Historical Society** in Helena houses the Poindexter Gallery, with its important collection of original works by artists of the New York school of modern art, including Willem DeKooning, Franz Kline, and Jackson Pollock. Also in Helena, the **Archie Bray Foundation** is one of the nation's leading centers for ceramic arts, featuring traditional and contemporary pottery, ceramics, and sculpture, including the works of Peter Voulkos, Rudy Autio, David Shaner, Ken Ferguson, Bernard Leach, and Shoji Hamada. **Paris Gibson Square** in Great Falls rotates exhibits in three galleries at its Center for the Contemporary Arts, and conducts classes, seminars, and tours.

Missoula Museum of the Arts features rotating exhibits, gallery talks, an annual art auction. **Hockaday Center for the Arts** in Kalispell has a permanent collection of regional works, plus rotating exhibits in three galleries, tours, and classes for students and adults. **Custer County Art Center** in Miles City is housed in the city's old water works plant, which provides spacious display areas for changing exhibits. **Beall Park Art Center** in Bozeman is a showcase for the city's vital arts community, with its exhibits, workshops, lectures, concerts, and performances. **Holter Museum of Art** in Helena has two spacious galleries for rotating exhibits of Montana and regional artists. **Arts Chateau** in Butte is housed in the old Charles Clark Mansion, where parlors and a second-floor kitchen have been transformed into art galleries, and the rest of the 26-room mansion has retained its elegance as a period museum.

In a state best known for its Western art, Billings' Yellowstone Art Center has built an impressive collection of contemporary art.

■ THE PERFORMING ARTS

The performing arts in Montana run from opera and Shakespeare to recitations by some of the top cowboy poets in the West. Nine Montana communities support symphony orchestras. They range from the state's largest orchestra in Billings (and the only one that pays all of its musicians) to an act of love called the **Prairie Symphonette** in the shrinking northeastern farm town of Scobey (pop. 1,150). In between are orchestras in Bozeman, Missoula, Great Falls, Kalispell, Helena, Butte, and Miles City.

Bozeman has the distinction of sustaining Montana's only opera company, the **Intermountain Opera,** anchored by Metropolitan Opera baritone Pablo Elvira, who lives in Bozeman during the off-season. Bozeman is also the home of **Shakespeare in the Parks,** a professional touring company that performs Shakespearean comedy for audiences in Montana and the region during the summer months. The company grew out of Montana State University's media and theater-arts department.

"Separated Spear Woman in Bird Headdress" by Winold Reiss. (courtesy of C. M. Russell Museum)

Missoula is Montana's other university town and it, too, nurtures an active community of performing artists. Theater groups include the **Montana Repertory Theatre**, a professional touring company based in the university's drama-dance department; the **Missoula Children's Theatre**, which tours nearly 300 communities annually; and the **Missoula Community Theatre**, which performs year-round. In addition to its symphony orchestra and chorale, Missoula is the home of the **String Orchestra of the Rockies**, an ensemble of top musicians that perform throughout the state, and the **Garden City Ballet**.

Three communities have made a specialty of summer theater. The **Bigfork Summer Playhouse**, the **Fort Peck Summer Theatre**, and the **Virginia City Players** draw residents and tourists to rotating schedules of comedy, vaudeville, and Broadway musicals. Other recommended acts are Bozeman's **Montana Ballet** and classical guitarist **Stuart Weber**; **Great Falls' Symphony, Montana Chorale, Cascade Quartet**, and **Daystar**, an Indian drama-dance company; Helena's **Grandstreet Theatre** and **Aleph Movement Theatre**; Kalispell's **Glacier Orchestra** and **Raphael Christy**, a one-man show featuring the wit and wisdom of Charlie Russell; Polson's **Port Polson Players**; Dillon's **Junior Fiddlers**; Big Sky's **New World Symphony**, and Billings' **Symphony, Chorale, Studio Theater, Actors Theatre Montana**, and **Calamity Jane's Dinner Theater**. The University of Montana, Billings, Bigfork, and Helena have recently completed showcase theaters for the performing arts.

■ THE LITERARY LANDSCAPE

In 1984, half a dozen Montana writers and historians hatched the idea of assembling an anthology of Montana literature as a birthday present to the state on the occasion of its 1989 statehood centennial. The result, four years later, was a five-pound, 1,161-page volume entitled *The Last Best Place,* now in its third printing. Acclaimed coast to coast as a literary milestone, the bestseller secured Montana's standing as an important, if remote, enclave for writers. As one reviewer put it, "There's something about Montana that makes Montanans write and makes other people arrive here with notebook in hand and typewriter in the back seat." Visitors have been recording their images of Montana ever since Lewis and Clark traveled up the Missouri River in 1804. Native peoples had developed a strong oral tradition long before that. Much of the appeal of *The Last Best Place* is in the

CROSSING MONTANA IN THE NINETEENTH CENTURY

Montana's first travel book appeared in 1865, after Captain John Mullan completed a wagon road that stretched more than 600 miles (960 km) across the Northern Rockies. The Mullan Road linked Fort Benton, Montana—the end of the line for Missouri River navigation—with Fort Walla Walla on the Columbia River in Washington. Designed as a military road, it was used far more by pioneers than by soldiers. Some of the admonishments and recommendations that Mullen made in his *Miners and Travelers' Guide to Oregon, Washington, Idaho, Montana, Wyoming and Colorado via the Missouri and Columbia Rivers* offer humorous insight into the human condition, as well as the travel conditions in the last century. He cautioned readers, for example, to govern their animals "as you would a woman, with kindness, affection, and caresses, and you will be repaid by their docility and easy management."

While leaving the gender gap wide open, Captain Mullan deserves some credit for narrowing the transportation gap that separated the northern plains from the Pacific. He also provided useful advice on equipment and supplies, including tips on where to find fresh vegetables along the trail, how many bushels of beans and sides of bacon to bring, and what to do when the wagon breaks down.

"Every article to be used in crossing the plains should be of the best manufacture and strongest material . . . Starting at dawn and camping not later than 2 P.M., I have always found the best plan for marching. . . . Never take anything not absolutely necessary. This is a rule of all experienced voyageurs."

re-telling of these native stories, many of which appear in print for the first time. Side by side traditional myths of Napi, the Ghost Owl, and Lodge-Boy are the contemporary observations of best-selling Montana authors like A. B. Guthrie, Jr., Tom McGuane, James Welch, and Ivan Doig.

The University of Montana's 70-year-old creative writing program, a seductive landscape, the "get-away" factor, and a low-rent lifestyle are often given as the reasons for the state's abundance of writers. Bozeman poet Greg Keeler narrows it down to the basics, "Some of us were born here, and some of us came for the trout." For whatever reason, Montana's writing tradition is firmly entrenched and now grows on its own strength. The university town of Missoula is the unrivaled capital of Montana's statewide literary community, supporting a surprising number of published authors, poets, and playwrights, and somewhere between 15 and 20 bookstores, many of them independent and locally owned. See "PRACTICAL INFORMATION" for a selected bibliography of Montana books and a listing of bookstores.

WINTER RECREATION

ALTHOUGH MONTANA IS GENERALLY VIEWED as a summer destination, winter is an attraction in its own right. The difference between the two seasons is in the way people travel. While summer travel is geared to the open road, the goal in winter is to ditch the car as soon as possible. Snow and ice take the pleasure out of exploring Montana's vast and diverse landscape, so winter travel is generally confined to a single destination. A number of attractive resorts and expanded winter services in nearby Yellowstone National Park make Montana an increasingly popular winter destination.

The mountains of western Montana begin filling up with snow in September and October, and by December the winter season is in full swing. Because of Montana's dry climate, snow piles up as deep, dry powder—perfect for skiing and snowmobiling. Each year, a growing number of skiers abandon the congestion and long lift lines of better-known ski areas in Colorado and Utah for the uncrowded, easygoing, and more affordable atmosphere of Montana's downhill ski areas. There are also a number of cross-country ski resorts within gliding distance of national forest and wilderness trailheads. Montana phone numbers are all area code 406.

■ DOWNHILL SKIING

Montana has 14 downhill areas, ranging from destination resorts to locally popular day-use areas. In the following brief descriptions, daily adult lift ticket rates are designated as: $ = under $20 and $$ = over $20. The largest ski areas are listed first.

The Big Mountain. West of Glacier National Park in northwestern Montana, this destination resort draws heavily on the western Canadian market as well as skiers from the Pacific Northwest who arrive by AMTRAK. The area has 50 marked runs, one quad chairlift, four triple chairs, and one double chair. On-site facilities include a variety of lodging options, several restaurants and bars, ski shop, ski school, day care, and Nordic center; $$. Write: P.O. Box 1400, Whitefish, MT 59937, or phone 862-3511, (800) 858-5439 (U.S.), or (800) 637-7547 (Canada).

Big Sky. About midway between Bozeman and Yellowstone National Park, this is one of Montana's top destination resorts. There are 55 runs on two mountains, two gondolas, two triple chairs, and four double chairs. Facilities include more than

Red Lodge Mountain is famous for its spring skiing. (courtesy, Travel Montana)

1,000 rooms and condominium units, several restaurants, bars and shops, ski shop, day care, and superb cross-country skiing at nearby Lone Mountain Ranch; $$. Write: P.O. Box 1, Big Sky, MT 59716, or phone 995-4211 or (800) 548-4486.

Bridger Bowl. Just minutes north of Bozeman, this is primarily a day-use area with limited lodging on the slope. Lots of powder, challenging runs, and full services in nearby Bozeman make this a popular area for serious skiers. There are 50 runs and five double chairs. Facilities include limited condominium units and private home rentals, day lodge with cafeteria and bar, ski shop, and day care; $$. Write: 15795 Bridger Canyon, Bozeman, MT 59715, or phone 587-2111 or (800) 223-9609.

Red Lodge Mountain. Located outside the friendly Western town of Red Lodge in the Beartooth Mountains of south-central Montana, this is a popular day-use area with lots of intermediate slopes and great spring skiing. As Montana's easternmost ski area, it draws heavily on skiers from the upper Midwest. There are 30 runs, one triple chair, and four double chairs. On-site services include a restaurant and cafeteria, a couple of bars, ski shop, kids' ski program, and gift shop; $$. Full lodging, food, and services are available in nearby Red Lodge. Write: P.O. Box 750, Red Lodge, MT 59068, or phone 446-2610 or (800) 444-8977.

Montana Snowbowl. Just 12 miles (20 km) northwest of Missoula, this is the home of the annual National Gelande Jump Championship. Steep slopes and deep bowls make this day-use area especially popular with advanced skiers. There are 30 runs and two double chairs. On-site facilities include cafeteria, saloon, ski shop, and nursery. Full lodging, food, and services are available in Missoula; $. Write: 1700 Snowbowl Road, Missoula, MT 59802, or phone 549-9777.

Showdown Ski Area. Part of the Kings Hill Winter Sports complex in the Little Belt Mountains of central Montana, this is a popular family area that draws heavily on the Great Falls market. There are 32 runs, one triple chair, and one double chair. On-site facilities include cafeteria, saloon, ski shop and nursery. Fine Nordic skiing and snowmobiling nearby. Limited lodging and food are available in nearby Neihart and White Sulphur Springs, 30 miles (48 km) south; full services in Great Falls, 60 miles (100 km) northwest; $. Write: Box 92, Neihart, MT 59465, or phone 236-5522.

Marshall Ski Area. Not far from Missoula, this is a beginners' and intermediates' day-use area with seven runs and one triple chair, along with night skiing. On-site facilities include day lodge, snack bar, and ski shop. Full services in Missoula, seven miles (11 km) west; $. Write: 5250 Marshall Canyon Road, Missoula, MT 59802, or phone 258-6619.

Discovery Basin. Located near Georgetown Lake and the Anaconda Pintler Wilderness, this is a popular day-use area for skiers in the Butte-Anaconda area. There are 13 runs and two double chair lifts. Facilities include a day lodge with cafeteria, ski shop, and nearby cross-country ski trails. Lodging is available at Fairmont Hot Springs, 32 miles (50 km) east, and in Anaconda, 20 miles (32 km) east, and Butte, 45 miles (72 km) east; $. Write: P.O. Box 221, Anaconda, MT 59711, or phone 563-2184.

Great Divide. About 25 miles (40 km) northwest of Helena near the ghost town of Marysville, this is the capital city's neighborhood ski area. There are 37 runs and two double chairs. Facilities include a day lodge with restaurant and bar, and a ski shop. Full services in Helena; $. Write: Box SKI, Marysville, MT 59640, or phone 449-3746.

Lost Trail Powder Mountain. Straddling the Montana-Idaho border about 90 miles (145 km) south of Missoula, this day-use area is known for its reliable snow and long season. There are 18 runs and two double chairs. Facilities include a day lodge with cafeteria and a ski shop. Limited lodging in Darby and nearby resorts; full services in Hamilton, 45 miles north (72 km), and Salmon, Idaho, 45 miles (72 km) south; $. Write: Box 191, Darby, MT 59829, or phone 821-3211 or 821-3508.

Rocky Mountain Hi. About 30 miles (50 km) west of Choteau on the Rocky Mountain Front, this is a locally popular, family day-use area that includes 25 trails and one double chair. Facilities include a day lodge with cafeteria and bar, ski shop, and day care. Lodging is available in Choteau; $. Write: Box 727, Choteau, MT 59422, or phone 466-2422.

Maverick Mountain. Located in the Pioneer Mountains northwest of Dillon, this is a locally popular day-use area that can be rented by groups for private skiing three days a week. There are 10 trails and one double chair. Facilities include a day lodge with food and beverage service and a ski shop. Limited lodging at nearby resorts; full services in Dillon; $. Write: Polaris, MT 59746, or phone 834-3454.

Two other neighborhood ski areas are **Beef Trail,** near Butte, and **Turner Mountain,** near Libby. Each has two single chairs serving about eight runs.

■ CROSS-COUNTRY SKIING

Montana has several, one-of-a-kind cross-country ski resorts, plus some excellent day-use Nordic centers and trail systems. Here are brief descriptions of the foremost resorts and areas:

Big Mountain Nordic Center. Located at the Big Mountain downhill resort near Whitefish, this has become an international training and racing center for cross-country and biathlon teams. For the public, there are nine miles (15 km) of groomed and tracked trails, plus instruction, rentals, and guided tours of nearby Glacier Park and other backcountry areas. Write: Box 1400, Whitefish, MT 59937, or phone 862-3511, (800) 858-5439 (U.S.), or (800) 637-7547 (Canada).

Bohart Ranch Cross Country Ski Center. Adjacent to Bridger Bowl Ski Area, the center has 18 miles (30 km) of groomed and tracked trails suitable for diagonal stride skiing and skating, plus rentals, lessons, and a warming cabin. There is also a biathlon range for year-round training and competition. Full services in nearby Bozeman. Write: 16621 Bridger Canyon Road, Bozeman, MT 59715, or phone 586-9070.

Skiers can rent a caboose for overnight stays at the Izaak Walton Inn, a popular cross-country ski lodge near Glacier Park.

Cross-country skiing at Lolo Pass, near Missoula.

Holland Lake Lodge. Just off Highway 83 in the Seeley Swan Valley, this comfortable lodge offers 15 miles (25 km) of groomed trails, plus rentals and guided trips. Lodging runs from about $35 per night for two people in the lodge to $60 for up to four in cabins, meals extra. Write: Condon, MT 59826, or phone (800) 648-8859.

Izaak Walton Inn. On U.S. Route 2 between Glacier National Park and the Great Bear Wilderness, this historic railroad inn has been described by *Cross Country Skier* magazine as "the coziest cross-country ski area in the Rockies." More than 18 miles (30 km) of groomed and tracked trails are augmented by a network of backcountry trails. AMTRAK stops at the back door. Rentals, instruction, and tours of Glacier Park are available. A one-week package ranges from $450 to $500 per person, double occupancy. Shorter stays can be arranged. Reservations recommended. Trail system is open to day skiers. Write: Box 653-D, Essex, MT 59916, or phone 888-5700.

Lone Mountain Ranch. Montana's finest Nordic resort, this guest ranch is within skiing distance of the Big Sky downhill ski resort, between Bozeman and Yellowstone National Park. The ranch offers 47 miles (75 km) of groomed and tracked trails for skiers and skaters, plus guided tours into Yellowstone Park, instruction and rentals, sleigh ride dinners, on-the-trail gourmet lunches, excellent food and lodging. Most trips are booked on a week-long, package basis at a per-person rate of around $800, double occupancy. Reservations are required. The trail system is open to day skiers. Write: Box 69, Big Sky, MT 59716, or phone 995-4644.

Nightingale Nordic. About 25 miles (40 km) southwest of Missoula on U.S. Route 12, this Nordic center is owned and operated by the Rossignol family. There are 10 miles (16 km) of groomed and tracked trails for skiers and skaters, plus rentals, instruction, a warming cabin, and food service. Lodging, food, and services are available in nearby Lolo or Missoula. Write: Box 369, Graves Creek Road, Lolo, MT 59847, or phone 273-2415 or 273-0655.

Red Lodge Nordic Ski Area. Just outside of Red Lodge, this trail system offers nine miles (15 km) of groomed trails for skiers and skaters, plus instruction, rentals, a skiathlon course, guided backcountry tours, and shuttle service to nearby Red Lodge Mountain downhill ski area. Full lodging, food, and services in town. Write: Box 283, Red Lodge, MT 59068, or phone 446-3158.

Sundance Lodge. This is a small, remote lodge in the Big Hole Valley of southwestern Montana. Located off Montana State Highway 43 between Wisdom and

Wise River, the lodge offers 15 miles (24 km) of groomed and tracked trails, plus additional trails in the Beaverhead National Forest. Ski rentals available. Lodging runs $40 to $60 per night for two, meals extra. Write: Wise River, MT 59762, or phone 689-3611.

Yellowstone Rendezvous Trail System. The town of West Yellowstone maintains 15 miles (24 km) of groomed and tracked trails that are used for early-season training by the U.S. Nordic and Biathlon teams. The trail system is next door to Yellowstone National Park. Full lodging, food, and services, plus rentals, instruction, and guided tours of the park, in town. Write: West Yellowstone Chamber of Commerce, Box 458, West Yellowstone, MT 59758, or phone 646-7701.

■ GLACIER AND YELLOWSTONE NATIONAL PARKS

Popular summer destinations, the Yellowstone and Glacier dazzle winter visitors with their quiet beauty and abundant wildlife. Of the two, Yellowstone is far more developed for winter visitors, with its many miles of groomed cross-country ski and snowmobile trails, ski and snowmobile rentals, guided ski and snowcoach tours, plus lodging and food service inside the park. Plenty of lodging awaits visitors just outside the park, in West Yellowstone, Gardiner, and Cooke City. No visitor services are open inside Glacier Park during winter, but the Park Service does maintain about a dozen cross-country ski trails. Lodging, food, and services are available just outside the park at West Glacier, East Glacier, and Essex. For more information about winter in the parks, Write: Superintendent, Yellowstone National Park, WY 82190, or phone (307) 344-7381; and Superintendent, Glacier National Park, West Glacier, MT 59936, or phone 888-5441.

■ SNOWMOBILING

Since 1977, when Montana set aside a portion of its gasoline tax for development of snowmobile recreation, nearly 3,000 miles (4,800 km) of trails have been designated for snowmobiling, most of them in national forests. Each year they are marked and groomed through cooperative agreements between local snowmobile clubs, the Montana Department of Fish, Wildlife and Parks, and the U.S. Forest Service. Easily the most popular destination for snowmobilers is **West Yellowstone,** which bills itself as the "snowmobile capital of the world." With 200 miles

(320 km) of groomed trails in Yellowstone Park and another 400 miles (640 km) on surrounding forests, West Yellowstone offers a vast trail system that begins in town, where snowmobilers share city streets with motorists. Snowmobile sales, service, rentals, instruction, and guide service, plus complete lodging and food service, are all available in town. Other locally popular snowmobile areas in Montana are Cooke City, Lolo Pass, Seeley Lake, Lincoln, Kings Hill, Polaris-Wise River, and Georgetown Lake. For more information about snowmobiling, write the Montana Snowmobile Association, Box 3202, Great Falls, MT 59403, or the Montana Department of Fish, Wildlife & Parks, 1420 6th Ave., Helena, MT 59620, or phone 444-2535.

■ GUIDED WINTER TOURS

Big Sky Alpine Guides. For downhill skiers who would like to sample more than one of Montana's ski areas, this company will make all of the arrangements, including transportation and lodging. Design your own tour or choose from one of the company's packages. Write: Box SCHUSS, Marysville, MT 59640, or phone (800) 666-8754.

Off the Beaten Path. This Bozeman-based travel consulting service designs personalized itineraries. You let them know what you're interested in seeing and doing, and they put the trip together using your guidelines. Emphasis is on high-quality facilities and services. Write: 109 East Main, Bozeman, MT 59715, or phone 586-1311.

TW Recreational Services. As the major concessioner in Yellowstone National Park, this company provides guided ski and snowcoach tours of the park, plus ski and snowmobile rentals, lodging, and meals. Write: TW Recreational Services, Inc., Yellowstone National Park, WY 82190, or phone (307) 344-7311.

Yellowstone Alpen Guides. Also based in West Yellowstone, this company provides snowcoach tours of Yellowstone National Park as well as guided ski tours inside and out of the park, skier drop-offs, and charters. Write: Box 518, West Yellowstone, MT 59758, or phone 646-9591.

Yellowstone Tour & Travel. This West Yellowstone company provides guided snowmobile tours of Yellowstone National Park and the surrounding backcountry, plus snowmobile rentals and instruction, and lodging and meal packages. Write: Box 369, West Yellowstone, MT 59758, or phone (800) 221-1151.

Snowmobile police bundle up for business in Yellowstone National Park. (photo by Don Pitcher)

S C E N I C   R O A D S

IN A STATE AS GRAND AND DIVERSE AS MONTANA, nearly every highway has scenic appeal. Depending on your preference for plains or mountains, gravel or blacktop, however, some are more inviting than others. When traveling on back-roads through western Montana's forests, it's always a good idea to have a forest map in addition to the state highway map (see "Useful Addresses" in "PRACTICAL INFORMATION" for Forest Service addresses and phone numbers). When driving on eastern Montana's back roads, it's important to keep your eye on weather conditions since even the slightest rain can turn the clay-like soil to gumbo and stop you in your tracks. Unpaved roads should be regarded as seasonal routes, best traveled in summer and early fall. The numbers in front of the following road descriptions are keyed to the Scenic Roads map.

■ EASTERN MONTANA

1) **Montana State Highway 200 from Lewistown to Sidney** (paved): Take to the open road through the heart of the Big Open. This trip is a meditation on sage and sky; for the sheer love of driving, it can't be beat (270 miles, 430 km).

2) **Crooked Creek, Hell Creek, and Pines roads** (gravel): These roads provide rugged, all-weather access to giant Fort Peck Lake and the C. M. Russell Wildlife Refuge. These are scenic routes through badlands and breaks, with few people and lots of watchable wildlife. All lead to recreation areas on the lake. Crooked Creek Road runs north from Winnett (about 40 miles, 65 km); Hell Creek Road is north of Jordan (about 30 miles, 48 km), and Pines Road runs southwest from Montana State Highway 24, north of the town of Fort Peck (about 25 miles, 40 km).

3) **Makoshika State Park** (gravel/unimproved): There are about 10 miles (16 km) of scenic roads in this badlands park, taking visitors to overlooks, vistas, and nature trails. Travelers are advised to check weather and road conditions before proceeding beyond Tower Junction toward Artists Point or the Sand Creek Overlook.

4) **U.S. Route 212 between Alzada and Crow Agency** (paved): Rough breaks and badlands, ponderosa pine forests, abundant wildlife, rivers that flower the plains, two Indian reservations, and the Custer Battlefield National Monument are all part of the view along southeastern Montana's major east-west artery (165 miles, 265 km).

5) **Route 314 between Busby and Decker** (paved): Red cliffs, wildlife, and the Rosebud Creek breaks are all part of the immediate view, while the Rosebud Mountains rise in the west (about 35 miles, 55 km).

6) **Tongue River Breaks** (gravel): Follow the Tongue River from Ashland to Birney, then down to the Tongue River Reservoir on a road that follows the river (after you pass the Diamond Cross Ranch, be on the lookout for a sign to the Tongue River Dam; follow the sign). You will drive through the austerely beautiful Tongue River Canyon, with views of coulees and breaks, red scoria rock, and weathered pines. Camping, boating, and good fishing for walleye, crappie, and bass at the reservoir (about 45 miles, 70 km).

7) **Ok-A-Beh** and **Bad Pass** roads at Bighorn Canyon National Recreation (paved): Ok-A-Beh, between Fort Smith and the Ok-A-Beh boat ramp, takes motorists through a short-grass prairie with expansive views of the Bighorn Mountains and Bighorn River Valley (11 miles, 18 km). At the south end of the canyon (entered via Lovell, Wyoming), the Bad Pass Road connects Horseshoe Bend and Barry's Landing. The best view of the canyon is along this road at Devil Canyon Overlook (17 miles, 27 km).

■ CENTRAL MONTANA

8) **Rocky Mountain Front** (paved): Follow U.S. Routes 89/287 from Glacier National Park to Wolf Creek. This is a dramatic landscape where the mountains meet the plains (about 140 miles, 225 km).

9) **Interstate 15, between Shelby and Great Falls** (paved): In late summer, precede the harvest through the heart of Montana's Golden Triangle grain-growing region. Rippling waves of grain break over an ocean of ripening wheat fields all around (85 miles, 135 km).

10) **Interstate 15, between Great Falls and Helena** (paved): Follow the Missouri River through Charlie Russell country as the suns sets over Square Butte and paints a picture as brilliant as the ones created by Russell himself. A paved recreation road between Cascade and Wolf Creek provides river access and more leisurely views of the river and the rock sculpture of Wolf Creek Canyon (90 miles, 145 km, total; recreation road is about 35 miles, 55 km).

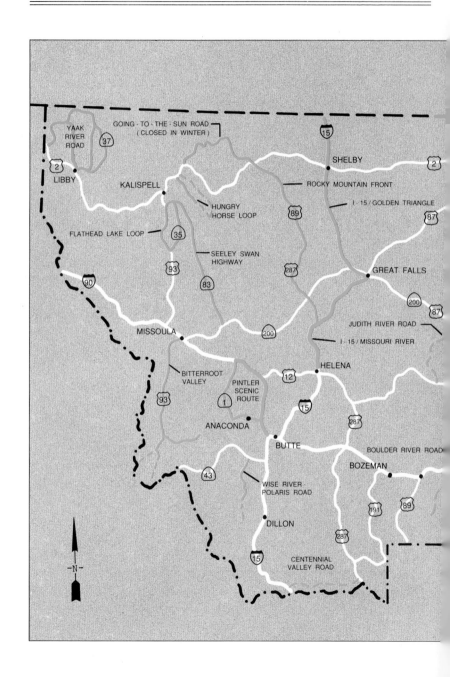

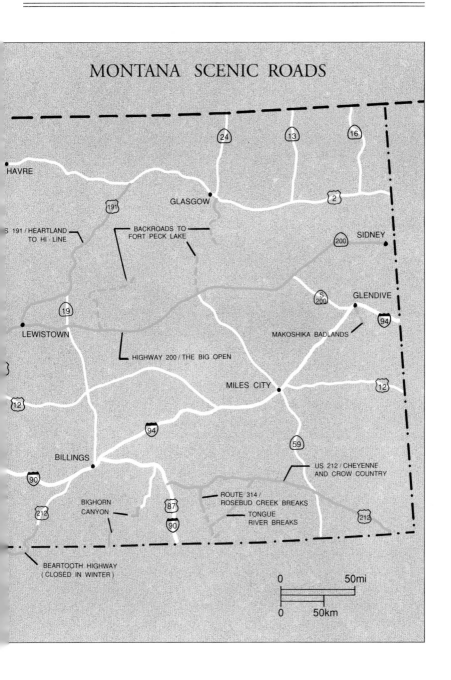

MONTANA SCENIC ROADS

HAVRE

GLASGOW

SIDNEY

GLENDIVE

S 191 / HEARTLAND
TO HI · LINE

BACKROADS TO
FORT PECK LAKE

LEWISTOWN

MAKOSHIKA BADLANDS

HIGHWAY 200 / THE BIG OPEN

MILES CITY

BILLINGS

US 212 / CHEYENNE
AND CROW COUNTRY

BIGHORN
CANYON

ROUTE 314 /
ROSEBUD CREEK BREAKS

TONGUE
RIVER BREAKS

BEARTOOTH HIGHWAY
(CLOSED IN WINTER)

0   50mi

0   50km

11) **Judith River Valley** (gravel): Follow this back road along the Judith and the South Fork of the Judith through the grass-rich valley where Charlie Russell lived when he first arrived in Montana. This is working cattle and dude-ranch country along the eastern edge of the Little Belt Mountains (about 50 miles, 80 km).

12) **U.S. Route 191 between Big Timber and Malta** (paved): View central Montana's "island" mountain ranges—the Crazies, the Snowies, the Judith Mountains and the Little Rockies—as you drive through the farm and ranch country between Big Timber and Lewistown, and the breaks and badlands of the Missouri River farther north (235 miles, 375 km). Inviting side trips (on mostly unpaved roads) include the ice caves and waterfalls in the Big Snowy Mountains, Judith Mountain ghost towns north of Lewistown, Slippery Ann Wildlife Viewing Area at the western edge of the C. M. Russell National Wildlife Refuge, the historic mining town of Zortman in the Little Rockies, and Mission Canyon at the south end of the Fort Belknap Indian Reservation.

13) **Boulder River Valley south of Big Timber** (pavement/gravel): Follow Route 298 past some of Montana's most beautiful ranches along a corridor that leads to the Absaroka-Beartooth Wilderness. The road turns from pavement to gravel to dirt before ending at a wilderness trailhead, with fishing, camping, and hiking along the way (about 45 miles, 70 km).

14) **Beartooth Highway/U.S. Route 212** (paved): Renowned as one of North America's most beautiful drives, the Beartooth begins at Red Lodge and climbs the glacially carved walls of Rock Creek Canyon en route to Yellowstone National Park. Switchbacks and hairpin turns twist higher and higher until the highway levels off at nearly 11,000 feet (3,360 m). This breathtaking route is generally open from late May to mid-October (68 slow miles, 110 km).

■ WESTERN MONTANA

15) **Yaak River Road** (paved): Route 508, north of Troy, follows the Yaak River through the Kootenai National Forest, with views of the Purcell Mountains. At Yaak, turn south on 508 to get back to Libby (loop is about about 100 miles, 160 km), or continue east on Route 92 to Rexford. There, you can cross Lake Koocanusa to Montana State Highway 37 or travel south on Forest Road 228 along the west side of the lake (loop is about 150 miles, 240 km).

16) **Going-to-the-Sun Road** (paved): This is Glacier National Park's magnificent east-west highway, starting at either St. Mary or West Glacier and crossing the Continental Divide at Logan Pass. It is normally open from early June into October. Summer crowds and many scenic turnoffs make this a slow trip (55 miles, 88 km).

17) **Hungry Horse Loop** (gravel): Make a full circuit around 34-mile-long (55-km) Hungry Horse Reservoir, along the west edge of the Great Bear Wilderness. There are plenty of campgrounds, boat launches, trailheads, and great views all the way around (115 miles,185 km; takes about six hours).

18) **Flathead Lake Loop** (paved): Montana State Highways 35, 82, and U.S. Route 93 form a loop around Flathead Lake, providing scenic views of the lake and the Swan Range, plus access to state parks and campgrounds (about 85 miles, 135 km).

19) **Seeley Swan Highway** (paved): Montana State Highway 83 follows a chain of lakes through dense forests, with views of the Mission Range and the Swan Range; access to several campgrounds, lakes, hiking trails, and fishing spots (91 miles, 145 km).

20) **U.S. Route 93, south of Missoula** (paved): This is a busy highway that follows the Bitterroot River and provides magnificent views of the Bitterroot Range and the Sapphire Mountains; the **East Side Highway** (County Road 269), between Florence and Hamilton, is a leisurely alternative, with access to the Lee Metcalf Wildlife Refuge. At the south end of the valley, the secondary **East Fork** and **West Fork** roads provide scenic access to fishing, hiking, and camping.

21) **Pintler Scenic Route** (paved): Montana State Highway 1, between Drummond and Anaconda, follows Flint Creek to Georgetown Lake, with views of the Flint Creek Range and the Anaconda Pintler Wilderness, and access to fishing, camping, and ghost towns (55 miles, 90 km). Interstate 90, east of Anaconda, forms a loop back to Drummond, via Deer Lodge and the Grant-Kohrs Ranch National Historic Site.

22) **Wise River-Polaris Road** (pavement/gravel): This is an enjoyable back road through the Pioneer Mountains, recently designated a National Scenic Byway. Besides great views of the East and West Pioneers, it offers access to camping, hiking, and fishing, the ghost town of Coolidge, and a rockhounder's playground called Crystal Park. Most easily traveled in the summer, but also popular with snowmobilers and skiers in the winter (40 miles, 65 km).

Motorists slowly make their way up the scenic Beartooth Highway; poles beside the road are snow markers.

23) Centennial Valley Road (gravel): This is a rough road to paradise, best traveled in summer. It lies west of Yellowstone National Park, between the Centennial Mountains and Red Rock Lakes National Wildlife Refuge. The refuge is home to the rare trumpeter swan and a tremendous diversity of waterfowl, shorebirds, songbirds, and raptors. Elk, moose, antelope and other wildlife species are abundant in the surrounding, sparsely settled valley (about 55 miles, 90 km).

Looking toward Mt. Reynolds from Logan Pass, Glacier Park.

PRACTICAL INFORMATION

■ TRANSPORTATION

Much of Montana's appeal lies in its detachment from urban America, but getting to Montana requires more time and expense than reaching more centrally located destinations. The high cost of transportation is generally offset by the relatively low cost of food, lodging, goods, and services, and by most U.S. standards, Montana is a travel bargain.

BY AIR

Because Montana is so far removed from the nation's major air routes, it is about as expensive to fly from Denver to Montana's capital city of Helena as it is to fly from Los Angeles to New York. Nonetheless, there are plenty of flights in and out of Montana. Four of the nation's major airlines—Northwest, Delta, United, and Continental—serve the principal cities, with commuter lines making connections from smaller towns. Montana's largest commercial airports, ranked in order of passenger boardings, are Billings, Bozeman, Great Falls, Missoula, Helena, Kalispell, and Butte. West Yellowstone has commercial air service in the summer, and the smaller towns of Miles City, Glendive, Sidney, Wolf Point, Glasgow, Havre, and Lewistown are served year-round by commuter flights.

BY CAR

Most of Montana's visitors arrive by car on interstate highways. Two east-west interstate highways (Interstates 90 and 94) converge in Billings, while Butte lies at the junction of Montana's major north-south and east-west routes (Interstates 15 and 90). State highways and secondary roads provide access to Montana's smaller towns and hidden places, while gravel roads reach deep into Montana's vast back-country and open spaces. The deeper they go, the better they get. Visitors should take note that eastern Montana is notorious for a soil condition that turns clay into greasy grabby gumbo and renders travel difficult to impossible after even the slightest rain. It is always a good idea in this part of the state to check on weather and road conditions before leaving the pavement. There are so few people out here that if you get lost or stuck, you may be on your own for quite awhile.

Highway rest areas appear sporadically along the interstates, but there aren't enough of them to satisfy most motorists, especially in winter, when many are closed. The Montana Highway Department does a fine job of maintaining roads in good driving condition year-round. Sudden storms occasionally block highways in winter, but not for long. Nevertheless, smart winter motorists are prepared for the worst. Although few motorists carry all of these items, the ultimate winter survival kit would include snow tires or chains, a shovel and window scraper, flares or a reflector, a blanket or sleeping bag, a first-aid kit, sand, gravel or traction mats, a flashlight with extra batteries, matches, a lighter or candle, paper, non-perishable foods, and a tow chain or rope.

Because distances are long and traffic is light, Montanans are notoriously fast drivers. While the state's highway patrol officers are generally tolerant of Montanans' 70-mph (112-kph) mindset, they have little tolerance for nighttime speeders and none at all for drunk drivers.

BY RAIL

AMTRAK'S *Empire Builder* parallels U.S. Route 2 across northern Montana, en route between St. Paul and Seattle. The passenger train makes daily stops at 11 stations along the Hi-Line. At East and West Glacier, it drops summer visitors off at Glacier National Park, and at Whitefish, it delivers skiers to The Big Mountain winter resort.

BY BUS

Greyhound Lines provides east-west service along Interstates 90 and 94, with stops in all major cities, including Glendive, Miles City, Billings, Livingston, Bozeman, Butte, and Missoula. Greyhound also travels U.S. Route 191 between

Bozeman and Idaho Falls, with a stop in West Yellowstone. Two local bus companies, Rimrock Stages and Intermountain Bus Co., provide passenger service to Anaconda, Dillon, Helena, Great Falls, Kalispell, Havre, Lewistown, Shelby, and Cut Bank. Kaarst Stage of Bozeman provides seasonal service from Bozeman and Livingston to Yellowstone Park, and a Wyoming bus line, Powder River Transportation, travels Interstate 90 south of Billings through Hardin.

■ SEASONS

Montana has two distinct travel seasons and two shoulder seasons. Although winter travel is growing each year, the vast majority of Montana's visitors prefer to explore Montana in the trusted comfort zone of summer. Warm-weather travel reaches its

Sheep wagons are still commonly seen across Montana; this one has been retired to the Sodbusters Museum in Windham.

An old gas pump stands outside the Utica Museum in Central Montana.

peak during July and August, Montana's hottest, driest period. This is Montana's high season: school is out, skies are clear, roads are dry, fishing, hiking, and camping are in full swing, and summer events are back to back. Autumn is Montana's sleeper shoulder season. An initial jolt of cold weather, usually in early September, scares most visitors away. But residents know the best time of year is at hand. Warm, bright days and crisp nights linger into October, even early November. Summer crowds have subsided, aspen and larch kindle Montana's fall colors, the air is exhilarating, and the fishing is prime. The other side of autumn is spring, which is received as a tonic by residents, but is too cool and wet for most visitors. Rivers are high, backroads and trails are still snowed in, and spring storms are frequent.

Montana often makes the national news with record low temperatures from a couple of notorious weather stations near Glacier and Yellowstone national parks. As a result, Montana has an undeserved reputation as an icebox. Unlike many areas of the nation, however, where winter settles in for keeps, Montana's cold spells are frequently interrupted by Chinook winds and mild periods. Its dry climate also makes Montana milder than most Midwestern states. While temperatures can be extreme in Montana, humidity is low, so the weather is never oppressively hot or cold. The coldest sub-zero day in Montana is never as cold as the coldest winter day in Minneapolis or Chicago. And the hottest summer day in Montana is never suffocating like a summer day in Washington, D.C. Humidity rarely reaches 70 percent, and generally ranges between 50 and 65 percent. Average annual rainfall is 15 inches (38 cm), varying from less than 10 inches (25 cm) on the plains to more than 100 inches (250 cm) in the mountains. Average daytime temperatures vary from 28° F (-2° C) in January to 85° F (29° C) in July.

Montana's weather patterns are generally more extreme in the east than they are in the west. Winters are colder and summers are hotter on the plains than they are in the mountains, where a milder, Pacific weather system prevails.

■ ESSENTIALS

Whatever the season, Montana's dress code is informal. Wardrobes run from shorts and slacks in summer to wool pants, flannel shirts, and sweaters in winter. Jeans are always in season and jackets or sweaters are never out of reach. Contrary to modern folklore, not every Montanan wears cowboy boots. Visitors are often amused, however, by the high proportion of Montana businessmen who combine boots and ties.

Most sports practitioners wouldn't leave home without their favorite fly rod, touring bike, or kayak. All of those toys and more can be put to good use in Montana. But if you're traveling far or just getting started, most sporting goods stores around the state will rent the equipment you need to sample the great outdoors. From backpacks to skis, mountain bikes to horses, all can be had on a rental basis.

■ ACCOMMODATIONS

Montana has a variety of lodging choices, covering the price and quality spectrum, but even the finest accommodations are affordable when compared to urban standards. The type of travel experience you seek will determine the type of lodging you need. Those planning an extended road trip will have plenty of motels, hotels, bed and breakfast homes, or campgrounds to choose from. If you plan to visit a single destination, you will want to plan ahead and select a ranch or resort based on its location or the kinds of activities it offers. Advance reservations are advised for lodging inside Glacier and Yellowstone national parks and for most ranches, resorts, and bed and breakfasts. Generally, reservations are not necessary for motels; however, rooms become scarce during July and August in communities around the parks and in communities holding special events.

For those who enjoy bed and breakfast travel, Montana has a growing number of distinctive homes that take in guests. **Bed & Breakfast Western Adventure** is a B&B reservation service representing more than 40 inspected B&Bs in Montana. For a free brochure or $5 directory, write P.O. Box 20972, Billings, MT 59104, or call 259-7993.

A partial listing of resorts, bed and breakfast homes, cabins, and condominiums appears below. Guest ranches are listed separately. Note that the telephone area code is 406 throughout Montana. For a more complete listing that includes motels, call Travel Montana (800-541-1447) to request a copy of the *Montana Travel Planner.*

B = Budget, under $35; M = Moderate, $35–50; L = Luxury, over $50

A B S A R O K E E
Oliver's; Main Street; 328-4813; historic bed and breakfast near Absaroka-
   Beartooth Wilderness; M

THIS IS NO BULL

YOU ARE IN NORTH CENTRAL MONTANA STOCKGROWERS COUNTRY! EAT BEEF

ANACONDA

Fairmont Hot Springs Resort; 1500 Fairmont Road; 797-3241 or (800) 443-2381; between Butte and Anaconda; L

BIGFORK

Burggraf's Countrylane; Rainbow Drive; 837-4608; on Swan Lake; L

The Gustin Orchard; East Lake Shore; 982-3329; on Flathead Lake; L

Marina Cay Resort; 180 Vista Lane; 837-5861 or (800) 433-6516; lake resort and convention center on Flathead Lake; L

O'Duach'ain Country Inn; 675 Ferndale Drive; 837-6851; between Flathead Lake and Swan Lake; L

BIG SKY

Big Sky Ski and Summer Resort; 995-4211 or (800) 548-4486; in Gallatin Canyon north of Yellowstone National Park; hiking, riding, fishing, golf, tennis, downhill and cross-country skiing; L

Golden Eagle Management; Meadow Village; (800) 548-4488; condominiums at Big Sky Ski & Summer Resort; L.

Triple Creek Management; 47650 Gallatin Road; 995-4847 or (800) 548-4632, condominiums at Big Sky Ski & Summer Resort; L

Montana's ranch culture and sense of humor manifests itself along highways and in hay fields.

BIG TIMBER

The Grand; 139 McLeod; 932-4459; historic bed and breakfast hotel near Boulder River and Yellowstone rivers and Absaroka-Beartooth Wilderness; M

BILLINGS

Feather Cove Inn; 5530 Vermilion Road; 373-5679; bed and breakfast inn 15 minutes from downtown; M

Sanderson Inn; 2038 S. 56th St. West; 656-3388; bed and breakfast in a renovated farmhouse on five acres west of the city; M

BOZEMAN

Bozeman Hot Springs; 133 Lower Rainbow Road; 587-3030; RV camping; B

Silver Forest Inn; 15325 Bridger Canyon Road; 586-1882; bed and breakfast home near Bridger Bowl Ski Area; L

Torch & Toes; 309 S. 3rd; 586-7285; historic bed and breakfast home; M

Voss Inn; 319 South Willson; 587-0982; a beautiful bed and breakfast home; L

CAMERON

Madison Valley Cabins; 682-4890; on the Madison River; B

Wade Lake Resort; 682-7560; cabins near Madison River and Yellowstone National Park; fishing, boating, hunting, cross-country skiing; lots of birds and watchable wildlife; B–M

CHOTEAU

Harvest Home; 36 4th Avenue SW; 466-5809; lovely bed and breakfast home near Bob Marshall Wilderness; M

CLINTON

Colonial House; 14265 Turah Road; 258-6787 or 259-7993; lovely bed and breakfast home near Missoula; L

COLUMBIA FALLS

Mountain Timbers; 5385 Rabe Road; 387-5830; near Glacier National Park; M

CONDON

Holland Lake Lodge; (800) 648-8859; near the Bob Marshall Wilderness; horseback riding, hiking, fishing, boating, hunting, cross-country skiing, snowmobiling; M–L

COOKE CITY

All Seasons Inn; 838-2251; close to Yellowstone National Park; M

CORVALLIS

Teller Wildlife Refuge; 1200 Chaffin Road; 961-3507; restored homestead on a private wildlife refuge; wildlife watching, fishing, floating, hiking, birding, duck hunting; L

DARBY

Nez Perce Ranch; West Fork Rt.; 349-2100; two log homes near the Selway-Bitterroot Wilderness; L

Triple Creek Guest Ranch; West Fork Stage Route; 821-4408; deluxe lodging and dining in the Bitterroot Mountains; horseback riding, hiking, swimming, tennis, mountain-bike riding, snowmobiling, cross-country skiing; L

West Fork Meadows Ranch; Coal Creek Road; 349-2468; Deluxe cabins and gourmet dining on the West Fork of the Bitterroot River; horseback riding, floating, fishing, hiking, gourmet cooking lessons, snowmobiling, downhill and cross-country skiing; L

EAST GLACIER

Backpackers' Inn; 29 Dawson Ave.; 226-9392; near Glacier National Park

ESSEX

Izaak Walton Inn; 888-5700; historic railroad inn near Glacier National Park; hiking, fishing, cross-country skiing; L

EUREKA

Grave Creek Bed and Breakfast; Grave Creek Road; 882-4658; near Ten Lakes Scenic Area; M

Trail's End; 57 Trail's End Road; 889-3486; M

GALLATIN GATEWAY

320 Ranch; 205 Buffalo Horn Creek; 995-4283 or (800) 243-0320; cabins and lease homes on a working stock ranch in the Gallatin Canyon near Yellowstone National Park and Big Sky resort; fishing, hunting, riding, downhill and cross-country skiing, snowmobiling; M–L

Gallatin Gateway Inn; 763-4672; beautifully restored railroad inn near Bozeman, fine dining; L

GARDINER

Absaroka Lodge; 848-7414; overlooks Yellowstone River, continental breakfast; L

GLACIER NATIONAL PARK

Belton Chalets, Inc.; Box 188, West Glacier, MT 59936; 888-5511; hike-in chalets, including three meals; L

Glacier Park Inc.; East Glacier, MT 59434; 226-5551; hotels, motor inns, lodges, and cabins in Glacier and Waterton national parks (summer only); B–L; between September 15 and May 15, use the following address for reservations: Greyhound Tower, Station 1210, Phoenix, AZ 85077; (602) 248-6000

GREAT FALLS

The Chalet; 1204 4th Avenue N.; 452-9001, bed and breakfast home across from C. M. Russell Museum; M

Three Pheasant Inn; 626 5th Avenue N.; 453-0519; Victorian bed and breakfast near C. M. Russell Museum; M–L

HAMILTON

Sleeping Child Resort; 363-6250; in the Sapphire Mountains; M

HARDIN

Kendrick House Inn; 206 N. Custer; 665-3035; Victorian bed and breakfast located near Custer Battlefield and the Bighorn River; M

HELENA

Feathered Pipe Ranch; 442-8196; cabins and yurts in mountains west of Helena; educational workshops on holistic health, yoga, and psychology; gourmet vegetarian dining; L

The Sanders; 328 N. Ewing; 442-3309; historic bed and breakfast near downtown and Original Governor's Mansion; L

Upcountry Inn; 2245 Head Lane; 442-1909; bed and breakfast in a rural setting close to town; M

KALISPELL

Ballymurry; 206 4th Avenue E.; 755-7080; bed and breakfast; M

Brick Farmhouse; 1946 Whitefish Stage; bed and breakfast; 756-6230; M

Peaceful Bay Condominiums and Resort; 150 Sherry Lane; 752-4783; luxury condominiums on Flathead Lake; L

Vacation Farm; 566 Creston Road; 756-8217 or (800) 882-8217; furnished farm home in Flathead Valley; swimming, lawn games; L

LIVINGSTON

Talcott House; 405 W. Lewis; 222-7699; historic bed and breakfast; L

LOMA

Virgelle Merc; Star Rt. l, Box 50; 378-3110; bed and breakfast rooms and cabins on the remote Wild and Scenic Missouri River; canoe rentals, shuttle service; B

MISSOULA

Birchwood Hostel; 600 S. Orange; 728-9799; B

Goldsmith's Inn; 809 E. Front; 721-6732; lovely rooms on the Clark Fork River, in town; L

NOXON

Bighorn Lodge; 710 Bull River Road; 847-5597; combination country inn and hunting lodge in Bull River Valley; trail rides, hiking, fishing, snowmobiling, cross-country skiing; L

PARADISE

Quinn's Hot Springs; 826-3150; on the Clark Fork River between St. Regis and Paradise in western Montana; B

POLEBRIDGE

North Fork Hostel; 756-4780; near Glacier National Park; B

POLSON

Bayview; 1221 Bayview Drive; 883-6744; bed and breakfast home on Flathead Lake; M

Hidden Pines; 792 Lost Quartz Road; 849-5612; near Flathead Lake; M

PRAY

Chico Hot Springs Lodge; 333-4933; near Yellowstone River and Yellowstone National Park; M–L

Davis Creek B & B; Route 38; 333-4353; bed and breakfast home near Yellowstone River in Paradise Valley; M

RED LODGE

Bear Mountain Guest House; 606 S. Broadway; 446-2207; private home, sleeps six; near Beartooth Highway and Red Lodge Ski Area; M

Creekside Cottages at the Red Lodge Resort and Golf Club; 2108 Broadwater; 656-0510 or (800) 444-8977; furnished townhouses and studio units on private golf course; L

Pitcher Guest House; 2 S. Platt; 446-2859; restored lodging house, sleeps eight; near Beartooth Highway and Red Lodge Ski Area; L

Rock Creek Resort; US 212 S; 446-1111; deluxe lodging, dining, conference facilities, and condominiums south of Red Lodge; tennis, swimming, hiking, horseback riding, biking, fishing; L

Willows Inn; 224 S. Platt; 446-3913; Victorian bed and breakfast home near Rock Creek, Beartooth Highway, and Red Lodge Ski Area; M

ROUNDUP

Ryan's Homestead Inn; 75 Turley Road; 323-2347; bed and breakfast horse ranch in Bull Mountains; M

SACO

Sleeping Buffalo Resort; Star Route 3, Box 13; 527-3370; B

SEELEY LAKE

Double Arrow Lodge; 677-2777 or (800) 468-0777; rooms, cabins, and RV sites in the Seeley Swan Valley; horseback riding, wagon and sleigh rides, hiking, fishing, hunting, swimming, tennis, cross-country skiing; M–L

SILVER GATE

Park View Cabins; 838-2371; near northeast entrance to Yellowstone National Park and Beartooth Highway; B

Pine Edge Cabins; 838-2222; near northeast entrance to Yellowstone National Park and Beartooth Highway; B

Whispering Pines Cabins; 838-2228; near northeast entrance to Yellowstone National Park and Beartooth Highway; B

SOMERS

Osprey Inn; 5557 US 93 S; 857-2042; on Flathead Lake, birders welcome; L

SULA

Broad Axe Lodge; 1151 East Fork Road; 821-3878; four cabins on East Fork of Bitterroot River; L

Lost Trail Hot Springs Resort; 821-3574; near Lost Trail Powder Mountain Ski Area; M

THREE FORKS

Sacajawea Inn; 5 N. Main; 285-6934; historic hotel near Headwaters State Park and Lewis and Clark Caverns; M

VIRGINIA CITY

Virginia City Country Inn; 115 E. Idaho; 843-5515; historic bed and breakfast home in a historic town; M

WEST GLACIER
Glacier Wilderness Resort; 888-5664; luxury log homes near Glacier National Park, M–L

WEST YELLOWSTONE
Firehole Ranch; 11500 Hebgen Lake Road; 646-7294; fly-fishing lodge; L
Madison Hotel Youth Hostel; 139 Yellowstone; 646-7745 or (800) 521-5241; near Yellowstone National Park
Sportsmen's High; 750 Deer Street; 646-7865 or (800) 272-4227; bed and breakfast home, fly-fishing spoken here; L
Yellowstone Cabins; 506 US 20; 646-9350; near Yellowstone; M

WHITE SULFUR SPRINGS
The Columns; 19 E. Wright Street; 547-3666; historic bed and breakfast home near Smith River and the Little Belt Mountains; M

WHITEFISH
Anapurna Properties; 3840 Big Mountain Road; 862-3687 or (800) 243-7547; condominium and private home rentals on The Big Mountain; L
Bay Point Estates; 300 Bay Point Drive; 862-2331 or (800) 327-2108; luxury condominiums on Whitefish Lake, near Glacier National Park and The Big Mountain; L
Big Mountain Ski and Summer Resort; 862-3511 or (800) 858-5439 or (800) 637-7574 (in Canada); near Glacier National Park; hiking, riding, mountain biking, downhill and cross-country skiing; L
The Castle; 900 S. Baker; 862-1257; L
Crestwood Resort; 1301 Wisconsin; 862-7574 or (800) 766-1181; condominium rentals near Glacier National Park and The Big Mountain; L
The Edelweiss; Big Mountain Village; 862-5252 or (800) 662-2270; luxury condominiums on The Big Mountain; L
The Garden Wall; 504 Spokane Avenue; 862-3440; lovely home in center of town; L
Grouse Mountain Lodge; 1205 US 93 W; 862-3000 or (800) 321-8822; on the Whitefish golf course, and near Glacier National Park and The Big Mountain; golf, tennis, cross-country skiing; L
The Lodge at Whitefish; 455 Blanchard Lake Drive; 862-2662; luxury home near golf course; L

WISE RIVER
Sundance Lodge; 689-3611; lodge and cabins near the Big Hole River; fishing, hiking, riding, hunting, cross-country skiing; M–L

YELLOWSTONE NATIONAL PARK
TW Recreational Services; Yellowstone National Park, Wyoming 82190; (307) 344-7901; advance reservations required at the park's lodges and cabins; M–L

ZORTMAN
Buckhorn Cabins; 673-3162; in the historic Little Rocky Mountains of north-central Montana; B

■ GUEST RANCHES

Montana's most distinctive accommodations are its many guest ranches, where Western hosts offer vacations with a flair and rooms with a view. No two ranches are alike, and rates vary widely, but most include lodging, meals, and activities. Many take guests only on a weekly basis. The ranches are listed below alphabetically by region. Write or call for detailed information and rates.

EASTERN MONTANA RANCHES
Bar Y Seven; Brusett, MT 59318; 557-6150; in the heart of the Big Open, near Fort Peck Lake and the C. M. Russell National Wildlife Refuge; horseback riding on working cattle ranch, hiking, fishing, hunting.
Hell Creek Guest Ranch; Box 325, Jordan, MT 59337; 557-2224; in the heart of the Big Open, near Fort Peck Lake and the C. M. Russell National Wildlife Refuge; working cattle ranch, fossil hunting, big-game hunting.
Schively Ranch; Box 281, Pryor, MT 59066 (summer); 1062 Road 15, Lovell, WY 82431 (winter); (307) 548-6688; near the Pryor Mountains and Bighorn Canyon National Recreation Area; serious horseback riding on a working cattle ranch; cattle drives and roundups.

CENTRAL MONTANA RANCHES
Circle Bar Ranch; Utica, MT 59452; 423-5454; Judith River Valley of central Montana; horseback riding, fishing, hunting, cross-country skiing, snowmobiling.

Elk Canyon Ranch; White Sulphur Springs, MT; 547-3373; on the Smith River, west-central Montana; horseback riding, fly-fishing, float fishing, swimming, tennis, trap and skeet shooting.

G Bar M Ranch; Clyde Park, MT 59018; 686-4687; in the foothills of the Bridger Mountains north of Livingston; horseback riding on a working cattle ranch; fishing.

JJJ Wilderness Ranch; Box 310, Augusta, MT 59410; 562-3653; near the Sun River Canyon and Bob Marshall Wilderness; horseback riding, fishing, hiking.

Klick's K Bar L Ranch; Box 287, Augusta, MT 59410; 467-2771 or 264-5806; near Bob Marshall Wilderness and Sun River Game Preserve; horseback riding, fishing, hunting.

Lazy AC Ranch; Box 460, Townsend, MT 59644; 547-3402; in the foothills of the Grassy Mountains near Townsend; horseback riding, fishing, square dancing.

Pine Butte Ranch; HC 58, Box 34C, Choteau, MT 59422; 466-2158; a Nature Conservancy property on the east slope of the Rocky Mountains near the Bob Marshall Wilderness; horseback riding, fishing, hiking, naturalist-guided tours, and workshops.

Seven Lazy P Ranch; Box 178, Choteau, MT 59422; 466-2044; on the Teton River and next door to the Bob Marshall Wilderness; horseback riding, fishing, hunting, cross-country skiing.

South Fork Lodge; Box 56, Utica, MT 59452; 374-2356; in the Judith River Valley of central Montana; horseback riding, fishing, hunting, snowmobiling, cross-country skiing.

YELLOWSTONE AREA RANCHES

Beartooth Ranch; Nye, MT 59061; 328-6194 or 328-6205; south of Columbus, near the Absaroka-Beartooth Wilderness; horseback riding, fishing, hiking.

Boulder River Ranch; McLeod, MT 59052; 932-6406; south of Big Timber, near Absaroka-Beartooth Wilderness; horseback riding, fly fishing, hiking.

Burnt Leather Ranch; West Boulder Road, McLeod, MT 59052; 222-6795 or 932-6155; south of Big Timber, near Absaroka-Beartooth Wilderness; horseback riding, cattle roundups, fly fishing, hiking, hunting.

CB Ranch; Box 604, Cameron, MT 59720; 682-4954; Madison River Valley near Ennis; fly fishing, horseback riding.

Diamond J Ranch; Box 577, Ennis, MT 59729; 682-4867; Madison River Valley near Ennis; horseback riding, fly fishing, hiking, trap and skeet shooting.

Hawley Mountain Guest Ranch; Box 4, McLeod, MT 59052; 932-5791; south of Big Timber near the Absaroka-Beartooth Wilderness; horseback riding, fishing, hiking, hunting.

Lazy K Bar Ranch; Box 550, Big Timber, MT 59011; 537-4404; in the foothills of the Crazy Mountains north of Big Timber; horseback riding on a working ranch; fishing, hiking, square dancing.

Lone Mountain Ranch; Box 69, Big Sky, MT 59716; 995-4644; near the Gallatin River, the Spanish Peaks, and Yellowstone National Park; horseback riding, fly fishing, Yellowstone tours, cross-country skiing.

Mountain Sky Guest Ranch; Box 1128, Bozeman, MT 59715; 587-1244 or (800) 548-3392; in the Paradise Valley north of Yellowstone National Park; horseback riding, fishing, hiking, tennis, swimming.

Nine Quarter Circle Ranch; Taylor Fork Road, Gallatin Gateway, MT 59730; 995-4276; north of Yellowstone National Park in the Gallatin Canyon; horseback riding, fly fishing.

Parade Rest Ranch; 7979 Grayling Creek Road, West Yellowstone, MT 59758; 646-7217; near the west entrance to Yellowstone National Park; fly fishing, horseback riding.

Rocking J Ranch; Park City, MT 59063; 633-2222; near the Yellowstone River west of Billings; horseback riding on a working cattle and registered quarter-horse ranch.

63 Ranch; Box 979, Livingston, MT 59047; 222-0570; south of Livingston near the Absaroka-Beartooth Wilderness; horseback riding, fly fishing, hiking, photo workshops.

Sweet Grass Ranch; Box 161, Big Timber, MT 59011; 537-4477 (summer) or 537-4497 (winter); in the Crazy Mountains north of Big Timber; horseback riding on a working cattle ranch, cattle roundups, fishing.

WESTERN MONTANA RANCHES

Blue Spruce Lodge and Guest Ranch; 451 Marten Creek Road, Trout Creek, MT 59874; 827-4762; in the foothills of the Bitterroot Mountains and near Noxon Reservoir in northwestern Montana; trail rides, float fishing, boating, hunting, cross-country skiing, and snowmobiling, all wheelchair accessible.

Double Diamond Guest Ranch; Box 501, Condon, MT 59826; 754-2351 or (800) 367-3612; in the Seeley Swan Valley between the Mission Mountains and Bob Marshall wilderness areas; horseback riding, hiking, fishing, cross-country skiing, snowmobiling.

Flathead Lake Lodge; Box 248, Bigfork, MT 59911; 837-4391; on the northeast
shore of Flathead Lake; horseback riding, tennis, fishing, water sports.

Hargrave Guest Ranch; Star Rt., Marion, MT 59925; 858-2284; Thompson
River Valley west of Kalispell; horseback riding on a working cattle ranch,
fishing, hiking, cross-country skiing.

Laughing Water Guest Ranch; Box 157, Fortine, MT 59918; 882-4680 or (800)
444-3833; between Glacier National Park and Lake Koocanusa; horseback
riding, fishing, hiking, swimming.

■ RESTAURANTS

The following Montana restaurants, cafés, and roadhouses provide a good cross
section of the state's diverse eateries. The area code is 406 throughout Montana.

> B = Budget; under $10 per person, excluding drinks
> M = Moderate; $10–20 per person, excluding drinks
> L = Luxury; over $20 per person, excluding drinks
> (R) = Reservations advised.

A L D E R

Alder Steak House; 842-5159; beef is taken seriously at this out-of-the-way
eatery; B–M

A N A C O N D A

Barclay II, 1300 E. Commercial; 563-5541; tenderloin steaks are the specialty;
also seafood, spaghetti, ravioli, and lots of extras; dinner only, nightly; B–M; (R
on weekends)

Jim & Clara's Dinner Club; 509 E. Park; 563-9963; traditional supper club
specializing in seafood, plus steaks, spaghetti and ravioli, and lots of extras; M

B A K E R

Sakelaris' Kitchen; 778-2208; homemade soups, cinnamon rolls, pies and much
more, all good, for breakfast, lunch and dinner; B

B E L T

Girdle Mountain Summer House; 277-3367; yet another one of Montana's
surprise dining rooms in unlikely places; dinner only, *prix fixe*, b.y.o.b.; advance
reservations a must; M

BIGFORK

Bigfork Inn; in the village; 837-6680; beef, including an excellent prime rib, plus seafood, pasta, chicken, and light dinners, all served in a rustic atmosphere; B–M (R)

Coyote Riverhouse; 600 Three Eagle Lane (north of Ferndale); 837-1233; fine dining on the Swan River; enjoy elegantly prepared steaks, pasta, and Mexican cuisine; M–L (R)

Coyote Roadhouse; 8083 Montana State Highway 35, north of the village; 837-4250; specializing in Cajun, Sicilian, and Mexican cuisine; *Travel and Leisure* declared it Montana's finest; M–L (R)

ShowThyme; next door to the Bigfork Summer Playhouse; 837-0707; have dinner before the show and desserts after; fresh pasta, seafood, and chicken entrées; substantial salads and desserts that speak for themselves, as in "Death by Chocolate Brownie Pie," M–L (R)

BIG SKY

Andiamo; Mountain Village; 995-2220; fine Italian cuisine; M (R)

First Place; Meadow Village; 995-4244; fine dining featuring regional American and continental cuisine; M (R)

Lone Mountain Ranch; 995-4644; gourmet dining in a rustic atmosphere; sleigh-ride dinners in winter; M (R)

BIG TIMBER

The Grand; 139 McLeod; 932-4459; elegant dining; M–L (R)

BILLINGS

Bruno's; 1233 N. 27th; 248-4146; authentic, affordable Italian cuisine; B–M

DeVerniero's; 513 N. 32nd; 252-9199; Italian cuisine for lunch and dinner; B–M (R)

Golden Belle; First Avenue N and Broadway; 245-2232; one of the few dining rooms in the state where blue jeans won't do; elegantly prepared and served entrées, appetizers, salads, and desserts; Billings' finest; M–L (R)

The Granary; 1500 Poly Drive; 259-3488; beef, seafood, chicken, and a great salad bar served in a restored flour mill; outdoor patio in summer; M (R)

Great Wall; 1309 Grand; 245-8601; Mandarin, Szechwan, and Cantonese for lunch and dinner, well prepared and served; B–M

Jade Palace; 2021 Overland; 656-8888; specializing in Mandarin and Cantonese gourmet cuisine for lunch and dinner; B–M (R)

Juliano's; 2912 7th Avenue N; 248-6400; fine continental cuisine served in an intimate atmosphere; lunch and dinner, plus gourmet take-out and tempting desserts; B–M (R)

Pug Mahon's; 3011 First Avenue N; 259-4190; good Irish stew, Reubens and other traditional Irish fare for lunch and dinner; B–M

The Rex; 24th & Montana; 245-7477; the best in beef, seafood, chicken and pasta, plus tempting appetizers and desserts; M–L (R)

Thai Orchid; 20 N. 27th; 256-2206; authentic Thai dinners and buffet lunch; B

Torres Café; 109 5th Street W; 248-5900; authentic Mexican food that reflects the influence of Montana's largest Hispanic population; B

B O Z E M A N

Bistro; 242 E. Main; 587-4100; imaginative menu, casual atmosphere; breakfast, lunch, and dinner; B–M

Ira's on Main; 233 E. Main; 587-9999; changing menu features new American cuisine for lunch and dinner; B–M

New Asia Kitchen; 1533 W. Babcock; 586-0522; Chinese and Thai food prepared with fresh ingredients; B–M

O'Brien's; 312 E. Main; 587-3973; fine cuisine, excellent wine list; M

Rocky Mountain Pasta Company; 105 W. Main; 586-1315; fine Italian cuisine; B–M

B R O A D U S

Montana Bar & Café; 436-2454; where the cowboys gather for coffee, homemade rolls, and pie, or a morning eye-opener from the bar; B

B U T T E

Gamer's Confectionery; 15 W. Park; 723-5453; no longer a confectionery but still a Butte tradition, right down to the Cornish pasties; owner-greeter-host Carl Rowan will make your day; B

Joe's Pasty Shop; 1641 Grand; 723-9071; these meat pies arrived in Butte with immigrant Welsh and Cornish miners; Butte lore has it that when a miner found a pasty in his lunch bucket, he referred to it affectionately as "a letter from 'ome"; pasties have endured as part of the Butte ethnic tradition; B

Lydia's; 5 Mile Harrison Avenue; 494-2000; traditional supper club with good service and lots of extras; the steaks and ravioli are memorable; M

M & M Bar & Café; 9 N. Main; 723-7612; a Butte classic, with a diner's counter on the right, bar on the left, and poker tables in the rear; B

Pekin Noodle Parlor; 117 S. Main; 782-2217; dating back to Butte's mining heyday, this no-frills walk-up is as popular for its atmosphere as it is for its pork noodles and boiled won ton; B

Uptown Café; 47 E. Broadway; 723-4735; arguably Montana's finest dining room, serving elegantly prepared seafood, poultry, veal, beef, and pasta; also great for lunch; M–L

CHARLO

Allentown Restaurant; U.S. Route 93; 644-2588; enjoy views of the Mission Mountains and Ninepipe National Wildlife Refuge while dining on beef, seafood, pasta, soups, and sandwiches; B–M

CHESTER

Red Onion; U.S. Route 2; 759-5335; spaghetti is the standout here; choose a traditional red sauce, or try the white with shrimp, oysters or scallops; also, small steaks cooked just right; B–M

CONRAD

Mom's Country Cooking; 319 S. Main; 278-5436; huge buttermilk and sourdough pancakes, plus homemade syrup, rolls, cakes, soups, and a full dinner menu (kids under eight eat dinner for under $1.75); open daily; B–M

COOKE CITY

Joan and Bill's Restaurant; 838-2280; family-style meals and famous homemade pies. B–M

DARBY

Karen's Montana Cafe; U.S. Route 93; where loggers and locals gather for good home cooking and perpetual coffee; breakfast and lunch; B

West Fork Meadows Ranch; West Fork Rt., Coal Creek Road; 349-2468; European cuisine prepared by nationally known chef Greg Patent and served in rustic elegance; one of Montana's finest dining rooms; L (R)

DELL

Yesterday's Calf-A; about 60 miles south of Dillon; take the Dell Exit; 276-3319; you won't know if you don't go; aim for the Sunday buffet; B

DILLON

Bannack House; 33 E. Bannack; 683-5088; Italian cuisine, plus locally grown veal, lamb, and beef; large selection of imported and domestic beers and wines; lunch and dinner; B–M

EAST GLACIER

Glacier Village Restaurant & Dining Room; 266-4464; wide variety for all budgets, just outside of Glacier Park; B–M

EKALAKA

Ekalaka Locker; Main St.; 775-6260; homemade soups and breads for lunch; also a popular gathering spot in the morning for coffee and rolls; B

EMIGRANT

Livery Stable; 333-4688; prime rib is the specialty, plus steaks, BBQ ribs, and chicken; dinner only, nightly, luncheon buffet on Sunday; B–M

Chico Hot Springs Lodge; 333-4933; one of Montana's most distinctive dining rooms in a most unlikely spot; M–L (R)

ENNIS

Continental Divide; next door to Jack Creek Saloon; 682-7600; fresh seafood, thick steaks, Cajun cuisine, fine desserts and wines; M–L (R)

Grizzly Bar & Grill; between Ennis and West Yellowstone on U.S. Route 287; 682-7118; half-pound burgers, steaks, and chicken with all the trimmings (especially good after a day on the Madison River); B–M

FORSYTH

Blue Spruce Café; 109 S. 10th; 356-7955; butchers its own beef to assure quality; breakfast, lunch, and dinner served daily, with good specials; B–M

GALLATIN GATEWAY

Gallatin Gateway Inn; 763-4672; seasonal menus and fresh ingredients bring out the best in seafood, beef, poultry, and lamb; the restored, Spanish colonial-style inn was built by the Chicago, Milwaukee & St. Paul Railway in 1927 as a hotel-depot for tourists en route to Yellowstone National Park; M–L (R)

GARDINER

The Ranch Kitchen; U.S. Route 89, 7 miles north of Gardiner; 848-7891; owned and operated by the Church Universal and Triumphant; great menu featuring fresh-baked breads and desserts, organically grown vegetables and meats, vegetarian entrees; B–M

The Loft; upstairs from Town Café; 848-7322; All-American food with a great view; B–M

GLASGOW

Sam's Supper Club; 307 First Avenue N; 228-4614; Hi-Liners travel miles for the steaks, seafood, walleye, and many other lunch and dinner specialties; B–M

GLENDIVE

Jordan Coffee Shop; 223 N. Merrill; 365-5655; don't miss the Klapmeier agate collection and the original J. K. Ralston mural and paintings; B–M

GREAT FALLS

Borrie's; 1800 Smelter (in Black Eagle); 761-0300; traditional Italian and American fare served in a festive, friendly atmosphere; B–M

Eddie's; 3725 2nd Avenue N; 453-1616; popular supper club known for its "campfire" steaks (arguably the best in Montana), burgers and homemade ravioli; there's also a coffee shop; B–M

Jake's; 1315 8th Avenue N; 727-1033; steaks, prime rib, fresh seafood and salads served in a classy dining room, once an iron works plant; M

Mama Cassie's; 319 First Avenue N.; 454-3354; Italian sandwiches, pastas, soups; deli-style sandwiches and salads, and desserts to die for; B

Morning Light Coffee Shop; 900 2nd Avenue N; 453-8443; a good place to start the day with fresh coffees, breakfast rolls, and soft music; B

Peking Gardens Restaurants; 801 Smelter; 727-3913, or 2408 10th Avenue S; 727-2194; best Chinese/Szechwan in town; eat in or take out; B

HAMILTON

Haigh's Hideway Deli; 163 2nd S; 363-4433; good deli selection; B

Mustard Seed; 149 Cherry St.; 363-3801; Asian; B

Signal Bar & Grill; 131 W. Main; 363-4648; burgers and steaks; B–M

HARDIN

Purple Cow; north end of town; 665-3601; popular breakfast spot; homemade soups, sandwiches, salad bar, buffet; B

HAVRE

The Lunch Box; 213 Third Avenue; 265-6588; choose from 69 different sandwiches, plus soup, cookies, and desserts, all homemade; B

Nalivka's Pizza Kitchen; 439 W. First; 265-5426; pizza and traditional Italian pasta dishes, plus sandwiches, soups, and salads; B

HELENA

Morning Light Coffee Roasters; 44 S. Park; 442-5180; breakfast rolls to accompany your fresh-ground coffee, espresso, cappuccino; B

On Broadway; 106 Broadway; 443-1929; regional Italian cuisine in a fine dining atmosphere; M

The Parrot; 42 N. Last Chance Gulch (on the downtown walking mall); 442-1470; the lunch menu says chili and tamales but it's the hand-dipped chocolates, chocolate malteds, chocolate parfaits, sodas, and sundaes that have kept people coming into this old-fashioned soda fountain and confectionery since 1922; B

Pasta Pantry; 1218 11th; 442-1074; eat in or take out fresh pasta, variety of sauces, soups, salads, light dinners, and elegant desserts; B

The Red Fox; 2245 Head Lane; 442-1909; dinners served *prix fixe* Friday and Saturday nights at the Upcountry Inn; M–L; in the afternoon, brewed teas are served with scones, tarts, and assorted tea sandwiches; B. Both by reservation only.

Windbag; 19 S. Last Chance Gulch; 443-9669; popular saloon that serves a variety of burgers, homemade soups, quiche, and light dinners; B–M

HUNGRY HORSE

Huckleberry Patch; 8858 U.S. Route 2 E; 387-5670; here is the place to sample western Montana's purple delicacies in the form of muffins, cookies, hotcakes, milkshakes, and more; B

Mike & Aggie's Hide-a-Way; 9050 U.S. Route 2 E; 387-5997; where the locals meet for hearty dinners featuring Montana beef and homemade desserts; B–M

INGOMAR

Jersey Lilly Bar & Café; 358-2278; this is a period-piece business; in fact, the only business in town; the owner and his signature pinto beans are legendary throughout the state; B

JORDAN

QD Café; 557-2301; this is the place to get a short stack or a steak sandwich and study the sociology of the Big Open; B–M

KALISPELL

1st Avenue West; 139 First Avenue East; 752-5757; fresh seafood, pasta, chicken, beef, and dinner salads, good wine selection; lunch, too; B–M

Moose's Saloon; 173 N. Main; 755-2337; lunch and dinner served in a lively Western bar, complete with swinging doors and sawdust on the floor; B–M

Sykes Grocery & Market Restaurant; 202 2nd Avenue West; 257-4306; home of the 10-cent cup of coffee and three affordable square meals a day, all homemade; if you need to know anything about Kalispell, this is the place to start; B

LEWISTOWN

Bar Nineteen; Fairgrounds Road; 538-3250; watch your steak, chicken, or seafood charbroiled to perfection, then head for the dance floor to learn the cowboy jitterbug; B–M

Whole Famdamily; 206 1/2 W. Main; 538-5161; a pleasing and nutritious menu features homemade soup, sandwiches, desserts, and dinner specials; B

LIBBY

Adam's Rib & Seafood; 1207 Utah; 293-3129; steak, seafood, prime rib, and chicken, served in a restored, turn-of-the-century church, complete with stained glass and pews; M

LIVINGSTON

Livingston Bar & Grille; 130 N. Main; 222-7909; a good-times bar with a serious kitchen, savory specials and wide selection of imported beers; B–M

The Sport; 114 S. Main; 222-3533; Western bar specializing in BBQ and jumbo burgers; B

LOGAN

Land of Magic Dinner Club; Exit 283 from Interstate 90; 284-3794; great steaks and prime rib; M–L

LOLO

Guy's Lolo Creek Steak House; 6600 U.S. Route 12 W; 273-2622; open-pit cooking, fresh ingredients, and a rustic atmosphere make this the best steak house in the valley; B–M

MILES CITY

600 Café; 600 Main; 232-3860; where the cowboys meet before dawn, and the kitchen keeps serving all day long; B

MISSOULA

Alley Cat Grill; 125 1/2 W. Main; 728-3535; imaginative menu offers French to Indonesian and Thai, and lots of seafood specials; lunch and dinner; B–M (R)

Casa Pablo's; 147 W. Broadway; 721-3854; authentic, affordable Mexican; B

The Depot; 201 W. Railroad; 728-7007; fresh seafood, choice beef, Cajun specialties; M (R)

Ekstrom's Stage Station; Rock Creek Road off Interstate 90, 20 miles (32 km) east of Missoula; 825-3183; family-style meals featuring homemade soups, breads, pies; lunch and dinner, summer only; B–M

Freddy's Feed & Read; 1221 Helen; 549-2127; gourmet and health food deli adjoining one of Missoula's best bookstores; heaven can wait; B

Goldsmith's; 809 E. Front; 721-6732; homemade ice cream is the draw; also a good stop for breakfast and lunch; B

Iron Wok; 2700 Paxson; 549-3965; Asian cooking prepared on tableside grills; prepared and served by members of Missoula's Hmong community; B–M

Kadena's; 231 W. Front; 549-3304; "gourmet take away" menu is small but imaginative; B

Mammyth Bakery Café; 131 W. Main; 549-5542; homemade breads, pastries, soups, sandwiches, and specialty desserts; a great place to ease into the day; B

Mustard Seed; 419 W. Front; 728-7825; "Fireworks Chicken" and "Tsing-Tsing Tofu" are just two selections on this original Asian menu; fresh ingredients, light sauces, and reliably good; B

Old Town Café; 127 W. Alder; 728-9742; healthful, whole grain cooking for breakfast, lunch and dinner; popular weekend breakfast spot; B

The Oxford; 337 N. Higgins; 549-0117; every university student has been to the Ox at least once for brains 'n' eggs or browns 'n' gravy; old-timers meet here for a beer, a game of poker, and an affordable meal; B

The Shack; 222 W. Main; 549-9903; one of Missoula's favorite breakfast places; beloved for its "browns," omelets, and hotcakes; lunch and dinner, too; B

Torrey's; 1916 Brooks; 721-2510; good, affordable, health-conscious home cooking; B

Zimorino Bros. Red Pies over Montana; 424 N. Higgins; 549-7434; giant, thick-crust pizza, plus spaghetti, ravioli, lasagne, and Italian sausage, all homemade; B

Zorba's; 420 S. Orange; 728-9259; authentic, affordable Greek cuisine in a casual atmosphere; lunch and dinner; B–M

M O N A R C H

Lazy Doe; 236-9949; renowned for the quality of its beef, plus occasional crab and lobster feeds, and imaginative salads; B–M

NORRIS

Schoolhouse Restaurant; U.S. Route 287; 685-3200; homemade Mexican food is the specialty here; B

NOXON

Bighorn Lodge; 710 Bull River Road; 847-5597; private guest lodge, open to the public for dining on weekends; prime rib is tops, plus seafood, chicken, pork, and lamb; M (R)

OLNEY

Point of Rocks; U.S. Route 93; 881-2752; steaks and seafood, plus trout, pork, and chicken; combos are a specialty; so are the quality and generous portions; B–M

PENDROY

The Rose Room; County Route 219; 469-2205; well-prepared shrimp and Montana beef are the specialties at this popular, out-of-the-way supper club, open nightly; B–M (R)

POLSON

China Garden; Jct. 93 & 35; 883-4048; enjoy Chinese or American fare and a close-up view of Flathead Lake; B–M

RED LODGE

Bearcreek Saloon; east of town on County Route 308; 446-3481; Mexican dinners served on weekends, but the big draw is the entertainment: pig races, Memorial Day through Labor Day; lizard races in winter; B

Bogart's Pizza; 11 S. Broadway; 446-1784; Mexican, too; B

Kalico Kitchen; 412 N. Broadway; 446-2568; this is a bakery that turns out good soups for lunch; B

Natali's Café and **Pius' International Room;** 115 S. Broadway; 446-3333; gourmet burgers and German, Austrian, and Italian cuisine, plus seafood specials and a memorable Caesar salad; B–L (R)

17 Broadway; 105 S. Broadway; 446-1717; gourmet-style, New American cuisine Friday and Saturday evenings; also, homemade soups, salads, and a delicatessen; B–M

ROSCOE

Grizzly Bar; 328-6789; a great place to stop for steaks or burgers en route to East Rosebud Lake; B–M

ROUNDUP

Busy Bee; Junction of U.S. Route 12 and 87; 323-2204; open 24 hours for truckers, hunters, locals, and visitors; extensive menu with lots of specials; B

ST. MARY

Johnson's of St. Mary; U.S. Route 89; 732-5565; down-home cooking served family-style, plus menu choices, at the east edge of Glacier National Park; B–M

SCOBEY

Cozy Café; 15 Main; 487-5370; extensive Chinese/American menu offers everything from biscuits and gravy to Peking duck; B–M

SEELEY LAKE

Seasons Restaurant; at the Double Arrow Lodge; 677-2777; seasonal products and fresh ingredients; dinner features imaginative variations on seafood, beef, chicken, and pasta; M–L (R)

STANFORD

Pump Bar; 71 Central; 566-9914; Rocky Mountain oysters served year-round, with a free oyster feed every fall; B

STEVENSVILLE

Marie's; 4040 S. U.S. Route 93; 777-3681; well-prepared Italian cuisine and tempting desserts; B–M

SULA

Broad Axe Lodge & Restaurant; 1237 East Fork Road; 821-3878; view bighorn sheep from the dining room of this rustic lodge; steaks, seafood, chicken, and prime rib; B–M

TOWNSEND

Rosario's Pizzeria; 316 N. Front; 266-3603; authentic Italian cuisine and pizza, steaks, seafood, and sandwiches; B–M (R)

UTICA

Oxen Yoke Inn; 423-5530; here, the burgers are all beef, and they're so big, they're called "haystacks"; B

WEST GLACIER

Glacier Highland Motel & Restaurant; U.S. Route 2 E; 888-5427; wide variety of well-prepared food, breakfast, lunch, and dinner, just outside Glacier Park; B–M

WEST YELLOWSTONE

Alice's; 1545 Targhee Pass Highway; 646-7296; German/American; B–M

WHITEFISH

The Bistro; 307 E. 2nd; 862-8922; pleasing combination of good food and contemporary art; breakfast, lunch, and dinner daily; B–M

Jimmy Lee's Chinese Restaurant; 6550 U.S. Route 93 S; 862-5303; imaginative menu that includes "Oriental Fajitas," "Shanghai Fire Pit," and "Buddha Pie"; a sure fix for anyone who loves Chinese; B–M

WOLF CREEK

Holter Lake Lodge; on Holter Lake; take the Recreation Road north of Wolf Creek; 235-4331; exceptionally well-prepared dinners Wednesday through Sunday; summer only; M

■ TOURS

The telephone area code is 406 throughout Montana.

The Fishing Widow; Box 548, West Yellowstone, MT 59758; guided tours and activities in and around Yellowstone National Park for non-fishing spouses or partners.

Montana Board of Outfitters; 1424 9th Ave., Helena, MT 59620; 444-3738; directory of licensed outfitters who provide hunting and fishing trips, trail rides, whitewater raft trips, scenic floats, and other guided outdoor trips.

Montana Outfitters and Guides Association, Box 1339, Townsend, MT 59644; 266-5625; another organization to contact for guiding information.

Off the Beaten Path; 109 E. Main, Bozeman, MT 59715; 586-1311; personalized itineraries by travel consultants who match clients' interests with outfitters, guest ranches, ski resorts, and tour operators.

TW Recreational Services; Yellowstone National Park, WY 82190; (307) 344-7901; horseback and stagecoach rides, bus tours, and guided fishing trips in summer; guided ski and snowcoach tours in winter.

Wilderness Walks; Montana Wilderness Association, Box 635, Helena, MT 59624; 443-7350; one-day and extended hikes led by Wilderness Association members into Montana's roadless backcountry.

Yellowstone Tour & Travel; Box 369, West Yellowstone, MT 59758; (800) 221-1151; full package summer and winter tours of the Yellowstone

National Park area, including bus tours, snowmobile tours, and guest ranch stays.

BIKE TOURS

Backcountry Bicycle Tours; Box 4029, Bozeman, MT 59772; 586-3556; van-supported, inn-to-inn mountain bike tours of Glacier, Yellowstone, and the Bozeman area; most tours on secondary and dirt roads.

Backroads Bicycle Touring; Box 1626, San Leandro, CA 94577; (800) 533-2573 or (415) 895-1783 (in California); van-supported tours of Glacier National Park.

Bikecentennial; 113 W. Main, Missoula, MT 59801; 721-1776; maps, itinerary assistance, and guided bicycle tours.

BOAT TOURS

Bighorn Canyon Boat Tours; S-S Enterprises, Box 717, Cowley, WY 82420; (307) 548-6418; 2-hour tours from Horseshoe Bend near Lovell, WY.

Far West; 857-3203; daily excursions on Flathead Lake in a 64-foot (20-m) cruise ship, departing from Somers on the north shore of the lake.

Gates of the Mountains; Box 478, Helena, MT 59624; 458-5241; cruise a portion of the Lewis and Clark route along the Missouri River north of Helena.

Glacier National Park SceniCruises; Box 5262G, Kalispell, MT 59903; 732-4430 (seasonal); daily tours of St. Mary, Many Glacier, McDonald, and Two Medicine lakes.

Lewis and Clark Cruises; 1414 Front St., Fort Benton, MT 59442; 622-5537; half-day to extended boat tours of the Upper Missouri River.

Port Polson Princess; 883-2448; daily cruises on the south end of Flathead Lake aboard a 41-foot (12-m) tour boat departing from Polson.

Questa; Flathead Lake Lodge, Bigfork, MT 59911; 837-5569; daily sailing excursions on Flathead Lake in a 51-foot (16-m) racing sloop.

WAGON TRIPS

Bozeman Trail Wagon Train; Box 36, Reedpoint, MT 59069; (800) 962-7483; four-day wagon trips along the historic Bozeman Trail in south-central Montana.

Old West Adventures; Box 1899, Whitefish, MT 59937; 752-5167 or 862-3511; 3- and 4-day horse and wagon trips in the Flathead.

Wagons West; Box 483, Broadus, MT 59317; 436-2350; six-day horse and wagon trips through southeastern Montana.

■ NATURE STUDY VACATIONS

The telephone area code for Montana is 406.

Elderhostel; Flathead Valley Community College, 777 Grandview Drive, Kalispell, MT 59901; 756-3836; week-long field study courses in and around Glacier National Park for people age 60 and over; April through October.

Glacier Institute; Box 1457, Kalispell, MT 59903; 752-5222; one-day to one-week summer field seminars on Glacier National Park geology, botany, wildlife, history, and photography, conducted by professional staff and instructors; college credit available.

Museum of the Rockies; Montana State University, Bozeman, MT 59715; 994-5257; one-day to two-week paleontology and archaeology field trips with professional scientists; college credit available.

Pine Butte Guest Ranch; HC58 Box 34C, Choteau, MT 59422; 466-2158; week-long natural history tours and workshops on birding, mammal tracking, photography, paleontology, and backcountry horsepacking at this Nature Conservancy property along the Rocky Mountain Front.

Rocky Mountain Front Exploratory Workshops; Seven Lazy P Guest Ranch, Box 178, Choteau, MT 59422; (406) 466-2044; week-long natural history tours and workshops on birds, plants, and grizzly bear ecology; hiking and horseback riding.

Yellowstone Institute; Box 117, Yellowstone National Park, WY 82190; (307) 344-7381; grizzly bear ecology, wilderness writing and photography, llama trekking, catch-and-release fly fishing, and kids' camping are just some of the more than 80 field courses conducted each year in Yellowstone National Park; college credit available.

■ CAMPING

Montana has much to offer campers and RV travelers, especially during summer and early fall. In addition to many private campgrounds located in cities and towns and near major attractions, Montana has hundreds of public campgrounds in national forests and state parks, as well as in the more crowded national parks. Whether it is near a mountain lake or a wilderness trailhead, by a trout stream, or next door to a wildlife refuge, each merits an entry in your Montana travel journal.

For a complete listing of public and private campgrounds, request a copy of the *Montana Travel Planner* from Travel Montana (800-541-1447). The U.S. Forest Service, National Park Service, and Bureau of Land Management can provide more detailed information about campgrounds. See "Useful Addresses" below for specifics.

■ MUSEUMS AND HISTORIC HOMES

Nearly every Montana county has a historical society, and most communities maintain a historic house or museum where visitors can learn about the people and events that shaped the area. Many charge no admission. A partial listing of notable historic homes and museums follows. The telephone area code throughout Montana is 406.

Aerial Fire Depot and Smokejumper Visitor Center; 5765 Highway 10 West; 329-4934; history of smokejumping.

Bighorn County Historical Museum and Visitor Center; Hardin; 665-1671; restored buildings, cultural exhibits about the homestead era.

C. M. Russell Museum Complex; 400 13th St. North, Great Falls; 727-8787; original paintings, bronzes, illustrated letters, and memorabilia of cowboy artist Charlie Russell in a gallery next door to his log cabin studio; also original works by many of his contemporaries.

C. W. Clark Mansion; 321 West Broadway, Butte; 723-7600; chateauesque-style mansion built in 1898 for William Clark's oldest son, Charles; now houses the Arts Chateau.

Carter County Museum; Ekalaka; 775-6886; impressive collection of fossils and artifacts from the dinosaur country of southeastern Montana.

Cascade County Historical Museum; Paris Gibson Square, 1400 1st Ave. North, Great Falls; 452-3462; rotating exhibits and lectures on homesteading, farming, mining, and railroading.

The Castle; 4th Ave. and Jefferson, White Sulphur Springs; 547-3744; stone mansion built in 1892 by rancher-businessman Byron Sherman; furnished with antiques from families throughout the area; now houses the Meagher County Museum.

Chief Plenty Coups Museum; Pryor; 252-1289; Crow Indian artifacts and history; the museum is part of a state park that preserves the home and burial site of Plenty Coups, last chief of the Crows.

Conrad Mansion; Woodland Ave. between 3rd and 4th streets, Kalispell; 755-2166; three-story, 23-room, Norman-style mansion built by the city's founder, Charles E. Conrad.

Copper King Mansion; 219 West Granite, Butte; 782-7580; three-story, 30-room Elizabethan-style residence owned by William A. Clark.

Copper Village Museum and Art Center; 401 Commercial, Anaconda; 563-2422; Anaconda Copper Company mining history.

Daly Mansion; East Side Highway, Hamilton; 363-6004; three-story, 42-room, Georgian Revival residence built by Butte copper king Marcus Daly.

Daniels County Museum and Pioneer Town; Scobey; 783-5691; restored, early-1900s town with 40 buildings, vintage machinery, cars, and tractors.

Fort Peck Museum; Fort Peck; 526-3431; impressive fossil collection and history of Fort Peck Dam.

Four Winds Historic Village; St Ignatius; 745-4336; history and culture of the Flathead Indians; historic buildings; railroad history.

Frontier Gateway Museum; Belle Prairie Road, east of Glendive; 365-4123; farm and ranch history, Plains Indian history and culture, and a frontier main street in miniature.

Grant-Kohrs Ranch; Deer Lodge; 846-2070; the ranch house at this national historic site was built in 1862, enlarged in 1890, and decorated over several decades with the finest furnishings available.

H. Earl Clack Memorial Museum; Fairgrounds, west of Havre; 265-9913; history and archaeology of north-central Montana; tours of Fort Assiniboine and a nearby bison kill site.

Historical Museum at Fort Missoula; 31st St. and South Ave., Missoula; 728-3476; history of the fort, built in 1877 for the protection of white settlers, plus history of Missoula County, forest management, and timber production in western Montana.

Livingston Depot; 200 West Park, Livingston; 222-2300; history, culture, and art of the Yellowstone region.

McCone County Museum; Circle; 485-2414; eastern Montana's ranch and homestead history; vast collection of machinery and artifacts.

Mehmke's Antique Farm Machinery Museum; Highway 87/89, east of Great Falls; 452-6571; large collection of tractors and antique farm machinery.

Mineral Museum; Montana Tech campus, West Park St., Butte; 496-4414; more than 1,300 mineral specimens on display.

Miracle of America Museum; US 93, Polson; 883-6804; 200 years of American history in artifacts and art.

Mondak Heritage Center; 120 3rd Ave. Southeast, Sidney; 482-3500; area history and art, turn-of-the-century street scene, and a Winchester rifle collection.

Montana Agriculture Center and Museum of the Northern Great Plains; Fort Benton; 622-3278; Montana's official museum of agriculture includes a homestead-era village and covers three generations of farming.

Montana Historical Society; 225 North Roberts, Helena; 444-2694; Montana Homeland exhibit uses 2,000 artifacts and works of art to illustrate Montana's past; also, the art of C.M. Russell and photographs of F. Jay Haynes.

Moss Mansion; 914 Division St., Billings; 256-5100; turn-of-the-century French Gothic mansion built by banker-developer Preston B. Moss; mixed interior styles include a Louis XVI French parlor, English Tudor dining room, and Moorish entry.

Museum of Fly Fishing; 200 Yellowstone Ave., West Yellowstone; 646-9541; part of the Federation of Fly Fishers' International Fly Fishing Center; history, art, and practice of the sport.

Museum of the Plains Indian and Craft Center; Browning; 338-2230; Northern Plains Indian history and culture; large collection of Blackfeet Indian artifacts.

Museum of the Rockies; Kagy Blvd. and Greek Way, Bozeman; 994-2251; four billion years of history and pre-history, plus a world-class dinosaur exhibit and planetarium.

Old Montana Prison; 1106 Main, Deer Lodge; 846-3111; built by convicts in 1871, it was one of the first prisons constructed in the Western U.S. and served as the Montana State Prison until 1979.

Old Trail Museum; Junction of US 89 and US 287, Choteau; 446-5332; fossils and Indian artifacts; fossil location and identification field trips.

Original Governor's Mansion; 304 North Ewing, Helena; 444-3115; Queen Anne-style, brick mansion built as a private residence in 1888 by entrepreneur William Chessman; served as Montana's official executive residence from 1913 to 1959.

Oscar's Dreamland; Route 9, west of Billings; 656-0966; antique farm machinery—including 500 tractors—and a dozen old buildings.

Range Riders Museum; US 10/12 West, Miles City; 232-4483; 400-piece gun collection, 1880s-era main street scene, military and cowboy memorabilia, Indian artifacts, and pioneer photographs.

Towe Ford Museum; 1106 Main, Deer Lodge; 846-3111; antique Ford car collection.

Western Heritage Center; 2822 Montana Ave, Billings; 256-6809; exhibits, tours, classes, and workshops emphasize the culture and history of the Yellowstone River Valley.

World Museum of Mining; West Park and Granite St., Butte; 723-7211; Hell Roarin' Gulch, a reconstructed, turn-of-the-century mining camp on the site of the old Orphan Girl Mine, with mining equipment and copper king memorabilia.

■ TOP MONTANA EVENTS

J A N U A R Y

Montana Winter Fair, Bozeman. Week-long celebration featuring livestock shows and sales, commercial exhibits, cooking and crafts, draft horse pulling contests, sheep shearing, and many more events.

Professional Rodeo Cowboys Association Circuit Finals, Great Falls. This national organization is divided into 12 competitive regions, or circuits; this is the final round of competition for the Montana circuit.

F E B R U A R Y

Montana 500 Sled Dog Race to the Sky, Helena-Holland Lake. A five- to six-day trek along the Continental Divide makes this second-only to the Alaska Iditarod in length.

Whitefish Winter Carnival, Whitefish. Three-day celebration features torchlight skiing, races, winter games, parade, fireworks, and a formal ball.

Yellowstone Art Center's Annual Art Auction, Billings. Montana's largest auction of contemporary art features up to 100 pieces of juried art by top regional artists (sometimes held in early March).

MARCH

National Gelande Jump Championship, Montana Snowbowl. Alpine ski jumping competition.

C. M. Russell Auction of Original Western Art, Great Falls. Widely recognized as the nation's largest and finest Western art auction, this is a four-day binge of auctions, quick-draws, seminars, receptions, and sales by about 100 exhibitors.

St. Patrick's Day, Butte. Easily Butte's biggest annual event, this Irish celebration draws upwards of 50,000 residents and visitors for a mid-day parade through uptown Butte, preceded by the annual Friendly Sons of St. Patrick's Day banquet and Shillelagh Shindig.

Western States Junior Olympics, Red Lodge Mountain. Week-long ski racing competition features top 16- to 18-year-old racers in the Western U.S.

APRIL

International Wildlife Film Festival, Missoula. Top wildlife films from around the world are screened during this week-long event, which also offers workshops, lectures, and seminars.

MAY

Intermountain Opera, Bozeman. One of Montana's most distinctive cultural events draws on considerable local talent and top professionals to create two nights of classical opera.

Miles City Bucking Horse Sale, Miles City. This cowboy classic features three days of bucking horse action, pari-mutuel horse racing, wild horse races, street dances, and a parade.

JUNE

Adult Chamber Music Festival, Bozeman. Professional musicians coach workshops during the day and perform nightly concerts.

American Legion Rodeo, Augusta. One of Montana's biggest small-town rodeos.

College National Finals Rodeo, Bozeman. Five nights of rodeo competition for college scholarships.

Montana Traditional Jazz Festival, Helena. Three-day party of outdoor concerts, jam sessions, and dancing on the city's downtown walking mall.

Red Bottom Celebration, Frazer, on the Fort Peck Indian Reservation. Traditional Indian celebration commemorating the Lower Band of the Assiniboine; dancing, contests, and hand games.

Red Lodge Music Festival, Red Lodge. A full week of evening performances by seasoned classical musicians who spend their days coaching young students.

JULY

Arlee Powwow, Arlee, on the Flathead Indian Reservation. Combined celebration of the Salish and Kootenai tribes over July 4th weekend; competitive dancing, stick games, horse racing, and rodeo.

Arts in the Park, Kalispell. Three-day summer fair features 65 artist booths, food, demonstrations, and entertainment.

Bannack Days, Bannack State Park. Horse and buggy rides, black powder rifle shooting, gold panning, frontier arts, crafts, music, and food at one of Montana's foremost historic parks.

Big Sky Arts Festival, Big Sky. Four outdoor concerts performed by the New World Symphony of Miami at the orchestra's summer residence.

Flathead Festival, Flathead Valley. Regional and world-class musicians perform everything from classical to jazz, and New Age to opera, during a two-week series of concerts.

Fourth of July Rodeo, Ennis. Another popular July 4th weekend rodeo, this one is organized by the National Rodeo Association.

Home of Champions Rodeo, Red Lodge. One of several July 4th rodeos, this three-day PRCA event is located at the base of the Beartooth Highway, en route to Yellowstone Park.

Last Chance Stampede, Helena. Three nights of rodeo featuring nationally known cowboys and professional entertainment.

Livingston Roundup, Livingston. Another July 4th PRCA rodeo, this one features three days of rodeo competition, plus a parade, fireworks, skits, and other entertainment.

Logger Days, Libby. Professional loggers use the tools of their trade to compete for prizes; games and contests for kids, too.

Montana State Fiddlers' Contest, Polson. Top fiddlers of all ages come together for two days of competition and jam sessions in this pleasant lakeside community.

Native American Indian Days, Browning, on the Blackfeet Indian Reservation. Highlights of this major Blackfeet celebration are dancing, singing, drumming, rodeo, parade, and games.

Northern Cheyenne Powwow, Lame Deer, on the Northern Cheyenne Indian Reservation. Annual celebration of the Morning Star People, also held July 4th weekend; parades, dance contests, drumming, singing, and feasting.

Summerfair, Billings. Regional arts and crafts fair featuring 90 artists in a juried show and sale on the campus of Rocky Mountain College; ethnic foods and entertainment add to the festive atmosphere.

Taste of Bozeman. Local restaurants serve their specialties to hundreds of guests on Main Street, which is closed to traffic (sometimes held in early August).

Wild Horse Stampede, Wolf Point. Located on the Fort Peck Indian Reservation, this event grew out of traditional Indian powwows and bucking contests. Wild horse races and other events draw a large crowd to the "granddaddy" of all Montana rodeos.

A U G U S T

Crow Fair, Crow Agency, on the Crow Indian Reservation. One of the nation's premier native cultural celebrations, Crow Fair draws Native Americans and spectators from throughout North America. Hundreds of teepees rise from the banks of the Little Bighorn River, making this the "Teepee Capital of the World" for five days of parades, rodeos, dancing, singing, feasting, gambling, horse races, and relays.

Festival of Nations, Red Lodge. Nine-day festival celebrating the European immigrants who built this once-booming mining community. Popular events are the international cooking pavilion, evening programs, street dances, craft demonstrations, and All Nations Day Parade.

Fiesta, Billings. Montana's largest Hispanic community combines Cinco de Mayo (May 5) and Mexican Independence Day (September 16) into a single, two-day celebration featuring Mexican music, dancing, games, and traditional foods.

Montana Cowboy Poetry Gathering, Lewistown. Two days of rhymes and recitations, jam sessions, music, and dance. This is no ersatz imitation or goopy reminiscence; this is the real thing.

Sweet Pea Festival, Bozeman. Headline musicians, artists' booths, kids' crafts and entertainment, a parade, sporting events, and a ball make this one of Montana's most festive summer weekends.

Western Rendezvous of Art, Helena. Three-day exhibition and sale of works by a select group of Western artists; includes receptions, auctions, and a popular quick-draw atop nearby MacDonald Pass.

SEPTEMBER

Herbstfest, Laurel. Initiated by the area's Russian German community as a harvest festival, this celebration has grown to include other ethnic groups, and two full days of music, dancing, drinking, and feasting.

Jaycee Rodeo, Dillon. Montana's largest Labor Day rodeo features top national and Montana cowboys and cowgirls in two days of competition, plus dances, a parade, and barbecue.

Nordicfest, Libby. Three-day celebration honors the Scandinavian peoples who settled this logging community in Montana's northwest corner. Highlights include crafts, food, dances, and sporting events.

Threshing Bee and Antique Show, Culbertson. Farm celebration and antique show with large display of old-time tractors and farm equipment.

OCTOBER

Northern International Livestock Exposition, Billings. Indoor rodeo at season's end brings some of the nation's top contestants to this growing event, which also features a stock show and commercial exhibits.

C. M. Russell Museum Benefit, Great Falls. A classy evening featuring the show and sale of up to 100 pieces of mostly Western art, and a formal reception attended by many of the artists.

NOVEMBER

U.S. Nordic and Biathlon Training Camps, West Yellowstone. Top U.S. athletes come here for their early season training.

DECEMBER

Christmas in Bigfork. Thousands of lights, greenery, carolers, sleigh rides, and special events make this attractive lakeshore community a festive destination from Thanksgiving to Christmas.

Christmas Stroll, Bozeman. Downtown heralds the season by closing the streets for two days of celebration and cheer.

◼ USEFUL ADDRESSES

The telephone area code for Montana is 406.

AMTRAK; (800) 872-7245

Beaverhead National Forest; 610 N. Montana, Dillon, MT 59725; 683-3900

Bitterroot National Forest; 316 N. Third, Hamilton, MT 59840; 363-3131

Custer National Forest; 2602 1st Ave. North, Billings, MT 59103; 657-6361

Deerlodge National Forest; Federal Building, Butte, MT 59703; 496-3400

Flathead National Forest; 1935 Third Ave. East, Kalispell, 59901; 755-5401

Gallatin National Forest; Federal Building, Bozeman, MT 59715; 587-6701

Glacier National Park; West Glacier, MT 59936; 888-5441

Helena National Forest; Federal Building, Helena, MT 59626; 449-5201

Kootenai National Forest; 506 US 2 West, Libby, MT 59923; 293-6211

Lewis and Clark National Forest; 1101 15th St. North, Great Falls, MT 59403; 791-7700

Lolo National Forest; Fort Missoula, Missoula, MT 59801; 329-3750

Montana Arts Council; 48 N. Last Chance Gulch, Helena, MT 59620; 444-6430

Montana Board of Outfitters; 1424 9th Ave., Helena, MT 59620; 444-3738

Montana Department of Fish, Wildlife & Parks; 1420 E. 6th, Helena, MT 59620; 444-2535

Montana Department of Highways; 2701 Prospect Ave., Helena, MT 59620; 444-6200

Montana Historical Society; 225 N. Roberts, Helena, MT 59620; 444-2694

Montana Outfitters & Guides Association; Box 1339, Townsend, MT 59644; 266-5625

National Weather Service; 449-5204

Travel Montana; 1424 9th Ave., Helena, MT 59620; (800) 541-1447; this is the primary source of statewide tourist information for Montana

U.S. Bureau of Land Management; Box 36800, Billings, MT 59107; 255-2882

U.S. Forest Service, Northern Region; 200 E. Broadway, Missoula, MT 59807; 329-3511

Yellowstone National Park; Yellowstone National Park, WY 82190; (307) 344-7381

Montana chambers of commerce offices with visitor information centers:

Anaconda Chamber of Commerce; 306 E. Park, Anaconda, MT 59711;
563-2400

Billings Chamber of Commerce; Box 31177, Billings, MT 59107; 245-4111

Bitterroot Valley Chamber of Commerce; 105 E. Main, Hamilton, MT 59840;
363-6518

Bozeman Chamber of Commerce; Box B, Bozeman, MT 59715; 586-5421 or
(800) 228-4224

Butte-Silver Bow Chamber of Commerce; 2950 Harrison Ave., Butte, MT
59701; 494-5595

Columbia Falls Chamber of Commerce; Box 312, Columbia Falls, MT 59912;
892-2072

Dillon Chamber of Commerce; Box 830, Dillon, MT 59725; 683-5511

Fort Benton Community Improvement Association; Fort Benton, MT 59442;
622-3761

Glasgow Chamber of Commerce; Box 832, Glasgow, MT 59230; 228-2222

Glendive Chamber of Commerce; Box 930, Glendive, MT 59330; 365-5601

Great Falls Chamber of Commerce; Box 2127, Great Falls, MT 59403; 761-4434

Hardin Chamber of Commerce; 204 N. Center Ave., Hardin, MT 59034;
665-1672

Havre Chamber of Commerce; Box 308, Havre, MT 59501; 265-4383

Helena Chamber of Commerce; 201 E. Lyndale, Helena, MT 59601; 442-4120

Lewistown Chamber of Commerce; Box 818, Lewistown, MT 59457; 538-5436

Malta Chamber of Commerce; Drawer GG, Malta, MT 59538; 654-1776

Manhattan Chamber of Commerce; Box 606, Manhattan, MT 59741

Missoula Chamber of Commerce; Box 7577, Missoula, MT 59807; 543-6623

Plentywood Chamber of Commerce; Box 4, Plentywood, MT 59254; 765-1810

Red Lodge Chamber of Commerce; Box 988, Red Lodge, MT 59068; 446-1718

Scobey Chamber of Commerce; Box 91, Scobey, MT 59263; 487-5961

Sidney Chamber of Commerce; 909 S. Central Ave., Sidney, MT 59270;
482-1916

West Yellowstone Chamber of Commerce; Box 458, West Yellowstone, MT
59758; 646-7701

Whitefish Chamber of Commerce; Box 1120, Whitefish, MT 59937; 862-3501

Wibaux Chamber of Commerce; Box 260, Wibaux, MT 59353

Wolf Point Chamber of Commerce; Box 237, Wolf Point, MT 59201; 653-2012

■ BOOKSTORES

The following booksellers (listed alphabetically by town) support Montana's literary tradition with strong regional sections and occasional book-signing parties to promote new releases. The telephone area code is 406 throughout Montana.

Montana Valley Bookstore; Railroad Avenue, Alberton; 722-4590; used and rare books.
Beyond Necessity; 401 E. Commercial, Anaconda; 563-3218.
Bay Books and Prints; Grand Street, Bigfork; 837-4646; used and rare books.
Electric Avenue Books; 490 Electric Avenue, Bigfork; 837-6072.
Big Timber Book Nook; 216 McLeod, Big Timber; 932-5514.
B. Dalton Booksellers; Rimrock Mall, Billings; 652-4200.
Broken Diamond Books; 19 N. Broadway, Billings; 259-3440; used and rare books.
Thomas Minkler Art and Books; 2907 Second Avenue N, Billings; 245-2969; used and rare books.
Country Bookshelf; 28 W. Main, Bozeman; 587-0166.
Graham/Timmer Books; 109 S. Fourth Avenue, Bozeman; 586-8032; used and rare books.
Museum of the Rockies; Kagy Blvd. & Greek Way, Bozeman; 994-2251.
Vargo's Books; 1 E. Main, Bozeman; 587-5383; used and rare books.
Books & Books; 206 W. Park, Butte; 782-9520.
Plaza Books; 3100 Harrison, Butte; 494-5817.
Second Edition; 129 W. Broadway, Butte; 723-5108; used and rare books.
The Bookstore; 26 N. Idaho, Dillon; 683-6807.
C. M. Russell Museum; 400 13th Street N, Great Falls; 727-8787.
Hastings Books & Records; 1017 10th Avenue S, Great Falls; 727-9550.
Chapter One; 219 Main, Hamilton; 363-5220.
Rocky Mountain House Bookstore; 140 N. Second, Hamilton; 363-2662; used and rare books.
Big Sky Books; 525 Second Ave., Havre; 265-5750.
Little Professor; 331 Last Chance Gulch, Helena; 443-0260.
Montana Historical Society Museum Store; 225 N. Roberts, Helena; 444-2694.
Blacktail Mountain Books; 42 First Avenue W, Kalispell; 257-5573; used and rare books.

Books West; First & Main, Kalispell; 752-6900.

Village Book Shop; Gateway West Mall, Kalispell; 752-8041.

Don's; 120 Second Avenue S, Lewistown; 538-9408.

Gallery Books & Cards; 508 W. Main, Lewistown; 538-7209.

Sax & Fryer's; 109 W. Callendar, Livingston; 222-1421.

The Bookmark; 907 Main, Miles City; 232-7776.

The Bird's Nest; 219 N. Higgins, Missoula; 721-1125; used and rare books.

Fact and Fiction; 216 W. Main, Missoula; 721-2881.

Freddy's Feed and Read; 1221 Helen, Missoula; 549-2127.

Great Northern Book Company; 133 N. Higgins, Missoula; 721-3311.

Sidney's Used Books; 518 S. Fourth Avenue W, Missoula; 543-5343; used and rare books.

Broadway Bookstore; 13 S. Broadway, Red Lodge; 446-2742.

The Book Peddler; 104 Canyon, West Yellowstone; 646-9358.

Bookworm; 14 Canyon, West Yellowstone; 646-9736.

Bookworks; 110 Central, Whitefish; 862-4980.

RECOMMENDED READING

There is a lifetime of good reading about Montana. Recognizing that there may be more to life than reading about Montana, here is the short list.

■ HISTORY

Abbott, E. C. and Helena Huntington Smith. *We Pointed Them North: Recollections of a Cowpuncher.* University of Oklahoma Press, 1955. One of Montana's best storytellers recounts the glory days of the open range.

Alderson, Nannie T. and Helena Huntington Smith. *A Bride Goes West.* University of Nebraska Press, 1969. One of the finest records of a woman's life on the Montana frontier.

DeVoto, Bernard, editor. *The Journals of Lewis and Clark.* (abridged) Houghton Mifflin, 1953. Meriwether Lewis and William Clark were better explorers than they were writers, but the journals they kept as they traveled up the Missouri and across the Northern Rockies are delightful reading for anyone following the same route, either by car or canoe.

Garcia, Andrew. *Tough Trip Through Paradise.* Comstock Editions, 1976. A lively account by a mountain man of life among the Indians.

Glasscock, C. B. *The War of the Copper Kings.* Bobbs-Merrill, 1935. Much of Montana's history was written in the mining city of Butte, and no one has written a more colorful account than this one.

Malone, Michael, Richard Roeder, and William Lang. *Montana: A History of Two Centuries.* University of Washington Press, 1991. The standard text on Montana history.

Rolvaag, O. E. *Giants in the Earth.* Harper & Row, 1965. You will taste the dust and dread the wind by the time you finish this classic about the homestead experience.

Russell, Charles M. *Trails Plowed Under.* Doubleday, 1937. Colorful yarns about the West by Montana's famed cowboy artist.

■ NATIVE AMERICANS

Brown, Mark H. *The Flight of the Nez Perce.* University of Nebraska Press, 1982. The definitive work on the Nez Perce War of 1877.

Bryan, William L., Jr. *Montana Indians: Yesterday and Today.* American Geographic Publishing, 1985. Words and photographs illustrate the diversity, cultural traditions, and contemporary issues of Montana's Indian tribes.

Bullchild, Percy. *The Sun Came Down.* Harper & Row, 1985. A collection of Blackfeet Indian stories acclaimed as one of the finest ever published of traditional Native American literature.

Deloria, Vine, Jr. *Custer Died for Your Sins: An Indian Manifesto.* University of Oklahoma Press, 1985. A witty and incisive polemic about this nation's dismal relationship with its native inhabitants.

Farr, William E. *The Reservation Blackfeet, 1882–1945: A Photographic History of Cultural Survival.* University of Washington Press, 1986. A graphic illustration of the impact of Euro-American civilization on native culture.

■ REMINISCENCES AND ESSAYS

Doig, Ivan. *This House of Sky: Landscapes of a Western Mind.* Harcourt Brace Jovanovich, 1978. A gifted Montana writer explores his connections to the land and the people who shaped his values.

Duncan, Dayton. *Out West.* Viking, 1987. Follow the same route Lewis and Clark did through the eyes of a modern explorer.

Frazier, Ian. *Great Plains.* Farrar Straus Giroux, 1989. From Custer and Crazy Horse to MX missiles, Frazier gives his readers a new look at America's heartland.

Kittredge, William, editor. *Montana Spaces.* Nick Lyons Books, 1988. Original essays about the land and the people of Montana by some of the West's finest writers.

Kittredge, William and Annick Smith, editors. *The Last Best Place.* University of Washington Press, 1988. The best in history, poetry, and literature, all wrapped up in one 5-pound (two-kg) volume.

Maclean, Norman. *A River Runs Through It and Other Stories.* University of Chicago Press, 1976. Humor and tragedy blend in this American classic about living and fishing in the Blackfoot River country of Montana.

McFadden, Cyra. *Rain or Shine.* Alfred A. Knopf, 1986. The daughter of a famous Montana rodeo announcer and dancer-turned-trick rider recounts her childhood on the rodeo circuit.

Stegner, Wallace. *Wolf Willow.* University of Nebraska Press, 1980. One of the West's great writers explores his boyhood on the plains of southern Saskatchewan, just north of the Montana border.

■ POETRY

Hugo, Richard. *The Lady in Kicking Horse Reservoir.* Norton, 1973. Before his death in 1982, this poet was mentor to many of Montana's leading writers as director of the University of Montana's creative writing program.

Keeler, Greg. *American Falls.* Confluence Press, 1987. Fishing is the metaphor for this poetry by a delightfully offbeat professor-writer-musician-angler.

McRae, Wallace. *It's Just Grass and Water.* Oxalis, 1986. One of Montana's favorite cowboy poets talks of life on the range.

Zarzyski, Paul. *Roughstock Sonnets.* Lowell Press, 1989. A refreshing and contemporary twist on cowboy poetry.

■ FICTION

Doig, Ivan. *Dancing at the Rascal Fair.* Atheneum, 1987. A chronicle of the American experience, beginning in Scotland in 1889 and ending three decades later on the Rocky Mountain frontier.

Dorris, Michael. *A Yellow Raft in Blue Water.* Warner Books, 1988. A sensitive and spellbinding portrait of three generations of contemporary Indian women.

Guthrie, A. B., Jr. *The Big Sky.* Houghton Mifflin, 1947. The best known of several historical novels by Montana's Pulitzer Prize winner.

Johnson, Dorothy. *A Man Called Horse* and *The Hanging Tree.* Ballantine, 1953, 1957. Two of the late Montana author's short stories that became motion pictures.

Welch, James. *Fools Crow.* Viking Penguin, 1986. A fictional account of the impact of white civilization on a band of Blackfeet Indians.

■ GUIDEBOOKS

Alt, David and Donald Hyndeman. *Roadside Geology of the Northern Rockies.* Mountain Press, 1927. An authoritative but non-technical explanation of the violent natural forces that shaped the landscape we see today.

Fischer, Carol and Hank Fischer. *Montana Wildlife Viewing Guide.* Falcon Press, 1990. Practical information on more than 100 easily accessible wildlife viewing sites.

Van West, Carroll. *A Traveler's Companion to Montana History.* Montana Historical Society, 1986. A motorist's guide to the past and its influence on today's landscape and communities.

■ GLACIER AND YELLOWSTONE NATIONAL PARKS

Depending on your field of interest (hiking, sightseeing, wildflowers, wildlife, natural history, geology, etc.), there are many guidebooks about Glacier and Yellowstone national parks available through each park's natural history association. For a complete list of field guides, general books, and maps, write **Glacier Natural History Association,** Box 327, West Glacier, MT 59936, (406) 888-5756, and **The Yellowstone Association** Box 117, Yellowstone National Park, WY 82190, (307) 344-7381.

■ MAGAZINES

Montana Magazine, American Geographic Publishing, Helena, MT. People, places, and lots of color photography (bimonthly).

Montana: The Magazine of Western History, Montana Historical Society, Helena, MT. Widely regarded as one of the nation's best history magazines (quarterly).

Montana Outdoors, Montana Department of Fish, Wildlife and Parks, Helena, MT. For sportsmen and all who love the outdoors (bimonthly).

I   N   D   E   X

■ ABOUT THE AUTHOR

Born and raised in Montana, Norma Tirrell brings to this guide a native's first-hand knowledge of the state and an insider's view of its travel industry. For six years, as publications specialist for Travel Montana, a division of the Montana Department of Commerce, she wrote and produced the state's official travel guides. A graduate of the University of Montana School of Journalism, her first book, *We Montanans,* was published in 1988 by American Geographic Publishing. She and her husband, Gordon Bennett, enjoy exploring Montana from their home in Helena, centrally located on the east slope of the Rocky Mountains.

■ ABOUT THE PHOTOGRAPHER

John Reddy, based in Helena, has been photographing landscapes and people since 1974. Reddy earned a degree in photography from Montana State University's Film and Television Production Department in Bozeman and subsequently lectured there for two years. He is widely published in Montana. His work has been seen in publications such as *American Heritage, Historic Preservation, Psychology Today, Sunset Magazine,* and the *Smithsonian Guide to Historic America.* Reddy has many commercial clients, but prefers working on books and magazines featuring outdoor subjects. In his free time, he enjoys spending his time with his family and continually strives to capture on film the many splendors of his beloved Montana outdoors.